CROSSTOWN CROSSFIRE

A game-by-game history of
a great American football rivalry
Updated from *Best Little Rivalry in Town*

BY JODY BROWN

Gridiron Publishers
P.O. Box 724201
Atlanta, GA 31139

Crosstown Crossfire by Jody H. Brown
(Update from *Best Little Rivalry in Town*)
Copyright (c) 1994 by Jody H. Brown

All rights reserved. No part of this book may
be reproduced in any form, except for quotations
in a review, without permission of the publisher.

Printed in the United States of America

Library of Congress Cataloging-in-Publication data:
1. History. University of Southern California - Football
2. History. University of California at Los Angeles - Football
3. History. College Sports - United States
4. History. Football - United States
Library of Congress Catalogue Number: 94-077119

ISBN 0-932520-55-3

Published in Atlanta, Georgia

1st Edition: 1982
2nd Edition: 1994

Jacket photograph by Wendall Adams & Associates
Atlanta, Georgia

Helmets courtesy of UCLA and
Southern California Athletic Departments

GRIDIRON PUBLISHERS
P.O. BOX 724201
ATLANTA GA 31139
(404)431-0962

Table of Contents

Dedication
Acknowledgments
Foreword by Terry Donahue
Foreword by John Robinson
1929 — The First Shall be Last ▪ 9
1930 — Pointless Progress ▪ 19
    — Back to the Drawing Board ▪ 26
1936 — No More Mr. Nice Guy ▪ 28
1937 — Too Little, Too Late ▪ 35
1938 — Moonlight for the Coach from Wabash ▪ 42
1939 — The Bruins' Rose: Gone With the Wind ▪ 48
1940 — Clash for the Cellar ▪ 56
1941 — Prelude ▪ 61
1942 — The Siege of Troy ▪ 66
    — The Victory Bell ▪ 76
1943 — Who's on First? ▪ 78
1943 — Bobbleville ▪ 82
1944 — Legs of Fizz, Cheeks of Fuzz ▪ 85
1944 — Troy Hardy-ness ▪ 91
1945 — How Jeff Doth Cravath Roses! ▪ 96
1945 — Same Song, Second Verse ▪ 100
1946 — A Case in Patience ▪ 105
1947 — Gray Colors Bruins Blue ▪ 113
1948 — Hi, Mom ▪ 118
1949 — Schneider Makes Dean's List ▪ 122
1950 — Boom, As in Bruin ▪ 127
1951 — Glory, Back-to-Back ▪ 133
1952 — Toast of the Coast ▪ 138
1953 — Two Bears, One Tale ▪ 145
1954 — All Dressed Up, No Place to Go ▪ 150
1955 — Triple Crown ▪ 154
1956 — (Ells)Worth of a Toe ▪ 162
1957 — Long-Suffering Trojans ▪ 167
1958 — Fit to be Tied ▪ 173
1959 — The Unbelievers ▪ 179
1960 — As the Worm Turns ▪ 185

1961 — Quack, Quack ■ 192
1962 — Knockout, In the Fourth ■ 197
1963 — Four Bees and a Gee ■ 203
1964 — You Win Some, You Lose Some ■ 208
1965 — Carnage, In Four Minutes ■ 215
1966 — The Dow Closes Up ■ 223
1967 — Star Trek ■ 229
1968 — OJ, the Trojan Way ■ 237
1969 — The Cardiac Kids ■ 243
1970 — No Joy in Troy ■ 248
1971 — All Things Being Equal ■ 254
1972 — A Bone to Pick ■ 259
1973 — Bruins Blow Ball, Bell, Bowl ■ 266
1974 — 1974, A.D. ■ 274
1975 — For Bobble or For Worse ■ 280
1976 — The Low Down on High Ranks ■ 288
1977 — Bruins Short, by a Foot ■ 294
1978 — A Game Divided ■ 300
1979 — A Lott of White ■ 306
1980 — Tip in History ■ 313
1981 — A Rose by Any Other Name ■ 319
  — Change of Venue ■ 328
1982 — Sack of Roses ■ 329
1983 — Tumbletown ■ 336
1984 — Blundering Herd ■ 343
1985 — Tollner Rolls Dice ■ 349
1986 — A Green Blowout ■ 355
1987 — An Ungroovy Win ■ 362
1988 — A Peete Repeat ■ 370
1989 — Crossbar Folly ■ 379
1990 — Point Parade ■ 386
1991 — A Sparkling Ale ■ 393
1992 — Paw Robs Rob ■ 400
1993 — Deja Vu ■ 408
  — Reflections, by Dick Vermeil ■ 416
  — Appendix ■ 417
The Author

To
Anna

Foreword

The USC-UCLA football rivalry is unique. Nowhere else in America are two schools of such national repute and tradition located in the same city. We live with each other 365 days a year, and the winner owns bragging rights in Los Angeles during that time.

The game is special to the athletes - many who are local products - because they are competing against players who may have been teammates or opponents from high school. That's what makes it fun for them: beating their buddies in this game and then holding it over them, razzing them about it all summer.

The game also offers a tremendous event for the fans. It brings on a division among people in offices, bars and families throughout the city. The Los Angeles Coliseum - or the Rose Bowl in Pasadena - is usually packed with 90,000 enthusiasts who are split down the middle in their support.

The contest is for the championship of Los Angeles, but usually the stakes are much higher. Often, this is the game which decides the Pacific-10 title and the Rose Bowl representative. Frequently, a high national ranking is on the line.

There is no bitterness in this rivalry. Some of the finest athletes in the country are pitted in what is usually a very physical matchup; yet, I can't recollect any incidents of fighting or unsportsmanlike conduct. It's a friend-against-friend and sometimes brother-against-brother. I've never had a feeling of hate in this rivalry.

USC-UCLA, two great universities represented by two outstanding football teams. It's a fun rivalry... and I love it.

John Robinson
Head Coach, USC

Foreword

The UCLA-USC game is the type of game where a coach doesn't have to give his players a pep talk. The excitement, tension and build-up during the seemingly endless weeks of preparation readies the players in a special way. They know it's the most important game of the regular season, and probably the biggest of their career.

Many Bruin-Trojan clashes have decided the league championship as well as the conference's representative to the Rose Bowl. With those stakes on the line, plus the sell-out crowd and media-hype, the game becomes the focal point of our season.

Every contest in this series has been fought with great intensity. Whether a player is a freshman or a senior, winning this game can be the highlight of an athletic career.

In my two years as defensive lineman on the Bruin varsity in 1965 and '66, we defeated the Trojans twice in close, tensely-fought games. Along with our 14-12 victory over Michigan State in the 1966 Rose Bowl, those two wins over the Trojans were the most exciting in my years as a player.

One of the most thrilling victories as head coach came in 1980 when we beat USC, 20-17... and Freeman McNeil rushed for 111 yards.

It's a unique rivalry because you have two outstanding football teams in one city. In my college career, the UCLA-USC series has epitomized what college football stands for: excitement, intensity, and great competition.

Terry Donahue
Head Coach, UCLA

Acknowledgments

A special acknowledgment is extended to both the University of Southern California and the University of California at Los Angeles for their generous cooperation in helping the author gather material for this book.

We extend gratitude to the offices of Sports Information at both institutions, especially to Tim Tessalone of USC, Marc Dellins and Patt Troutman of UCLA, plus Duane Lindberg of the PAC-10 office.

Appreciation is expressed to the Library Systems of Southern California, UCLA and the University of Georgia, especially the Copy Services Departments.

There were many individuals who made contributions, so a heartfelt *thank you* is offered to Dick Vermeil, Pat Howell, Fulton Kuykendall, Bob Neal, Vic Kelley, Charles Dayton, John Robinson, Terry Donahue, Ann Brown, Barry Munz, Lee Perkins, Trey Perkins, Lyn Billings , Bill Cromartie, Bill Dixon, Ray Tapley, Pete McDonald, Pepper Rodgers and John Copland. A special note of gratitude is extended to Dr. Jim Peterson whose cooperation made possible this book.

A book of this format would have been impossible to compile without the newspaper files of the Los Angeles *Times*, as well as its predecessor newspapers in Los Angeles, such as the *Herald-Examiner* and the *Mirror*.

These papers were the source of the vast majority of the factual material included in this book. And to their sportswriters, past and present, we sincerely offer a grateful and admiring salute. They were the eyewitnesses to the drama and color as it unfolded year after year. They recorded the facts and quotations from which a large portion of this book has been drawn.

1929
Game 1

The First Shall Be Last

Nineteen-Twenty-Nine, the end of the "Roarin' Twenties"... and the beginning of a new roar—a vociferous noise that would be heard for decades deep into the future.

On September 28th, 1929, a clear, chilly day, football teams representing the University of Southern California and the University of California at Los Angeles glared eye-to-eye at each other across the 50-yard line of Memorial Coliseum... and thus was born one of the most storied—and bitter—rivalries throughout the nation.

The contest emerged as a David-versus-Goliath confrontation. Little David - UCLA - was barely ten years old, had played only 74 games with nothing to brag in the way of laurels, and was just recuperating from its campus move from Vermont Avenue to Westwood Village. Big Goliath - USC - was a football veteran of 36 seasons, had gone to the gridiron front 226 times, boasted a 14-3 Rose Bowl triumph over Penn State in 1923 ('22 season), was just coming off back-to-back Pacific Coast Conference titles, and was defending a mythical national championship.

It should now be understood: the Biblical script was not followed. Nay, David did not slay Goliath. So guess which team won.

And take another guess as to what phenomenon was going head-to-head against football, as well as other forms of entertainment, that year. It was the new kid in town, a two-year-old little fellow named "Talkies". Even so, the inaugural USC-UCLA battle drew well—reports range from 35-to-over 50,000 spectators ... despite the colossal attractions over in Hollywood; such as Ronald Colman in "Bulldog Drummond", Colleen Moore in "Smiling Eyes" and Richard Dix in "The Love Doctor".

The old Atwater-Kent claimed its addicts, too. And it had fans on the way to the game humming such just-released songs as "Louise", "Am I Blue?", "Lover Come Back to Me", and of course the immortal "Stardust". Thanks, Hoagy.

Earlier in the year—on New Year's Day, to be exact—football had jumped off to a most bizarre start. You remember: Georgia Tech 8, California 7, and the never-to-be-forgotten wrong way run by Roy Riegals. How did it happen, Roy?

"Well, in eluding tacklers, why, I became confused and turned around and ran the other way, uh, down the other end of the field. On the way down, why, I could hear my teammate, Benny Lom, er, hollering at me to stop, I was going the wrong way, and I thought he was completely off his rocker. Just about that time I was hit by the whole Georgia Tech team, and I landed about two feet from the goal line. If I could have dug a hole in that turf, I'd crawled in and covered myself up and not appeared again."* Well, Roy, the sports world is glad you didn't.

The *California Trojan*, USC's student newspaper, opined that the "Bruin eleven hopes to find the Troy Varsity over-confident", then, though being facetious, became near-prophetic by adding "... the Bruin players expect to be beaten about 70 to nothing".

That was close. For the record, the final score was Southern California 76, UCLA 0.

Actually, the Uclans played the Thundering Herd on equal terms for the first ten minutes, but when quarterback Russ Saunders broke loose on a 50-yard sprint for a touchdown—well, let UCLA's *Southern Campus* yearbook tell it:

"... the Bruins were playing three teams, not one. And their endurance and stamina ebbed as equally capable Trojan replaced equally capable Trojan in endless succession. No apologies can be made for the Bruins in their first conference game with the Trojans. It merely remains a task for succeeding Bruin teams to build up a reputation that will erase this defeat."

Saunders, of course, earned the distinction of scoring the first points in this grand series, and before USC reserves flooded the field, he tallied twice more, on runs of 55 and 12 yards. Joining him in the TD parade with two touchdowns each were Erny Pinckert, later in his career to become a consensus All-American, Gaius Shaver and Jesse Hill, himself learning the rudiments to one day become

USC's head coach. James Musick, Rockwell Kemp and Charles Willingham rounded out the crossing of the double-stripe. And one who didn't score in the game, but who later scored big in another arena was a fellow named Ward Bond.

For those who would like to mull over the minute details of this slaughter, the multiple marches by the men of Troy went like this:

— The 50-yard dash by Saunders. This drive started on the Trojan 23-yard line and required only four plays. Musick went around left end for six, Saunders hit center for a first down to the 34, then Musick advanced the ball to mid-field, setting up the Saunders spin. Musick went through right guard for the extra point.

— Pinckert's two-yard dive ended a six-play, 23-yard campaign.

— Starting from the Bruin 24-yard line, The Herd tamed the Bruin in two plays as Hill went the last 15 yards around left end, untouched.

— Stan Williamson intercepted an Eddie Soloman pass and carried to UCLA's 44-yard line. On the first play, Hill broke through the middle, shook off three would-be tacklers, and scored. Shaver converted.

— Norm Duncan quick-kicked to USC's 28-yard line. Shaver failed to gain on the first play, but then took off around right end and streaked 72 yards for another Trojan tally. Score at intermission was 32-0.

["*Be it forever remembered that the Bruins were courageous martyrs . . .*"]

MAURICE GOODSTEIN
Center

THEODORE DENNIS
Halfback

MEYER ZIMMER
Tackle

Bruins 0 . . . .

HARDLY could a tougher opening struggle than that which faced Bill Spaulding and his untried Bruins on the 28th of September, 1929, be selected. The Light Brigade on its memorable charge had nothing on the Bruins when they rammed into the super-gridded Trojans from across the way. The results, 76 to 0, were just about as disastrous. Pinckert to left of them, Musick to right of them, Saunders in front of them volleye[d] thundered. And those pugnacious Trojan[s] ered by a rolling barrage of potent interf[erence] volleyed and thu[ndered] all afternoon. No[t until] the declining su[n] cold shadows ov[er the] Coliseum was a [halt] called, and some [very] weary Bruins st[aggered] to the training q[uarters] as 35,000 shiverin[g, be]wildered fans dr[ifted] from the scene of t[he mas]sacre. But be it [forever] remembered tha[t the] Bruins were cour[ageous,] praiseworthy mar[tyrs]

HIGHLIGHTS OF THE GAME

The Bruins attempted 6 forward passes and completed one, Solomon to Roberts, for 30 yards.

According to the figures, Saunders of Troy made 231 yards; Duncan headed the Bruins with 17.

Saunders averaged 16 yards to the try, Duncan 2. The Bruins made 4 first downs, 2 on a drive in the first quarter, 2 in the last minutes of play.

Southern California got the worst of the penalty deal, losing 85 yards to the Blue and Gold's 28. Don Jacobson, mainstay in the Bruin line, left the game in the first quarter with a broken ankle.

Coach Spaulding gave more than 40 men a chance; Coach Jones used 45 men out of a squad of 50; 35,000 saw the first game between these schools.

["Duncan headed the Bruins with 17 yards . . ."]

IFF SIMPSON
Quarterback

ARTHUR SMITH
Guard

JERROLD RUSSOM
Halfback

.... Southern California 76

THAT Duncan and Thoe and Simpson and Brown and French and Jacobson and all the rest defended the Bruin until the final despite overpowering odds in number, and experience, e as a vivid picture minds of all who essed the game. ring the first ten the Bruins out-emselves. Taking koff, they pushed into Trojan territory, and stayed there until Saunders knifed through the line and raced fifty yards to the goal line. But the Bruins were playing three teams, not one and their endurance and stamina ebbed as equally capable Trojan replaced equally capable Trojan in endless succession. ¶ No apologies can be made for the Bruins in this first conference game with the Trojans; it merely remains a task for succeeding Bruin teams to build up a reputation that will erase this defeat. Westwood begins siege of Troy.

THE LINEUPS

Bruins		Trojans
Rasmus	L.E.R.	Steponovich
Brown (C)	L.T.R.	Anthony
Gibson	L.G.R.	Galloway
French	C.	Dye
Noble	R.G.L.	(C) Barragar
Jacobson	R.T.L.	Hoff
Bishop	R.E.L.	Tappaan
Simpson	Q.	Saunders
Forster	L.H.R.	Mortensen
Thoe	R.H.L.	Edelson
N. Duncan	F.	Musick

Bruin substitutes: Dennis, Solomon, J. Duncan, Russom, Roberts, Grossman, Brenniman, Stoeffen, Duffy, Remsburg, Mulhaupt, Wellendorf, A. Smith, Huse, McMillan, Lloyd, Milum, Goodstein, Nelson, etc.

Trojan substitutes: Practically the whole squad.

- On the first play from scrimmage in the second half, Saunders followed Captain Nate Barranger through the Uclan defense, manipulating 55 yards and TD Number six.
- Next, Musick culminated a 69-yard drive in six plays, going the final 11 over left guard.
- Not to be outdone, Saunders scored over right guard from 12-yards out, ending a 50-yard, five-play push.
- Then it was Pinckert from four yards out, again through right guard, and that finalized a 68-yard, 12-play effort. After three periods, it was 56-0.
- Fourth frame: Shaver, one yard plunge, the eighth play of a 56-yard assault. Kemp converted.
- USC recovered a fumble on UCLA's 38-yard line. Three plays later, Kemp reversed his field and scampered 37 yards for a TD. Adding insult to injury, he then proceeded to tack on the PAT.
- The onslaught ended when Barry Stephens intercepted a Soloman aerial and hot-footed to the Bruin 37. Eight plays later, Willingham went off tackle and crossed the double-stripe from seven yards out. That made it 76-0, and the UCLA fans suddenly found themselves wishing Los Angeles was on Mountain Standard Time.

Early in the game, USC was backed up to its one-yard line. What happened thereafter is unclear, but according to the *Times* "... there was something goofy and the officials finally gave SC the pigskin on their 20-yard marker". Huh?

Leading rushers for the Troymen were Saunders with 229 yards and Hill with 152. Sophomore Duncan's 21 yards paced the Ukes.

USC completed only one pass, that a 24-yarder from Saunders to Tony Steponovitch in the initial quarter. Bruin Buddy Forster stopped the play.

Stout in heart, but lacking in manpower, UCLA never seriously threatened the scoreboard. It was not, however, without its stalwarts. Captain Carl Brown was outstanding both on offense and defense. And others cited for stellar efforts were Cliff Simpson, Don Jacobson, Reubon Thoe and Duncan.

Howard Jones, starting his fifth season as head coach of the Trojans, put every member of his squad on the field of action (not at the same time, of course), but SC still amassed 735 total yards (some reports say 750), a figure that stands today as a Trojan record.

As the USC yearbook, *El Rodeo*, surmised "... it will be remembered as a game that produced enormous Trojan yardage ... it will be remembered by grand-dads to come as a complete rout of the Westwood Bruins."

USC's Russ Saunders, far right, scored the first touchdown of the series, 1929.

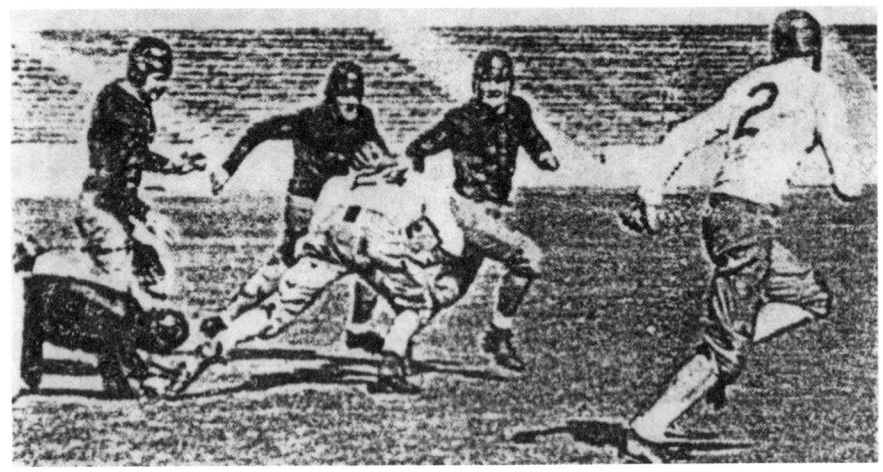

USC's Russ Saunders leads Jim Musick around end as Bruin defenders move in.

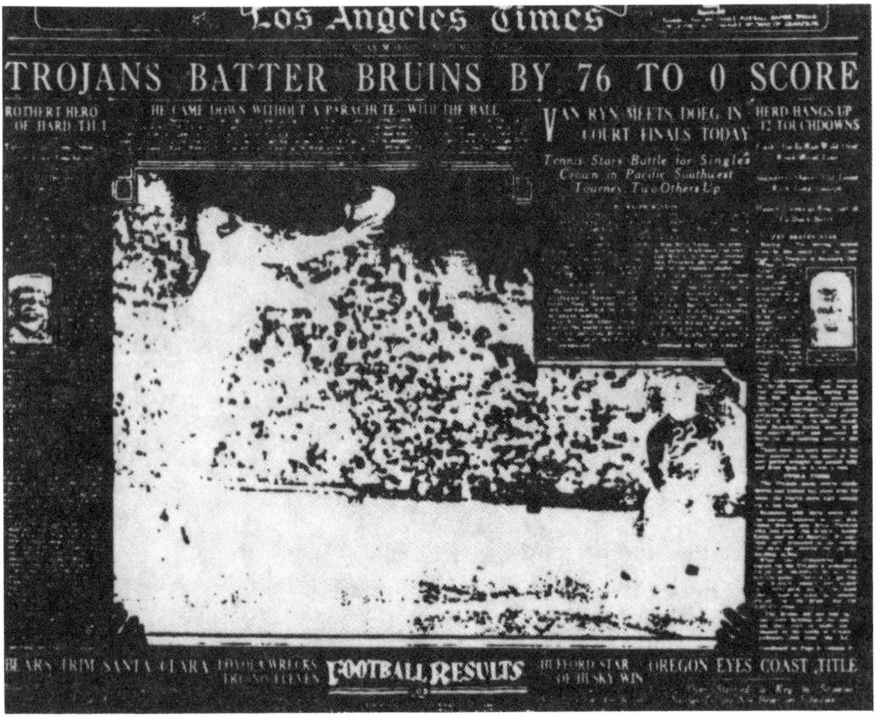

Los Angeles Times

TROJANS BATTER BRUINS BY 76 TO 0 SCORE

ROTHERT HERO OF HARD TILT

HE CAME DOWN WITHOUT A PARACHUTE—WITH THE BALL

VAN RYN MEETS DOEG IN COURT FINALS TODAY

Tennis Stars Battle for Singles Crown in Pacific Southwest Tourney; Two Others Up

HERD HANGS UP 12 TOUCHDOWNS

BEARS TRIM SANTA CLARA

FOOTBALL RESULTS

OREGON EYES COAST TITLE

Coach Bill Spaulding

Bill Spaulding, UCLA Head Coach, 1925 to 1938.

Across the field was William H. Spaulding, and he too, was beginning his fifth season at the helm of the Ukes, who, by the way, were starting their second year as members of the Pacific Coast Conference. Although out-classed, UCLA did manage to gain 124 total yards.

If the initial meeting of USC and UCLA created a stir from Santa Monica to Long Beach, it caused hardly a ripple up the coast in San Francisco. Buried on page two of the *Chronicle's* sports section was a one-column report that told the story in four insignificant paragraphs attached to an inconspicuous 14-point headline. It even editorialized: "... the fans went home wondering what the 76-to-nothing count might mean—if anything". Well, after all, weren't the Cubs and the A's warming up for the World Series? And hadn't Jack Sharkey just stopped Tommy Loughran in the third round?

And so, San Francisco notwithstanding, the beginning of the Southern Cal-UCLA rivalry took its niche in the bustle of 1929, sandwiched between the infamous Valentine Massacre and the massive crash of the stock market.

The Wall Street demise prompted Will Rogers to say: "We'll hold the distinction of being the only nation in the history of the world that ever went to the Poor House in an automobile." Maybe so, Will, but gasoline wasn't a buck-forty then, either.

The 76-0 pasting has turned out to be the biggest margin ever inflicted upon UCLA by USC in the more than six-decade-long series, and because of the present-day parity in college recruiting, it is unlikely it will ever be matched. The first shall be last.

The season was certainly not a calamity for the Bruins, though. To their eternal credit, they bounced back the next week and clobbered Fresno State, 56-6. They then split their six remaining games and finished the year at 4-4-0. Included was a 14-0 verdict over Montana, their first conference victory. Other victims were Caltech and Pomona.

Southern Cal finished the season with a 9-2-0 slate, then pounded Pittsburgh in the Rose Bowl, 47-14. It was a fitting finish to a season that ignited the long and healthy series with their cross-town rivals.

Voted the best motion picture of the year was "All Quiet on the Western Front". It was all quiet on the Westwood front, too . . . because of that 76-0 bombardment by USC.

Starting Lineups: USC—Ends, Tappaan and Steponovitch; Tackles, Hoff and Anthony; Guards, Barranger (c) and Shaw; Center, Dye; Quarterback, Saunders; Halfbacks, Edelson and Mortenson; Fullback, Musick. UCLA—Ends, Bishop and Rasmus; Tackles, Jacobson and Brown (c); Guards, Noble and Gibson; Center, French; Quarterback, Simpson; Halfbacks, Thoe and Forster; Fullback, Duncan.

Summary

	USC	UCLA
First Downs	26	4
Yards Rushing	712	99
Yards Passing	23	34
Total Yards	735	124
Passes Attempted/Completed	4/1	6/1
Passes Had Intercepted	1	2
Fumbles Lost	4	3
Punts/Average	3/35	13/37
Penalties, No./Yards	8/80	5/17

Scoring by Quarters:

USC	7	25	24	20	—	76
UCLA	0	0	0	0	—	0

*Taped from WSB radio broadcast in 1975.

1930
Game 2

Pointless Progress

It had been 12 months and 12 touchdowns since Southern California blasted the upset hopes of an upstart neighbor which bore letters for a name—UCLA.

And with the drubbing still humming in their ears, the Bruins figured they had only one way to go: up.

But, among the fans, the thought of the second challenge by the Westwood youngsters was lacking in anticipation, compared to the first, which, with its property of uncertainty, had planted a seed, be it ever so tiny, that just maybe, perhaps, somehow an upset, be it ever so huge, might blossom.

But visions of the second contest were more harsh in reality. If the Bruins weren't mature enough to walk with the men of Troy last year, how could they be expected to match strides so quickly?

Nevertheless, the day of the game—September 27th—broke with promise. It wouldn't be as disastrous as last year, said the Bruin faithful.

The day also broke with shocking news from the Merion Cricket Club in Pennsylvania that spun the sports world agog. Bobby Jones had just captured the United States amateur golf championship, his fourth straight national victory of the year, the unforgettable "Grand Slam" of golf.

And, on the lighter side, the populace mused over their morning coffee with chuckles that leaped from the comic strips of Winnie

Winkle, Gasoline Alley, the Gumps, Ella Cinders and Little Orphan Annie. Leapin' Lizards, they wondered, would the USC-UCLA game that afternoon be a laugher, too?

It wasn't. Well, not a knee-slapper, anyway. Although still unable to penetrate the Trojan end zone, the Uclans yielded less points than in the first encounter, and ended up on the short end of a 52-0 score. That was a 24-point margin of improvement. That was, despite an absence of points, progress.

Both school yearbooks thought so, too.

"The defeat was complete but the game never took on the semblance of a rout," reported UCLA's *Southern Campus*. "It was in no sense a victory, not even a moral one, but it was a big improvement over last year, with indications of strength ahead," it added.

And from USC's *El Rodeo* came a prediction. "It seems to be the consensus of opinion among all fans that UCLA will gradually improve its football program and will be our main contender within the next five years."

Right on, *El Rodeo.*

If the army of the Trojans wasn't already deep in heroes, it surprisingly reached down and unveiled yet another Hector to slash wounds in the hide of the Bruin. His name was Orv Mohler, sophomore.

Mohler Star of Trojan Victory . . . headlined the *Los Angeles Examiner*, whose poetic lead went on to say: "A new phantom of the gridiron appeared out of the sweet mysteries of sophomore life yesterday to stalk the white-barred field where Southern California mowed down the defenses of the UCLA Bruins in the season's opener, 52-0. A new phantom it was, named Orv Mohler, the Alhambra Moor, making his debut . . ." etc.

The Jonesmen gained 550 yards from scrimmage, with 470 coming from the rush, and of these, Mohler contributed 176. He scored twice, and for his overall effort, Mohler was named by the *Los Angeles Daily News* as one of the top 12 backs in the Pacific Coast Conference. Two other Trojans also were tapped—Marshall Duffield, who thrice increased numerals on the scoreboard, and Erny Pinckert.

It was a fast turf under clear skies that awaited the second clash of the Trojan and the Bruin. About 40,000 people were in the Coliseum, some cocky, some with fingers crossed.

— If nothing else, the Bruins appeared more confident than their fans. Capt. Eddie Soloman won the toss and elected to— kickoff! (Alas, that may have been the turning point in the game.) Anyway, Norm Duncan did the honors and his leg sailed the ball

Los Angeles Times

SUNDAY MORNING, SEPTEMBER 28, 1930

TROJANS ROLL UP 52-TO-0 SCORE AGAINST BRUINS

FOURTH IN ROW FOR ATLANTAN

Vines Conquers Mangin in Title Court Battle

JONES'S TEAM IMPRESSIVE

PASADENA STAR TAKES LAURELS

UP AND OVER WITH MUSICK AND MOHLER

S.C. RESERVES LACK STRENGTH

CUBS THUMP REDS AGAIN

Chicago Makes it Three in Row Over Cincinnati Ball Club, Wilson Raises Record

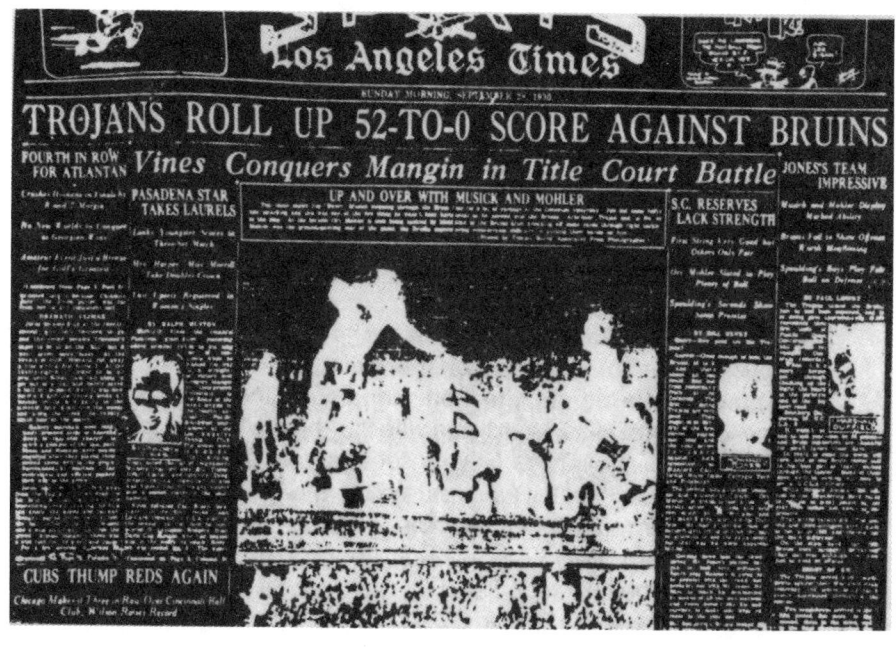

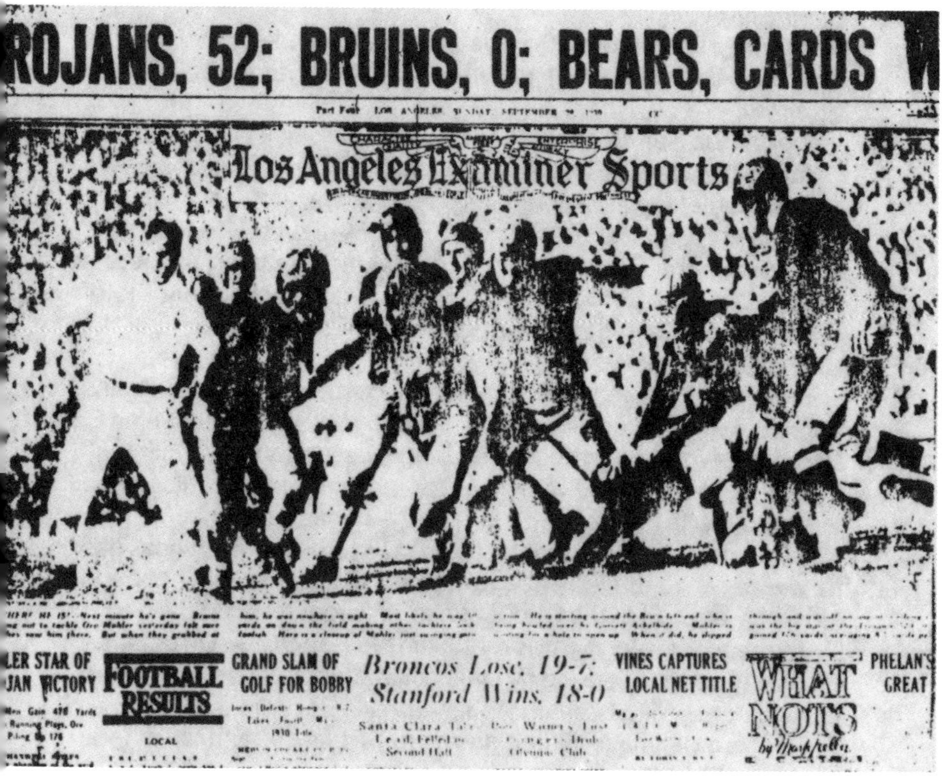

ROJANS, 52; BRUINS, 0; BEARS, CARDS W

Los Angeles Examiner Sports

LER STAR OF JAN VICTORY

FOOTBALL RESULTS

GRAND SLAM OF GOLF FOR BOBBY

Broncos Lose, 19-7; Stanford Wins, 18-0

VINES CAPTURES LOCAL NET TITLE

WHAT NOTS

PHELAN'S GREAT

down to USC's two-yard line. There it was gathered in by Marshall Duffield, who sped down the right side all the way back to UCLA's 28-yard line. From that point, the Trojans required nine plays before Jim Musick crashed over from the one.
— The second touchdown covered 45 yards and took four plays, aided by a Bruin penalty. Duffield got this one on a 16-yard dash and Johnny Baker converted.
— USC's Garrett Arbelbide smeared Soloman, causing a bobble which Jesse Shaw covered on the Bruins' 29. These yards evaporated in three thrusts with Mohler ringing up the six-pointer on a one-yard buck. His 20-yard gain was the "biggie" in the drive, too.
— A quick-kick by UCLA's Howie Roberts was partially blocked, then fielded by Mohler, who returned to the Bruin 29. Four plays later, Mohler found a gaping hole at left tackle and zoomed 13 yards for an untouched, stand-up touchdown. Kirkwood converted and the half ended at 26-0.
— In the third quarter, Duffield circled right end for 13 yards, putting the signature to a 65-yard mission. Big gainer was a Duffield-to-Pinckert toss.
— The Troy team drove 70 yards for its next marker, with Duffield spearing through right tackle for the final yard. Musick converted.
— Trojan Bob Hall blocked an attempted quick-kick by Bob Decker, then embraced the ball on the Uclans' 25. Aided by a penalty, the Troy soldiers racked up another TD in a brace of plays, Musick smashing over right guard from the 17. He then added the PAT.
— To set up the last touchdown, Al Maloney returned a Roberts punt 30 yards to the Bruin 25. Paydirt was reached in a trio of plays, with Bart Ritchey going over right guard for the final 16. That made it 52-0.

The Trojans figured they had done a days work, but the Bruins weren't ready to punch the clock. Instead, they started punching El Trojo, and with Len Bergdahl heaving passes to Dick Mulhaupt, moved inside Troy's 30-yard line. The passing combo missed on third and fourth downs, however, and the threat was erased.

As mentioned earlier, Mohler netted 176 yards (on 20 rushes), and he was assisted by Duffield, who carried 15 times for 84 yards, and Musick, whose 18 rushes brought him 77 yards.

Bergdahl showed 15 yards on six runs to lead UCLA. On defense, the Westwooders were led by Linebacker Aubrey Grossman, Guard Gordon Jones, End Leonard Wellendorf and Back Duncan.

Southern Cal made 19 first downs to UCLA's six, and led in total yardage, 488 to 130.

Erny Pinckert, USC All-American, 1930 and 1931.

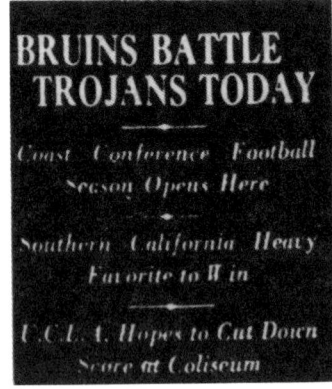

Orville Mohler
Quarterback

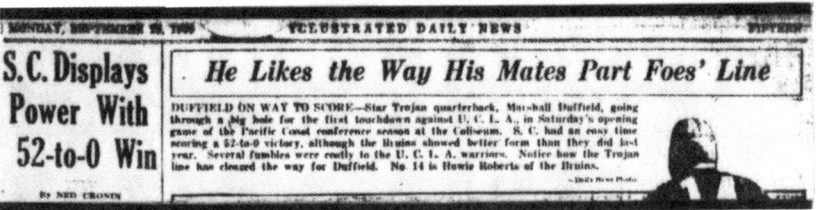

It was the beginning of the 1930 season for both schools. Likewise, something else was on the horizon... an era we now lovingly call the *Golden Age of Radio.*

So it is probable the supporters of UCLA trudged home after the game and drowned their sorrows while listening to the antics of *Amos 'n Andy* or *Myrt and Marge* or *Billy Jones and Ernie Hare.*

And it is just as probable they were joined by elated USC fans as the air waves were filled with the *Lux Radio Theatre* and Bing Crosby's *Philco Radio Time,* as well as Rudy Vallee, who would earnestly crave your attention and strive earnestly to please you. Hi-ho, everybody.

And hi-ho to the rest of the season, too. Duplicating the previous year, Coach Bill Spaulding's tribe rebounded from the USC tumble to blank Pomona, 21-0. After a two-touchdown setback to St. Mary's, the Bruins then shut out Caltech, 30-0. They then felt the sting of point-poverty themselves, failing to score in successive losses to Stanford, Oregon and Oregon State. Undaunted, UCLA closed its 1930 season with a 20-6 decision over Idaho, and that inscribed a 3-5-0 record for the year.

If the Trojans did themselves proud in their 52-0 smacking of UCLA, they smiled even broader in two other affairs. California crumbled before the Trojan terror, 74-0, and Utah State was almost as shaky at 65-0.

Other victims of the Jonesmen were Oregon State, Stanford, Denver, Hawaii and Washington. Enroute to the Rose Bowl, Washington State was a one-point victor over USC, and nemesis Notre Dame won, 27-0, in the season finale. Post an 8-2-0 slate for Troy.

Pinckert was a NCAA consensus All-America for Southern California in 1930, while Mohler and Arbelbide were named on at least one All-America team.

Oh—there can be no farewell to 1930 without quoting the following squib from Braven Dyer's "Grid Gossip" in the *Times:*

"When 'The Big Trail' opens Thursday at Graumman's Chinese Theatre, the lead will be played by John Wayne. You never heard of him, probably, but if you followed the Trojans several years ago, you saw 'Duke' Morrison play tackle now and then. Wayne and Morrison are one and the same."

So, ol' Duke may not be remembered too well around Vermont and Exposition, but you gotta' admit he made quite an impression over at Hollywood and Vine.

Summary

	USC	UCLA
First Downs	19	6
Yards Rushing	421	31
Yards Passing	67	99
Total Yards	488	130
Passes Attempted/Completed	11/4	14/6
Passes Had Intercepted	2	1
Fumbles Lost	1	3
Punts/Average	4/28	9/31
Penalties No./Yards	9/75	11/51

Score by Quarters:

USC	13	13	20	6	—	52
UCLA	0	0	0	0	—	0

Back To The Drawing Board

1931 Through 1935, the Hiatus

True, Southern California had soundly trounced UCLA in the first two meetings... decimated may be a better description.

But, in all fairness to both institutions, the game should be put into proper perspective.

As mentioned in Chapter One, the Bruins were inexperienced in big-time football. The ambition was there, the tradition was not. Ten years in the arena, only one in the Pacific Coast Conference... that was their heritage.

Why, Southern Cal had been in existence for almost four decades before the Los Angeles State Normal School became a part of the University of California in 1919. The Trojans, who, incidentally, were so named in 1912 by Owen Bird, then sports editor of the *Los Angeles Times,* had been to the top of the mountain: conference crowns, national champs, Rose Bowl winner, All-America players.

Of course, USC cannot be chastised for taking on this uptown upstart. Obviously, those people who sat on the council of Troy were aware of their own superiority; just as obviously, they envisioned the future magnitude of the series, as well as the vast potential of their young opponent.

And so, after a double dose of famine, UCLA apparently decided its program needed time to regroup. The next five years could be better spent in "X's" and "O's" than by being mauled by those gladiators from University Park.

The two schools went their separate ways... USC to even greater heights, UCLA to maturity.

As it turned out, the Westwooders picked a splendid time to abstain. In the three years that followed—1931-32-33—Howard

Jones and his Thundering Herd collared 30 victories while suffering only two losses and one tie. Included were back-to-back Rose Bowl triumphs (21-12 over Tulane and 35-0 over Pittsburgh), a mythical national championship, and two PCC titles.

The next two seasons, however, were far less productive: nine wins, 13 defeats and a tie. Indeed, swordless Trojans.

During the five-year hiatus, USC produced five bona-fide All-America players–guards Johnny Baker and Aaron Rosenberg, backs Gus Shaver and Irving Warburton, tackle Ernie Smith. Three others–back Erny Pinckert, center Stan Williamson and tackle Tay Brown were named to at least one All-America team.

Meanwhile, back at the Westwood corral, Coach Bill Spaulding and his Uclan clan were doing what they planned to do . . . mold their program into a winner. There it was: 30 victories, 17 losses and two ties. And get this: Number One in the PCC in 1935, UCLA's first conference championship.

Bruins selected on the All-PCC first team between 1931 and 1935 were Leonard Wellendorf, end; Homer Oliver and Lee Coats, centers; Verdi Boyer, guard; and Chuck Cheshire, back.

Others receiving various awards included Ransom Livesay, Sherman Chavoor, Raymond Olmstead, Mike Frankovitch and Sam Stawisky.

The honors were coming, the titles were coming, the Bruins were growing up. Now, were they ready for that rugged juggernaut of Cardinal and Gold?

Read on, and see.

1936
Game 3

No More Mr. Nice Guy

Cuddly and cute no more, Master Bruin was now Mr. Bruiser Bruin. He had come of age. Okay—so it took two lickings and five years of preparation, but that was the price to pay. Finally, he was ready—ready to face the guns mounted behind the walls of Troy.

Thanksgiving Day, 1936, was a clear day, and you could see that the UCLA-USC rivalry—now resumed—would last forever. Over 85,000 people came to the Coliseum to dispatch its delayed launching.

The fact that neither club was rated by the *Associated Press* in the Top 20—Minnesota was Number One—seemed immaterial to both coaches on the eve of the battle, even though this was the first year *AP* put out its rankings.

"The Bruins are going into tomorrow's battle with a foundation that will make for a good game on their part. They are really looking forward to this game with a spirited mental attitude that will do much more than mere physical perfection. Regardless of the ultimate outcome, you will view a creditable performance by the Blue and Gold. Tomorrow's game will mark the beginning of a new 'Big Game' tradition in the Southland. It remains for UCLA to uphold its half of this tradition. In this at least, you can be certain we will not fail."–Coach Bill Spaulding, UCLA.

While not quite as verbal, Coach Howard Jones of USC agreed in principle. "I rate the game a toss-up," he said. "My boys are in perfect condition physically and mentally. The best team will make its own breaks, and these will be enough to win the ball game after a hard-fought battle."

Jones also decided to put his finest men on the field against his adversary, an adolescent no longer.

"Trojan Two-Team Idea Shelved by Jones", blared a headline in the *Times*, which then subbed it with "Southern Cal Coach to Play Eleven Best Men on Field in Bruin Game".

The Colisuem stage was set for a pigskin battle. So why would anyone go to Loew's State Theatre to see "Pigskin Parade" with Stuart Erwin and Arline Judge? Even at 30-cents!

Southern Cal entered the fracas with a 4-2-1 mark, and was tabbed a 2-1 favorite to win. Oregon State, Oregon, Illinois and Stanford had yielded to the will of the warriors, while California and Washington had scorned their might, and Washington State went away on equal terms.

UCLA's slate was 6-3-0 going into the fray. The Bruins started with a bang, blanking Occidental, Pomona and Montana. Next came a defeat by Washington, then victories over California and Oregon State. Sandwiched between losses to Stanford and Washington State was another shut-out, this one over Oregon.

Boys-will-be-boys, so they say, and lads from the two schools proved they could match pranks with any group of boys-will-be-boys anywhere. A few days—or most probably, nights—before the long-awaited clash, the Trojan statue on the USC campus was daubed with blue and gold paint, while the letters "SC" were burned on the lawn of the main quadrangle at Westwood. Tsk, tsk.

As mentioned earlier, the Spring Street bettors favored USC, 2-1. So why did Bill Henry, *LA Times* Sports Editor, pick UCLA?

First It's → **BRUINS 7** *Then It's Also* → **TROJANS 7** *So All Ends*

Touchdown! The official signals UCLA's first points against USC. Billy Bob Williams scored midway the second quarter.

"Because, on the day they played California, the Bruins could have beaten any team I've seen this year, with the possible exception of Washington—and I've an idea they're going to play like that again today. If so—look out!"

And while Mr. Henry was half-right, the genuine soothsayer was Braven Dyer, also a *Times* columnist. In his "Sports Parade" dated September 13th (over two months before kickoff), Mr. Dyer wrote "That's (the game) going to be a tie, 7 to 7".

The popular scribe couldn't have been closer. At the final gun, there were two "sevens"—one for each eleven—on the scoreboard. In more simple terms, a 7-7 deadlock.

The only scoring came in the second and third quarters, and it was the Bruin rooters who had the first chance to howl.

Billy Bob Williams, shown here exhibiting his kicking prowess, scored UCLA's first touchdown in the series, 1936.

Captain George Dickerson, 185-pound tackle, won the toss for UCLA and elected to kickoff. Dickerson, later to become a member of the Bruin coaching staff, was making a cameo appearance, the victim of a wrecked knee. After Walter Schell planted his toe in the football, Slats Wyrick replaced the veteran leader.

Dickerson, who now resides in Laguna Hills, has not been directly connected with football for the past few decades, but his memory of the UCLA-USC series is vivid.

"The UCLA/USC football game has to be one of the most emotional rivalries due to the proximity of the universities," he stated, "and the fact that many players on both teams played with each other in their high school days. It is truly an intracity (community) rivalry, as well as a nationally-recognized tradition."

Back to the action. Starting from their 19 after the kickoff return, the Trojans proved immobile, and Davie Davis punted.

Wasting no time, the Bruins went right to work. With Don Ferguson and Schell carrying the load, UCLA moved in ten plays from its own 48-yard line to the shadow of USC's goal. But on third down from the seven, Schell and the ball were abruptly divorced on a jarring tackle by Miles Norton, and USC's Phillp Duboski took custody of the wayward oval on the one-foot line. End of threat.

The Uclans, however, would not be denied. Read on.

The ball exchanged hands seven times, winding out the first quarter and moving into the second. And then came a fatal turnover by Southern Cal. Ambrose Schindler fumbled going into center, and Sherman Chavoor, shaking off an injury from the previous play, recovered for UCLA on Troy's 40-yard line. Let's take it from there.

Freddie Funk followed Wyrick around left end for a first down on the 29. Hal Hirshon swept right end for two, and Billy Bob Williams hit center for three. Izzy Cantor went overhead to Bob Nash for a first down on the 15. After Funk flunked on a reverse, Cantor drove over right tackle for six, then added three more through the middle. On fourth down, Williams slashed off tackle for a possession-preserving first down on the four.

Williams punched right guard for two yards, took a welcome rest while USC rallied its forces with a time-out, then bulled over left guard for a touchdown, the very first points ever hung on the Trojans by the Bruins. If the UCLA supporters were delirious—and they were—forgive them.

The PAT didn't seem so all-fire important at the moment, but Williams added it anyway, so the young colts from Westwood led, 7-0.

SC had visions of locking the score by intermission, but Bill Gaisford's bobble was surrounded by UCLA's Earle Harris on his 13-

yard line. Funk boomed a 71-yard punt and the half ended a few plays later.

The third period belonged to the Jonesmen. Beginning on its 48-yard line after a Funk punt, USC knotted the contest in 13 plays. Schindler made two through tackle, Jimmy Jones passed incomplete, then Schindler tossed to Duboski for a first down on the Bruin 40. After Jones gained one, Schindler threw a strike to Homer Beatty in the left flank for a sticks-mover on the 27. Schindler plowed off tackle for seven, and Jones punched center for a first down on the 17. Schindler picked up two, threw incomplete, added two more through right tackle, then projected an aerial to Beatty in the right flank for a first down on the five.

Schindler bucked tackle for a single, then Jones drove over left tackle for the six-pointer. When Jim Henderson tacked on the extra point, it was a new ball game at 7-7.

If ever there was an Achilles to torment the Trojans, his shining armor appeared in the name of Merle Harris. Although not a starter, Harris halted four Trojan drives with three pass interceptions and a fumble recovery . . . all in the fourth quarter.

To a man, the SC squad was disappointed with the tie, and felt ". . . we should have won". But then, over in Hollywood, Mae West was complaining because ". . . the censors take out my best cracks." Hmmm, there may be some correlation here.

El Rodeo, the USC yearbook, reviewed the tussle most admirably. "The meeting of the two universities this year will set a tradition that will last as long as either school participates in football competition," it read. "From a crowd of 90,000 people, this grid natural received a thunderous approval. The Thanksgiving Day game was spectacular and exciting, ending in a 7-7 tie to the satisfaction of the attending masses. The fine sportsmanship displayed by both schools on the field and in the stands warrants the beginning of a classic. Already, the SC-UCLA combat has been titled by sports scribes as 'The Big Game'."

Top gainers for USC were Davis with 81 yards and Schindler with 44. Both carried the ball 11 times. Williams and Ferguson each had 33 yards for UCLA.

As might be suspected by now, turnovers assumed an important role in the game, especially hurting the Trojans, who counted eight.

Players cited in newspaper reports for outstanding efforts were Bill Radovich, Captain Gil Kuhn, Norton, Don McNeil, Davis and Schindler for USC; Ferguson, M. Harris, Williams, Schell and Cantor for the Westwooders.

Both teams had one game remaining before closing the season. For Southern Cal, it was another tie—13-13 against Notre Dame.

The Uclans were looking forward to a gridiron feast against the University of Hawaii in Honolulu on December 19th. It never came off. A maritime strike on the nation's waterfronts kept the Bruins in dry dock and the luau was finally canceled. (Where were you, Delta?)

After the game, officials of the two institutions decided to have the game ball bronzed and made into a perpetual trophy, the team winning each year to hold it for 12 months.

Also, after the game, uptight fans went home to unwind. Many turned to the ever-faithful radio for help—Ben Bernie, Easy Aces, Jimmy Fidler—the 7-to-7 draw faded into history.

Starting Lineups: Southern Cal-Ends, Hibbs and C. Williams; Tackles, Belko and Norton; Guards, Hansen and Radovich; Center, Kuhn (c); Quarterback, Davis; Halfbacks, Duboski and Beatty; Fullback, Berryman. UCLA-Ends, Schroeder and Robinson; Tackles, Barber and Dickerson (c); Guards, Barr and Hastings; Center, Chavoor; Quarterback, E. Harris; Halfbacks, Funk and Ferguson; Fullback, B. Williams.

Summary

	USC	UCLA
First Downs	9	8
Yards Rushing	142	129
Yards Passing	28	10
Total Yards	170	139
Passes Attempted/Completed	11/3	5/1
Passes Had Intercepted	3	0
Fumbles Lost	5	1
Punts/Average	7/34	12/40

Scoring by Quarters:

USC	0	0	7	0	—	7
UCLA	0	7	0	0	—	7

1937
Game 4

Too Little, Too Late

Nobody from Los Angeles was going anywhere. No title hung in the balance. Not an All-American was in sight. Those were the dull conditions under which UCLA and Southern California met in 1937.

But the weather was good, general admission was just $1.65, and between 65-and-70,000 loyal aficionados streamed into the Coliseum.

Both clubs entered the game batting less than .500, although both had turned in credible performances the week before. The Bruins had white-washed Missouri, 13-0, while the Trojans had journeyed to South Bend and held powerful Notre Dame to a 6-13 score.

Troy's other losses were to Washington, California and Stanford; victories came over College of Pacific, Ohio State and Oregon; while struggles with Washington State and Oregon State ended even. So USC needed the Bruins' hide to prevent a losing season.

Other than the Missouri verdict, the Ukes' only other bright spots were an opening-season triumph over Oregon and a tie with Oregon State in Game Three. UCLA drew the short end of the stick against Stanford, Washington State, California, Washington and Southern Methodist. By count, that's a 2-5-1 record. Conquer Troy, and . . . well, that would be some salvage.

Following habit, the commissioners of Spring Street installed USC as a slight favorite, predicated no doubt, on the Trojans' stout showing against the Irish.

Bill Henry, then sports editor of the *Times,* viewed the upcoming tussle with objectivity.

"It takes a year like this one to demonstrate that the Trojan-Bruin football game has what it takes to become a classic," he wrote. "Here are a couple of football teams meeting in the Coliseum with nothing in their season's record to recommend them—but we'll probably have the best crowd of the year. Probably the best game, too."

Henry, who was to announce the contest over radio station KFI, was off-target on the crowd, but man, was he ever right about the calibre of the game!

It will be recorded as one of the most thrill-packed games in the long and exciting series between the two universities.

Details will follow, but in a nutshell, the battle, if it could be so labeled after 51 minutes, evolved like this:

USC tallied in the first, third and fourth periods to hold a commanding 19-0 lead with only nine minutes to play. To that point, UCLA's net gain from rushing was a mere 25 yards and from passing just 46—a total of 71 yards. The Bruins had picked up only four first downs, and only once had they advanced the ball into Troyland. Some fans wondered if the team could remain afoot for nine more minutes. The fans, that is, that stayed for the final gun.

Others, long since turned the color of Pepto-Bismol, had gone home to swallow some . . . or to drown their misery in the homespun humor of Lum and Abner.

Then, faster than the Lone Ranger could fire a silver bullet, the Bruins struck . . . infused by the arm of Kenny Washington plus the hands and legs of Hal Hirshon. In the span of three plays (with a Trojan kick off in-between), UCLA's passing combination put 13 points on the scoreboard and jubilation in the hearts of their supporters.

What's more, the Westwood Whizzes weren't through. With reborn vigor—after forcing a Trojan punt—they stormed toward the winning touchdown, an achievement that so far in the brief series had eluded them.

Down, down, down to Troy's 14-yard line . . . a scant three minutes left on the clock. Coach Howard Jones paraded up and down the sideline like a caged mad man. The Trojans stiffened, gathering themselves together to stymie this do-or-die, furious assault by the Bruins.

And they did. Pushed back to the 15, and with 70-seconds to play, Washington's bullet failed to connect with Woodrow Strode, and USC took possession, thereby preserving a 19-13 victory.

Hal Hirshon was on the receiving end of the longest in-air pass in the series history, 1937.

For the first time in nine action-packed minutes, the Trojan rooters breathed.

Washington's second TD bomb to Hirshon established a record that stands unmatched today. In the air, the ball sailed 72 yards, 62 from the line of scrimmage. The people in the top row of the Coliseum thought they were seeing a Stinson flying the mail to San Diego.

The only aerial feat that challenged Washington's heave happened the day before when Jacqueline Cochran flew nonstop from New York to Miami in four hours, 12½ minutes. But her record didn't last very long.

Unable to locate Jones in the bedlam of the post-game turf, UCLA's Coach Bill Spaulding, he being a sportsman true, plowed his way to SC's dressing room to congratulate his conquerer, only to find the door closed and locked.

In truth, the Trojans were in the process of electing a captain for their 1938 season (Don McNeil), but in jest, Spaulding seized upon the opportunity to josh his opponent.

"You can come on out now, Howard," he shouted, "we've stopped throwing passes."

Both squads entered the melee minus important cogs in their machines. USC's fine quarterback, Amby Schindler, was out with a damaged knee, and he was joined on the bench by Phil Gaspar and Mickey Anderson. Although a well-kept secret until game-time, UCLA did not have the service of Billy Bob Williams, hero of the 1936 tie. Earl (Two Gun Tex) Harris was also idle.

The Bruins won the coin-flip, decided to kick off, and Walter Schell smacked the ball over the end zone. With Bill Sangster and Grenville Lansdell packing the ball, the Trojans moved to UCLA's 31-yard line where Sangster fumbled and Mladin Zarubica enfolded the ball for the Ukes.

SC held, UCLA held and SC held again. But Lansdell returned the last Bruin punt 28-yards to put Troy in business on the Westwood 39-yard line.

After four rushes, Sangster and Company were camped on the eight, but on fourth down from the one, Sangster was stopped shy of the goal by four inches. Look, that's what the report read—four inches.

Undaunted, back came the men of Troy. This time, they scored from UCLA's 24 in seven plays.

Lansdell threw incomplete, Sangster gained five, then Boyd Morgan on a reverse got a first down on the 12. Sangster's lateral to Lansdell carried to the five. Sangster plunged to the four. Lansdell threw incomplete, but then went through a hole at left tackle for a touchdown. Bob Hoffman added the PAT and it was 7-0, Trojans. The second period drew a blank.

After five exchanges of the ball in the third frame, Lansdell returned a Schell punt to the Bruin 38-yard stripe. A Lansdell-to-Sangster strike picked up 11 and Morgan executed his reverse again for seven more. After Lansdell went overhead to Hoffman for a first down on the 9-yard line, Morgan reversed again for five. Lansdell then circled right end for the marker. Hoffman's conversion attempt failed, so at the end of three periods, it was 13-0.

The Jonesmen increased their lead the first time they had possession in the final quarter. And they gained possession when Schell's punt was blocked by Owen Hansen and McNeil, permitting Harry Smith to scoop up the bouncing beauty on the Ukes' 27-yard line.

Joe Schell lost a yard, Lansdell's long pass was batted down and his next fell incomplete. On fourth down, Lansdell found Schell open on the 10 and he went in for a six-pointer: 19-0, ho-hum.

The game was over. Or was it?

The Trojans kicked off, and after getting their first down of the second half, the Bruins punted. Enter a break for the Spauldingites.

Roy Engle fumbled a bad snap from center and Lawrence Murdock claimed the pigskin for the Uclans on SC's 44-yard line.

Hirshon's deep pass was incomplete, then Washington put one up which Hirshon gathered in on the 10-yard line and waltzed in for a touchdown. Schell tacked on the extra point, and the 19-7 margin awoke some Bruin fans from their slumber.

Still confident, Troy elected to kick off (the team just scored on had the option in those days). Schell received the ball on his 10 and garnered 17 yards. On the first play, Washington faded back, wound up and uncorked his record-shattering bombshell which the ever-present Hirshon grabbed on USC's 12-yard stripe and trotted across the goal line. The conversion failed, but SC's lead was trimmed to six.

Why did Southern Cal kick off to the Bruins after they had caught fire with their first TD? Captain Chuck Williams opined he guessed he had erred in letting UCLA get its hot hands on the ball.

"But I've been going along on the theory that it's a good policy to let the other team receive when we're tied or ahead," he explained, "but in this instance, it didn't work out so well."

Lesson learned. After strike Number Two, Williams, defying an adage, decided it was better to receive than to give.

But the revved-up Uclans forced the Trojans to punt, then started

TROJANS CONQUER BRUINS, 19 TO 13, IN THRILLER
Los Angeles Times Sports

SUNDAY MORNING, DECEMBER 5, 1937

SANGSTER AND TROJAN ROOTERS UP IN AIR AS BRUINS STIFFEN ON GOAL LINE

their final effort on their 43, having returned Lansdell's punt 21 yards on a Hirshon-to-Washington lateral.

Hirshon rifled eight yards to Strode. Washington raced for a first down on Troy's 40. Washington passed to Slats Wyrick on a tackle-eligible play and the big lineman lumbered across the double-stripe; but, alas, his knee touched the ground on the 31. Washington lost a yard, then tossed to John Baida for a sticks-mover on the 21.

There followed an incomplete pass by Hirshon, then Washington hit Jim Mitchell for a first down on the 14.

Far enough, said the Trojans, unified to a man. Washington's pass to Strode lost two yards, but the sophomore sensation retrieved one with an aerial to Baida. On third down, Hirshon's pass, aimed at Washington, failed to connect.

This was it. All the pounding, the agony, the pain of 58 minutes and 50 seconds was reduced to one single play.

The obvious came. Washington passed. Intended for Strode, who stood open on the four, the sizzling oval zipped through his eager arms.

"Sorry, Kenny," lamented Strode in the dressing room, "but that potato was just too hot to handle. It went right through my hands."

"Okay, Buddy," replied Washington, "I knew it was hard but I just had to open up on that one. Those Trojans were charging in too fast."

USC's Lansdell paced all rushers with 98 yards on 19 carries. Next came Bruin Washington with 54 on 16 attempts, followed by Trojan Oliver Day, who rushed 11 times for 46 yards.

Joe E. Brown, a famous comedian and leader of the Bruins' fan club, joined the throng of UCLA players congratulating Johnny Ryland and Schell for their heroic defensive roles. And, without hesitation, the Bruins voted Hoffman as the enemy's greatest player, closely followed by Smith, Lansdell, Williams and McNeill.

USC's *El Rodeo* had this to say about the game: "The USC lads returned from their eastern jaunt with a renewed vigor and wound up the season on December 4th by ripping the hide of the UCLA Bruins in a smashing 19-13 triumph."

That says it. But it doesn't tell the story.

Starting Lineups–UCLA: Ends, Nash and Strode: Tackles, Wyrick and Zarubica; Guards, Pfeiffer (c) and Frawley; Center, Ryland; Quarterback, Baida; Halfbacks, Washington and Hirshon; Fullback, Schell. USC: Ends, Hibbs and Williams (c); Tackles, Stroecker and George; Guards, Hansen and Smith; Center, McNeil; Quarterback, Lansdell; Halfbacks, Hoffman and Morgan; Fullback, Sangster.

Summary

	USC	UCLA
First Downs	14	8
Yards Rushing	237	73
Yards Passing	76	198
Total Yards	313	271
Return Yardage	81	131
Passes Attempted/Completed	16/6	25/14
Passes Had Intercepted	0	0
Fumbles Lost	3	0
Punts/Average	6/37	10/33
Penalties No./Yards	2/20	6/50

Scoring by Quarters:

| USC | 7 | 0 | 6 | 6 | — | 19 |
| UCLA | 0 | 0 | 0 | 13 | — | 13 |

**Bruin Woody Strode,
All-Conference End, 1939**

1938
Game 5

Moonlight for the Coach from Wabash

Unlike the previous year when pride was the dominant factor in the outcome of the game, the result of the 1938 fracas could wield some influence on which team would go to Pasadena. Or to Hawaii.

Oh—UCLA had no dancing thoughts of sugarplum roses, but the juggernaut put together by Coach Howard Jones down on University Avenue did have a shot at Flowerland, and the Bruins might just be a convenient stepping stone.

Actually, the affair shaped up in rather bizarre fashion.

The Bruins, by winning, would knock themselves out of a trip to Hawaii, where a couple of assemblages out there wanted to play some gridiron group from stateside.

Conversely, the Trojans, by losing, would capture the coveted prize to those magic islands out in the blue. But USC, by winning, would tie the University of California for the Pacific Coast Conference crown, thereby forcing a showdown within the league as to who would host the Rose Bowl.

And lastly, UCLA, by losing, could claim the ocean voyage and many happy days in Honolulu—provided the conference vote favored Troy for Pasadena.

Oh-kaaaay. With all those buts-ifs-and-whens jogging the equilibrium, some folks should be forgiven if they overlooked the fact that, after 14 years as head master at UCLA, Coach Bill Spaulding was hanging up his blackboard. It would be his last game against archrival Southern California. It was, you might say, moonlight for the man from Wabash College.

Spaulding and Jones had been meeting on the field of combat, off and on, since 1922 when Bill masterminded the Minnesota Gophers and Howard was the key man down the road at Iowa.

During this 16-year period, Jones gained a distinct edge over Spaulding with four victories, one defeat and a tie. But on the golf links, where the two were just a couple of old cronies, it was different. In fact, Spaulding, a prankish wise-cracker, often referred to Jones as his favorite "pigeon".

It was not unusual for USC to be favored to win. It had been the handicappers' choice every year since the series started. And, similar to previous ratings, this year, too, was justified.

The Trojans had waded through eight games, losing only to Alabama by 12 points and to Washington by one. Playing the role of "Gangbusters"—which, by the way, was airing over KNX—the Jonesmen had shot down Oregon State, Ohio State, Washington State, Stanford, Oregon and California.

While not looking at a great season, UCLA was focusing on a good one. The school listed Iowa, Washington, Idaho, Stanford and Washington State in its victory column, but placed Oregon, California and Wisconsin in the loss ledger. Entering the game, then, USC was 6-2-0; UCLA, 5-3-0.

And so on this Thanksgiving Day, 1938, some 65,000 people put down the comic strips of "Buck Rogers" and "Joe Palooka" . . . complained about a company named Pioneer Builders asking $3,265 for a six-room, FHA-approved house (why, that would make the payments $27 a month—outrageous!) . . . took a quick look at the financial pages (Hudson Motors was $9 a share, NCR 25 1/2) . . . consumed their turkey . . . and headed for the Coliseum.

If they were anticipating a close contest, they were disappointed. As Braven Dyer wrote in the *Times:* "It was UCLA's misfortune to be standing between the Trojans and a bid to the Rose Bowl." He was leading up to this: "Southern Cal crushed the hapless Bruins, 42-7."

Perhaps the Westwood eleven made a mistake by scoring first. But, after all, SC gave them a glorious opportunity, so why not?

UCLA won the toss and, as was the current custom, kicked off. John Frawley's short projectile was fumbled by Trojan Ralph Stanley, and Ernie Hill recovered for the Bruins on Troy's 34-yard line.

Four running plays, the last two by Kenny Washington, picked up a first down on the 24. Then, on third-and-seven, Joe Schell stole a pass by Washington, but when tackled, bobbled the ball back to the Uclans, the recipient being Woody Strode on the Bruin 23. Yes, it seemed USC was determined for UCLA to score.

So they complied. On second down, Washington broke through to the 10-yard stripe. Then, after two running plays, he hit Strode with a strike just inside the end zone. Frawley tacked on the PAT amid whoops from the Uclans and gasps from across the field.

Inoculated by this surprising circumstance, the Bruins battled the Trojans to a standstill throughout the rest of the quarter and well into the second.

But it couldn't last. Might would come to light in the fleet legs of Jimmy Jones, who broke away around left end on a reverse for 50 yards, stopped two yards shy of Trojan-Heaven by Frawley. On the next play, Jack Banta burst through right guard for a TD. Hope by Bruin fans remained alive, faintly, when John Ryland blocked Phil Gaspar's try for conversion.

Shortly thereafter even these weak spirits faded away. With the Bruins in Trojan territory, Washington's short flank flip was intercepted by Al Krueger, and the Trojan end scampered 52 yards for a touchdown. This time, Gaspar's kick was true and USC led at halftime, 13-7.

Southern Cal added nine points in the third stanza, then packaged the Bruins for a Hawaii trip with 20 digits in the fourth. That made the final score a lop-sided 42-7.

Bill Spaulding, UCLA Head Coach, 1925-1938.

Grenny Lansdell got the third period tally, going over from the 3-yard line to cap a 47-yard campaign in six plays. He also added the extra point.

Forthwith came a safety after the Bruins had stopped SC on fourth down on their one-foot line. Warren Haslam's attempted pass was batted down by Harry Smith in the endzone, giving Troy two points under existing rules. After three frames: Trojans, 22-7.

In the final quarter, Oliver Day registered twice, and Engle once to ring up the final margin of victory. Day's first marker culminated a 57-yard drive as he banged in from the one-yard line. The conversion by Jones failed.

Day's next tally was a one-yarder, too, and it followed a strange occurrence. From a spread formation, Bruin Hal Hirshon's lateral to Washington hit the ground and was picked up by SC's Stanley. The players thought it was simply an incomplete pass, but when no whistle sounded, Washington tried to snatch the ball from Stanley, causing a loose ball which was claimed by Banta on the UCLA 16-yard stripe. The play was ruled legitimate, and the Trojans went to work, advancing the score to 35-7.

Another pass interception (the Bruins threw four) set up Troy's final touchdown. Mickey Anderson leaped in the air, snagged a steal from Washington, and returned to the Bruins' 20. On third down from seven yards out, Engle raced around end for a six-pointer and Ray Wehba secured SC's 42nd point.

Lansdell accumulated 55 yards on 15 rushes to pace the Trojans. Smith, USC's fine guard who made three first-team All-America squads, was awesome for the defense, as was his replacement, Floyd Phillips.

For UCLA, Washington led the offense and his overall efforts were assisted most noteworthy by Frawley, Hill and Ryland. Teamwise, SC led in first downs, 14-4, and in total yardage, 287-64.

In summary, the *El Rodeo,* USC's annual, had this comment: "It was an infuriated set of Trojans that returned to the Coliseum on Thanksgiving Day and chased the UCLA Bruins clear back to the woody hills of Westwood, running up a 42-7 score."

So it was splash, splash to Hawaii for Bill Spaulding as he pulled down the curtain on his coaching career. It was a memorable finish, too, as his Bruins devastated the Honolulu Town team, 46-0, then sliced the University of Hawaii, 32-7. The Ukes slate read 7-4-1, indeed a long season.

And, after a tremendous 13-0 triumph over Notre Dame, it was on to the Rose Bowl for Coach Jones and his warriors, their first visit since 1932. The result was the same . . . another victory. The victim was Duke, by 7-to-3, and Southern Cal's slate at Pasadena remained perfect—five-for-five. Duke, with a 9-0-0 record, had surrendered not a single point during the season.

Starting Lineups: USC–Ends, Fisk and Stanley; Tackles, Stoecker and George, Guards, Smith and Tonelli; Center, McNeil; Quarterback, Lansdell; Halfbacks, Shell and Morgan; Fullback, Sangster. UCLA–Ends, Strode and MacPherson; Tackles, Broadwell and Hill; Guards, Frawley and Pfeiffer; Center, Ryland; Quarterback, Mathews; Halfbacks, Washington and Hirshon; Fullback, Sutherland.

Summary

	USC	UCLA
First Downs	14	4
Yards Rushing	272	36
Yards Passing	15	28
Total Yards	287	64
Passes Attempted/Completed	7/1	17/5
Passes Had Intercepted	0	4
Fumbles Lost	2	0
Punts/Average	5/35.4	6/36.8
Penalties No./Yards	7/65	2/20

Score by Quarters:

USC	0	13	9	20	—	42
UCLA	7	0	0	0	—	7

1939
Game 6

The Bruins' Rose: Gone With the Wind

Dusk was falling across the Coliseum greensward as the game, a brutal defensive struggle, ebbed into its twilight moments. A scant four minutes and 45 seconds remained to play. In more than 55 minutes, neither undefeated UCLA nor undefeated Southern California had registered a single point.

The underdog Bruins, cramming every ounce of determined force into one last, desperate attack, had marched to the Trojans' three-yard line. Now it was fourth down and the ball rested on the four.

There was one play left to unlock the scoreless tie. One play to decide which team would capture conference laurels and host the Rose Bowl. One play to snap USC's dominance over UCLA, now aged a decade.

Taciturn and undemonstrative Howard Jones, King Priam of Troy, was off the bench with a look of distress on his face. Across the turf, Edwin C. "Babe" Horrell, interning his first year as Westwood's headmaster, was emulating his older adversary, and then some.

Fourth down. Clearly, quarterback Ned Mathews was on the spot.

Mathews, a junior, looked to his teammates for suggestions, knowing a running play was out of the question (three had just failed). Five Bruins, puffing and pumped-up, opted for a pass. The

A crucial moment in the 1939 tussle as UCLA's Jackie Robinson and Ned Mathews tackle USC's Grenny Lansdell, causing a fumble into UCLA's endzone.

UCLA's Kenny Washington demonstrates the hard-running style that earned him All-American honors in 1939.

other five, pumped-up and puffing, leaned toward a field goal attempt, which, by today's standards, would be an automatic call. From the four-yard line, it would be a chip shot. Co-captain John Frawley's kicks had been adequately reliable throughout the season, and while 3-to-0 might not be as rosy as 7-to-0, a win is a win is a win.

USC's burly defense dug its cleats into the sod as the huddle broke. Mathews barked his signals, took the snap and drilled a dart into the end zone, intended for the arms, cradled and anxious, of Don MacPherson.

The dart never struck. From out of the dust rose Trojan Bob Robertson, weary from toil. Mustering unknown agility, he knocked down the spiraling oval behind the goal line, and the opportunity for Rose Bowl glory, as well as all the other goodies that had flirted with the Bruins, vanished.

There were cheers from 51,651 1/2 fans and moans from 51,651 1/2 fans. For that was the number in attendance — 103,303 — the largest crowd ever to witness a game west of the Mississippi River.

Hollywood was at its peak in 1939. Magnificent movies by the dozens rolled from camera to theatre, most notable being Margaret Mitchell's searing "Gone With the Wind". And, as a pair, USC and UCLA peaked in '39, too. Both entered the showdown skirmish with nary a loss on their records. And frankly, my dears, the fans did give a damn.

Sure, the blemish of an opening season tie with Oregon tainted the Trojan slate. And the Bruins left the field knotted with Stanford, Santa Clara and Oregon State. But the fans pointed to victories in all other engagements.

USC earned decisions over Washington State, Illinois, California, Oregon State, Stanford, Notre Dame and Washington, and all that figured into 7-0-1 credentials. Victims of UCLA were Texas Christian, Washington, Montana, Oregon, California and Washington State, and all that figured into 6-0-3 credentials.

Paul Zimmerman, writing in the *Times,* labeled UCLA "lucky", but qualified his description by saying the Bruins had abilities of desire, speed and deception, and possessed an uncanny knack of "coming from behind". He foresaw the conflict as Bruin speed versus Trojan brawn, then picked USC, four touchdowns to two.

Season-long statistics nodded in favor of El Trojan, and despite the flu-bug bites on Amby Schindler, Roy Engle and Ben Sohn, plus the absence of Bob DeLauer, bettors installed the warriors 5-to-2 favorites.

It was open season for scalpers, who reaped a golden harvest of

Kenny Washington was UCLA's first All-American in 1939.

up to $15 for a choice-seat ticket. That's not much? Eight-cylinder Buicks were selling in downtown LA for $895.

Both coaches Jones and Horrell closed their practice gates as grid fans stormed the sessions.

"If we had opened our gates, there wouldn't have been room for the team in there," explained Horrell.

Horrell was playing the role of yearling in this face-off against Jones, the veteran. Only 15 years removed from his playing days, Horrell was serving his apprenticeship as head mentor. Jones, still imbued with the decorum of his Yale background, was in his 15th year at the bridge of the Trojan ship. His record at Troy was 117-32-9.

"We realize that we'll be facing probably the most dangerous offense in the country," related Jones in a pre-game statement. "It'll be a hard game and a thrilling one. I hope we play our best ball of the season, for we'll need it," he added.

Coach Horrell's sentiments were about the same. "We do not know whether we will be good enough to stop the Trojans," he stated, "but we are in top mental and physical condition and if we aren't good enough, then we don't deserve to win. I have every confidence in our boys and know that they'll never stop trying, win or lose."

Notice he didn't say "win, lose or draw"?

The magnitude of the contest drew comments from other coaches up the coast.

-"A close game which could go either way, but Southern Cal's superior line play gives them a slight advantage"-James Phelan, Washington.

-"USC is too well fortified in all departments to yield to individual UCLA stars"-Lon Stiner, Oregon State.

-"It's strictly a toss-up and one that might easily be decided by luck and breaks; I cannot see how Southern Cal can be installed as favorite"-Gerald Oliver, Oregon.

-"If both clubs play up to top form, the game will be closer than the next second"-Leonard Allison, California.

Over at the race track, Seabiscuit, Kayak II and Challedon topped a list of four-legged nominations for the Santa Anita Handicap — but some pretty fancy two-legged horses were chomping at the bit at the Coliseum, too.

UCLA's Jackie Robinson was considered by some experts as the greatest broken field runner ever to grace a West Coast gridiron. Then there was his accomplice in skill, versatile Kenny Washington, the Bruins' first All-American, plus All-Coast player Woody Strode.

Counter those with Trojans Grenny Lansdell and Harry Smith, All-

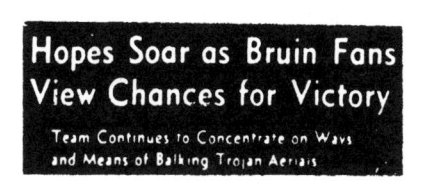

> **Hopes Soar as Bruin Fans View Chances for Victory**
> Team Continues to Concentrate on Ways and Means of Balking Trojan Aerials

Americans both, not to mention Schindler and Doyle Nave.

The sky was overcast and the dreary banner headline of the day- "Nazi Fleet Bombed by British off Helgoland"-was an omen of things to come. But December 9th was the day of the "Big Game". Nothing else mattered.

Southern Cal started with a rush, giving the impression that the Bruin was due for a spanking. But Lansdell, after gaining 39 yards in six rushes, fumbled on UCLA's 19-yard line, and Gene Adler covered it for Westwood.

The Uclans couldn't stand prosperity, however, so on third down, Washington bobbled the ball, which was pounced upon by Troy's Ed Dempsey on the 28-yard stripe of the Blue and Gold.

In two plays, Bob Peoples punched for six yards, and Robertson caught Lansdell's flat pass for four more. Lansdell and Peoples alternated to the 11-yard line. Then Lansdell drove through the line to the two-yard stripe where he was grabbed by Robinson and Mathews. The precious cargo of pigskin spun from the grasp of Lansdell and squirted into the end zone where it was caressed by Strode for an automatic touchback.

"I can't hit a man hard enough to make him fumble," joshed Robinson after the game. "It must have been Kenny." But Washington denied his participation, so Robinson gets official co-credit for the tackle.

Shaking hands after the game with Jones, Lansdell apologized for his miscue. "I'm sorry, coach," he said.

"Forget it," was Jones' response, "you played a fine game."

Although passing mid-field several times later, USC's only other serious penetration, engineered by Nave early in the fourth quarter, became a corpse on UCLA's 25-yard line.

The Uclans's ill-fated, last-ditch assault on victory started on their own 20-yard line. In 13 plays they were on Troy's three-yard stripe, first down.

> **Trojans and Bruins in 0-0 Tie Before 103,300**

Washington slammed left guard, but Sohn and Smith jammed his interference and there was no gain. Then the Bruins opened a momentary hole, but it was quickly plugged by Ben Hoffman as Leo Cantor drove to the two-yard line. On third down, Sohn jumped into the Bruin backfield and dropped Cantor for a yard loss.

The stage was set for the pivotal fourth down decision which, right or wrong, is now history. At any rate, Trojan Robertson's paws seemed bigger than those attached to any Bruin as he batted down Robinson's bullet in the end zone. And that was that.

Contrary to thousands of armchair quarterbacks, Coach Horrell refused to "second-guess" his field general, even refused to comment on the choice of play. "Mathews," he simply said, "is a good signal-caller."

There were accolades galore handed out, and while USC's gritty guard Smith came in for his share, he modestly pointed to a couple of associates. "Give Ben Sohn and Bob Hoffman plenty of credit for their work in that goal line stand," he exclaimed. "They were the ones that stopped 'em."

Sohn played the game under dual pressure. His father, enroute from San Diego to watch the brawl, suffered a heart attack, and spent the afternoon at Georgia Street Hospital instead of at the Coliseum.

Both leading rushers were from Troy; Lansdell getting 100 yards on 15 carries, Nave 55 on 13. Washington lugged the ball 18 times for UCLA, netting 49 yards, while Robinson went four for 35.

Coach Jones described UCLA "... a much improved squad over previous representatives, but we were not up to their physical peak so the result was a scoreless tie. I was proud of the Trojans' goal line stand. It proved again that they have what it takes."

Naturally, being the underdog and never having topped USC, some folks called it a "moral victory" for UCLA.

"Maybe so," wrote Davis Walsh in the *LA Examiner*, "but as such it is as worthless as a politician's promise. For the tie put the Trojans in the Rose Bowl."

If the Bruins could have had their way, they would just as soon replay the Trojans in the Rose Bowl. "Why give that $100,000 to some Eastern team?" asked Robinson, a question echoed by his mates.

But give it Pasadena did, and the University of Tennessee was the recipient. As usual, Southern Cal was a noble representative for the Pacific Coast Conference in the Rose Bowl, repelling the previous undefeated, untied and unscored on Volunteers, 14-0. It was the second straight year the Trojans had speared a Southern team boasting perfect credentials in the battle for the roses. It was also the fourth Rose win in the past five years for a West Coast team.

The outcome was no surprise to Bill Leiser, sports editor of the *San Francisco Chronicle,* who, upon learning of their selection, expressed deep sympathy for Tennessee.

So, it could be said a funny thing happened to the Bruins on their way to Pasadena. A bunch of boys from University Avenue gave new meaning to the word "defense".

Starting Lineups: USC-Ends, Fisk and Winslow; Tackles, Gaspar and Stoecker; Guards, Smith and Sohn; Center, Dempsey; Quarterback, Lansdell; Halfbacks, Hoffman and Robertson; Fullback, Peoples. UCLA-Ends, Strode and MacPherson; Tackles, Lyman and Zarubica; Guards, Sommers and Frawley; Center, Matheson; Quarterback, Mathews; Halfbacks, Washington and Robinson; Fullback, Overlin.

Summary

	USC	UCLA
First Downs	11	10
Yards Rushing	183	89
Yards Passing	39	72
Total Yards	222	161
Passes Attempted/Completed	11/5	18/7
Passes Had Intercepted	1	1
Fumbles Lost	1	1
Punts/Average	7/33	8/34
Penalties/No. Yards	3/20	0

1940
Game 7

Clash for the Cellar

If there was a reason for Southern California and UCLA to match virtues in 1940—other than the fact that a contract to play was legally recorded—it was purely to determine which maligned squad would escape the dankness of the cellar in the Pacific Coast Conference.

The previous year, these two teams met with the Rose Bowl at stake, and the experts figured they would take up where they left off and mold 1940 into another banner-searching escapade.

But, as Paul Zimmerman wrote in the *Times,* "... someone threw their grid machinery in reverse".

That they did, Paul.

Through seven games, the Trojans had managed to win only twice, 13-7 over Illinois, 13-0 over Oregon. They salvaged a couple of ties, too, against Washington State and Oregon State. But then came consecutive losses to Stanford, California and Washington.

Even without computers, that programmed into a 2-3-2 record, hardly par for the criteria of Howard Jones who was in the sunset of a brilliant coaching career. UCLA, then Notre Dame, and Jones, though unknown at the time, would depart USC after 16 years as head mentor. The legendary coach deceased July 27th, 1941 at Tolvea Lake, NY, a month shy of his 56th birthday.

For the record, his won-loss-tie ratio at Southern Cal was quite admirable: 121-36-13. And his life-time career of 194 victories rank him today 15th on the list of all-time winning coaches.

A headline of the day read: "Wendell Wilkie Calls for More Aid to Britain". While Mr. Wilkie may have been unaware of their predicament, UCLA probably needed help more than did the British; for the Bruins, going into the Trojan tussle, had been victorious in just one of nine starts.

Their first seven opponents—Southern Methodist, Santa Clara, Texas A&M, California, Oregon State, Stanford and Oregon—had all paddled the Bruin backside, before Washington State became a morsel. Then the Huskies of Washington ran roughshod over the Ukes, dropping their slate to 1-8-0.

Neither team had shown much offense prior to their meeting: SC had averaged 7.7 points per game; UCLA, only 7.4. Defensively, the Jonesmen had allowed 10.8 points a game, while Coach Edwin "Babe" Horrell's Uclans had yielded an average of 16.2 points.

Perhaps these figures were the basis of Troy being installed a 2-1 favorite, despite injuries that would sideline speedy Mickey Anderson, end Bob Jones and guard Floyd Phillips.

On the other hand, UCLA faced the battle without the services of wingman Milt Smith and fullback Bill Overlin.

It was written that Bobby Robertson, a key man for USC, had the "hurts", and would play under a severe handicap.

Don't tell the Bruins or the 70,000 people who took seats in the Coliseum that November 30th about those "hurts". They wouldn't believe it.

All Mr. Robertson did was score three touchdowns, roll up 170 yards rushing (more than the Uclan backs combined) and return one kickoff 60 yards, another 30. Needless to say, these antics led USC to a verdict over UCLA, the score being 28-12.

It was the fifth victory for the Trojans over the Westwooders in seven encounters, with the other two ending in draws. At this point in the series, USC had scored 224 points, UCLA only 39.

UCLA, however, was the first to activate the scoreboard. It happened in the first quarter, like this:

Robertson, back to pass, fired the ball on a dead run from his 30-yard line, the sphere traveled 10 yards and there was big Jack Sommers, a 240-pound Bruin tackle, to snip it from mid-air and rumble down to Troy's 22-yard stripe.

In three plays, with little Ted Forbes inflicting the damage, UCLA was on the six. On the next play, Jackie Robinson skirted left end for a touchdown without so much as a Trojan hand to impede him. The try for extra point failed when Captain Ed Dempsey smashed through the Uclan defense and blocked Robinson's attempted

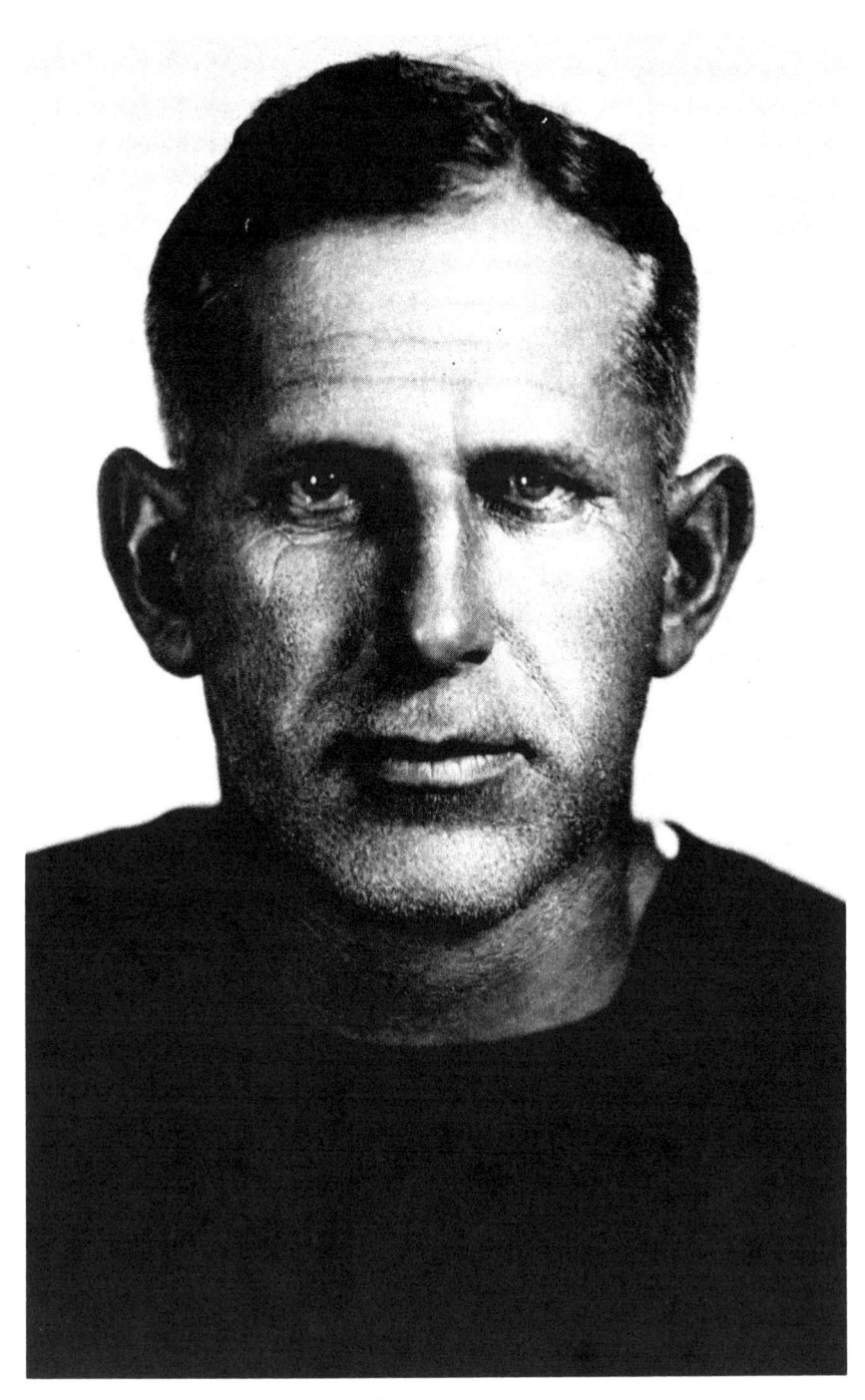

Howard Jones, USC Head Coach, 1925 to 1940.

placement.

The lead, however, was clothed in brevity, as Robertson returned the ensuing kickoff 30 yards and El Trojan went the remaining 61 in 10 plays. Bob de Lauer's conversion put Southern Cal ahead, 7-6, and UCLA never caught up.

On this drive, which was born on USC's 39, Jack Banta and Robertson consistently slipped through the Bruin defense, as the ball moved steadily downfield. Finally, Robertson leaped over outstretched paws to score from the two-yard line.

Late in the second period, Southern Cal engineered another attack which carried 60 yards to UCLA's seven before it fizzled out. So, the spectators watched the half-time show with SC holding a narrow one-point advantage.

The Trojans didn't waste much time before rolling to their second TD, cracking 67 yards in 11 plays early in Frame Three. Again, it was Robertson who hauled leather six times during the drive, and it was his 16-yard explosion to UCLA's 8-yard stripe that positioned Troy for the marker. Banta circled end for half the distance and Robertson slashed to the 1. It was then an easy task for Peoples to hurdle his body into the end zone. A swing of de Lauer's foot widened SC's lead to 14-6.

Not content, the Trojans scored again on their very next possession. Jones had inserted his "B" backfield, consisting of Bob Beeson, Bob Berryman, Bill Bledsoe and Mel Bleeker, and this quartet buzzed to a touchdown early in the final stanza with a 62-yard push. Berryman did the honors from one yard out and Quentin Klenk kicked the PAT. The horde from Westwood trailed, 6-21.

UCLA stopped SC's next drive, then closed the gap to 12-21 when Forbes tallied, but Robinson's conversion kick failed.

The final count was posted when Robertson took the ensuing kickoff on his six-yard line and raced 60 yards to the Bruin 34. Next, Robertson turned the corner for 23, then slid through the middle on two plays to UCLA's five. Banta went the remaining distance and de Lauer split the uprights. That was it, 28-12.

The game ended the season for UCLA, and a record of 1-9-0 could be reason for distress.

"Keep your spirits up, boys," came the lifting words from Coach Horrell, himself relieved from the agony of a season nine miles long.

"Our spirits are up, coach," replied one of his Bruin players. "We just met a good football team all fired up to go places today." Horrell agreed.

Nobody needed to pump up the emotions of the Trojans. As Al Wolf of the *Times* described it: ". . . the dressing room looked like a convention of models for a toothpaste ad".

The smiling theme of the Trojans was "if we can just stay this way for Notre Dame".

And, you know, they almost did. The Irish won, but only by four points: 10-6. The season ended at 3-4-2 and with it ended a legend. For Howard Jones had coached his last game at USC.

In addition to Robertson's net gain of 170 yards on 31 carries, Banta contributed 55 yards on eight rushes for the Trojans, who amassed 407 yards, all on the ground.

UCLA's total yardage was 143 of which Robinson accounted for 56 on 13 snaps.

"UCLA found out that the Thundering Herd is not dead and that the Jones system still works, when Joe Bruin emerged at the short end of a 28-12 count," harked *El Rodeo,* USC's year book. "The much-feared Jackie Robinson was completely fettered and shackled, making 21 yards his longest trip of the day," it concluded.

The blocking of Bill Bundy played a major role in the Trojan's success story. Addressing the blond halfback, Coach Jones said, "Your father was a champion, and you needn't take your hat off to him after today. You played a great game."

And so while the innuendoes of Hedda Hopper spilled from newspaper ink, the Bruins went into their off-season hibernation, dozing dolefully in the dreary cellar of the conference.

Starting Lineups: USC–Ends, Krueger and Davis; Tackles, Willer and de Lauer; Guards, Benson and Sohn; Center, Dempsey (c); Quarterback, Robertson; Halfbacks, Bundy and Banta; Fullback, Peoples. UCLA–Ends, Anderson and MacPherson (cc); Tackles, Fears and Sommers; Guards, De Francisco and Cohen; Center, Matheson; Quarterback, Mathews (cc); Halfbacks, Robinson and Forbes; Fullback, Curtis.

Summary

	USC	UCLA
First Downs	22	7
Yards Rushing	407	62
Yards Passing	0	81
Total Yards	407	143
Passes Attempted/Completed	4/0	19/8
Passes Had Intercepted	1	0
Fumbles Lost		
Punts/Average	4/34	9/42
Penalties, No./Yards		

Scoring by Quarters:

| USC | 7 | 0 | 7 | 14 | — | 28 |
| UCLA | 6 | 0 | 0 | 6 | — | 12 |

1941
Game 8

Prelude

As the Bruins of UCLA and the Trojans of Southern California met in combat at Memorial Coliseum Saturday afternoon, December 6th, the striking force of Vice-Admiral Nagumo's Japanese fleet had long before departed Tankon Bay, churning the Pacific toward its target: Pearl Harbor on the island of Oahu.

Twenty hours from kick-off, the mission would be accomplished.

The 60,000 fans who came to the Coliseum to encourage their favorite sons that Saturday afternoon were aware of evil winds stirring the world, but at the moment, they were concerned with two victory-starved schools whose mutual and single stake in the outcome of the game was — honor.

Between them, USC and UCLA had lost 11 games. Bowl scouts were conspicuous by their absence. Neither team could rise to the Pacific Coast Conference championship. Sure — there were outstanding heroes on both teams, but for the most part, the squads were endowed with unsung players.

Even so, Paul Zimmerman of the *Times* had faith in the followers of the schools. "There probably is no city in the nation where football commands so much interest," he wrote. "Even in these doldrum years like the last two, the fans refuse to stay away from these contests."

A pair of Bobs carried hopes of victory for the teams — Bob Robertson of USC, Bob Waterfield of UCLA.

Going into the contest, Robertson, a senior, had advanced the ball 859 yards, tops in the conference. The All-Coast star was also noted for his prowess as a pass defender, and ranked as a better-than-fair passer.

Waterfield, a sophomore, was best known for his passing ability. Because of his 43 completions for 692 yards, the Uclans were recognized as owning the best air attack in the league.

"I've been passing a football since I could first grab one," said Bullet Bob. "And yes, I think we have a good chance against the Trojans."

Naturally, he would say that. Any young lad who was dating actress Jane Russell—as was Bob—would have an optimistic outlook on life. Carry on, Bob.

Speaking of personalities, they turned out en masse for Southern Cal's Friday night homecoming banquet. Edward Arnold was toastmaster, Rudy Vallee was MC, Kay Kyser and Ginny Sims provided the music. And in attendance were Pat O'Brien, Mickey Rooney and Allan Jones, among others.

The standards of the teams may have been sub-par, but the head coaches, playing the role of head coaches, saw nothing but strength in their adversary.

Coach Justin M. "Sam" Barry, replacing the late Howard Jones, and in his only season as head coach at Troy, stressed the importance of kicking extra points.

"Inasmuch as we seem inclined to let the other fellow score as many touchdowns as we get," spoke Sam, "the best thing we can do is learn how to get that extra point."

And, up at Westwood, Coach Edwin "Babe" Horrell warned his players not to become cocky about their potent passing game, pointing out that USC had, in truth, outscored UCLA through the air.

"When the Trojans throw, they mean business," Horrell stated. "They seem to get'em when they need'em. We can't afford to relax for a moment."

And while these coaches were preparing their teams for combat on a friendly field of battle, words more stern were being uttered in the rolling waters several hundred miles off the coast of Hawaii.

"The rise and fall of the Empire depends upon this battle," Admiral Yamamoto addressed his rigid troops. "Every man will do his uttermost."

Doing their utmost came as a habit to the troops of Troy and Westwood. The fact that USC had lost to Ohio State, Oregon, California, Stanford, Notre Dame and Washington while besting only Oregon State and Washington State was no reflection on their

Los Angeles Times

JAPS OPEN WAR ON U.S. WITH BOMBING OF HAWAII

City Springs to Attention | **F.D.R. Will Ask Congress Action Today** | **Berlin Shy About Aid to Tokyo** | **Toll Feared High in Attack Against Isles** | **Fleet Speeds Out to Battle Invader**

effort. The fact that UCLA had lost to Stanford, Washington, California, Oregon State and Santa Clara while besting only Washington State, Montana, Oregon and Camp Haan was no reflection on their effort, either.

As usual, the Trojans were installed as favorites to win, the odds set at 7-5. But writer Zimmerman had an angle. "Both beat Washington State, 7 to 6," he explained. "That would make the outcome a tie today."

The outcome of the game was a tie, 7-7... the third knot since the series resumed in 1936.

All 14 points were manufactured in the third period. The Ukes cashed in first, as halfback Vic Smith took a lateral from Waterfield and tallied from Troy's 12-yard line. The Bruin lead was shortlived, however, as the Thundering Herd took the following kick off and marched 63 yards to paydirt, Robertson diving over from one foot out.

Ken Snelling nonchalantly kicked the PAT for UCLA, but a few minutes later when USC's Bob Jones assumed his stance for the all-important seventh digit, the pressure was thick. But his boot sailed through the posts, the score was even, 7-7, and that's the way it ended.

Each club made a stab for points in the first half, both futile. And SC threatened seriously near game's end, to no avail.

El Trojan's first campaign went to the Uclan 14-yard stripe and was interrupted by a fumble. Robertson was the loser of the ball, UCLA's Nate DeFrancisco the founder.

"It was the same in 1939 when we drove the length of the field and fumbled almost on the goal line," observed Coach Barry.

Robertson had a thought about it, too: "Shucks—if I hadn't fumbled that ball down there near the goal line, I think we'd have won easily."

The first half gun halted UCLA's initial threat. A 16-yard punt return by Clarence Mackey placed the Bruins on the Trojan 36, and after a five-yard penalty, Waterfield hooked up with Burr Baldwin, who was tackled on Troy's 10 as time expired.

The Bruins exploded early in the second half, thanks perhaps to a change in tactics from their regular "Q-T" formation to a "single wingback" setup.

Captain Teddy Forbes returned Ralph Heywood's punt from his 25 to his 39-yard line. In 11 plays, UCLA scored, aided by a couple of Waterfield aerials, one to Milt Smith for 24 yards, the other to Smith for nine.

The jaunt, which gave Joe Bruin his 7-0 lead, was featured by a supercharged line, headed by DeFrancisco and Jack Lescoulie, that opened holes for Noah Curti and Smith to scoot through. And, after 61 yards of progress, Smith cradled Waterfield's lateral to his chest and went in to score.

"That was a cinch," Smith said, beaming. "Soon as I got the ball every Trojan in sight seemed to be falling over, so I just ran for the goal. Believe me, I really got blocking."

But if the Bruins had visions of pulling off an upset, the Trojans thought otherwise. Within two minutes after the UCLA TD, the Trojans had the ball on Mr. Bruin's three-yard line, first down. Here's how they arrived there:

Robertson took the kick off on his 10 and roared upfield 27 yards. On second down, the Cardinal-and-Gold whippet whipped a long pass to Paul Taylor, who tucked the ball to his bosom on the Uclan 43, then scampered to the 33. Robertson then hit Dick Manning with two tosses, one good for seven yards, the other for 23. So there the ball was, on the Bruin three-yard line.

It required Robertson three plunges to break the plane, then in came Jones for his pressure-packed conversion.

The game ended on a twist. With USC driving for a go-ahead marker, Bob Musick threw deep for Heywood. UCLA's Forbes leaped high and wrestled the ball from Heywood on the one-yard line, but his momentum carried him into the end zone. Squirming his way back out, he fumbled and the ball rolled out onto the field of play where it was covered by an unknown Bruin.

Had Forbes not fumbled, he would have been charged with a

safety, and the Trojans awarded two points. The tie would have been broken.

But there were many "if's" in the battle, and Horrell remembered those that affected his team: "If Mackey hadn't had to slow up on the double reverse, he'd have gone all the way . . . if we had stopped Manning behind the line on the play that set up their touchdown, and we had had a good chance to stop him . . . if we had had time for another play in the first half . . . if," his voice trailed away.

Curti, who netted 64 yards on 11 rushes, drew praise from both coaches.

"Didn't Curti do a great piece of work?" asked Horrell.

"Curti played a fine game for the Bruins," declared Barry.

Leo Cantor also carried 11 times for UCLA, picking up 46 yards. Robertson with 48 and Manning with 27 yards paced the Trojans.

Statistics bore out the closeness of the game. UCLA led in yardage, 250 to 246; SC led in first downs, 16 to 12.

It was the curtain-dropper for USC, whose final slate read 2-6-1. But UCLA had one more to go—an engagement clear across the country against the University of Florida. It turned out well, a 30-27 squeaker for the Bruins, wrapping up their season at 5-5-1.

So the play ended. And the war began.

Starting lineups: USC-Ends, Heyward and Jones; Tackles, Willer and de Lauer (c); Guards, Thomas and Verry; Center, Green; Quarterback, Bundy; Halfbacks, Robertson and Bleeker; Fullback, Manning. UCLA-Ends, Anderson and Smith; Tackles, Finlay and Fears; Guards, Lescoulie and DeFrancisco; Center, Alder; Quarterback, Waterfield; Halfbacks, Cantor and Forbes (c); Fullback, Curti.

Summary

	USC	UCLA
First Downs	16	12
Yards Rushing	108	185
Yards Passing	138	65
Total Yards	246	250
Passes Attempted/Completed	22/10	12/4
Passes Had Intercepted	2	1
Fumbles Lost	1	0
Punts/Average	8/35.7	8/45.5
Penalties Yards	10	35

Score by Quarters:

USC	0	0	7	0	—	7
UCLA	0	0	7	0	—	7

1942

Game 9

The Siege of Troy

At long last. The worm turns. The drought breaks. The silver lining. Think of any similiar cliche and it will apply to the 1942 conflict between the University of Southern California and the University of California at Los Angeles. For this was the long-awaited year that the Bruins, after more than a decade of frustration, finally whipped the Trojans. Even the sun beamed down on the scoreboard, brightly exhibiting the 14-7 numerals for one and all to see.

Not only did UCLA gain some measure of revenge against its cross-town rival, but the belated conquest also projected the Bruins into the Rose Bowl, their first visit to Pasadena.

So, to say 1942 was a banner year in UCLA's football history would indeed be an understatement.

Actually, the game, as it did in 1939, would decide whether USC or UCLA would smell the coveted odor of roses. And, for the first time in the series, the Spring Street handicappers did not favor the Trojans. It was 9 to 10, and take your choice. The *California Daily Bruin*, however, disagreed, rating SC a slight favorite.

Despite the Uclans' dazzling offense—they had put points on the board in their last 13 games (dating back into the previous year)—Coach Edwin "Babe" Horrell stressed defense in his pre-game scrimmages.

Undoubtedly, he was thinking about a Trojan offense that was strong enough to score twice on sturdy Ohio State, lay 26 points on front-running Washington State, and scorch Oregon (which beat UCLA) for 40 points.

Both squads had representatives on the Associated Press All-Coast team. For Troy, there was Mickey McCardle, a junior, in the backfield; for Westwood, senior Jack Lescoulie was at guard and junior Bob Waterfield was the QB.

Despite the gory headlines emanating from World War 2, the day before the game, as always, was loaded with festivities. Comedian Joe E. Brown, Bruin rooter supreme, appeared at a mid-day rally at Royce Hall; Rudy Vallee presented his variety show at Kerckhoff Hall; the opposing coaches joshed at the Rotary Club; and the UCLA-USC Victory War Bond Drive entered the eve of its 2-million dollar mark. Incidentally, any patriotic citizen could obtain a 50-yard seat or sit on the players' bench for the purchase of a $5,000 bond.

Crocodile-sized tears flooded the Biltmore Ballroom when opposing coaches took the lectern and decried their own woeful little team, while lauding that juggernaut of his opponent with a spewing flow of superlatives.

"Troy can't miss," moaned Babe.

Bruins are a shoo-in," mocked USC's rookie head coach, Jeff Cravath.

CALIFORNIA DAILY BRUIN
UNIVERSITY OF CALIFORNIA AT LOS ANGELES

Rose Bowl Bid at Stake as Bruins, Trojans Vie in Big Game of Year

S.C. Favored by Small Odds

Bruins Drive for Victory with Vallee

Bond Drive Reaches Climax at Big Game

Joint Hop Prepared by A.W.S.

Variety Show, Dance Scheduled Tonight

And if The Horrell and Cravath Show wasn't enough, on hand as toastmaster was Gloomy Gus Henderson, originator of the crying towel for the California coaching profession.

"Dan Clark at left guard weighs 192 tons—I mean pounds," wailed Horrell, "and when Mickey McCardle carries the ball, we're going to need four men off the bench to stop him." (McCardle justified that billing, too, by rushing for 97 yards in the game.)

But Cravath had the last word. "Babe Horrell is the finest gentleman and the finest coach I ever met and he played the same way as he coaches," cracked Jeff. "He's tops. I wish him the very best of luck... between now and 2:30 tomorrow afternoon."

The Bruins and Trojans seemed more like turtles in the early stages of the season. Through its first five games, USC suffered setbacks to Tulane, Ohio State and Stanford, managed a tie with Washington and owned a lone win over Washington State. And UCLA was defeated in its first two games by Texas Christian and St. Mary's Pre-Flight.

At this stage, a bowl of genus rosa seemed remote.

But the Uclans went on to handle Oregon State, California, Santa Clara, Stanford, Washington and Idaho, slipping only to Oregon on a muddy field. So they carried a 6-3-0 ledger into the fray. The second half of SC's season listed verdicts over California, Oregon and Montana with a loss to Notre Dame. So it carried a 4-4-1 ledger into the fray.

So how did the experts of the Fourth Estate foresee the Coliseum clash?

Braven Dyer—"These teams have played three ties in eight games and it looks like another draw today. If either team can muster enough stuff to win, it'll probably be by a field goal."

Paul Lowery—"I have a sneaking suspicion the Trojans will win because of a sturdier defense. It should be a free scoring battle between two well-balanced teams which possess spectacular offensives."

Paul Zimmerman—"Too much Waterfield. UCLA 14, SC 6."

Al Wolf—"This is the day when Solari explodes. That's one UCLA touchdown. Waterfield will throw for another. The Bruins can't bottle McCardle all afternoon, so call it 14-7."

Can you believe that Wolf? Not only did he predict the winner and the score to its precise point, he also called two of the three touchdowns—Waterfield throwing for one, McCardle throttling in for one. He was right about Solari, too, as the 177-pound halfback led his team with 63 yards net gain, though not crossing the doublestripe.

Jack Lescoulie played in UCLA's first series victory, 1942.

It was somewhat of a surprise when UCLA designated its infantry troops to shoulder the bulk of the burden, rather than its vaunted air attack, piloted by Bullet Bob Waterfield.

And, ironically, it was an aerial thrust by Troy that led to UCLA's initial six-pointer. It happened like this:

From his 23-yard line, McCardle went overhead with Joe Davis the intended receiver. But at mid-field the ball was picked off by Waterfield, who returned 15 yards. SC was then penalized five yards, so for Westwood, it was a 30-yard jaunt in seven plays to the Promised Land.

Vic Smith garnered five, two and four yards to the 19. Then Waterfield, who seldom ran with the ball, faked to Smith, ambled around right end and set sail downfield. He was knocked out of bounds at the six by Jim Hardy and Dick Manning.

Waterfield's sneak may have been the most dramatic play of the day, and here's how one radio announcer described it: "It's a reverse. No, no, no, Solari has it—he's down. No, no, no, Waterfield has it himself. No one's near him. There he goes."

Now, from that station break, pick up the action at the six again. Backfield in motion cost the Ukes five, but Smith got it back with an

UCLA defenders await USC's Mickey McCardle in 1942 upset.

Bob Waterfield, UCLA quarterback in its first Rose Bowl game, January 1, 1943.

extra yard to spare, then cracked guard for two more. From the three, Ken Snelling ploughed into the end zone. He also made the conversion, giving UCLA a 7-0 advantage.

The Bruins' vim carried past intermission and into the third period, but was momentarily cooled when their opening drive sputtered on Troy's 27-yard line.

Still, touchdown Number Two materialized midway this period. Smith, Solari and Ev Riddle punched the ball from UCLA's 31 to SC's 42. Then, calling a pass for the first time in the second half, Waterfield heaved a strike into the arms of Burr Baldwin at the 20, and the speedy reserve sped the rest of the way. Snelling's toe lifted the score to 14-0.

"I had a feeling everything was going to be all right when I saw that pass heading my way," expounded Baldwin. "It was all I could do to keep from yelling 'Come to Papa!' "

The Trojan troops were down, but not out.

UCLA's Bob Waterfield looks for running room as UCS's Bill Seixas and Don Clark prepare a blockade in the 1942 contest.

Bruins Rip Trojans, 14-7;
Win Title, Rose Bowl Bid

BRUINS VOTED TO PASADENA

What D'ya Say Joe-- Let's Go!

90,000 SEE U. S. C. LOSE FIRST TIME

Bob Musick fielded Waterfield's boot and El Trojan set up shop on UCLA's 43-yard stripe. Hubie Kerns split the middle for three, then McCardle delivered a swing pass to Doug Essick, who dashed to the Bruin 10. On the next play, ol' No. 28 — McCardle — drove off tackle and eradicated those 10 yards in one fell swoop. Dick Jamison kicked true and the Trojans now trailed by only seven.

In no time, USC was knocking at the Bruin door again, reaching the 16 before the effort fizzled with two incompletions.

SC engineered two other threats earlier in the game, too. One was interrupted when Roy Kurrasch stole a Hardy toss in the first quarter. Then, in the second frame, the Trojans moved 61 yards to Westwood's 13 before the Bruins took charge on downs.

After the game, the Bruins lingered long in their dressing room, mulching sweet gulps of victory. All except Solari.

"Let's wait until after January 1st," he cautioned. "We've got Georgia, yet, don't forget."

The Bulldogs had already been selected as the visiting team for the battle of roses. Their scout, Howell Hollis, was impressed with the Bruins.

"They're plenty tough," he reported, "particularly Solari and Waterfield."

BRUINS BREAK EIGHT-YEAR TROJAN GRID JIN[X]

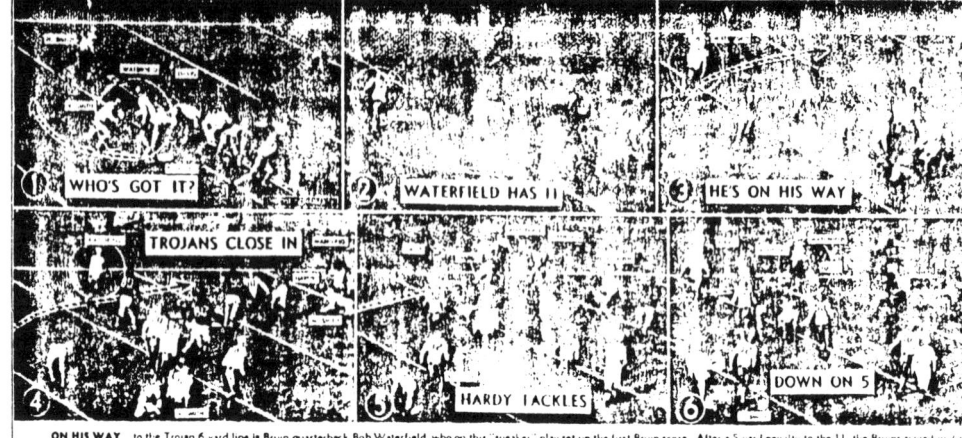

1. WHO'S GOT IT? **2.** WATERFIELD HAS IT **3.** HE'S ON HIS WAY
4. TROJANS CLOSE IN **5.** HARDY TACKLES **6.** DOWN ON 5

ON HIS WAY to the Trojan 6 yard line is Bruin quarterback Bob Waterfield, who on this "sneak" play set up the first Bruin score. After a 5-yard penalty to the 11, the Bruins scored in...

CALIFORNIA DAILY BRUIN Sports

Snelling, Baldwin Tally for Bruins
Uclans End 'Best Ever' Season with Clean 1942 Conference Victory

'Sneak' Play Leads Bruins to Rose Bowl
by Bob Wilcox

Uclans Stagger Scots in First City Cup Tilt
Ramos, Chang, Storn, Stanziola Sparkle in Sensational Victory
by Bud Sewell

THOSE TWO LITTLE YARDS TO HEAVEN

Gridders Gain Rose Bowl Bid with Georgia

Dressing Room Wild After First Victory

Fifth Down

Troy Fans 'Glad' of Bruin

PASADENA BOUND!

U.C.L.A. WINS 14-7 BATTLE
VICTORY CLINCHES ROSE BOWL BID FOR LOCALS
by Milt Wilner

UCLA 14; USC 7.

74

Waterfield, by the way, played the full 60-minutes, his sixth ironman performance of the year and a feat that earned him a school record of 557 minutes of playing time during the season.

One of the happiest invaders in the Westwood dressing room was Kenny Washington, their former All-American. "What a team," he exulted. "I always felt bad that we didn't make the grade but that's over now."

And the UCLA yearbook, *Southern Campus,* capped the occasion like this: "This sunny afternoon will long be remembered as the great day in UCLA grid history, for at long last, the ambitious Bruins emerged victorious over their traditional cross-town rivals. Came nightfall, and the festive guys and gals were all over at the big moonlight rally and street dance on Gayley, whooping it up all over again."

While the Bruin players hung slow, the Trojans dressed rapidly, evacuating their quarters in record time.

"Guess there had to be a first time for the Bruins to win," remarked Musick. But even in their swift retreat, the Trojan players did find time to wish the Bruins well in the Rose Bowl.

"The Bruins played heads-up football and deserved to win," stated Cravath. "We made too many mistakes to win."

But win they did the following week when St. Mary's Pre-Flight was grounded by USC, 21-13. The triumph enabled Troy to finish the season at an even .500.

Of course, Georgia awaited UCLA in the Rose Bowl, and the Bulldogs, sparked by Fireball Frankie Sinkwich, spoiled the debut of the Bruins, 9-0.

Starting Lineups: USC—Ends, Heywood and Davis; Tackles, Verry and McCall; Guards, Clark and Seixas; Center, Bianchi; Quarterback, Bleeker; Halfbacks, McCardle and Taylor; Fullback, Musick. UCLA—Ends, Smith and Weiner; Tackles, Finlay and Fears; Guards, Lescoulie and Sparlis; Center, Armstrong; Quarterback, Waterfield; Halfbacks, Solari and Riddle; Fullback, Snelling.

Summary

	USC	UCLA
First Downs	9	9
Yards Rushing	135	156
Yards Passing	36	54
Total Yards	171	210
Passes Attempted/Completed	17/6	6/2
Passes Had Intercepted	2	1
Fumbles Lost	0	0
Punts/Average	7/42.1	8/38.2
Penalties No./Yards	3/15	2/20

Score by Quarters:

USC	0	0	0	7	—	7
UCLA	0	7	7	0	—	14

A Sidebar

The Victory Bell

Once clanging proudly through hill and dale, through woodland and plain, through meadow and bush, the meandering of The Victory Bell is now confined to a 13-mile trek between University Park and Westwood. And that only once a year . . . or less.

The destination of The Victory Bell is solely dependent on which school—Southern California or UCLA—is victorious in the annual clash of its football teams. Once decided, The Victory Bell rests with dignity in that location for 12 months . . . or more.

For many years, The Victory Bell rang from atop a Southern Pacific freight engine. Since 1942, it has been the symbol of supremacy in each year's gridiron battle between the two cross-town rivals.

To the victor belongs the spoils. That's Minnesota and Michigan fighting for the Little Brown Jug . . . Texas and Oklahoma vying for The Golden Hat. That's Stanford and California arguing over The Ax . . . Indiana and Purdue battling for the Old Oaken Bucket . . . Ole Miss and Mississippi State crowing about The Golden Egg.

And that's USC and UCLA cracking for The Victory Bell.

When did it start? How?

In 1939, the UCLA Alumni Association secured a large, gold-plated bell which once adorned a locomotive, mounted the bell on a wagon, and presented it to the Uclan student body.

Weary from years of travel, the bell was happy to settle down, so it rang loud and clear at every UCLA pigskin party, tolling each and every point posted on the scoreboard by the Bruins . . . for two years.

Then the bell, wagon and all, disappeared in 1941. In the Ukes' opening game with Washington State, several USC students slipped into the Bruin rooting section, offering — at game's end — to assist in loading the bell aboard a truck bound for Westwood.

One of the Trojan rascals confiscated the key to the truck, and when the Bruins (wearing white hats, no doubt) went to fetch another, the Trojan guys (wearing black hats, no doubt), scratched off, amid gleeful howls, with truck, bell, clapper, wagon and key.

The search began. But the Trojan snipers were always one step ahead, moving their loot from Hollywood Hills, to a haystack, to Orange County, to . . . well, who knows?

A truce. That was the only solution. Bill Farrer, student body president of UCLA met with Bob McKay, his counterpart at USC.

The negotiation. Southern Cal would return the bell, with assorted accessories, and share whatever expenses might have accrued, if UCLA would agree to designate it as a trophy for the big game winner.

The Bruins agreed, and in a fateful act of poetic justice, proceeded to whip the Trojans for the first time since the series began, thus becoming the initial host. Since then, however, the bell and the Trojans have become bosom buddies.

Long ring The Victory Bell!

1943
Game 10

Who's on First?

The winning streak of UCLA over its crosstown rival was snapped at one straight, alas. Yes, just 40 weeks after their throbbing triumph, the Bruins were waylaid and whitewashed by Southern California, 20-0. (Oh well, you can't win 'em all.)

The year 1943 started the annual home-and-home UCLA-USC football arrangement—one game in September, another in late November, dictated of course, by the upheavel in peacetime routines.

It was a dilemma of uncertainty in which coaches found themselves, as players, controlled by V-12 and other government training programs, shifted from one school to another.

"My quarterback? Sure, it'll be old what's-his-name."

"Do you mean who started at left tackle last week, or who'll be there this week?"

Some programs were depleted of quality athletes, while the squads of others were filled to the brim with talent.

Sadly, the purge was too much for some colleges to endure and the manly art of football became a war casualty at Washington State, Oregon State, Idaho, Montana and Oregon, to name just a few.

UCLA and USC could not escape the far-reaching effects that sifted down from the war effort. The Bruins became a thin group of "have-nots"; the Trojans a puffing roster of "haves". And it was on this note of imbalance that the first of 1943's tandem meetings was constructed.

Dotting the Southern California line-up were many ace performers from other institutions: Eddie Saenz, halfback from Loyola; Lou Futtrell, halfback from Fresno State; Dick Handley, a center from the same school; Bill Gray, center from Oregon State; Jack Pattee, fullback from Fresno State; and, among others, Ted Ossowski, a two-letter Rose Bowl tackle from Oregon State.

Adding salt to the wound, Troy even inherited a prize of Westwood—Bill Patapoff—a 205-pounder who had been a first-stringer in UCLA's spring practice sessions.

A few rays of light did shine for the undermanned troops of Coach "Babe" Horrell. Herb Weiner, a three-year letterman at end who was slated for Navy duty, was given a reprieve by naval authorities and rejoined his Bruin mates. And from Stanford, UCLA latched onto quarterback Bob Andrews and Dave Brown, an end. But on the other hand, Art Markel, right tackle starter, was declared ineligible.

Though USC appeared superior at most positions, a matchup of major proportions loomed at the center spot between Trojan Gray, a transfer, and Bruin Don Paul, a 19-year-old fellow fresh out of Los Angeles High School.

"It's been a long time since I've seen a boy as alert on defense as Bill (Gray)", observed Coach Jeff Cravath, of USC.

To which Horrell responded "He (Paul) may be a bit green, but I'll bank on him to hold his own with any of the Trojans. He's a great prospect".

To the surprise of no one, Southern Cal ruled as the choice to win among those who wager on such things. The odds ranged from 3-to-1 all the way to 10-to-1.

And, also to nobody's surprise, Hollywood was flicking out war movies, 24 frames to the second. "Salute to the Marines" with Wallace Beery was pulling in crowds at the Ritz. And United Artists had Gary Cooper and Ingrid Bergman starring in "For Whom the Bells Toll".

Perhaps they clanged for UCLA. For the Bruins, despite a noble effort, yielded to the Trojans, 20-0.

The autumn day of combat was a scorcher—over 100 degrees. The Brotherhood of Railway Trainmen had struck against the Pacific Electric Railway, and the combination of heat and motionless trolleys kept the crowd at the Coliseum down to less than 50,000.

But the aspirations of the Bruins were not down and, scraping every ounce of gun powder from their arsenal, finished the first quarter on even terms with the warriors.

UCLA recovered a fumble on its 19-yard line to stop one Trojan drive, then held Troy for downs on the six to stymie another.

But the inevitable was bound to surface, and that it did as Southern Cal broke out for two markers in the second stanza.

UCLA's Don Malmberg toed a boomer from his end zone and Mickey McCardle returned it 10 yards to mid-field. Chuck Page rambled for five and then McCardle spun an aerial downfield which was snagged on the Bruin 34 by Ralph Haywood, USC's All-American end. When Andrews rushed over to sock the Trojan captain, Haywood flipped a soft lateral to Howard Callanan on the 25, and fleet Howard skipped into happy land. Dick Jamison converted as SC led, 7-0.

After two pass interceptions by McCardle, which sandwiched a fumble recovery by UCLA's Brown, the Trojans ignited their second TD journey from the Bruin 46.

McCardle lofted a strike to Don Hardy on the 14-yard line, and with the clock ticking its waning first-half tocks, Duane Whitehead blistered the Bruin defense for a touchdown. The conversion failed and the half ended at 13-0.

After intermission, Malmberg orbited a 54-yard punt out of bounds on SC's 14-yard stripe. On the first play from scrimmage— and on a direct snap to the runner—Saenz turned the left end corner and streaked 86 yards for Troy's third six-pointer. When Jamison tacked on the PAT, the final 20-0 score was posted.

Although any hope for victory seemed remote, the kids from Westwood provided a lift for their supporters in the fourth quarter by surging downfield with an 83-yard jaunt that carried momentarily into the end zone. Fullback Troy Horton's two-yard TD plunge, however, was nullified by an offside penalty, and a repeat performance was not in the cards.

UCLA generated only three first downs, all in the final period. Its total yards gained amounted to only 71, compared to 310 by USC.

But Coach Cravath was gracious in victory. "Say," he exclaimed, "Babe's going to have quite a ball club before the year's over. Those Bruins never quit trying. We'll have our hands full next time we meet."

And while lauding his opponent, Cravath was critical of his Trojans.

"We had lousy blocking, especially in the line," he fumed.

As usual, Horrell took the thumping in style. "I think our boys did a pretty fair job, all things considered," he pointed out. "Our line made several swell stands and our backfield, though green, picked up valuable experience. I think you'll see a difference next week."

Thanks to his 86-yard sprint, Saenz was the game's leading ground gainer with 109 yards on eight carries. The other USC backs came in for plaudits, too... McCardle, Callanan and Page.

Cited for stellar efforts on the Bruin's side were Paul, Malmberg, Mike Marienthal and Weiner.

USC used the UCLA shutout as a springboard for things to come, blanking its next five opponents. That's right, Troy yielded not a single point in its first six games. Besides UCLA, other teams to feel the anvil of USC's devastating defense were California, St. Mary's Pre-Flight, University of San Francisco, College of the Pacific, and California again.

The Trojans then lost by three points to San Diego Navy and were clobbered by March Field before meeting UCLA for the second encounter.

Due to travel restrictions, the Rose Bowl was an all-in-the-family affair that saw Southern Cal scrub Washington, 29-0. It was the seventh appearance by the Trojans at Pasadena and their victories numbered the same. For the season, their slate was 8-2-0.

After losing to SC in the opener, the Bruins were humbled by College of the Pacific, March Field, California twice, San Diego Navy and Del Monte Pre-Flight. Their lone moment of joy was gained at the expense of St. Mary's just before tangling with USC in the season finale.

The outcome of that curtain dropper was... but that's another story.

Starting Lineups: USC-Ends, Haywood and MacPhail; Tackles, Jamison and Audet; Guards, Verry and Garzoni; Center, Gray; Quarterback, J. Hardy; Halfbacks, Callanan and McCardle; Fullback, Page. UCLA-Ends, Brown and Wiener; Tackles, Malmberg and Vannatta; Guards, Munro and Marienthal; Center, Paul; Quarterback, Andrews; Halfbacks, Boyd and Stiers; Fullback, Horton.

Summary

	USC	UCLA
First Downs	10	3
Yards Rushing	236	11
Yards Passing	74	60
Total Yards	310	71
Passes Attempted	4	9
Passes Completed	2	4
Passes Had Intercepted	0	4
Fumbles Lost	3	1
Punts/Average	4/39.2	9/32.5
Penalties No./Yards	4/30	3/15

Score by Quarters:

USC	0	13	7	0	—	20
UCLA	0	0	0	0	—	0

1943
Game 11

Bobbleville

Oh where, oh where did my little ball roam? That was the dominant theme when Southern Cal and UCLA met for a football encore in late November, 1943. For the teams—oops—combined for a total—oops—of 14 fumbles—oops.

And even though the Trojans dropped the seemingly lubricated pigskin eight times, they still managed to drop the Bruins, 26-13 . . . calling upon a second-half rally to turn the trick.

Earlier in the season—September 25th to be exact—the Thundering Herd had slapped a 20-0 paddling on the Uclans, and now, bridled by wartime travel restrictions, the two institutions were meeting for the second time.

Whereas the fortunes of Westwood had plummeted to a record of 1-7-0 (their lone decision having come the previous week over St. Marys, despite a one-man show by the Gaels' Herman Wedemeyer), those of Troy soared to a 6-2-0 plateau. And, whereas the Bruins could look forward only to a bus ride back to the confines of Hilgard and Sunset Boulevard, the Trojans entertained visions of a rosy trip to Pasadena, their favorite post-season stomping grounds.

The reader though, had to be a little confused with advance headlines that appeared during the week: "New Bruins May Sweep Troy Clean" and "Uclans Stock Boosted for Win Over Trojans" and "Trojans in Top Shape for Clash with Bruins."

UCLA Coach Babe Horrell seemed to put more stock in the last one. When questioned, he replied: "Naturally, I can't get away from picking the Trojans. The odds favor them, but I think both teams will score."

He was correct on both counts. Southern California did win and both teams did score.

The warriors did it first, thanks to a couple of Gray hounds. From his 23-yard line, Bruin Don Malmberg dropped back to punt, but Trojan Bill Gray crashed through and blocked his boot-to-be. His buddy, Gordon Gray (no relation) scooped up the errant pigskin on the six and trotted in, unmolested, for a touchdown. The point-after failed.

This little act of easy-come-TeeDee apparently infuriated Malmberg. So, moments later, he tore through and blocked a Jim Hardy kick at mid-field, UCLA's Dave Brown staked claim to the ball, then tried to lateral it off. Nobody could find the handle, but a bouncing ball is like a magnet to a football player, so Bruin Mike Marienthal finally attached himself to it on Troy's 24-yard stripe. One play—boom—Don Borden off tackle—six points—Malmberg PAT good—UCLA 7, USC 6.

USC threatened to regain the lead in the second period but UCLA had contrary notions. With the ball on Westwood's 23-yard line, Hardy's lateral was stolen by Brown, and the lanky end breezed 84 yards for a touchdown. The conversion was missed, but UCLA led at intermission, 13-6.

Downtown, the Hollywood Grand Opera Company was making plans to perform "I Pagliacci"—but at the Coliseum, there were no plans by Tommy Trojan to play the role of clown in the second half.

On the first play of the third stanza, Ted Ossowski pounced on a Bruin fumble 20 yards from glory-land. Eddie Saenz ripped off seven, then George Callanan whizzed around end, cut back and scored. Dick Jamison's toe tied the tussle at 13-13.

The remainder of Frame Three was spent in the spirit of the match: exchanging fumbles.

But a spectacular run by Johnny Evans in the final quarter tipped the Trojans toward paydirt and they capitalized on the opportunity. Evans' sojourn was 32 yards, to the Blue-and-Gold six, from where Earl Parsons scored in two plays. Jamison upped the count to 20-13.

Evans then essayed a repeat performance, bolting 18 yards to the Bruin 17, but the Uclans recovered a fumble inches from their goal line to thwart that would-be game-clincher.

USC did, however, clinch the game as the scoreboard clock panted into its last breaths. Saenz simply returned a Malmberg punt 40 yards for a marker. It mattered not the PAT failed.

Speaking of Saenz, his net gain for the game amounted to 49 yards, a figure matched by both Tom Duddleson and Jack Boyd of UCLA.

"We gave everything we had," mumbled Bruin Coach Horrell, visibly shaken, "and it wasn't enough. Our boys tired out badly toward the end. We didn't have enough adequate replacements."

Coach Jeff Cravath was stunned by the epidemic of fumble-itis that attacked his Trojans.

"Everything I've got to say I can say in three words," he huffed. "Fumble, fumble, fumble." Then he added "It looked like for a while we might lose our fumble championship, but I guess we managed to retain it."

And he further added "I thought UCLA was very high out there and I had anticipated they would be, but I couldn't get my kids up for the game".

Cravath may have been disappointed in some aspects of his team, but could he fault the defense? Hardly. UCLA made only one first down during the entire conflict and its yards gained totaled only 93.

It was a mutual opinion by players from both squads that Malmberg, burly Bruin All-Coast tackle, was the most outstanding athlete on the field. And mate Brown was not far behind.

Be that as it may, there was faint reason for rejoicing at Westwood, for the loss to USC shaded their season to 1-8-0.

SC wound up with an 8-2-0 mark after blanking neighbor Washington in the Rose Bowl.

After 11 games, the series of crosstown crossfire stood at 7-1-3 with USC on top. The point differential was 284 to 73.

A popular comic strip of the day was "Smilin' Jack". He had nothing on Tommy Trojan.

Starting Lineups: USC-Ends, G. Gray, J. Callanan; Tackles, Ferraro, Ossowski; Guards, Jamison, Garzoni; Center, W. Gray; Quarterback, J. Hardy; Halfbacks, Saenz, G. Callanan; Fullback, Whitehead. UCLA-Ends, Markel, Brown; Tackles, Vannatta, Malmberg; Guards, Rohrer, Marienthal; Center, Paul; Quarterback, Andrews; Halfbacks, Boyd, Beling; Fullback, Duddleson.

Summary

	USC	UCLA
First Downs	9	1
Yards Rushing	188	86
Yards Passing	50	7
Total Yards	238	93
Passes Attempted	12	11
Passes Completed	3	1
Passes Had Intercepted	0	2
Fumbles	8	6

Score by Quarters:

USC	6	0	7	13	—	26
UCLA	7	6	0	0	—	13

1944

Game 12

Legs of Fizz, Cheeks of Fuzz

Many of the 60,000 spectators had left the Coliseum on September 23rd, 1944, when an unheralded, teenage freshman entered the game off the UCLA bench. Why not? There were less than three minutes to play in the game, ol' Sol was blistering the stands with rays in excess of 100 degrees, and USC had a comfortable (everyone thought) 13-0 advantage. Farewell.

But those die-hard fans who stuck around for the final gun were witnesses to one of the most pulsating, whirlwind finishes in the series history of these crosstown rivals.

For Johnny Roesch, a carbonated speedster with fizz in his legs, burned the Troy defense for two lightning-quick touchdowns, enabling the Bruins to convert a sure-fire loss into a 13-13 tie. On his second TD, Roesch actually crossed the goal after the final shot sounded, as did Bob Waterfield's breathtaking PAT.

And guess what? There wasn't even a picture of the Beverly Hills youngster in the official game program.

It was the first game of 1944's wartime twin-bill between the Los Angeles institutions, and the curtain-raiser for both.

Street and Smith's Football Yearbook, crystal-balling the season, put the finger on the Trojans: "Winner of the Rose Bowl game, Southern California once again rates favoritism within the (Pacific

Coast) Conference. It hopes to field a full starting lineup of players with 1943 varsity or junior varsity experience. SC may make Pasadena once more."

And, concerning UCLA, *Street and Smith* predicted: "The Bruins figure to hit their stride this fall and with a break or two could top the parade again. (Coach) Babe Horrell has half a dozen regulars back from last year, along with enough new blood to make the Westwood critter an entirely different animal."

As it turned out at kickoff, Coach Jeff Cravath's club lined up with eight lettermen, Horrell's with four. Perhaps this edge in experience influenced the Spring Street moneychangers, as odds were quoted at 9-10 on the Herd from University Park.

Cravath was ready to field a veteran backfield of Jim Hardy, George Callanan, Gordon Gray (shifted from end) and Duane Whitehead. Horrell could counter with two backfield vets—Waterfield and Jack Boyd.

But it was apparent that both coaches would rely on substitute backs to spell their veterans . . . folks like Bill Fade, Don Burnside and George Murphy for the Trojans; like Vic Smith (who played in 1941 and '42, but not '43), Dean Witt and Jerry Shipkey (an SC transfer), as well as Saturday's Hero, Roesch himself, for the Bruins.

The *LA Times* described these and some of their first string counterparts as jitterbacks, prophesying that ". . . if any is sprung into the open he can spell touchdown in a hurry." Are you listening, Mr. R.?

And those scribes who like to look for such things foresaw a battle royal on the brew between quarterbacks Hardy and Waterfield, who like Smith, were absent from college action in '43.

The day of the contest dawned hot, very hot, but the mercury would soon submit to action even more torrid on the gridiron turf.

Southern Cal scored first . . . and second—both markers coming in the last five minutes of the first half. The initial TD was shrouded with controversy.

On third-and-14 from the Bruin 25, Hardy threw a pigskin into the sky . . . it fell to earth, no one knew why. But umpire Vern Landreth ruled that Bruin Bert West had interfered with Trojan Gordon Gray's opportunity to catch the pass and handed the ball to USC at UCLA's one-yard line, first down. Whitehead inched the ball a mite closer, then Hardy rammed it into the end zone, but an unnamed Trojan was offside, so the ball came back out to the five. On the next play, Gray circled end for the six pointer, but Wally Crittendon's PAT try was wide.

Did the umpire adjudge the interference call right, Coach Horrell?

John Ferraro, USC All-American tackle, 1944.

"Of course not."

What's your opinion, Coach Cravath?

"Sure, it was interference."

No solution there. Let's go to the players involved. How did you see it, Trojan Gray?

"The ball was right in my hands when West grabbed my left arm and pulled it down."

And you, Bruin West?

"When I saw the ball coming, I made a big leap for it, but at the last second there was a big collision and it got away. I don't know whether I touched the ball or not."

Well, since the ump always has the last word anyway, let's hear it from Landreth:

"West was guilty of two violations. As he ran along with Gray, he waved his hands in the air. Then, instead of going after the ball as they went into the air, he doubled up his body and obviously hipped Gray."

'Nuff said.

A few moments later, Burnside (you knew him in later years as Don Doll) pilfered a Waterfield aerial on the Bruin 38 and hot-footed it down to the 25. On the next play he darted to the two, and after Hardy failed to gain, SC was penalized back to the seven.

Pat West plunged to the four, then Burnside flung his body into TeeDee territory. West's conversion didn't seem all that important at the time, and shortly thereafter the teams retired to hear some half-time oratory with USC ahead, 13-0.

UCLA gave birth to some cheers in the third period when it drove from its 16-yard line to SC's 18. But the cheers abated when J. Hardy intercepted Waterfield's pitch on the Trojan seven.

Then USC attempted to stretch its lead, but in vain. On the first play from his seven, Whitehead scampered 42 yards, just shy of midfield. The Trojans kept moving until the Bruins got their dander up and took over on downs at their 20.

Now—in the final quarter—and with doom lurching for Joe Bruin in the late afternoon shadows, Bob Russell enfolded Trojan Murphy's bobble on the Ukes' 49. A break, sure, but less than three minutes remained in the game.

Waterfield hurled a pass to Russ Tausheck for 17 yards to Troy's 34. Enter, Johnny Roesch . . . and see Johnny run. Three yards on a lateral, 16 through tackle, 12 more over the same spot, and on his fourth carry, across the double stripe.

Waterfield's kick was blocked, but the Uclans had closed the gap to 6-13.

Still, time was running out. Less than two minutes showed on the clock, and the Trojans had possession after Tausheck's kick off.

Three penalties prevented SC from making a first down, so with fourth-and-19 from his 16 yard stripe, Hardy spiraled a long, high punt.

When Roesch snared the ball on his 20, the second hand on the clock had wound down to 10 seconds. Let's pick up Braven Dyer's observation at this point.

"Roesch shifted into high gear, sped down the sideline nearest the Trojan bench, appeared to be cornered at midfield, broke loose again, stumbled near the 20, regained his stride and then swept into the promised land as pandemonium reigned."

Roesch had been bedded by the flu bug until a few days prior to the game, making even more amazing his 80-yard touchdown trip. He said he was very tired when he positioned himself to receive the punt, ". . . but when I got my mitts on the ball, I forgot all about it, I guess."

Time had expired, but the game was not over. USC still led by a point as Waterfield lined himself up for the all-important extra-point attempt, pressure prevailing.

The foot swung, the ball hit the right upright, bounced crazily for a tantalizing eternity, then fell over the crossbar to knot the score at 13-13.

Bronko Nagurski, the Bruins' new assistant coach, sighed. "If this is the way they always play football out here, I'll never live through the season," he commented.

Leading rushers for UCLA were Boyd with 53 net yards, Roesch with 32 and Myers with 25. Whitehead topped USC with 63 net yards, followed by Burnside with 47 and Gray with 41. Teamwise, the Uclans outgained the Trojans, 226 yards to 182, and first downs favored UCLA, 14 to 10.

The brush with the Bruins was as close to defeat as the Cravathmen would encounter during the rest of the season, save for another draw (with California). College of the Pacific, St. Mary's Pre-Flight, Washington, St. Mary's, San Diego and California (second meeting) all succumbed to the wrath of Troy before the Westwood lads appeared for their second challenge in November.

Prior to that match-up and after the USC tie, the Bruins racked up verdicts over St. Mary's, Alameda Coast Guard, California and College of the Pacific, while yielding to California (second meeting), San Diego Navy, St. Mary's Pre-Flight and March Field.

All of this meant that when the two clubs met for the second time in 1944, USC was sporting a 6-0-2 record, and UCLA stood at 4-4-1.

Would the second contest be as exciting as the first? Would another yearling steal the show? For these and other answers, see the next chapter.

Starting Lineups: USC-Ends, D. Hardy and J. Callanan; Tackles, Ferraro and Romer; Guards, Crittendon and McGinn; Center, Anties; Quarterback, J. Hardy; Halfbacks, G. Callanan and Gray; Fullback, Whitehead. UCLA-Ends, Sheller and Tauscheck; Tackles, Boom and Vannatta; Guards, Watts and Simms; Center, Paul; Quarterback, Waterfield; Halfbacks, Rossi and Boyd; Fullback, Myers.

Summary

	USC	UCLA
First Downs	10	14
Yards Rushing	181	147
Yards Passing	1	79
Total Yards	182	226
Passes Attempted	6	17
Passes Completed	1	9
Passes Had Intercepted	2	3
Fumbles Lost	2	1
Punts/Average	4/50.5	5/51.8
Penalties No./Yards	9/65	7/94

Scoring by Quarters:

USC	0	13	0	0	—	13
UCLA	0	0	0	13	—	13

Bruin Grids Roar Back to Tie Trojans, 13-13

1944
Game 13

Troy Hardy-ness

Things were looking up on the war fronts when UCLA and Southern California returned to the Coliseum front in late November for another growl at each other.

Yanks Cross the Rhine.
Superforts Blast Tokyo.
Great Allied Drives Raise Victory Hopes.
And of course, Ernie Pyle was still telling the GI Story.

Closer to home, Moss Hart's "Winged Victory" was playing at Philharmonic Auditorium and Noel Coward's "Fallen Angels" was at the Wilshire Theatre.

There might be an analogy in these titles concerning the outcome of the game; USC with the former, UCLA with the latter. For the Trojans were the victors and the Bruins were the fallen, and it wasn't even close... unless a trace of compatability can be found in a 40-13 score.

Because of their superior record (6-0-2), gamboleers along Spring Street were taking Troy and giving seven. That was logical, because the Uclans had split nine games at 4-4-1. And SC had fared better against common foes.

Tommy Trojan had the incentive, too—a sniff of rose buds to excite his olfactory sense. And how that fellow did like Pasadena!

Both squads had the usual good news and the usual bad news. For USC, letterman Milt Dreblow would not be able to play, but freshman whiz Don Burnside would. For UCLA, guard Jack Watts was doomed by injury to the bench, but end Al Blower returned from the disabled.

Some interesting match-ups were forecast. First, consider the head coaches, USC's Jeff Cravath and UCLA's Babe Horrell. This would be their fifth scuffle against each other, with Cravath boasting a 2-1-1 edge. Truth is, their personal rivalry dated back to their playing days in the mid-twenties, when Horrell was the Bruin captain and Cravath piloted the Trojans.

The other anticipated duel of intrigue between QB's Jim Hardy and Bob Waterfield did not materialize, mainly because the Trojans shut Waterfield down to a sprinkle, while Hardy was pure devastation in leading the hardy men from Troy to their convincing conquest.

Many of the 78,000 fans who trudged into the Coliseum that late November afternoon were still studying their depth charts when Burnside of Troy recovered Jake Myers' fumble on the Bruin 47.

Captain Jim Hardy passed to Jim Callanan who lateraled to Burnside and that picked up 17 yards. Three plays later, Hardy, behind great interference, rolled for 16 yards and a first down on Westwood's nine. On fourth down, Duane Whitehead slanted off tackle from the one for Troy's first touchdown. Pat West kicked his first of four conversions.

SC tallied twice in the second quarter, the first drive consuming 61 yards on 14 running plays and one pass. Don Garlin slammed over from two yards out, and West passed the toe test.

Southern Cal's third TD jaunt required just six plays to eradicate 56 yards. Jim Hardy started it by intercepting a Waterfield pass, and he finished it by diving into the end zone for the last yard. That put the Trojans up at halftime, 20-0.

Hardy apparently thought the grass was greener in the end zone, so shortly after the second half began, he pointed his mates in that direction again. Eight plays—64 yards—Hardy in six point-land again, this time scoring from the seven. Big play in the assault was Jim pitching to brother Don Hardy for 20 smackers.

Then, after Garlin scored again to stretch SC's lead to 34-0, Cravath yanked his starters and began sweeping his bench. At this point, the Trojans had amassed 19 first downs to just one for the Bruins.

With Freshman George Murphy at the controls, USC nailed its final touchdown by cavorting 29 yards in eight plays, Murphy doing the honors from the one-foot stripe.

Trailing by 40 points, UCLA searched its arsenal to at least make

Edwin "Babe" Horrell, UCLA Head Coach, 1939 to 1944.

the score respectable.

Pass interference set up the Bruins on Troy's nine, and after Myers bolted to the two, Dean Witt swung a lateral to Smith who put six points on the board for Joe Bruin. Then Smith's drop kick made it seven.

And UCLA was still not through. With half-a-minute remaining, Witt rifled a strike to Nelson King for a 21-yard touchdown. The point-after failed . . . final, 40-13.

Two Trojan reserves, Bob Morris and Garlin, proved most adept at traveling with the pigskin, Morris netting 105 yards on a dozen carries, Garlin 58 on 15. Myers' 26 yards stood high for the Bruins.

Teamwise, USC rolled up 403 yards to UCLA's 148 and 21 first downs to seven.

"The Trojans were easily the best team we saw all season," lamented Coach Horrell, of the wiped-out. "Yes, and I am including March Field. My hat's off to Jeff Cravath and his boys."

A visiting coach, Jimmy Phelan of St. Mary's, echoed the praise:

"SC displayed the best T formation running attack I've ever seen in college ball. And Jim Hardy deserves most of the credit. His was an absolutely perfect performance."

Even Coach Cravath was shocked by the "bravo" performance of his warriors. "I never dreamed we'd be able to run like that against them," he stated.

Then he addressed Al Wolf, writer for the *LA Times:* "And many thanks to you for tearing us down and building the Bruins up. You were great for our morale. The boys were out to make you look bad."

Cravath was putting a royal roast on Wolf, who, prior to the game, wrote: "Troy is a heavy favorite. But this writer thinks it could go either way by a touchdown or two, depending on the breaks. And this writer thinks that this, the 13th game in the traditional series, will be unlucky for Troy."

Entering the wild celebration permeating the Trojans' dressing room, Wolf said he knew exactly how Daniel felt when he was tossed into the lion's den.

There was another colorful little vignette associated with the contest. B.B. Robinson, vice-president of the Beverly Hills Hotel, purchased a $50,000 War Bond for the privilege of sitting in the press box and writing a sidebar.

"The press box was so high my ears popped," he penned. "The football players looked like a group of midgets." Then, becoming more serious, Mr. Robinson opined, "Thrill packed, the game each year is becoming more hotly contested until now its rivalry conjures such traditional contests as Yale-Harvard, Minnesota-Michigan,

Georgia-Georgia Tech and others."

The only player to make All-America in 1944 from either team was John Ferraro, USC's 235-pound right tackle.

It was the final skirmish for UCLA, which strung out the season at 4-5-1, third in the conference. It was also the last game for Horrell as UCLA's head coach. The Babe, who was at the helm for six years, departed with a record of 24 victories, 31 losses and six ties.

It was on to Pasadena for Southern Cal, and as usual, another Rose Bowl triumph, the eighth without a blemish. Tennessee was the goat and the score was 25-0.

Starting Lineups: USC–Ends, D. Hardy and J. Callanan; Tackles, Ferraro and Pehar; Guards, Curtis and Wall; Center, Anties; Quarterback, J. Hardy; Halfbacks, G. Callanan and Burnside; Fullback, Whitehead. UCLA–Ends, Wheeler and Tausheck; Tackles, McCabe and Asher; Guards, Keefer and Simons; Quarterback, Waterfield; Halfbacks, Smith and Rossi; Fullback, Myers.

Summary

	USC	UCLA
First Downs	21	7
Yards Rushing	335	34
Yards Passing	68	114
Total Yards	403	148
Passes Attempted	10	21
Passes Completed	5	7
Passes Had Intercepted	1	2
Fumbles Lost	0	2
Punts/Average	5/38	6/44
Penalties No./Yards	5/47	3/15

Scoring By Quarters:

USC	7	13	14	6	—	40
UCLA	0	0	0	13	—	13

QB Jim Hardy Led Trojans To Victory in 1944

1945
Game 14

How Jeff Doth Cravath Roses!

'Tis a bit premature, methinks, at this point (before delving into all the intricacies the 1945 season had to offer), but yea, let's get it out: for the third consecutive year, Coach Jeff Cravath guided his warriors to Pasadena . . . the first school to achieve this distinction in the 43-year history of the Rose Bowl.

That fact seemed to contain proper import for a deserving introduction; now, let's investigate the trail that led the Trojans to this record-shattering appearance among the roses. The first step was UCLA and it was a giant one, as the Bruins surely forced SC to put its best foot forward.

In a nutshell, the Troy terrorists overcame a six point deficit to chalk up a 13-6 verdict before 81,000 Friday night spectators. And USC was on its way.

Street and Smith's Football Yearbook foresaw the Trojan potential: "If Jeff Cravath can dig up a quarterback to run the T formation as well as doughty Jim Hardy did during the past two years, the Trojans are the team to beat on the West Coast."

But then the *Yearbook,* as such purveyors of prognostication often do, straddled the proverbial fence by adding: "But the Uclans are pre-season favorites to enter the Rose Bowl when the shooting is all over. They have—a brand new coach, 18 lettermen, a flock of promising newcomers, and the Bruin fight."

Local odds-makers were more decisive. They installed, without hesitation, USC as a solid choice to open its season on a winning note.

Their logic could not be faulted. Why change horses in midstream? And it was common knowledge that the equestrians of Troy were riding a path of only two losses in their last 21 games.

The new Westwood coach to whom the Yearbook alluded was Bert LaBrucherie, who was jumping into college competition after a highly successful stretch as head mentor at Los Angeles High School.

The Trojan task of filling the enormous QB gap vacated by Hardy seemed destined to fall upon the young shoulders of a triple-threat sophomore with the euphonic name of Verl Lillywhite. Another newcomer in Cravath's backfield was Ted Tannehill, by way of Notre Dame.

And if Hardy's void at Troyland was a problem, so was the quarterback vacuum created by the departure of Bob Waterfield at Westwood. But the military smiled upon the Bruins as Ernie Case, a southpaw flinger, returned from the wars. Case was a substitute quarterback in 1941.

The armed forces sent back a couple of other fellows, too ... Johnny Aquirre, a tackle, to the Trojans; George Robotham, an end, to the Bruins.

As kick-off time drew nigh, it was apparent that Joe Bruin would rely on speed, and that Tommy Trojan, while no slow poke himself, would depend on his bulk and weight advantage (a team edge of 16 pounds to the man).

And so, with their new coach and their new look, the Uclans sped onto the Coliseum turf, an inspired flock indeed. Across the sod were the methodical, the confident, the been-there-before, the Trojans.

Neither club activated the scoreboard in the opening quarter, but, true to form UCLA called upon its superior speed to break the ice

Armed Forces Give Aid to Trojan, Bruin Squads

HERITAGE HALL

midway in the second period.

Marching 79 yards in just six plays, the scrappy Bruins took a 6-0 lead when Skip Rowland, a sub halfback from Long Beach, negotiated the final 10 yards to pay dirt. What's more, he went in standing up.

Prior to the touchdown dash, the Bruin drive went like this: Rowland 19 yards from the 21 to the 40 . . . SC penalized 15 yards . . . Cal Rossi: 24 yards, to the Trojan 21, then three more to the 18 . . . Rowland fumble recovered by Bob Wheeler on the 15 . . . Jack Porter to the 10 . . . and, lastly, the Rowland sweep.

That ended the Bruin scoring for the game, however. Because Rossi, holding for the attempted PAT, fumbled a high snap from center, and Case's foot found nothing but air at which to swing.

Tannehill returned the ensuing kickoff to his 34-yard line and the Trojans chewed up 66 yards in 10 plays to lock the score at 6-6.

Despite a gash over an eye, it was Lillywhite who piloted the flight. Twice he hurled aerials to Henry McKinney which covered 46 yards, and once he skirted end for 14. Now on the Bruin 14-yard stripe (after runs by Bobby Morris, Lillywhite and Tannehill), Lillywhite tossed to Morris in the left flank and the swift halfback crossed the double-stripe standing up, eluding would-be tacklers on the way.

Walter McCormick tacked on the extra point with three minutes left in the first half, so it was 7-6, USC, at the break.

The third frame was scoreless, but the Cravathmen bought some insurance in the final quarter, going 55 yards in eight plays for TeeDee No. Two.

Starting from his 45-yard line, Roy Cole took a lateral and scooted 15 yards to the Bruin 40. Tannehill, fleet of foot, bolted through tackle for 19 yards to the 21, then erased 15 more yards with his next two sprints. From the four, terrific Ted crashed through the tiring Bruin line for the marker. McCormick's kick was wide right, leaving the final score 13-6 in favor of Troy.

Statistics for the scrap were close, but nodded toward USC, 245 to 230 in total yardage; 16 to 12 in first downs.

Foremost contributors to UCLA's attack were Rossi, who netted 106 yards on 15 carries, and Rowland, who compiled 83 on 10 rushes. Tannehill ran 19 times for 78 yards to top the Trojans, followed by Morris' 18 lugs for 68 yards.

Other players accorded special mention for outstanding performances included Tom Asher, Al Sparlis and Marion Childers for Westwood; Jack Musick, Lillywhite and Jim Callanan for Troy.

So, after 14 head-on collisions with its intracity rival, Southern Cal had emerged victorious nine times, with four bouts ending in a stalemate. El Trojan led in points scored, 350 to 105.

Down at the Cinema Theatre, it was "adults only" to see Hedy LaMarr in "Ecstasy", but this probably didn't appeal to the Trojan fans, who were relishing the sweet taste of an opening day victory. After all, they were in their own state of euphoria.

Starting Lineups: USC-Ends, Callanan and McKinney; Tackles, Rae and Pehar; Guards, Musick and Heinberg; Center, McCormick; Quarterback, Lillywhite; Halfbacks, Morris and Tannehill; Fullback, Cole. UCLA-Ends, Hansen and Tausheck; Tackles, Malmberg and Asher; Guards, Woelfle and Sparlis; Center, Childers; Quarterback, Case; Halfbacks, Boyd and Rossi; Fullback, Steffen.

Summary

	USC	UCLA
First Downs	16	12
Yards Rushing	177	212
Yards Passing	68	18
Total Yards	245	230
Passes Attempted	12	12
Passes Completed	7	2
Passes Had Intercepted	0	0
Fumbles Lost	3	0
Punts/Average	7/38.2	8/30.1
Penalties No./Yards	5/45	5/35

Score by Quarters:

USC	0	7	0	6	—	13
UCLA	0	6	0	0	—	6

1945
Game 15

Same Song, Second Verse

A metaphorical aroma of rose petals drifted across Memorial Coliseum on December 1st when UCLA and Southern California met for the second time in their 1945 wartime double-header arrangement. It was the fifth time in their limited series that the outcome of the game would designate the Rose Bowl host.

Since the September session, which was captured by the Trojans at 13-6, the lads of Troy had measured California twice, St. Mary's Pre-Flight, College of the Pacific and Oregon State. On the other side, SC had been ruled by San Diego Navy, Washington and St. Mary's, all of which compiled into a 6-3-0 slate, with Joe Bruin upcoming. The *Associated Press* ranked SC 16th, with Army first and Navy second.

After their opening game loss to USC, the Bruins whipped San Diego Navy, College of the Pacific, California, Oregon and St. Mary's, while yielding to St. Mary's Pre-Flight and California (second meeting). This staked UCLA to a 5-3-0 record, with Tommy Trojan upcoming.

Pasadena would invite Southern Cal, UCLA or Washington State, depending on the Trojan-Bruin survivor. A victory or even a tie would propel SC into the Rose Bowl. A triumph by UCLA would scramble the choice among the three schools under consideration.

With a slightly superior record, the warriors of Jeff Cravath rated a 6-5 favorite to win. Deke Houlgate, a renowned football handicapper, picked USC by 12 points.

"They (SC) have twice the incentive to win—their goal being the Rose Bowl, plus another win over the Bruins," explained Houlgate, who further supported his selection with ". . . they (SC) roll at their best in late November and early December. Also, I think the Trojans have a definite backfield edge with (Ted) Tannehill and (Verl) Lillywhite."

There would be some personnel changes since the two clubs met in September. Half of UCLA's early-season backfield was gone; Cal Rossi to Harvard via a Naval transfer, and Jack Boyd to the inactive shelf via an injury. Rocky Childers, regular center, was also missing.

Southern Cal would be without both of its ends who started in September: Jim Callanan and Harry McKinney, both of whom received walking papers from the Navy.

But the Troy backfield came back intact: Lillywhite, Bobby Morris, Tannehill and Roy Cole. And behind this group was another solid quartet, headed by Jerry Bowman.

The Trojan bench was so deep, in fact, that Cravath toyed with the idea of using one combination of players for offense, another for defense. The pros were doing it, except they called it "two-platooning".

Duplicating the initial 1945 clash, this second battle also shaped up as swiftness versus bulk; Joe Bruin being the rapid one, Tommy Trojan the massive one.

The nation's largest crowd of the season—over 103,000—watched in awe as the Trojan Horse, a scent of roses swelling in his nostrils, broke from the gate and galloped to a 26-15 haymaker over the gallant, but outmanned, Bruins.

Tannehill, who outdistanced all runners with 107 net yards on 10 carries during the game, electrified the crowd with early scampers of 10 and 54 yards, but the end result was negative as UCLA stopped that threat on its six-yard line.

It turned out to be only a postponement, however, as the Trojans scored on their next possession. From his 45-yard stripe, Bowman lofted a lateral to Tannehill, who first utilized his interference, then exhibited some fancy open field running which didn't end until he was in the end zone, a 55-yard tour. Lillywhite's attempted conversion was wide, but USC had jumped to a 6-0 first-quarter lead.

Southern Cal then generated two more touchdowns in the second period and enjoyed a 19-0 cushion at intermission.

The second marker required a movement of just 21 yards. Jack

Al Sparlis, UCLA All-American guard, 1945.

Porter punted from his end zone and Morris brought the ball back 13 yards to the Bruins' 21.

With fourth-and-eight from the 19, Bowman rifled a bullet to Harry Adelman, good for a first down on the nine. A penalty set the Trojans back to the 14, but Bowman, unaddled in thought, simply spotted Adelman in the end zone and pitched to him again. Walt McCormick's PAT try was blocked.

Touchdown No. Three also required short yardage. The Trojans' John Rea wrapped himself around Skip Rowland's fumble on the Uclans' 26-yard line to set it in motion.

UCLA stiffened for three plays, but on fourth-and-nine, the duo of Bowman to Adelman clicked once more and USC had a first down on the seven. Joe Scott, on a brace of runs, advanced the swineskin to the one, from which point Cole grabbed a lateral from Bowman and turned right end for a marker, untouched. The score became 19-0 after Lillywhite found his kicking groove.

The squads matched points in the third stanza, but the Bruins, dispelling any hint of becoming a drop-out, got theirs first . . . and quickly.

Rowland had two successive runs (one for 49 yards, and an apparent touchdown, the other for 10 yards) nullified by penalties, so UCLA was forced to start its campaign from its 31-yard line.

Undaunted, Case hooked up with Rowland on SC's 45 and Skip skipped into the end zone, a 69-yard pass play. The margin narrowed to 19-7 after Case converted.

But the warriors got those seven digits back when Joe Bradford picked off a Case pass, setting up the Trojans on Westwood's 23.

Scott was thrown for a two-yard loss, but on the next play Tannehill tore around left end to score standing up. Lillywhite booted true and USC was in control at 26-7 with half-a-quarter to play.

Ol' never-say-die Joe Bruin wasn't throwing in any towel, though. First, he blocked a punt by Joe Peterson and earned two points on a safety when the ball bounded beyond the end zone.

Then, with less than a minute to play, Porter uncorked a bombshell that settled into the anxious arms of Bob Wheeler, good for 44 yards and a touchdown. Case's failure to convert stationed the score at 26-15, USC.

"I guess it wasn't quite my turn for the Rose Bowl yet," lamented Bert LaBrucherie, UCLA's rookie coach, "but Southern Cal, at least in the first half, was the best club we faced all season."

Al Sparlis, the Uclans' fine All-America guard, lent credence to his coach. "Wow, what a line the Trojans have got now," he elucidated, "they are three times as good as they were in the first game against us."

Cravath, though aware his Trojans were Pasadena-bound for the third straight year, appeared calm.

"I think we played by far our best game of the year," he related. "All our fellows played swell ball – Tannehill, Bowman, Bradford, Musick, Adelman, all of 'em. And it would have been a pretty rugged afternoon if UCLA hadn't got some bad breaks in the first quarter," concluded Cravath.

When listing his nominations for outstanding contributions, *Times* writer Dick Hyland led off with Tannehill, and then handed out plaudits to Bowman, Adelman, John Aguirre and Rowland.

As mentioned earlier, Tannehill's 107 net yards was the game's pace setter, but the next best effort was by a Bruin reserve, Brooks Biddle, who churned for 43 yards on 11 jaunts.

Despite being outscored, UCLA had an edge in statistics, piling up 275 total yards to SC's 261, and getting 11 first downs to eight.

Scouting the Trojans from the University of Alabama were H.D. (Red) Drew, Dixie Howell and Fred Sington. All were impressed.

"Say, those Trojans are big, they're rugged, tough as nails, and they're fast," expounded Drew. "When our Tide players read my report, they won't be overconfident." Neither Howell nor Sington would dispute his assessment.

But the trio must have done a pretty fair job of scouting. For the undefeated Crimson Tide, led by Harry Gilmer, dealt Southern Cal its first Rose Bowl setback in nine appearances. And the blow was solid, 34-14.

Starting Lineups: USC-Ends, Adelman and Williamson; Tackles, Musick and Aguirre; Guards, Rea and Vasicek; Center, Bradford; Quarterback, Lillywhite; Halfbacks, Morris and Tannehill; Fullback, Cole. UCLA-Ends, Hansen and Tausheck; Tackles, Asher and Malmberg; Guards, Woelfle and Sparlis; Center, Fyson; Quarterback, Case; Halfbacks, Rowland and Solid; Fullback, Porter.

Summary

	USC	UCLA
First Downs	8	11
Yards Rushing	164	50
Yards Passing	97	225
Total Yards	261	275
Passes Attempted	8	26
Passes Completed	4	10
Passes Had Intercepted	1	4
Fumbles Lost	2	2
Punts/Average	8/33.3	8/36.7
Penalties No./Yards	5/29	5/45

Scoring By Quarters:

USC	6	13	7	0	—	26
UCLA	0	0	7	8	—	15

Trojans Trample Bruins, 26-15, Before 103,000 to Cinch Rose Bowl Bid

1946
Game 16

A Case in Patience

UCLA mixed the talents of Ernie Case with 60 minutes of patience in 1946 to gain its second victory over Southern California, as well as its second visit to the Rose Bowl. The score was 13-6.

Heavy rains during the week had produced a soggy turf at Memorial Coliseum, but there was nothing muddy about the game plan Coach Bert LaBrucherie had decided upon. The Bruins would play it close to the vest, a waiting strategy designed to take advantage of the breaks. This, mind you, despite the fact that UCLA would go into the game rated the top offensive club in the nation . . . 3,279 total yards in eight games, an average of 409.9 yards per event.

The Uclans had conquered all eight of those foes, too—Oregon State, Washington, Stanford, California, Santa Clara, St. Mary's, Oregon and Montana.

Small wonder, then, that Southern California was a seven-point underdog, a role unfamiliar to the Trojans.

Reacting to those odds, LaBrucherie informed his squad that across the line of scrimmage come Saturday would be the men of Troy, not the bookies of Spring Street.

"We'll have to work just that much harder now," he wailed, "because that underdog label is going to pump the Trojans full of fight."

Besides, SC's record going into the game wasn't all that atrocious. In fact, it could be said it wasn't bad at all. The truth is, 5-2-0 was pretty good. The two set-backs—to Ohio State and Oregon

State—had come early in the season, and they had been overshadowed with triumphs over Washington (twice), Stanford, Oregon and California.

LA Times' writers Al Wolf and Paul Zimmerman selected the Bruins while Braven Dyer nodded toward the Trojans.

Coach Jeff Cravath told reporters his roster was in the best condition of the year, although he would not have the services of Ted Tannehill, Johnny Rea nor Edsel Curry.

While Cravath was undecided about his starting quarterback – Verl Lillywhite or Mickey McCardle – LaBrucherie was set with Case.

Former Bruin wonder-boy Bob Waterfield, later with the Los Angeles Rams, had worked with Case during Spring practice.

"I consider Ernie the best T quarterback in college today," stated Waterfield, "and I have seen Arnold Tucker (Army) and Johnny Lujack (Notre Dame)."

In his *Sportscripts* column, Zimmerman proved quite prophetic when he wrote: "If the Bruins trip the Trojans this afternoon, the chances are strong that Ernie Case, their quarterback, will be the biggest deciding factor. Yes, as Case goes, so go the Bruins."

Well, it wasn't exactly a one man show, but Case did punch over the tie-breaking touchdown mid-way in the fourth quarter that spelled doom for Troy and delight for Westwood.

Threatening weather reduced the attendance—still 93,714 seats were occupied—and the fans weren't fully settled in them when UCLA struck for six points on the 12th play of the game.

With SC's Lillywhite punting from his 25-yard line, tackle Bill Chambers crashed through and blocked the ball. It was scooped up by the other Bruin tackle, Don Malmberg, on the 16, from which point there was nothing but daylight to the end zone. Case's attempted PAT was slightly wide, and the initial period ended, 6-0.

But the half ended, 6-6, as USC, led by McCardle, fashioned a 43-yard drive which ended in paydirt-land early in the second frame.

McCardle accounted for 19 of those 43 yards, and also tossed an 11-yard pass to Don Hardy for a first down on the Bruin seven. Don (Burnside) Doll crossed the double stripe in two plunges, but Johnny Naumu's conversion try wasn't close.

UCLA, sticking to its conservative game plan, almost endorsed another break into points before intermission when Benny Reiges booted out of bounds on Troy's three. The Trojans were forced to kick out from deep, so the Uclans started back down from SC's 35. They generated one first down to the 22, but the SC line arose and said—far enough.

Burr Baldwin, UCLA All-American end, 1946.

UCLA's Ernie Case, hero of the 1946 game.

The teams retired to their dressing rooms to learn their half time lessons, but it was LaBrucherie who almost became the pupil in Bruinland.

"The boys wanted to quit playing defensive ball and go out after points," he revealed. "They gave me quite an argument, but when I ordered them to stick to our prearranged system of watchful waiting—playing it close to our belt and kicking early—they went right out and did it."

So the defensive struggle continued with neither team reaching mid-field in the third stanza.

Then came the rewards of patience. Case punted to the Trojan goal line where McCardle attempted to field the ball. A second after the ball reached McCardle, so did little Al Hoisch, and his tackle jarred the ball loose from McCardle. The wayward oval squirted up to the five, and there was West Mathews, Johnny-on-the-spot, to claim it for UCLA.

Jack Myers inched the ball to the four, then the warriors stopped Hoisch just shy of the goal. On third down, Case followed the bulk of Don Paul into the end zone, then kicked true on the point-after to stake UCLA to a 13-6 margin.

"Whoever tackled me hit my arm and the next thing I knew I didn't have the ball," explained McCardle, whose one "goat" play should not distract from an otherwise outstanding performance.

Anyway, there was still time for USC to catch and overtake UCLA.

Gordan Gray returned the Bruins' kickoff 23 yards to his 27. McCardle passed 27 yards to Capt. Doug Essick, then for five more to Naumu, but the Bruins broke up the next two passes to take possession.

The Trojans gave it one more fling, reaching UCLA's 33 before Paul intercepted an aerial, to the relief of all Joe Bruin fans.

With very little offense to be seen, most plaudits for heroism went to players for their defensive actions ... such as Myers, All-American Burr Baldwin, Case and Paul for the winners; such as John Ferraro, Mike Garzoni, Walt McCormick, McCardle and Art Battle for the losers.

"We were just unlucky," was the unified summation of the Trojans, who blamed a couple of mistakes for their loss.

Cravath agreed: "We made a couple of mistakes and they cost us the game. That's about all there is to it."

Don Paul, the Uclans' versatile center, thought the goo on the field was a great neutralizer. "Sure, I love the mud," he beamed. "It makes everybody else just as slow."

BRUINS BEAT TROY, 13-0

93,714 See Uclans Nab Bowl Bid

QUARTER	1	2	3	4	TOTAL
SC	0	6	0	0	6
UCLA	6	0	0	7	13

UCLA BALL ON 34 YARD LINE
2 DOWN 12 YARDS TO GO
FIRST DOWNS SC 9 UCLA 4

The clock tells the story of the 1946 results.

The battle of statistics favored the Trojans, who racked up nine first downs to the Bruins' four, and led in yardage, 176 to 67.

Southern Cal went on to split their last two games, losing to Notre Dame while nudging Tulane. Six-four-oh was it for the season.

UCLA, the conference champs, still had to play Nebraska before hosting the Rose Bowl. Call it a warmup, if you like, for the Bruins emerged an 18-0 victor. At that point, UCLA stood proudly at 10-0-0.

Then came the Rose Bowl. But not before a ruckus of major proportions cast a sinister shadow over its future.

By a vote of 6-2, the Pacific Coast Conference signed a pact with the Western Conference which would automatically bring the winner of that league to the Rose Bowl for at least the next five years, starting immediately.

And that agreement knocked out the possibility of Army coming to Pasadena . . . Army, the greatest team in the nation for the past three years . . . Army, the team with such stalwarts as Glenn Davis, Doc Blanchard, Tucker, and others.

And the thought of not getting Army for the Rose Bowl knocked a lot of people for a loop.

The Troy alumni appointed a committee to survey the advisability of USC withdrawing from the conference. A petition to the Coast Conference president with names of 563 "disgusted fans" denounced the pact.

Sports editors, such as Bill Leiser, *San Francisco Chronicle;* George Bertz, *Portland Journal;* Rube Samuelson, *Pasadena Star-News;* Curly Grieve, *San Francisco Examiner;* Charlie Park, *Glendale News-Press;* and Bob Segall, *Daily Bruin,* all wrote with disdain about the immediate tie-up which would freeze Army out. Most, however, did foresee beneficial rewards in store on a long-range basis.

The two negative votes from the PCC to bind the two conferences came from Southern Cal and UCLA (Oregon and Oregon State did not vote). Two schools voted nay in the Big Nine poll, too. Ironically, one was Illinois, the eventual league winner and first to visit Pasadena under the terms of the pact. (Michigan State had not yet joined the conference; hence, the "Big Nine.")

Whatever the merits or demerits of the agreement, the Fightin' Illini did come west, and if Army had been any tougher, pity Joe Bruin. At the end of the day, the bruised fellow found himself licking his 45-14 wounds, and trying to console his sole loss of the season.

As for Army, it received an invitation to play in the Sugar Bowl, but decided to just take a furlough and stay in West Point for the holidays. Air mail postage was only a nickle, so the players could write to all their West Coast friends . . . on what might have been.

Starting Lineups: UCLA-Ends, Baldwin and Fears; Tackles, Malmberg and Chambers; Guards, Dimitro and Clements; Center, Paul; Quarterback, Case; Halfbacks, Rowland and Shipkey; Fullback, Myers. USC-Ends, Essick and Callanan; Tackles, Ferraro and Hendren; Guards, J. Musick and Garzoni; Center, McCormick; Quarterback, Lillywhite; Halfbacks, Garlin and Battle; Fullback, B. Musick.

Summary

	UCLA	USC
First Downs	4	9
Yards Rushing	67	81
Yards Passing	0	95
Total Yards	67	176
Passes Attempted	4	18
Passes Completed	0	8
Passes Had Intercepted	0	2
Fumbles Lost	1	3
Punts/Average	16/35.6	13/30.8
Penalties No./Yards	4/50	4/30

Scoring By Quarters:

| UCLA | 6 | 0 | 0 | 7 | — | 13 |
| USC | 0 | 6 | 0 | 0 | — | 6 |

Bert LaBrucherie, UCLA Head Coach, 1945-1948.

1947
Game 17

Gray Colors Bruins Blue

For the sixth consecutive year, the annual duel between UCLA and Southern California would decide which team would represent the Pacific Coast Conference in the Rose Bowl. To be sure, California and Oregon were in the running, too, but a verdict by the Trojans would spell "also-ran" for any and all challengers.

To eliminate suspense, let it be known that the warriors from University Park eked out a slim 6-0 decision when Jim Powers passed 33 yards to Jack Kirby, but the most breathtaking play occurred during the final minute of the conflict.

Leading by a scant six, USC found itself with its back to the wall as the Bruins lined up a mere four yards from the goal line, 55 seconds to play, fourth down. (Actually, the Uclans could earn a first down by just reaching the three.)

Ernie Johnson ran to his right and pitched toward Bill Hoyt in the end zone. But there was an obstacle. From out of the late afternoon dusk loomed Troy's Gordon Gray who pilfered the toss and lumbered out to his 15-yard stripe as the clock wound down to 15 seconds. Victory was preserved, the conference crown was secured, a date at Pasadena was confirmed.

Southern Cal, going into the fracas with a record of 6-0-1 and ranked as the fourth best team in the country, was a slight choice of the oddsmakers to win. Like the title of the movie starring Gary Cooper and playing at the Palace, SC was "Unconquered". The Trojans had waded through Washington State, Ohio State, Oregon State, California, Washington and Stanford, thanks in part to a stout defense that had blanked four of those headhunters. The lone blemish was a 7-7 knot with Rice.

UCLA, playing to the tune of an up-and-down rhythm, exhibited 5-3-0 credentials. The Bruins, rated 18th nationwide, beat Iowa, lost to Northwestern, slammed Oregon and Stanford, was shut out by Southern Methodist and California, then blasted Oregon State and Washington.

In pre-game studies, sports writers settled on passing as the key to victory and further put the bee on SC as having the better QB.

"On the record, George Murphy and Jim Powers have it over our Benny Reiges and Carl Benton," admitted UCLA Coach Bert LaBrucherie. "We're underdogs and we should be."

Fearsome John Ferraro, All-American tackle, and Johnny Naumu (out with an injury) were named co-captains for Troy; Don Paul and fearless Tom Fears, both All-Coast honorees, received the same appointment for Westwood.

Dwell upon the names of Ferraro and Paul a moment. These two competitors earned the unique distinction of opposing each other in six Trojan-Bruin games . . . twice in 1943, ditto in '44, once in '46 and in '47. As Fran Tarkenton would say — that's incredible.

Paul tabbed Ferraro as USC's best lineman. "I ought to know," he said, "I've played against him often enough."

Three of Troy's 16 seniors had special incentives to bang up the backside of Joe Bruin. Neither Fred McCall nor Don Clark had ever tasted the sweet flavor of Bruin meat. And Mickey McCardle had a burning desire to atone for mishaps he figured had throttled Westwood to its two decisions over El Trojan. This, in addition to not ever having played in the Rose Bowl, influenced McCardle to forego an opportunity to turn professional, instead returning to USC for his final year of eligibility.

The Uclans boasted a stable of fleet backs . . . such as Al Rossi (421 yards rushing), Al Hoisch, Ernie Johnson, Johnny Roesch and Skip Rowland, hobbled by injury to just a hop-and-a-jump.

Unlike the previous year when torrential rains soaked the Coliseum sod, the day of the 1947 contest broke crisp and clear. And a huge throng of 102,050, largest in the nation, was on hand for the festivities.

USC kicked off and UCLA, on short jabs by Rossi and Hoisch moved to midfield before having to punt. That — the punt — was the

Royce Hall, landmark at UCLA.

main ingredient of the first quarter. Just before it ended, Rossi boomed a 61-yarder that died on SC's five-yard line.

From this unenviable spot, the Trojans marched 77 yards to the Bruins' 18, where four straight passes fell incomplete. Kirby was the noise maker in the campaign, sprinting once for 21 yards and latching on to three aerials.

Though unsuccessful, the drive backed-up the Bruins, who, after a penalty, found themselves punting from their five. Gray accepted the kick on UCLA's 45 and reeled off 13 yards before Reiges, the punter, brought him to earth.

From off the SC bench came Powers, relieving Murphy for the first time. And, without further ado, Powers faded back behind good protection and jetted a long missile toward the end zone. Meanwhile, Kirby had slipped behind Reiges, snatched the ball from midflight, and stepped over the goal line. USC, 6-0.

"Coach Cravath told me to use that pass play when he sent me in," related a happy Powers. "He called the turn."

Tommy Walker tried for seven, but his kick was wide.

That was it until the desperate gasp by the Bruins in the waning ticks of the contest ... unless you count the murmur of hope that thrilled the Uclan fans when Rossi intercepted a Lillywhite pitch and meandered 32 yards into enemy territory. But Doll's theft of a Carl Benton heave on his six-yard stripe terminated that menace.

With some signs of tiredness by the Trojans, the Bruins started their foray at one last bid for victory with Johnson returning Newell Oestreich's boot from his 20 to his 35.

The legs of Art Steffen and Jerry Shipkey plus the arm of Benton and the hands of Phil Tinsley, all went to work and the Bruins were soon on Troy's 33, first down.

Roesch spun for eight, Benton went airborne to Fears for 13 and Shipkey cracked to the five, then to the four. When Roesch failed to gain, it was fourth down and the dramatic now-or-never act took center stage.

In retrospect, it was revealed that Tinsley was supposed to be Johnson's target, but when Tinsley was held up, Johnson went to Hoyt, his secondary receiver. And you already know about the blur of Gray that colored Joe Bruin blue.

A reporter asked Tinsley about being "held up" while running his pattern.

"I wasn't only held up, one of their tackles was sitting on me," replied the tall end. "I didn't have a chance to go for that pass."

Cravath was a gracious winner, as usual.

"The Trojans are the luckiest team in the country and the Bruins have had more hard luck than any team I ever saw," he stated.

Looking at the team statistics, he may have had a point, seeing as how they were neck-and-neck in yardage; UCLA 204, USC 203. And there were a lot of "ifs" in the game that could have gone either way.

LaBrucherie was philosophical in his appraisal. "USC was easily the best ball club we met," he muttered, "even better than Southern Methodist. But I just hope we had all our bad luck for the next few years rolled up in this one season," added Bert, who then asked "How often can you lose these photo finishes?"

The amiable coach was well aware that his Bruins had lost four games during the season by a total of a mere 20 points. Of course, they had five wins to off-set this.

Some of the names mentioned for stellar work were All-Americans Paul Cleary and Ferraro, Clark, Kirby, Walt McCormick and Gray for the Trojans; Fears, Paul, Hoisch and Mike Dimitro for the Bruins.

The UCLA battle did not finish USC's slate. Lurking two weeks away was Notre Dame, always a power. Coach Frank Leahy scouted the Trojans and was most lavish in his praise.

And, regarding the game, Bob Snyder, head coach for the Los Angeles Rams, wrote in the *Times:* "I give Southern Cal a good chance against Notre Dame—you can figure they'll be just right for a good effort."

Welllll—maybe not. Would you believe the Irish 38, the Trojans 7?

And Coach LaBrucherie told Harry Culver of the *Los Angeles Herald-Express:* "The best team on the coast (USC) is in the Rose Bowl."

Maybe so. But the best team on the coast was matched with Michigan, the best team in the country. And the Wolverines fitted Tommy Trojan into another straight jacket with a humiliating 49-0 thrashing. But a 7-2-1 record was nothing at which to yawn.

Oh-by the way-about the time UCLA and USC were playing in 1947, there was planned a marriage of regal status in Great Britain between two people named Elizabeth and Phillip. A headline in the newspaper read: "All England is Gay over Royal Wedding". Well, okay.

Starting Lineups-USC-Ends, Tolman and Cleary; Tackles, Ferraro and Hendren; Guards, Clark and McCall; Center, McCormick; Quarterback, Murphy; Halfbacks, McCardle and Doll; Fullback, Lillywhite. UCLA-Ends, Clements and Fears; Tackles, Chambers and Pastre; Guards, Nikcevich and Dimitro; Center, Paul; Quarterback, Reiges; Halfbacks, Rossi and Hoisch; Fullback, Myers.

Summary

	USC	UCLA
First Downs	13	9
Yards Rushing	86	98
Yards Passing	117	106
Total Yards	203	204
Passes Attempted	25	20
Passes Completed	11	11
Passes Had Intercepted	2	3
Fumbles Lost	0	0
Punts/Average	7/37.0	8/42.2
Penalties No./Yards	6/30	6/84

Scoring by Quarters:

| USC | 0 | 6 | 0 | 0 | — | 6 |
| UCLA | 0 | 0 | 0 | 0 | — | 0 |

1948
Game 18

Hi, Mom

It had to happen. Sooner or later, the electronic eye known as television would invade the sanctity of the trenches, peer into secrets of the huddles, pose doubt into the efficiency of the officials and emblazon the fiery emotions of young players along the sidelines. The pioneer station was KLAC-TV and the year was 1948. Yes, Joe Bruin and Tommy Trojan were on the tube.

Too bad it wasn't a typical match-up of the two performers, slugfests which usually decided who would go to Pasadena.

But this was a lean year. No crowns waited in the wings. No scent of roses filtered the air. No Hector to lead the Trojans into battle. No Smokey to guide the Bruins from the wilderness.

Entering the game, it was just a 5-3-0 season for Troy; only 3-6-0 for Westwod. Mediocrity at its best.

Both ledgers could be defended to some degree. UCLA was a young team with only seven seniors. Of those, only Bill Clements, Phil Tinsley and Art Steffen were regulars.

Southern Cal's roster listed just 14 seniors, including five starters — Don Doll, George Murphy, Ernie Tolman, Bob Bastien and Bill Betz.

"We are probably in the best shape we've been all year," said Coach Jeff Cravath, "but you can't take anything for granted in football. We definitely are not looking past the UCLA game to Notre Dame."

Cravath would be without halfback Don Garlin and tackle Bob Hendren while Harold Hatfield and Jim Monson would see limited action.

For Coach Bert LaBrucherie's Bruins, running ace Gene Rowland had been out for weeks with injuries. Starter Mike Dimitro had been dropped from the squad, and the chance of halfback Howard Hansen playing was slim.

Considering USC's better running backs, its superior defense and its slight advantage in maturity, bookies decided UCLA would lose by two touchdowns.

Perhaps they were just basing this margin on history. In the 17 previous games between the two schools, USC's average was a shade over 22 points per game, UCLA's just under eight . . . a difference of 14 points.

The upcoming tussle offered one player a chance to ascend a throne. Bruin quarterback Ray Nagel could eclipse Bob Waterfield's single season pass completion mark—if he could find at least seven open receivers. Waterfield's campus record was 57, accomplished in 1942, and going into the game, Nagel stood at 51. Did he break it? Did his hurling arm lead UCLA to an upset?

Yes and no. Nagel did complete eight passes to overcome Waterfield's record, but the feat did not defeat the foe.

After a stupendous struggle on the field and considerable nail-biting in the stands, USC outlasted UCLA, 20—13. The bookies took a bath.

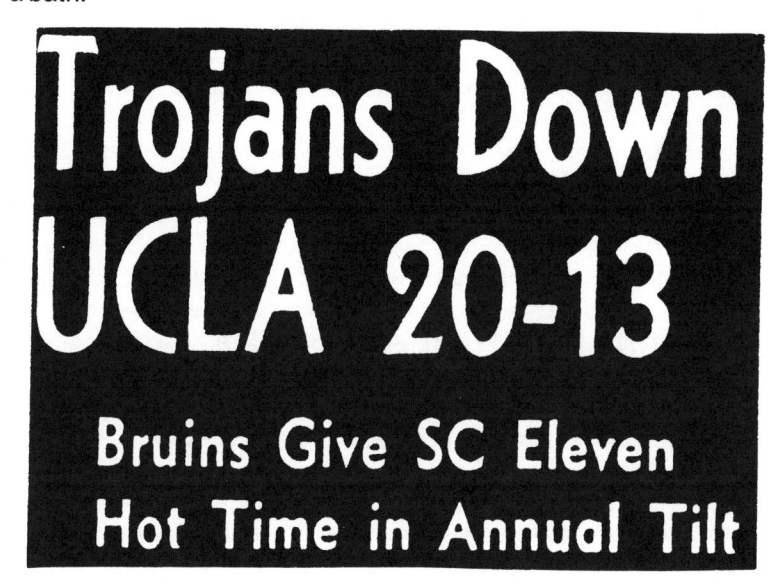

Trojans Down UCLA 20-13
Bruins Give SC Eleven Hot Time in Annual Tilt

Over 76,000 fans were on hand and saw the Bruins get two early breaks, cashing neither. First, Eddie Eaton and Leon McLaughlin recovered Jim Powers' fumble on the SC 40 but that opportunity sputtered. Moments later, after a Trojan penalty and a punt from deep down, the Bruins were on Troy's 15-yard line, but that fizzled on a bobble by Bill Stamper.

Midway in the second quarter, the Trojans decided it was their turn, so they marched 80 yards in 12 plays to take a 7-0 lead. Most notable events in the jaunt were a crippling penalty against UCLA, followed by a 23-yard pass completion from Powers to Jack Kirby, spotting the ball on the 17. Jay Roundy went to the 13, Powers bootlegged for 11 yards, and Kirby scored from two yards out. Dean Dill delivered, 7-0.

Taking a cue, the Blue and Gold decided to emulate the action. Starting from their 28 after the kickoff, the Bruins moved uninterrupted into the end zone. Nagel fueled the advance by firing passes to Willis Duffy and Don Hunt, Duffy racking up the six points on a five-yarder. Bob Watson's missed PAT left the Uclans one point in arrears.

Just before intermission, the Cravathmen struck swiftly to bolster their advantage to 14-6. John Kordich returned UCLA's kickoff to the SC 40. Dill's first pass was incomplete, but his second was arched into the arms of Kirby on UCLA's 32. The fleet halfback dodged Hunt and crossed the double stripe with two seconds showing on the first-half clock. Dill drilled, 14-6.

Both teams tallied in the third period, the Trojans doing it first.

Doll returned a punt 17 yards to the UCLA 44-yard stripe, and later barged over from the six after a series of power plays by the Trojans. Dill dipped, 20-6.

The oddsmakers were breathing easier now, but they were soon holding their lungs again. For the Bruins took the ensuing kickoff, and in six plays ate up 75 yards and a TD. Nagel heaved to Clements for 21 yards, then for 30. Ernie Johnson circled end for 25 yards and Watson piled across the goal line from the one. His kick narrowed the gap to seven points, and that's the way it ended, 20-13.

USC consumed a large portion of the final frame with a 56-yard effort that expired on UCLA's 16.

"Bert LaBrucherie did a good coaching job," remarked Cravath, "but we still have a long way to go for the Notre Dame game two weeks away."

They must have made some progress, because the Trojans tied Notre Dame, 14-14. That gave them a 6-3-1 record for the season. The Bruins wound up at 3-7-0.

"Our kids were in there playing real ball," expounded LaBrucherie, "but the Trojans were hitting awful hard on their running plays."

When LaBrucherie left the dressing room, Bruin supporters swarmed around and hoisted him to their shoulders.

"We'll be seeing you next fall, Bert," they chanted.

Unknown to those rooters, LaBrucherie had just coached his last game for UCLA. During his four-year tenure, the popular headmentor had won 23 games and lost 16, with no ties. And he had carried the Uclans into the Rose Bowl.

His last game of crosstown crossfire against USC was a humdinger. And it was on TV. Hi, mom.

Starting Lineups—USC—Ends, Tolman and Stillwell; Tackles, Bird and Schutte; Guards, Bastien and McMurtry; Center, Hachten; Quarterback, Powers; Halfbacks, Doll and Battle; Fullback, Betz. UCLA—Ends, Hunt and Clements; Tackles, Stroschein and Pastre; Guards, Eaton and Nikcevich; Center, Vujovich; Quarterback, Stamper; Halfbacks, Watson and Johnson; Fullback, Steffen.

Summary

	USC	UCLA
First Downs	19	13
Yards Rushing	268	96
Yards Passing	89	140
Total Yards	357	236
Passes Attempted	15	24
Passes Completed	5	11
Passes Had Intercepted	1	11
Fumbles Lost	2	0
Punts/Average	6/40.0	7/37.7
Penalties No./Yards	6/51	5/35

Scoring By Quarters:

| USC | 0 | 14 | 6 | 0 | 20 |
| UCLA | 0 | 6 | 7 | 0 | 13 |

1949
Game 19

Schneider Makes Dean's List

When a team loses its first string quarterback, the coach moves up his back-up. And when the second stringer is also hurt, the coach turns to the next back-up. And when the third stringer is not available, the coach screams and calls upon his fourth stringer.

Admittedly, such a series of events doesn't happen . . . unless you're Coach Jeff Cravath preparing your Trojans for the annual confab with UCLA.

But two days before the conflict, Jim (Mystic) Powers was hospitalized with a hip injury, ending his season.

Powers' back-up, Wilbur Robertson, had previously been cut down by an injury, and Frank Gifford, from the third team, was recuperating from an appendectomy. Cravath didn't scream, but his eyes searched the breadth of Bovard field and finally came to rest upon a bright-eyed youngster who had been around for a while but who had not played one second of varsity ball at quarterback during the season. Dean Schneider, you're it.

What say, let's not unravel right now the cheers—or jeers—that accompanied Schneider's performance in the game. A little suspense is good for the soul.

Until Powers, who had enjoyed a sensational season, was relegated to the sidelines, USC had been established as a seven point favorite. But now the contest was rated even, a toss-up.

Pappy Waldorf, the California coach, predicted a tie. Communicating to Braven Dyer of the *Times*, Waldorf wired: "With the loss of Powers, the Trojans are very seriously handicapped. The Bruins have come along in great style, and probably have an edge. However, I will make a guess of a 20-20 tie."

The Trojans were bringing 4-2-1 credentials into the battle; while the Bruins boasted a 6-2-0 inventory. The men of Troy had vanquished Navy, Washington State, Oregon and Washington while drawing with Ohio State. The men of Westwood had conquered Oregon State, Iowa, Oregon, Stanford, Washington State and Washington. Both teams lost to California, and it was Stanford who handed SC its other loss; while Santa Clara was the other culprit for the Bruins. Neither team was in the *Associated Press* top 20.

UCLA had a new coach, Henry "Red" Sanders. And he had installed a single wing offense built around Ernie Johnson, a little man with big talents.

"We all expect SC to hit its peak performance against us," Sanders told reporters on the game's eve. The Trojans are big and rugged and it's going to be hard for us to move the ball. I hope we can make them earn everything they get," he concluded.

Of course, sly ol' Cravath could not be hoodwinked. "We suffered a tough blow in the loss of Jim Powers," he responded, "but I don't think Dean Schneider will make us ashamed. We'll be out there and we'll play a ball game."

In addition to Powers, Cravath faced the fracas with injuries to halfbacks Al Cantor, Bill Bowers and Jay Roundy, though all three, unlike Powers, were expected to play.

Bob Watson, splendid defender and blocker deluxe, was listed as doubtful for the Bruins.

If incentive was to be a factor in determining the result, UCLA had the advantage. In 31 years of competition, the Uclans had won 129 games, lost 130 and tied 18. See, a victory over SC would square things at 130-130.

Also, UCLA was still nursing a slim, faint and weak chance of sharing the league title, which was tantamount to nursing a slim, faint and weak chance of getting into the Rose Bowl.

So, November 19th arrived in Los Angeles and a crowd of just over 75,000 arrived at the Coliseum for the 2 pm kickoff.

They saw a rough-and-tumble brawl highlighted by the scintillating performance of Schneider that nudged Southern California to a 21-7 victory. The game was closer than the margin indicated.

The opening quarter was scoreless, as UCLA muffed two scoring

Schneider Skippers Trojans to 21-7 Triumph Over Bruins

opportunities, and USC blotched one.

And, as the embroilment became rougher and tougher, Referee James Cain ejected Bruin George Pastre from the game, allegedly for kicking a Trojan. The incident prompted Sanders out onto the field for a discussion with Cain.

"I wanted to know why the Trojan involved (Fullback Bill Martin) also wasn't ejected," he explained. "Cain had just told me both players were involved."

When things settled down, the Trojans launched an armada from their 33 that sailed into Touchdown Harbor just before the half ended.

During this cruise, Skipper Schneider, hurling from the port side, completed six-of-ten passes, the anchor toss being a four-yarder to Bill Jessop.

To sustain the drive at UCLA's 34, Schneider on fourth down faked to Battleship Bill Martin and fired a torpedo to Jessop for a first down on the 25. Schneider then connected with Jessop to the nine, and then on third down to the same fellow for the TD. Gifford, on orders from his physician to confine his activities to place-kicking, upped the score to 7-0, as the half ended.

UCLA apparently got a shot of stick-it-to-'em during intermission, and Johnson was injected with the biggest needle.

Starting from his 20, the diminutive scatback ripped off 15 yards, then pitched to Roy Vujovich to the 48. Howard Hansen was on the receiving end of an aerial which gave the Bruins a first down on Troy's 17. Johnson picked up five, then passed softly to Bob Wilkinson, who had eluded defenders in the end zone. Watson locked the score at 7-7.

Wilkinson's grab was his 10th touchdown tally of the season, and his 546 total yards broke the PCC record.

Southern Cal pushed over two touchdowns in the fourth period to seal its victory, but only after two stabs at the Bruin goal had failed.

The first unsuccessful thrust was stopped on UCLA's three, and

Francis Mandula encircled a Trojan fumble on Westwood's 30 to halt the second.

But early in the final quarter, USC drove 81 yards for the clincher. Don Burke handled the ball 11 times and eradicated 35 of those yards. Then, with fourth-and-four on the 18, Schneider lofted the ball to Johnny Williams, who nestled it to his chest without breaking stride in the end zone. The conversion failed.

The Bruins, still spirited, charged from their 17 to midfield, but Williams interrupted that spurt by intercepting Johnson's long heave and rambling back to UCLA's 18-yard stripe.

But the Trojans consequently fumbled and Nagal wrapped himself around the ball to afford UCLA one last chance from its 17. Three plays failed and Johnson, gambling on fourth down, was smothered on his eight-yard line with 35 seconds to play.

Schneider picked up four on a sneak, SC stopped the clock, Burke rammed to the one, SC stopped the clock, and Burke blasted over with two seconds to play. Gifford kicked with accuracy, making the final count, 20-7.

"We got beat by two touchdowns," moaned UCLA assistant coach Tom Prothro, "and when did they happen? Forty-five seconds before the half, and two seconds before the game ended," he answered himself.

Bruin players and fans complained about the officials, who dealt seven assessments for 70 yards on the losers, in addition to kicking Pastre from the game.

"What a way to go out—sitting on the bench like a criminal," cried the heartbroken senior. "I was rushing the passer and knocked over Martin. They said I kicked him and expelled me. I didn't kick him," Pastre added.

Sanders would not comment on the officiating. "We played our best game of the year," he observed, "but I think SC hit a peak, too."

Cravath was high in his praise of Schneider, the unknown fourth stringer who almost quit the team earlier in the year.

"There's a great lesson in stick-to-itiveness in Dean's fine showing," lauded Cravath.

The SC coach also singled out Jim Bird, Volney Peters, Burke and Bob Stillwell for potent contributions, along with Harold Hatfield, Jack Nix, Paul McMurtry and Jess Swope.

Bruin stickouts were Johnson, who passed for 165 yards, Wilkinson, Jim Buchanan, Leon McLaughlin and Hansen. Their season ended at 6-3-0.

Southern Cal was tortured by Notre Dame in the season finale, closing its registry at 5-3-1.

The Victory Bell remained at University Park another year, but it may have felt the ring of Wilkinson's vow, who, as spokesman for the Uclans, proclaimed "We'll get 'em next year!"

Starting Lineups—USC—Ends, Hatfield and B. Stillwell; Tackles, Peters and Bird; Guards, Swope and McMurtry; Center, Barnes; Quarterback, Schneider; Halfbacks, Williams and Duff; Fullback, Martin. UCLA—Ends, Wilkinson and Vujovich; Tackles, Thompson and Pastre; Guards, McLachlan and Niccevich; Center, McLaughlin; Quarterback, Buchanan; Halfbacks, Johnson and Hansen; Fullback, Schroeder.

Summary

	USC	UCLA
First Downs	20	13
Yards Rushing	172	43
Yards Passing	127	169
Total Yards	299	212
Passes Attempted	26	23
Passes Completed	13	12
Passes Had Intercepted	0	2
Fumbles Lost	4	0
Punts/Average	4/27.2	7/33.2
Penalties No./Yards	3/15	7/70

Scoring By Quarters:
USC	0	7	0	14	—	21
UCLA	0	0	7	0	—	7

1950
Game 20

Boom, As In Bruin

Take all the UCLA-USC clashes of years gone by and label each what you wish. But take 1950 and there's only one title: The Year of the Bruin.

On a late Saturday in November, the spirited Uclans, playing near-flawless ball, annihilated the Trojans, 39-0. For Southern Cal, it was the worst defeat ever administered to its Pacific Coast conference record and the second worst in its long and noble history (Michigan 49-0 in 1948 Rose Bowl, exceeded it.)

Naturally, it was the most satisfying triumph in the annals of Westwood history.

Some say the great victory could be credited to the fancy running of a slender sophomore from New Jersey; or to a brutal defense that barricaded the Trojans' every move; or to a game plan executed to perfection. Those were physical attributes.

Perhaps the great victory was one of inspiration. After all, California had clobbered UCLA, 35-0, just seven days previous, so who could expect such a drastic turn-around if only physical prowess was the weapon?

No, the Bruins were a team possessed.

Mrs. LaVon Hansen, wife of UCLA's senior wingback, Howard Hansen, deceased two days before the game.

Coach Red Sanders left the decision of playing or not playing entirely up to Hansen.

Howard Hansen played under sad circumstances in UCLA's 1950 victory.

Hansen played. "I know she would want me to play," he said. "Besides, I feel I owe it to my school."

So the Bruins went out and won one for Howie.

The tragedy was real to those closely touched, but so were the festivities of pre-game frivolity to others . . . the usual hoopla, roots, toots, etc. KFI-TV featured the Victory Bell on the Eddie Koontz Show.

It had been a season of famine at Troyland . . . the most sparse since 1941. Believe it or not, USC had only one win to show for its seven game effort, and that was over impotent Oregon. Two ties — with Washington State and Stanford — helped to off-set losses to Iowa, California, Navy and Washington. So it was 1-4-2 for the Trojans going into the skirmish.

UCLA's index was better, but nothing about which to rave. Joe Bruin had out-growled Oregon, Washington State, Stanford, Purdue and Oregon State, while submitting to Washington, Illinois and California . . . a 5-3-0 scroll.

Throughout the week, the odds favored UCLA by a touchdown. Braven Dyer of the *Times* rated it a tossup.

Both squads were beset with injuries . . . Joe Marvin, Johnny Florence, Dave Williams and Bob Moore for Westwood; Bill Bowers, Frank Gifford, Dean Schneider and Ralph Pucci for Troy.

A crowd of slightly less than 52,000, blessed with good weather, jammed Memorial Coliseum expecting to witness a struggle of titanic proportions.

They saw, instead, a lop-sided affair that, once past the first quarter, contained little suspense as to its end result.

And what little suspense still existed was erased when the crowd saw Ted Narleski start cavorting up and down the field. The Uclan sophomore scored three touchdowns, rushed for 138 net yards and completed two of three passes.

His first six points ended a 50-yard opening quarter drive that required eight plays. Important cogs in the drive were two passes — Narleski to Hansen for 13 yards, Luther Keyes to Ernie Stockert for 11. From USC's 18, Narleski ground out yardage to the three, then scored. Capt. Bob Watson converted.

In the second quarter, USC manipulated its only viable thrust of the game, but lost the ball on the Bruin 20. Thereafter, the Trojan offense went into seclusion.

The Bruins' second marker was ignited by Cappy Smith when he pilfered a Wilbur Robertson aerial on the SC 46. In five plays, the most electrifying of which was a 27-yard dazzler by Narleski, UCLA was on the scoreboard again. Reddy Teddy marked this one up from five yards out, but Watson's toe was untrue . . . 13-0.

Tally No. Three came easy. As Robertson was trying to pass from his end zone, he was blind-sided by Darrell Riggs, causing a fumble. Guard Fran Mandula fulfilled a lineman's dream by pouncing on the ball and getting himself a touchdown. Watson missed again, so it was 19-0 at the half.

Taking up where they left off, the hungry Bruins sliced away 63 yards of acreage in 10 plays. Narleski lugged leather seven times on this jaunt, finally cashing his third TeeDee on an off-tackle slant. Watson's kick upped the count to 26-0 and that's the way the third period ended.

Just to be safe, Joe Bruin nailed tight the coffin of Tommy Trojan with 13 points in the final stanza.

The first covered 73 yards in nine plays, with Dave Williams hammering left tackle for the final six feet. One play evaporated 42 yards on this foray, a Keyes to Herb Lane missile.

Williams set up Westwood's final touchdown, too, bolting through tackle and blasting 38 yards to Troy's three-yard stripe. Two plays later, Joe Marvin piled into glory land, Watson split the bars, and the final 39-0 score was posted.

"My," blurted Notre Dame Coach Frank Leahy who was scouting USC, "I am surprised at how good that Bruin team is. They appeared to have been inspired."

Coach Sanders underscored Mr. Leahy's comment. "I'm certain this is the best ball game we've played in two years, maybe the best any of my teams have played."

The statistics bore him out. UCLA amassed 423 total yards to SC's 79, and racked up 18 first downs to six.

Behind Narleski's 138 net yards was Hansen with 61 and Williams with 56. Bruins making the game's defensive honor roll were Riggs, Cliff Livingston and All-American Donn Moomaw, among others.

The UCLA yearbook diverted from speedy two-legged creatures to make an analogy about four-legged ones. "The Trojan horse," it read, "looked more like the old gray mare."

Tops for the Trojans was Al Carmichael, whose 13 yards may have been heroic under the conditions.

"That was a good football team Red Sanders had out there today," stated USC Coach Jeff Cravath. "We can't say that about ourselves."

It was the last season for Cravath as Southern Cal's head coach, but fortunately he had one more game to play. Fortunately, the players had a chance to redeem themselves for the sake of their

This formidable group of iron gridders was THE 1950 Bruin varsity squad. From left to right, first row, they are DONN MOOMAW, JOE HORTA, BOB MOORE, BOB WATSON, JIM BUCHANAN, ED FLYNN, FRANK MUNOZ, JULIE WEISSTEIN, JOHNNY FLORENCE, JOE MARVIN, BILL COPE, XAVIER MENA; second row, HERB LANE, DAVE OWEN, CLIFF LIVINGSTON, BOB WILKINSON, CAPPY SMITH, TEDDY NARLESKI, HAL MITCHELL, LUTHER KEYS, GUY WAY, ALAN RAFFEE, CHUCK FRAYCHINEAUD, ROY JENSON; third row, BILL SMITH, TOM BUSH, ERNIE STOCKERT, DAVE WILLIAMS, JIM THOMAS, DICK SHORT, WHITNEY ARCENEAUX, LEO HERSHMAN, BOB ZELINKA, JOE SABOL, DARRELL RIGGS, DON COGSWELL; fourth row, WERNER ESCHER, FRANCIS MANDULA, JOHN SENDE, GEORGE MORGAN, RAY LEWAND, GAYLE PACE, BILL WILCOX, ED MILLER, ORAN BREELAND, BRUCE MACLACHLAN, BRECK STROSCHEIN, ISSAC JONES.

The UCLA 1950 Varsity Squad.

Jeff Cravath, USC Head Coach, 1942 to 1950.

coach. And showing true grit, they did. Notre Dame fell to the Trojan sword, 9-7, enabling Cravath to depart on a winning keel.

During his nine years as headmaster, Cravath compiled a record of 56 victories, 28 losses and eight ties. Against UCLA, he was 6-3-0.

UCLA's captain, senior Bob Watson, accepted the game ball as symbolic of one of the Bruin's greatest triumphs, then graciously awarded it to Hansen.

And Ted Narleski, the pint-sized speedster who made so much happen, gleefully summed it up: "I am happy we could help Howie Hansen finish his college playing like this. He's one of the greatest guys I ever met."

Summary

	UCLA	USC
First Downs	18	6
Yards Rushing	322	30
Yards Passing	101	49
Total Yards	423	79
Passes Attempted	9	28
Passes Had Intercepted	0	3
Fumbles Lost	1	1
Punts/Average	6/38.3	9/33.8
Penalties No./Yards	6/55	1/5

Scoring By Quarters:

| UCLA | 7 | 12 | 7 | 13 | — | 39 |
| USC | 0 | 0 | 0 | 0 | — | 0 |

Editor's Note: With the arrival of two-platoon football, starting line-ups will not be included in future chapters.

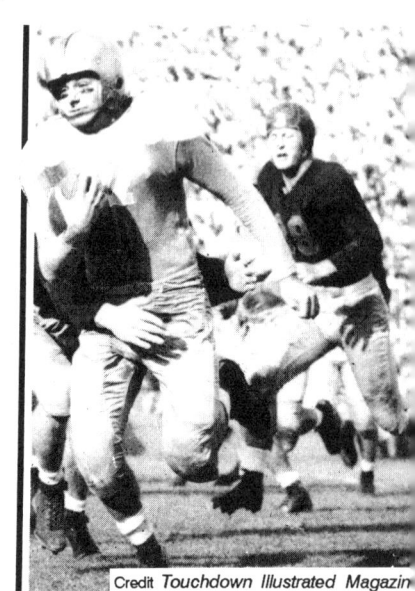

Ted Narleski ran for 138 yards and three TDs while leading the Bruins to a 39-0 victory over USC in 1950.

Credit *Touchdown Illustrated Magazin*

1951
Game 21

Glory, Back-to-Back

It must have been habit, pure and simple, that induced bookmakers to take Southern California and lay seven in its autumn date with UCLA.

How else could the odds be justified? The Bruins were coming off that 39-0 knockout of the previous year, and so far in 1951, their stats were better than the Trojans in seven of 11 categories.

UCLA's averages were better in rushing, passing, touchdown passes, total offense, punting, returning punts and pass defense.

USC's averages were better in rushing defense, total defense, returning kick offs and intercepting passes.

But heed the words of Howie O'Dell, Washington head coach: "SC is a shoo-in. SC is stronger, man for man. SC is bigger and rougher."

And of seven writers picking for the *Times*, five gave the nod to Troy (Al Wolf and Dick Hyland were in the minority).

True, USC was rated 11th by the *Associated Press*, which didn't list UCLA in the Top 20.

True, USC's won-lost record was superior, 7-1-0 to 4-3-1.

The Trojans conquered their first seven opponents—Washington State, San Diego Navy, Washington, Oregon State, California, TCU and Army, before falling to Stanford.

The Bruins defeated Santa Clara, Oregon, California and Oregon State, tied Washington and fell to Texas A&M, Illinois and Stanford.

BRUINS FIND GOLD MINE IN THE SKIE

Bruins Hand Troy Decisive Setback

Cameron Sets School Offense Mark; Uclans Repeat 1950 Walkaway

Several unit duels were in prospect. Offensively, the Uclans would match their Paul Cameron and Teddy Narleski against Troy's All-American Frank Gifford and Al Carmichael. Defensively, it was Bruin Donn Moomaw versus Trojan Pat Cannamela, All-Americans both. And in the area of masterminding, it was Red Sanders opposing Jess Hill, squaring off against each other for the first time.

Cameron, a flashy sophomore, would be shooting for a school record, needing 41 total yards to shatter Kenny Washington's campus record of 1394 yards.

Sanders made some late personnel switches, inserting Ike Jones, Joe Sabol and Bob Zelinka into his starting lineup. Some critics interpreted the presence of Jones as an indication that Sanders would rely on a passing game for victory.

Neither team could win the conference title, but second place was open and awaiting the outcome of the game.

More than 71,000 fans poured into the Coliseum to see what that outcome would be. In the process, they saw a little chunk of history. Because UCLA, for the first time since the series began in 1929, put together back-to-back victories by outclassing its crosstown rival, 21-7.

Two in a row for Joe.

SC fell heir to the first break, recovering a fumble on UCLA's 39. With Rudy Bukich at the stern, the Trojans moved to the 27, but no farther.

Still in the initial period, Gifford fumbled when creamed by Lyman Ehrlich and Sabol sprawled around the ball for UCLA on Troy's 42.

On a reverse, Don Stalwick legged 16 yards, then the Uclans were penalized back to the 31. On third down from the 24, Cameron lobbed the ball over Duck Nunis and into the arms of Stalwick in the end zone. A pop by Gayle Pace put the Bruins out front, 7-0.

"I could see it coming right on the beam from Cameron," said Stalwick, beaming, "but at the last second I was sure Nunis would deflect it." He didn't.

Nothing of consequence happened before intermission, except a 60-yard drive by UCLA that bogged down on SC's 20.

The Westwood eleven tacked on seven more digits in the third quarter to go up by 14.

Stalwick set fire to this excursion by zooming 36 yards to the SC 19. After two plays, the Bruins had gone nowhere; in fact, they had lost a yard. Then, from a seldom-used page of their play book, the Uclans pulled a double reverse that sent Jones prancing across the goal line. Pace converted.

UCLA's final tally was sort of a gift, but not entirely. It came on an intercepted pass early in the fourth frame.

Trying to throw to Cosimo Cutri, Bukich was rushed, and pitched into the eager arms of Moomaw, who rumbled (linebackers always rumble) 21 yards into gloryland. Enter Pace, enter 21-0.

Southern Cal avoided a shut-out with a 65-yard sojourn capped by Jim Sears' plunge across the double stripe. The drive was illuminated by the passing of Schneider and by a 20-yard dash (backs always dash) by Sears. Gifford toed the final point of the game, which ended 21-7.

As probably expected, Cameron did set a new UCLA school record by netting 40 yards on the ground and 88 in the air. This boosted his season aggregate to 1472 yards.

Cameron showed little emotion. "I don't feel anything—except proud to be a member of this team. The other fellows did it, no fooling," he spoke with modesty.

Naturally, Coach Sanders was elated.

"Men, my hat is off to you," he addressed his squad. "You responded magnificently to a challenge."

Later, he told reporters: "It was Joe Marvin, Bill Stilts, Joe Sabol and the rest of that defensive unit which won the game for us."

Captain Hal Mitchell and Pace also graded high for the Bruins.

Assistant Bruin Coach Tommy Prothro had a good word for his QB, too. "You are the finest quarterback I ever coached," Prothro told Julie Weisstein.

Trojan Coach Hill endorsed the appraisal. Referring to Weisstein, Hill said, "Now there's a really fine blocker."

Turning to the game, Hill admitted, "We were outcharged, outblocked and outtackled," but then quickly added, "we were not outfought."

Troy's All-American back, Gifford, made his first start against UCLA, an operation and an injury depriving him of this honor two years running.

But the senior was totally bottled up by the Bruins all afternoon, netting only 17 yards.

"I thought I could see daylight several times when I had the ball," remarked Gifford, now of television fame. "But when I got to the scrimmage line, it wasn't there."

After losing to UCLA, the Trojans spun out their season with a 12-19 loss to Notre Dame. So, after seven consecutive wins, the Hillmen dropped their last three.

Frank Gifford, USC All-American back, 1951. Gifford is now a network television announcer.

UCLA ended its season at 5-3-1.

With Cameron racing to the four corners of the field, hurling passes and breaking records, there was very little opportunity for Narleski, bona fide hero of the 1950 triumph, to strut his stuff. Most of the game, he sat glued to the bench, unnoticed ... while the rooters stomped, clapped and cheered for Cameron.

How soon they forget.

Summary

	UCLA	USC
First Downs	13	11
Yards Rushing	183	33
Yards Passing	88	117
Total Yards	271	150
Passes Attempted	16	36
Passes Completed	6	15
Passes Had Intercepted	1	2
Fumbles Lost	1	1
Punts/Average	9/43.3	10/38.7
Penalties No./Yards	10/60	3/15

Scoring By Quarters:

| UCLA | 7 | 0 | 7 | 7 | — | 21 |
| USC | 0 | 0 | 0 | 7 | — | 7 |

1952
Game 22

Toast of the Coast

Unlike their B.C. ancestors, an army of terrific Trojans were duped not by any wooden horse tricks from Westwood, as had been the case for two years running. Nay, this time the Southern Cal defense kept shut the gates of Troy and, in a gigantic struggle of unbeatens, came from behind to shade UCLA, 14-12.

Prestige galore was on the line for this late November clash. For the first time since the crosstown rivalry was born, both teams would enter the contest unbeaten and untied. Both were 8-0-0; truly, the toast of the coast.

So the Pacific Coast conference crown was at stake and with it an invitation to the Rose Bowl, not to mention the fruits of a perfect season.

While each club's offense was averaging four touchdowns per game, the hallmark of both was defense. Southern Cal ranked seventh in the nation in rushing defense and in pass defense, third in total defense. The Uclans were not in the Top Ten in total defense, but were rated second in rushing defense.

On a television show a week before the game, the opposing coaches predicted the score of the game. Their guesses were sealed and not opened until after the game.

Red Sanders, of the Bruins: UCLA 13, SC 7.

Jess Hill, of the Trojans: SC 17, UCLA 14. Not bad, Coach Jess.

Al Sparlis, former star guard at UCLA, bumped into sports writer

Los Angeles Times SPORTS
PART 3
GAME OF THE YEAR--TROJANS VS. BRUINS!

Rose Bowl Bid Prize to Victor; Sellout Crowd to See Game

Braven Dyer at a luncheon. "I don't see how they'll be able to score," said Big Al.

"Who?" inquired Braven.

"The Trojans," replied Big Al.

One of the teams brushed aside by the Bruins during their victory parade was Wisconsin, 20-7. Unknown at the time, it would be the Badgers who would test the PCC champ, come Rose Bowl Day.

Other victims of UCLA were Oregon, 13-6; TCU, 14-0; Washington, 32-7; Rice, 20-6; Stanford, 24-14; California, 28-7; and Oregon State, 57-0.

On the way to their unscathed slate, the Trojans hijacked Washington State, 35-7; Northwestern, 31-0; Army, 22-0; San Diego Navy, 20-6; Oregon State, 28-6; California, 10-0; Stanford, 54-7; and Washington, 33-0.

So, based on comparative scores of common foes . . . well, that's meaningless anyway.

Southern Cal received a blow when it was learned Bob Van Doren, its co-captain and most authoritative lineman, would not play due to a head injury.

"We'll win this one for Bob," pledged his mates.

Hill planned to replace Van Doren with lightly-used Mario DaRe, brother of the movie star, Aldo Ray. "As far as I'm concerned, it is still an even ball game," spoke Hill.

A couple of sidelight duels commanded interest: tailback, between SC's shifty All-American Jimmy Sears and UCLA's versatile Paul Cameron; and linebacker, where Trojans George Timberlake and Marvin Goux would match talents with Bruins Donn Moomaw, All-American, and Terry Debay.

Despite rain drops that kept falling on their heads, lightly, a monstrous crowd of 96,867 men, women and children packed themselves into Memorial Coliseum.

And when the first break of the game sided with the Bruins, they capitalized upon it.

Sears fumbled when splattered by Jack Ellena, and Myron Berliner recruited the ball for Westwood on Troy's 32-yard line. Don

Stalwick and Cameron combined efforts for nine yards, then Cameron swept end to the 15. Three plays gained only one yard, so Pete Dailey booted a field goal from the 22. It was the first field goal of the lengthy Bruin-Trojan series.

Not content, UCLA sought Point Heaven again, as Cameron clicked with a 29-yard strike to Stalwick to the Trojan 38. But a demon named Dick Nunis burglarized Cameron's next toss on the 16, then lateraled to Lindon Crow, who carried to his 25.

After Sears picked up five, the Hillmen came up with a biggie. From the Trojan 30, Carmichael eluded defenders and sped to Westwood's 36-yard line. Seemingly stopped by Berliner, Carmichael wafted a lateral to Sears who waltzed into the end zone with nary a paw to hinder him. Sam Tsagalakis' kick gave USC a 7-3 lead.

There was some controversy about the legality of the lateral, some observers saying Carmichael's forward motion was stopped, which, if so, would have ended the play at that point.

"I saw a white jersey coming up and heard a yell," confided Carmichael. "He (Sears) was in a heck of a lot better position to run than I was, so I threw a lateral."

A reporter asked Sanders if the Carmichael-Sears TD escapade was illegal.

"I don't remember seeing it called back," Sanders shot back.

Several minutes later, UCLA's Bob Heydenfeldt punted dead on Troy's 10-yard line. Harold Han then bobbled a snap from center and retrieved it in the end zone where he was collared by Berliner—a safety for the Bruins. The scoreboard resembled the end of a good tennis set . . . 7-5.

Now that the Uclans had a field goal and a safety, their greedy appetite wanted a touchdown.

SC's Desmond Koch, punting from his end zone, laced a boomer, but Sabol brought it back 15 yards to the Trojan 30-yard line.

Cameron pelted for four, then threw to Stalwick on the six. A Troy penalty moved UCLA to the two, then Bill Stits found the haven of six-points in two plays. Dailey's PAT gave UCLA a 12-7 cushion and that's the way it was at recess.

Southern Cal rallied in the third spasm to make the go-ahead and stay-ahead touchdown; but only after UCLA showed misleading signs of packing the game away.

When the Uclans took the second half kickoff and marched all the way down to SC's 18-yard stripe, it looked like church was out for the Trojans.

But the Hillmen must have met their tithes, especially All-American Elmer Willhoite. For it was he who intercepted a well-

Al Carmichael (left) and Jim Sears are all smiles after leading USC to a 14-12 victory, 1952.

Donn Moomaw, UCLA All-American linebacker, 1950 and 1952. Moomaw is considered one of the greatest linebackers in UCLA history.

intended aerial by Cameron and it was he who didn't stop running until Cameron knocked him out of bounds on the Uclan eight. That was 72 yards from where he stole the pitch.

"I don't know just what happened," Cameron told reporters. "It was intended for Stockert, but went right to Willhoite. I don't know if somebody hit my arm or not. It was my fault," his voice trailed away.

Carmichael lost three on a reverse, but Leon Sellers slashed to the four. Sellers failed to gain, so Sears deftly dumped a pass to Carmichael, who swept into the end zone. Tsagalakis kicked true, staking USC to a 14-12 lead, which turned out to be the final score.

"We'd worked up the play, figuring the Bruins would be looking for an off-tackle smash," related Carmichael. "All Jim Sears told me in the huddle was 'catch it'."

The jubilant Trojans gave their coach a dousing, fully clothed, in the shower, but Hill came out praising the Uclans.

"UCLA is by far the strongest team we've met, particularly on defense," he acknowledged, dripping water to his toes.

Concerning the Crown City classic, Hill pointed out "It's the Coast's turn to win and we'll give the Big Ten team the battle of its life on New Year's Day."

DaRe, the fill-in tackle, and his replacement, Frank Pavich, were congratulated by Hill for their clutch performances.

The Bruins were not convinced that they were the second best team on the field.

"We made all the points," blurted Jack Peterson. "Theirs' came on our mistakes and not on their own doing."

Moomaw backed up his mate. "I don't mean to sound like sour grapes," he stated, "but I think we'd best them six times if we played seven more times." (The linebacker who was destruction personified, later became Rev. Donn Moomaw, minister of the Bel-Air Presbyterian Church in Los Angeles, the church attended by Ronald Reagan before he became president. Rev. Moomaw, now retired, delivered the invocation at Mr. Reagan's inauguration.)

Coach Sanders took a realistic view.

"Well, we just lost," he said, forlorn. "We played our best, our best of the year. But we lost to a great team. SC deserved to win. They had the best defense any team of mine ever faced," he added.

Perhaps UCLA won the battle and lost the war inasmuch as the Bruins outgained the Trojans, 199 yards to 168, and rolled up 10 first downs to six.

And maybe USC left too much of their energy and spirit on the Coliseum turf, because its untainted string was spoiled by Notre Dame the following week, 9-0.

But, as Hill predicted, it was the Coast's turn at Pasadena, and the Trojans bounced back to trim Wisconsin, 7-0. And nobody could complain about a 10-1-0 season. Indeed, they were the toast of the coast.

Summary

	USC	UCLA
First Downs	6	10
Yards Rushing	80	84
Yards Passing	88	115
Total Yards	168	199
Passes Attempted	23	20
Passes Completed	10	7
Passes Had Intercepted	2	4
Fumbles Lost	2	0
Punts/Average	10/42.2	11/43.7
Penalties No./Yards	7/87	8/65

Scoring By Quarters:

USC	0	7	7	0	—	14
UCLA	3	9	0	0	—	12

Three-Year UCLA Letterman Paul Cameron Made All-America in 1953

1953
Game 23

Two Bears, One Tale

Bears are probably clannish. They probably stick together. Especially those that live in California.

How else could you rationalize the undeniable fact that the Golden Bears from the University of California slapped a tie on sturdy Stanford, an unsuspected exploitation that catapulted the bruising Bruins of UCLA into the Rose Bowl?

Sure, Joe Bruin had to do his part, too. That was to ambush Southern California. And that he did, 13-0, on the same day the "Big Game" was taking place in Palo Alto. (That's what they call it up there; everybody in the Southland KNEW where THE big game was being played.)

UCLA, on the strength of a 7-1-0 entry, was the favorite to win, by a touchdown.

But this was an analysis not fully shared by the seniors—and there were 16 of them—on the Southern Cal roster.

A self-appointed spokesman spoke out: "Sure, we know UCLA is good, but that doesn't mean they're unbeatable. After all, Stanford beat'em and we beat Stanford."

Not only that, but SC's record going into the fray (6-1-1) almost matched the Uclans.

Take a look. The Trojans' path to the Coliseum left Washington State, Minnesota, Indiana, Oregon State, California and Stanford wounded along the way. Washington held its ground with a tie,

You're Wrong—This Is Not About War and Russia

Credit *Los Angeles Times*

while—surprise—frail Oregon succeeded in piercing the Trojan shield.

Stanford nipped UCLA by one point in the fifth game, but it was a downhill ride for the Bruins against Oregon State, Kansas, Oregon, Wisconsin, Washington State, California and Washington.

A couple of former celebrities were on hand to vent their opinions, and Paul Zimmerman let them do it in his "Sportscripts" column.

"I like the Bruins by a touchdown," opined Bob Waterfield, erstwhile AA at UCLA. "Defensively, SC isn't what it was last year, so I think the Bruins will be able to run on the Trojans."

Then John Ferraro, AA star of yore for Troy, countered: "I predict the Trojans will eke out a win. I don't think Troy has yet played its best game—and SC at its best should win. This is the time."

Strange, the ex-Bruin picks UCLA, the ex-Trojan picks SC.

Of the 14 seniors who would give their all for the Blue and Gold, perhaps none would be missed more than Paul Cameron, leader of the Pacific Coast Conference in both rushing and scoring, and destined for All-America honors.

The crew of NBC-TV was in town to eyeball every facet of the game to a national audience. Mel Allen would handle the play action with Lindsey Nelson doing the color. (Well, after all, Howard was still a practicing lawyer back in New York.)

So, with the glitter of 80-million television viewers plus the presence of 85,366 loyalists in a combat zone known as the Coliseum, the head-to-head Joe and Tommy Show began to roll.

It was a story of missed opportunities, mistakes, being at the right place at the wrong time ... that type of thing—but, as the script unfolded, it was also a rough, tough, rock-and-sock clash of brutality that wound up with a happy ending and a sad ending, depending on individual sentiments.

High spots in the first quarter were the time-outs and commercial breaks, which gave fans and viewers a chance to replenish their beer supply.

Then came the second quarter and with it Southern Cal's lone opportunity to fiddle with points.

A vicious tackle by Leon Clarke separated the ball from Cameron and Ed Fouch adopted it for SC on the Bruin 40. Aramis Dandoy immediately turned right end, and behind a bevy of blockers, swept 24 yards to the 16. Three running plays by Bill Riddle, Dandoy and Addison Hawthorne left Coach Jess Hill with a decision to make, for it was fourth-and-two on the eight.

The decision was to go for three, but Sam Tsagalakis' kick from

THE MIRROR

Bruins, Spartans Celebrate as Teams Picked for Bowl

the 17 floated wide to the left.

Hill defended his decision. "Sure, our field goal attempt was a proper call," he said. "The game could have ended 3-0 or 10-7 if the kick had been good. UCLA tried two, didn't they?"

Several plays later, SC's Des Koch was forced to punt from his end zone, and Milt Davis, breaking tackles right and left, stormed back to Troy's 10-yard stripe.

From there, UCLA unraveled the scoreless tie in four plays. First, it was Primo Villanueva for two and Bob Davenport for two more. Villanueva then crashed to the one, and Davenport dived over the goal line. Pete Dailey drilled the PAT, and UCLA led as the teams withdrew for the break, 7-0.

The Bruins came out steaming to open the second half, puffing to SC's 21-yard line where Don Stalwick fumbled and Ed Pucci claimed the ball for Troy.

Three more times in that same period, Sanders' club made gestures for points, but none succeeded. The Uclans penetrated to SC's 15, 10 and 13. Two of these drives ended with Dailey missing on FG attempts.

But the Trojans were bearing gifts on this day, and it was their fifth fumble in the last stanza that led to the Bruins' insurance deposit.

Bob Buckley did the bobbling, and Hendenfeldt recovered for UCLA on the Trojan 43. With Dailey, Bill Stits and Cameron taking turns, the Westwooders poked the ball to Troy's six, from which point, Cameron started to his right, then cut back inside and scored. The jaunt took eight plays and was spearheaded by Dailey's 17-yard burst. That was it; UCLA, 13-0.

It did appear that the Uclans would add to their point total when Dailey trucked 41 yards to the SC 13. But on fourth down from the 10, Jim Contratto intercepted a Cameron pass and the Trojans escaped. And SC made one last jab, marching 40 yards to the UCLA 45, but it was terminated when Joe Ray pounced on a Trojan fumble.

Only the die-hards could debate the result, as UCLA controlled the flow practically from kickoff to curtains.

"UCLA deserved to win, without a doubt," acknowledged Hill. "Red (Sanders) has the toughest team we met this year."

If there was a turning point, it was probably Davis' 31-yard punt return that cemented the way for UCLA's primary touchdown.

Coach Sanders heaped accolades upon his pass defense. "The manner in which we contained that Trojan passing attack was the key to the game," he commented. SC netted only 38 yards on four pass completions.

By holding USC scoreless, the Bruins wound up second in the nation (behind Maryland) for allowing the fewest points—48.

A sports writer singled out UCLA's Hardiman Cureton and USC's Ed Pucci as the two best linemen on the field.

"It was a good, hard ball game," remarked Pucci, "and we played our hearts out."

Maybe the Trojans left their hearts on the Coliseum floor, because they were no match for Notre Dame the following week, losing 14-48.

For UCLA, it was on to Pasadena (thanks again, Golden Bears) and a date with Michigan State. First, Trojans; then, Spartans. How many wars can a Bruin win? Not all. The visitors carried back to the land of lakes a 28-20 squeaker, but UCLA could be proud of its 8-2-0 season of 1953. United Press ranked Westwood fourth in the country.

Summary

	UCLA	USC
First Downs	11	6
Yards Rushing	250	71
Yards Passing	-2	38
Total Yards	248	109
Passes Attempted	12	21
Passes Completed	2	4
Passes Had Intercepted	1	2
Fumbles Lost	1	3
Punts/Average	6/40.5	10/41.6
Penalties No./Yards	9/75	3/33

Scoring By Quarters:

UCLA	0	7	0	6	—	13
USC	0	0	0	0	—	0

1954
Game 24

All Dressed Up, No Place to Go

The 1954 edition of UCLA's Bruins was crowned National Champions by *United Press,* and was runner-up in the Associated Press poll. They slaughtered Southern California, 34-0, to win the Pacific Coast Conference title. They won nine, lost none and tied none, the first team in the illustrious history of Westwood to reach perfection. And yet they stayed home for the holidays.

The reason, of course, was UCLA was not eligible for a repeat performance in the Rose Bowl, having represented the league the previous year.

"The members vote for the team which they believe will best represent the conference in the Rose Bowl, exclusive of the team last in the Bowl, which is not eligible to repeat under the present rules." proclaimed Victor Schmidt, commissioner of the conference.

So, since Pasadena was off-limits and PCC schools were barred from accepting bids elsewhere, the Uclans found themselves all dressed up and no place to go.

Since nobody during the season had found a method to spank Joe Bruin, the bookies wisely figured Tommy Trojan couldn't either. So they established the Uclans a $12^1/_2$ point favorite on the morning line, down from 13 earlier in the week.

Writers for the *LA Times,* Dick Hyland and Braven Dyer, both lined up with the handicappers, but, there was one group of interested partisans who was not fully in accord . . . the Trojan football team.

Dyer asked Jim Contratto, Troy's splendid quarterback, about this. Come on, Jim, do you think SC can win?

"Yes, I do," replied the man whom many thought held the key to a Trojan win. "A lot of us are seniors, you know, and it's our last shot at the Bruins."

Contratto was the lead pony in a fine stable of Trojan running backs that included Aramis Dandoy, Jon Arnett, Lindon Crow and Gordon Duvall.

But if Troy was formidable in the backfield, Westwood was peerless up front where it counts . . . in the line. There gleamed a galaxy of stars, the brightest of which may have been All-American candidates Jack Ellena, Jim Salsbury, Bob Long and Hardie Cureton.

"It's as good a collegiate line as I've seen," boasted Red Sanders.

Nor would the Bruin coach undersell his backfield. "Bob Davenport is the best fullback I ever coached," boasted Sanders again. "In fact, I'm not sure he isn't the best fullback I've ever seen."

The polls placed UCLA tops throughout the land with Southern Cal sixth.

"We're impressed with the fact that UCLA is considered the No. 1 team in the nation," USC coach Jess Hill told the Rotary Club, "but I'm from Missouri and so are my players. We will have to be shown."

Sanders spoke next. "We're not interested in national ratings and all like that. The only thing my players are interested in is being the No. 1 team in Los Angeles."

Only one club, Washington, had scored more than one touchdown on the Bruins, and it was the Huskies who came closest to spoiling the slate (UCLA won, 21-20). The other decisions — over San Diego Navy, Kansas, Stanford, Oregon State, California and Oregon — came with more ease. And mighty Maryland fell.

Going into the game, USC had lost only to Texas Christian, and that on a day when Contratto was incapacitated. The Trojans bushwhacked Washington State, Pittsburgh, Northwestern, Oregon, California, Oregon State, Stanford and Washington.

A nation-shattering record of 102,548 persons filled the Coliseum to its brim . . . and each had a place in the sun. Would you believe 110-degrees at kickoff?

Those people who didn't pass out from heat prostration saw a close ball game for three quarters, at which time UCLA was clinging to a narrow 7-0 lead.

Then, to paraphrase Coach Hill's post-game remark, the dam broke. Dissolved. Disintegrated. Evaporated. Crumbled. Twenty-

Los Angeles Times SPORTS

BRUINS EXPLODE IN 4TH, ROUT SC, 34-0

seven big points in the fourth period plus the seven they already had gave the Bruins a whopping 34-0 triumph.

The Uclans leaped to an early lead with an heretofore unseen play they must have devised while toiling behind closed gates during the week. It was a 48-yard air bomb from tailback Primo Villanueva to end Bob Heydenfeldt, who burned defender Lindon Crow to make the reception. Johnny Hermann's conversion ended the scoring until the fateful fourth.

A tie ball game loomed in the making when Southern Cal's Marvin Goux (later to become a coaching fixture at his alma mater) stole a Bruin pass in the third stanza and trotted 37 yards to UCLA's eight yard line.

But the Troy rooters were soon disheartened. On first down, Contratto hurried a pass intended for Leon Clarke. From his defensive position came a blur named Jim Decker, who snatched the ball on the goal line and sped the length of the field. His 100-yard excursion didn't count, however, as the Bruins were nabbed for clipping. Then Ron Calabria popped up to intercept Villanueva's pitch, and the Bruins, too, came away empty handed.

So the action moved into the very late stage of the third frame when UCLA started its second TD jostle. Hermann got it started by pilfering a Contratto aerial and hauling the ball to SC's 22. Five plays later, Davenport plunged over from the one, as the fourth quarter got underway. Hermann found the range and the Bruins rested easier at 14-0.

UCLA kicked off, Arnett fumbled, Cureton recovered on the 15, and on the second play, Villanueva hit Terry Debay with a twelve-yard scoring strike. Hermann upped it to 21-0.

The Bruins' last two markers were manufactured by reserves. Sam Brown ignited the first when he returned a Dandoy boot 27 yards. Then Rommie Loudd pulled in an eight-yard heave from Doug Bradley for six points. . . followed by Hermann's fourth PAT. Now it's 28-0.

After a mild intrusion by SC to UCLA's 29, the Bruins notched their final TD, and it, too, was set up by a pass interception. Warner Benjamin injected himself into the path of a Frank Hall toss, returning the ball four yards to SC's 12. Two running plays lost seven, but then Brown hooked up with Bruce Ballard in the end zone. And that added up to the final 34-0 count.

Dandoy tried with earnest to get Troy on the scoreboard by taking the adjacent kickoff and darting 52 yards into enemy territory, but the scoreboard clock, as did the Bruins, objected to SC's intentions.

One could imagine the dismay of Coach Hill, scratching his head in disbelief as he took one last look at the quartet of goose eggs on the scoreboard, a telltale resume of 60 minutes spent in paydirt poverty.

There was a movie at the Paramount starring Elizabeth Taylor titled "The Last Time I Saw Paris". And there was a sequel at University Park titled "The Last Time I Saw Points Against UCLA". That would be 1952, for the Trojans had now labored through nine straight quarters of scoreless production against the Bruins.

So awesome was the Uclan defense on this day that El Trojan was restricted to a mere five net yards rushing.

"This Bruin team has provided me and our other coaches with the highest point in our lives," Sanders said.

Hill echoed the praise of Sanders. "The Bruins richly deserved their No. 1 rating in the nation," he stated. "Their line is very powerful. But we weren't doing too badly until the dam broke."

UCLA's Long was a standout, but actually you could run down the Bruin roster and you would be identifying the stars of the game. Of course, the Trojans had some, too . . . like Goux, Ed Fouch, Orlando Ferrante and Clarke.

At game's end, the huge card section of the Bruin rooters flashed a pathetic message to the Trojan fans across the field. It read: "We can't go, so we're sending you".

But that was no favor. Ohio State came in and mashed the Trojans, 20-7. That, along with a season-ending loss to Notre Dame, created an 8-4-0 record, for USC.

And, as stated earlier, UCLA was 9-0-0. It wasn't stated that, in so doing, the Bruins amassed 367 points while allowing only 40.

Summary

	UCLA	USC
First Downs	15	8
Yards Rushing	121	5
Yards Passing	139	103
Total Yards	260	108
Passes Attempted	13	23
Passes Completed	7	9
Passes Had Intercepted	2	5
Fumbles Lost	0	2
Punts/Average	8/32.1	8/37.8
Penalties No./Yards	2/30	6/36

Scoring by Quarters:

| UCLA | 7 | 0 | 0 | 27 | — | 34 |
| USC | 0 | 0 | 0 | 0 | — | 0 |

1955
Game 25

Triple Crown

By winning the Derby, Preakness and Belmont, Citation was the most recent winner of racing's Triple Crown. Of course, the sleek colt did it in one year. And, while it took UCLA three years to do it, the Bruins, too, became Triple Crown winners . . . champions of the Pacific Coast Conference in 1953, in '54—and now 1955.

During this span, the men of Westwood won 26 of 30 games, with two of their four losses coming in Rose Bowl encounters. The only regular season setbacks were to Stanford by one point and to Maryland by seven.

That loss to the Terps, by the way, was the only blemish on the Bruins' ledger as they prepared for battle with Southern California in 1955. Eight opponents were slotted in the UCLA "W" column: Texas A&M, Washington State, Oregon State, Stanford, Iowa, California, Pacific and Washington.

The Trojans had played to a 5-3-0 tune, waltzing past Washington State, Oregon, Texas, Wisconsin and California, but playing second-fiddle to Washington, Minnesota and Stanford.

The early line gave Troy and ten, but later dropped to eight when reports leaked that UCLA was not in top condition, mentally or physically.

Out of action, for sure, would be Ronnie Knox, the Bruins' talented tailback. Concerning the loss of Knox, a reporter asked Coach Red Sanders what he had in mind. "Lots of Prayerful

Mirror News SPORTS SECTION

Vol. VIII—No. 35 • SATURDAY, NOVEMBER 19, 1955 PART III MA 5-2311

BRUIN STARTERS
- LE—JOHN SMITH
- LT—ROGER WHITE
- LG—HARDIMAN CURETON
- C—STEVE PALMER
- RG—JIM BROWN
- RT—GIL MORENO
- Q—BRUCE BALLARD
- LH—SAM BROWN
- RH—JIM DECKER
- F—BOB DAVENPORT

TROJAN STARTERS
- RE—BING BORDIER
- RT—FABIAN ABRAM
- RG—ORLANDO FERRANTE
- C—MARVIN GOUX
- LG—GEORGE GALLI
- LT—DICK ENRIGHT
- Q—ELLIS KISSINGER
- LH—JON ARNETT
- RH—DON HICKMAN
- F—GORDON DUVALL

Bowl Bid At Stake as UCLA Battles SC Before 102,000

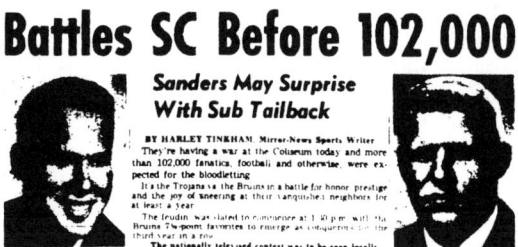

Sanders May Surprise With Sub Tailback

BY HARLEY TINKHAM, Mirror-News Sports Writer

They're having a war at the Coliseum today and more than 102,000 fanatics, football and otherwise, were expected for the bloodletting.

It is the Trojans vs the Bruins in a battle for honor, prestige and the joy of sneering at their vanquished neighbors for at least a year.

The feudin' was slated to commence at 1:30 p.m. with the Bruins 7½-point favorites to emerge as conquerors for the third year in a row.

The nationally televised contest was to be seen locally over KRCA (4) starting at 1:15 p.m.

Several hundred tickets were on sale this morning at the Coliseum, but they were hardly choice seats, being located in the east End zone.

The Bruins needed a victory today to clearly establish their right to represent the Pacific Coast Conference in the Rose Bowl.

A Trojan win combined with an Oregon State victory over Oregon would leave the Bruins and Beavers in a virtual tie and necessitate a vote that could prove embarrassing.

Minus the passing arm of Ronnie Knox, the Bruins were expected to fasten mainly on the ground with Sam Brown, Bob Davenport and Jim Decker making most of the advances.

Should this get them nowhere, Red Sanders was prepared to...

Turn to Page 3

INJURY DOUBLY COSTLY

Bruins to Miss Long Knox Punts

BY JACK TOBIN, Mirror-News Sports Writer

There's no question but that Ronnie Knox's injury virtually eliminates UCLA's passing threat against SC today, but even more important factor, which many have overlooked is the loss of the kicking edge which Knox's presence would give the Bruins.

Knox, who boasts a fine long kick, puts the pressure on the safetyman and cuts down the possibility of punts being run back to scores...

With Troy boasting Jon Arnett, a master hand at returning punts to touchdowns, the Bruins need that type of a kicker. Knox has a 40-yard punting average this fall on 19 kicks, second best in the conference.

Miami Runs Away From Bama, 34-12

MIAMI, Fla., Nov. 19 — Paul Cameron...

Tribe Choice to End Long Bear Jinx

SC-UCLA TV LINE-UPS

TODAY, 1:15 P.M., KRCA (4)

UCLA BRUINS

No.	Name	Pos.	Ht.	Wt.	Yr.

TROJANS

thought," he replied.

Then, in a more serious vein, Sanders said "The squad looks tired and 'stove up'. We haven't released any stories on injuries but we have had to secure an extension on our adhesive tape budget. We're going to line'em up out there, cheek to cheek, and see how long they last." Or was he still kidding?

Jesting or not, USC Coach Jess Hill wasn't about to let his adversary escape with all that jargon.

"We have quite a few boys we are going to have to nail together using tacks, baling wire and tape, too," he countered. "But, like Red, we're willing to put them out there, cheek to cheek, and see who outlasts the other."

Win, lose or draw, the Rose Bowl plum already belonged to Westwood. The Uclans were undefeated and untied in conference standings, and their mathematical advantage was beyond reach, regardless of who did what anywhere.

Railbirds anticipated a battle royal between the clubs' tailbacks—Jon Arnett, an elusive, breakaway All-America runner for SC; Sam Brown, a sturdy, pounding plodder for UCLA.

Behind these, and other outstanding backs, the Bruins during the season had piled up 268 points, the Trojans 216.

But on defense, the Uclans seemed superior, yielding only 50 points to Troy's 121. Suspect area of the Trojans was pass defense.

Would Sanders exploit that deficiency?

"Everybody says we can't throw," he responded, "so what difference does it make?" Then Sanders added: "SC is a big, strong team physically with lots of speed in the backfield, and has a man who's the best runner I've seen in a long time (Arnett)."

Arnett must have liked the compliment, so to show his gratitude, he took the opening kickoff on his three-yard line, moved with caution for a few steps up the middle, then shifted into high gear. When he applied brakes, he was in the Bruin end zone, 97 yards downfield.

The great run didn't count. Five members of the Trojan forward wall had lined up offsides, so the play was nullified. Many of the 95,878 folks who were filing into the Coliseum, frozen in their tracks during the stunning sprint, now continued to their seats.

"That was the turning point of the game," agonized Hill. "I always thought the officials were supposed to help the players line up properly," he continued. "Frankly, I never saw the penalty called before."

After the kickoff that did count, there followed an exhange of punts. On SC's second boot, Bing Bordier interfered with Brown's

Jon Arnett, USC All-American back, 1955.

fair catch effort and UCLA was in business on its 45-yard line. Brown and Bob Davenport picked up a first down to the 34, the Bruins lost five on a penalty, then Brown passed to Rommie Loudd for a 21-yard gain. Davenport sliced the middle for eight, and a Trojan penalty advanced the ball to the five-yard stripe. Davenport tried the middle for two, then Brown crashed over with a neat cut inside tackle. Jim Decker's PAT brought UCLA a 7-0 lead, which was the score as the first quarter ended.

The Bruins added a field goal in the second period to take a 10-0 advantage into the recess break.

The drive started 76 yards from Troy's goal. Brown, faking a quick kick, bolted to the Trojan 48 to start the momentum. Ground plays moved the Bruins to the 34, then Brown threw 29 yards to John Smith, who made a miraculous catch, over the objection of Ernie Merk. Davenport bulled to the two and the Uclans were penalized back to the 17. When the drive sputtered, Decker booted a 29-yard field goal.

The third fiesta was scoreless, although USC drove from its 16-

USC co-captains Marv Goux and George Galli meet UCLA leaders Hardiman Cureton and Gil Moreno before start of 1955 game. Goux later joined the USC coaching staff.

UCLA Downs SC by Score of 17-7

Bruins Grind Out Gains on Ground to Conquer Trojans Before 95,878

yard line to UCLA's 24. Outstanding defense by Hardiman Cureton and Bruce Ballard put the red light to this effort.

Now USC had a 10-point deficit to overcome and just 15 minutes to do it. An 89-yard mission consumed five of those minutes but it accomplished seven digits for the Trojans.

It went like this: Ernie Zampese for 10 and Gordon Duvall for 3. Then C.R. Roberts, on a pitchout, scampered 34 yards before Loudd shouted "whoa". When tackled, Roberts lost possession, but his mate, Ben Lardizabel, recovered.

The situation seemed apropos to go airborne, so Jim Contratto went overhead to Leon Clarke for a first down on the Bruin 26. Grinding yardage, inch by tough inch, Roberts and Arnett backed UCLA to its four-yard line, fourth-and-two. The Trojan rooters erupted, then, as Contratto concealed the ball on his hip and whirled into the end zone, unmolested. The conversion sliced the margin to three points, 10-7.

But the Bruins promptly retrieved the seven points they had just given up.

Smith returned the Trojan kickoff to his 40-yard line, and, behind the power of Brown and Davenport, plus the aid of a 15-yard penalty, the Bruins posted their insurance touchdown. It took Davenport three plunges from the Trojan four, but he finally got in. Decker's boot was on target and the final 17-7 score was etched in history.

"That was the sweetest march, that last one, that we ever made," exuberated Sanders.

The Bruin lineup contained four players of All-America stature—Davenport, Loudd, Cureton and Jim Brown, but it was generally conceded by observers that UCLA's Sam Brown was, indeed, the man of renown. His output for the day—153 yards—increased his season total to 829, and this was sufficient to pass Kenny Washing-

Hardiman Cureton, UCLA All-American guard, 1955.

ton's 812 yards for a new Bruin record.

Contratto, Troy's veteran QB, was impressed. "Brown is the best back I've played against this season. But the Bruins as a whole are a real good ball club."

Other Bruins left their mark on other Trojans, too. Like lineman Dick Enright, who uttered "That (Gil) Moreno is the best tackle I've met all year. Cureton was good, too."

Consequently, Sanders poured the saccharine on the SC team. "We haven't played anyone all year who tried harder than the Trojans," he avowed.

Other top rushers were Davenport for Westwood with 78 yards; Duvall and Roberts for Troy with 69 and 60, respectively.

UCLA threw only two passes, completing both. Its total yardage exceeded SC, 294 to 247, while first downs were 16 to 13. None of which convinced Hill.

"This is the weakest UCLA team of the last three years," he professed. "I thought my players gave a good team effort, but I was certainly disappointed that the Bruins moved as they did when they were leading, 10-7."

Following the loss to UCLA, Southern Cal whipped Notre Dame, 42-20, to wind up a 6-4-0 season.

The Uclans had a date in the Crown City classic. "I hear Michigan State is the best in the Big Ten," observed Sanders. "Well, we'd like to play the best team."

It was a tight contest, but UCLA kept consistent its record of never being a victor in the Rose Bowl, as the Spartans nicked out a 17-14 conquest. After this, both press polls ranked the 9-3-0 Bruins in fourth place.

The city rivals had now met in combat 25 times. USC led, 14 to seven, with four games ending even. In points, the Trojans had scored 457, the Bruins 289.

Summary

	UCLA	USC
First Downs	16	13
Yards Rushing	244	201
Yards Passing	50	46
Total Yards	294	247
Passes Attempted	2	8
Passes Completed	2	4
Passes Had Intercepted	0	0
Fumbles Lost	0	0
Punts/Average	40.6	47.0
Penalties No./Yards	8/78	8/70

Scoring By Quarters:

UCLA	7	3	0	7	-	17
USC	0	0	0	7	-	7

1956
Game 26

(Ells)Worth of a Toe

By his own admission, Southern California's senior quarterback, Ellsworth Kissinger, had never kicked a field goal. Not in high school, not in college. But it was his three-pointer that provided the margin of difference as the Trojans trimmed UCLA, 10-7, before 63,709 sweltering fans at the Coliseum on a late November afternoon.

And it was Kissinger's field goal that enabled victory-starved USC to snap a three-game losing streak to Joe Bruin, temporarily curbing the appetite of that ravenous beast.

Not that Kissinger's kick occurred in the dying moments of the game to snatch victory from defeat, mind you. It just wasn't all that dramatic. But it did turn out to be a winner. Also, it was the first time any SC player had ever kicked a field goal against UCLA.

By a toe, by a leg, by an arm — it mattered not to the Trojans how victory was attained.

"Now we can live in this town," shouted C. R. Roberts to a screaming bunch of SC rooters.

The two institutions brought records of close comparison to their 1956 clash. The Bruins stood at 7-2-0; the Trojans at 6-2-0. But the slight Bruin edge meant nothing to the bookies, who installed Troy as a two-point favorite.

Red Sanders' Uclans ruled such teams as Utah, Oregon, Washington State, California, Stanford, Washington and Kansas, but were measured by Michigan and Oregon State.

Jess Hill's Trojans brushed aside Texas, Oregon State, Wisconsin, Washington, Washington State and California, while feeling the broom from Stanford and Oregon.

Numerous players on both squads were akin to aching. Frank Finch wrote about that in his "Here's the Pitch" column:

"To hear tell, tomorrow's tilt between the lame (SC) and the halt (UCLA) should be advertised as the first annual Blue Cross Bowl. Hill's team is shot to hell with injuries and Sanders ain't got nobody to use but a batch of stretcher cases."

"We are in the worst physical condition I have seen a team," wailed Sanders a few days before the game.

But, on the other side of the coin, the Trojans would play with their injured, as well as minus Jon Arnett, their All-American senior.

The scoreboard operator could have overslept and not have been missed. Because there was nothing but nothings on the board when the weary players retired for intermission: SC 0, UCLA 0.

The Trojans penetrated four times during the half—to the Bruins 15, six, 29 and 25—but it was all pointless, thanks mainly to stellar defensive work by Jim Methany, Esker Harris and Don Shinnick. Troy moved the sticks nine times to only once for Westwood.

The Bruins did thrust to midfield in the second quarter, but Barry Billington's fumble was pounced upon by SC's Karl Rubke.

UCLA essayed to regain this momentum early in the third period, strutting to SC's 31-yard line. But Ed Griffin had the ball knocked from his grasp, and Bob Voiles claimed it for Troy.

Enough is enough, thought the Trojans. So they proceeded to march 67 yards in 12 plays for the tie-breaking touchdown. Roberts, Dan Hickman, Rex Johnston and Jim Conroy took turns lunging at the Bruins' porous defense until the ball reached the 14-yard line. Then, to break the monotony, Roberts wafted a blooper to Hillard Hill for the six-pointer. Add Kissinger's conversion and you've got a 7-0 situation.

Speaking of Robert's fling, which resembled a shot-put toss, Hill, the end, ribbed, "I thought it would never come down."

And, from his defensive position, Shinnick admitted, "We knew they had that play, but we weren't expecting it, and didn't react."

Kissinger's field goal was next on Troy's scoring agenda, and a 29-yard dash by Johnston gave impetus to its birth.

With two minutes ticked away in the fourth stanza, a Trojan drive came to rest on the Bruin 10-yard line, fourth and three. SC took a five yard penalty to get Kissinger in the game, but it was worth it. His trajectory was low . . . but high enough, and SC led, 10-0.

Trojan Sums It Up: Now We Can Live in This Town

Doggedly, the Bruins kept fighting back. Sophomore Phil Parslow pulled in a 33-yard aerial from Kirk Wilson but fumbled at midfield when hit by Ernie Zampese and Conroy recovered. Then Lou Elias broke for 50 yards on a punt return, but nothing materialized. Again, Wilson combined with Dick Wallen for a 36-yard pass gain, but that hope deceased on Troy's 19.

Meanwhile, the powerful backs of the Trojans—Roberts, Johnston, Zampese, Conroy, Tony Ortega, Ed Isherwood, et al—kept hammering big chunks of real estate away from Bruinland.

After the dust had cleared following one of those pile-driving poppers, assistant Bruin Coach Bill Barnes turned to Sanders and asked if that particular gain was a "trap play." "I am not sure," responded Sanders, "but it sure sounded like it."

Finally, Pat Pinkston blocked Zampese's punt to give the Ukes the ball on Troy's 42-yard line. Wilson threw three passes . . . to Bob Enger for eight, to Pinkston for 13 and to John Brown for 17. On the eighth play on the drive, Stu Farber smashed over from one yard out and Dan Duncan converted. That made the score, 10-7, but only 52 seconds remained in the game.

One bright spot for the Bruins was the 51.5 punting average of Wilson. His six kicks gave him a season mark of 49.3, which booted him into a new NCAA season record.

On the ground, UCLA was held to a measly 23 net yards, such was the forte of Monte Clark, Mike Henry, Rubke, Laird Willott, Ben Lardizabal, Walt Gurasich, Voiles and other Trojans.

"Our defense did it, but it was a team victory," put forth Hill, who also had high praise for Conroy, his quarterback.

Roberts, however, was Hill's top rusher, with 102 yards. Johnston, with 79, was next.

"The score wasn't indicative of how badly we were outclassed by SC," remarked Sanders. "The power of the Trojan line was too much for us."

Sanders concurred with Hill concerning the merits of Conroy.

"He is a fine looking back," said Sanders, "He runs that split-T very well."

Tommy Trojan

After all the statistics were totaled, and after all the comments were examined, and after all the armchair quarterbacks had been surveyed, it all was reduced to one non-debatable item: it was a very one-sided, close game.

And now the fans could go home and watch Jack Webb's new television show, "Dragnet". Well, the Trojans fans could. The Bruin fans had seen enough cleaning up for one day.

Midnight was approaching for the coaching career of Jess Hill at Southern Cal, for only Notre Dame remained as an adversary. Though involuntary, the Irish cooperated, and Hill departed in a golden chariot with a 28-20 victory.

The former SC player headed Troy's task force for six years, accumulating 45 wins. He endured 17 losses and one tie. His record against Enemy No. 1, however, did not stack up with his overall slate. Against UCLA, he won two and lost four.

Summary

	USC	UCLA
First Downs	17	5
Yards Rushing	314	23
Yards Passing	13	116
Total Yards	327	139
Passes Attempted	6	13
Passes Completed	2	6
Passes Had Intercepted	1	1
Fumbles Lost	1	3
Punts/Average	3/33.0	6/51.5
Penalties No./Yards	4/20	0

Scoring by Quarters:

USC	0	0	7	3	—	10
UCLA	0	0	0	7	—	7

1957
Game 27

Long-Suffering Trojans

Opportunists. Courageous. Determined. These words were synonymous with the 1957 UCLA Bruins, which—according to sports scribes of the day—"have done more with less talent than any team on the coast".

So, when the big spree with SC arrived, the Uclans were adjudged a one touchdown favorite, and the writers hinged this advantage on the anticipated performance of three exalted Bruins: Tackle Bill Leeka, End Dick Wallen (both on their way to All-America honors) and Tailback Don Long.

The designation of all three was on target, but it was Long who stood tall in leading UCLA to a 20-9 thumping of the Trojans. And it was the Long-led defeat that pummeled Southern California to the worst and most suffering season of its far-reaching and magnificent history.

The surprising Bruins brought a record of 7-2-0 to the conflict, having tamed Air Force, Illinois, Washington, Oregon State, California, Washington State and Pacific. Only Oregon and Stanford had escaped the Bruin corral.

"I privately thought we'd have trouble breaking even this year," confided Coach Red Sanders.

Former assistant Coach Don Clark had moved up to the helm of the Trojan ship and, since pulling anchor, had wallowed in rough waters. The first five opponents—Oregon State, Michigan, Pitts-

Dick Wallen, UCLA All-American end, 1957.

Don Long led UCLA to a victory over USC, 1957.

burgh, California and Washington—all put a hook in the Trojans' side. Then SC decked Washington State, but was later put in dry dock by Stanford and Oregon . . . one lone victory in eight sailings.

USC had a reputation for fumbling, having lost the pigskin handle 37 times in those eight games.

In statistics, the Bruins showed better than the Trojans in total offense, rushing, passing, pass interceptions, punting, returning kickoffs, total defense and rushing defense. Only in the area of punt returns and pass defense did Troy lead.

The contest had been reduced to one of pride as neither team was eligible for conference honors or post-season trips. In fact, by edict of the Pacific Coast Conference, both teams were stripped of their players in the senior class, were denied participation in the Rose Bowl, and were deprived of a chance to win the league championship. So upset was the SC alumni that it called for a secession from the PCC at its annual pre-game gathering.

Injuries dotted the rosters of both squads, which added to the other negatives of the game, but the "Seniorless Bowl" was scheduled and the "Seniorless Bowl" would be played.

A crowd of 64,818 was on hand to attest to that.

Southern Cal took the opening kickoff and defaced the Coliseum turf from its 26-yard line all the way to UCLA's 24, rolling up four first downs in the process. Then, just when things were looking up for the Trojans, the old fumble booger cropped up and stifled an opportunity to register some points. Little Don Buford was the fumble-or and Bruin Phil Parslow was the fumble-ee.

"While UCLA deserved to win, that fumble hurt us tremendously," ventured Coach Clark. "The one game we won this year, we scored first. But I'm not blaming Buford. It was just one of those things," he added.

After an exchange of punts, UCLA drove from its 40 to Troy's 19, utilizing nothing but running plays. So Long changed tactics and went overhead. It was a dying-duck push-pass, but uncomplaining Steve Gertsman nabbed it on the five and dived into the end zone. The missed conversion left UCLA ahead, 6-0.

Late in the first quarter, Trojan Ed Isherwood hemmed in Long in the end zone for a safety. (Not content with pacing the Bruins, Long even figured into points for the Trojans.)

The first period ended, 6-2, as did the half . . . as nothing of consequence happened in the second frame.

But after three quarters, it was 13-2 in favor of the Ukes, thanks to a 70-yard, seven-play TD jog.

Long connected on three passes along the way, first a 25-yarder to Bill Mason and then one of 11 yards to Wallen. From SC's 34, Long romped for five, and the Trojans drew a penalty to their 19. Long promptly hit Mason again, this time to the one. Next play: Long . . . for a touchdown. Kirk Wilson passed the toe test.

Early in the final stanza, SC staged an escapade that carried to UCLA's 27, but barely missed a much-needed first down by inches.

If the Uclans needed more incentive, that was it, as evidenced by a subsequent 80-yard, six play jaunt for a tally.

Long and Barry Billington combined for 15 yards, then Long passed to Glen Almquist for eight. Now it was time for El Bingo, so Long rared back and fired a missile which Wallen took in stride on Troy's 25 and sauntered into the promised land. After Wilson's PAT, the Uclans were in the driver's seat, 20-2.

Late in the tilt, the Trojans' Tom Maudlin starting filling the air with pigskins, and USC dented the scoreboard.

The drive covered 64 yards, mostly consumed by Maudlin's seven aerials. The first recipient was Lindsy Hubby, good for 14 yards. Then Maudlin clicked twice to Larry Boies, to Bob Arnett and again to Boies. From the one-yard line, Maudlin lunged over, Buford added another digit, and the game concluded shortly thereafter. UCLA 20, USC 9.

After the game, the victorious Bruins gathered around their coach in front of the UCLA cheering section.

"I asked the boys to join me here because they are the reason for our victory," announced Sanders. "This season has been like a beautiful dream, and I think they brought you a happy new year."

Later, in defiance of the blackball hanging over his team, Sanders declared, "I'm personally going to buy the biggest banner I can find, have 'PCC Champs' put on it, hang it up at our football banquet and see what happens."

Long, who netted 62 yards rushing, completed nine of 13 passes for 181 yards including two touchdowns, and ran for another TD, drew a drawl from Sanders: "I guess you could safely say that Long's presence meant a lot out there."

Sanders also handed kudos to Wallen, Billington and Dan Peterson, before putting in a kind word for the losers.

"SC was no patsy. The Trojans were all steamed up, hustled all the way and were real tough to handle."

Clark returned the compliment: "UCLA is a good, sound team, one that you can't afford to make mistakes against. That (Don) Long has been a great passer since his prep days."

Clark singled out Bob Violes, his right end, for an excellent performance. "He's a real champ," cited Clark. Other Trojans in the

Red Sanders, UCLA Head Coach, 1949 to 1957.

limelight were Maudlin and Mike Henry.

Still to be met by USC was Notre Dame, and Trojan fortunes didn't improve at South Bend. The Irish won, 40-12, to wrap up Troy's dismal season at 1-9-0.

In his closing remarks, Sanders, still elaborating about his Bruins, said: "This is the most spirited team I ever coached."

It was also his last as UCLA's mentor.

The doughty leader had given UCLA nine straight years of winning football, a national championship, three PCC titles and two visits to the Rose Bowl. His record showed 66 victories, against only 19 losses and one tie, surely the most prodigious chapter of the Westwood story. What's more, he had bested that crosstown rival in six of nine outings. As Sanders once said: "Beating SC is not a matter of life and death; it's more important than that."

Summary

	UCLA	USC
First Downs	17	12
Yards Rushing	157	110
Yards Passing	181	116
Total Yards	338	226
Passes Attempted	16	20
Passes Completed	9	10
Passes Had Intercepted	0	1
Fumbles Lost	0	2
Punts/Average	7/37.8	8/33.5
Penalties No./Yards	5/45	4/36

Scoring by Quarters:

UCLA	6	0	7	7	—	20
USC	2	0	0	7	—	9

Joe Bruin

1958
Game 28

Fit to be Tied

Two plus two equals 15. That was the formula used by UCLA and Southern California when they squared off on a hot day at the Coliseum for Game No. 28.

The Trojans capitalized on two big plays that brought the fans to their feet to accumulate 15 points. And the Bruins capitalized on two alert plays that brought the fans to their feet to accumulate 15 points.

Mathematically speaking, that was the ol' ball game—a 15-15 deadlock. The underdog Uclans, battered and bruised, found some consolation in the stalemate. The favored Trojans, still clinging at kickoff to a feeble and long shot at the Rose Bowl, were fit to be tied.

"It wasn't a win, but close to it," said Bruin Captain Jim Steffen as he presented the game ball to Coach Bill Barnes.

USC, under second-year Coach Don Clark, brought 4-4-0 testimonials to the conflict, administering defeats to Oregon State, Washington State, Stanford and Washington, while dropping verdicts to Michigan, North Carolina, Oregon and California. Three of those four games were lost by a total of only four points.

UCLA, which played under two coaches in '58, didn't quite have a balanced ledger. Under George Dickerson, the Ukes beat Illinois but lost to Pittsburgh and Oregon State. Under Barnes, the Uclans jumped on Washington and Oregon but submitted to Florida, Stanford, Washington State and California. Combined, that was 3-6-0.

So, no one was unduly surprised when the oddsmakers tabbed USC a seven point favorite, then upped it to seven-and-a-half.

"SC is the toughest team on the coast in my book," commented Barnes, endorsing the odds. "The Trojans should be substantially favored."

Then, as an afterthought, Barnes added, "But if we play our best game of the season and get a couple of breaks, we might win."

As usual after a rigorous schedule, both teams were beset with wounded. But this was minimized by Barnes. "We've got a lot of problems," he said, "but so have the Trojans."

Topmost among the Bruin lame were Chuck Kendall, Tony Longo and John Brown. For the Trojans, neither Willie Wood nor Al Prukop would play, while Monte Clark and George Van Vliet might play, but only in low gear.

The loss of Wood and Prukop cut the SC quarterback corps to two activists—senior Tom Maudlin and untested Ben Charles. But this was a situation in which previous Troy clubs had found themselves. Remember 1949 and Dean Schneider? Remember 1956 and Jim Conroy?

It would be the last crosstown clash for 14 Trojans, while 10 Bruin seniors would end their college careers.

Al Wolf, *LA Times* writer, must have kept a crystal ball next to his typewriter. "The Bruins are the ball-hawkingest outfit in the conference," he wrote, "which may provide the breaks Barnes seeks for upset ammunition."

Indeed, alertness was the key to the Uclans' "victory of morale".

In the first quarter . . . well, nothing happened, so let's go to the second. In the second period . . . well, nothing happened, so let's go to the third. In the third stanza . . . well, a lot happened.

USC had possession on its 17-yard line. Scooter Don Buford, in two plays, scooted to the 30. Hillard Hill bulled for three, then the Trojans came up with Big Play No. 1. A gaping hole was opened in the Bruin line, and the smallish Buford popped through it, picked up his interference—Hill and Clark Holden—and zipped 66 yards before Trusse Norris hauled him down, one yard shy of the Bruin goal line.

On the next play, Maudlin plowed over center, Don Zachik converted, and SC had itself a 7-0 tiebreaker.

The Trojans kicked off, forced a Bruin punt, and started out again from their 17. Don Kasten kneaded his way to the 20. Then came Alert Play No. 1 for the Bruins. Maudlin, when boxed in on a keeper, turned and flipped a backward pass, intended for Kasten. A bouncing ball, however, is unpredictable, and this particular one was

A DEADLOCK IN THRILLER, 15-15

Trojans Held Off by UCLA
BY AL WOLF

58,507 See Wild Windup
BY BRAVEN DYER

pounded upon by Bruin Rod Cochran, not Kasten.

"Some official got in the way," explained Maudlin. "Kasten told me he didn't see the ball."

With spirits lifted, UCLA now needed only six yards for a marker.

Two plunges by Bill Kilmer, injured and inactive since UCLA's third game, spotted the ball on Troy's one, from where Ray Smith nose-dived over. The new two-point conversion was now an option in college football, and Barnes opted for it, sending Kilmer around end. It worked. And, as Harry Mehre, former Georgia and Ole Miss coach, used to say: "We had a commanding one point lead."

Barnes, who still resides in Los Angeles, was recently asked to identify the most significant item affecting football while he was coaching.

"The choice to go for two points following a TD," he responded. "I knew that field goal kicking was to gain in importance."

Quarter Number Four started with UCLA ahead, 8-7, but on defense. Starting from their 26-yard stripe, the Trojans had advanced the ball 51 yards to UCLA's 23, first down. Here the Bruins bristled, so on fourth-and-two, Clark gambled on a field goal. Zachik's boot was long enough, but a bit wide. Not as wide, however, as the grins on the faces of Bruin rooters.

UCLA could not move, so Kilmer punted and the Trojans made a first down from their 30 to their 45-yard line.

Enter Alert Play No. Two for Westwood. Maudlin ran to his right, then pitched out to Angie Coia. A good call, no doubt, except the ball never reached Coia. Big Bruin John Brown, supposedly hobbled, swiped the toss and trundled 45 yards to pay dirt, with no Trojan to hamper his progress. Steffen's PAT stretched UCLA's lead to 15-7.

"I was worried about Coia going wide," stated Brown. "I thought Maudlin's lateral was over my head, but I just reached up my hand and there was the ball. It seemed like I moved in the same spot for several seconds before I got going."

UCLA invaders pierce USC vigil and douse Tommy Trojan with paint, blue of course.

But UCLA's prosperity was doomed for an early depression. Big Play No. Two was ready.

Luther Hayes, starting his first game for Troy, took Steffen's kickoff in full flight on his 26, saw open daylight after 20 yards of probing, then unlimbered his gams to complete a 74-yard TD scamper.

"It was a short kick," said the pumped-up Hayes. "I caught the ball and looked for somebody to lateral it to, but then I decided I'd better take off."

"We kicked short to keep the ball away from Buford," said a deflated Barnes. "Naturally, we didn't figure on Hayes getting the ball and going for the easy TD."

Trailing by two, everyone in the stadium knew the truculent Trojans would go for two. Maudlin decided if he had been the goat so far, he might as well be a turkey, too . . . or make some amends. He did the latter. Taking the snap, Maudlin ran to his left and swept into the end zone, barely, for two points.

Now tied at 15-all with seven minutes to play, USC figured it could still be a winner.

After a Bruin punt, a pass interception by Kilmer and another Bruin punt, the Trojans started an excursion from their 17 with just over three minutes remaining.

Maudlin passed 47 yards to Hillard Hill, who was tackled by Paul Oglesby on the Uclans' 32. Two plays later, Phil Parslow pilfered a Maudlin aerial, but fumbled when tackled, and Gary Finnerman retrieved the oval for SC on Westwood's 31.

Maudlin threw incomplete, was sacked for an eight yard loss by Bob King, then hit Larry Boies with a strike to the 19. Alas, the gun sounded as the Trojans rushed to the line of scrimmage.

"We just didn't have any more time-outs to stop the clock." Clark explained.

So there it was, one of the most stirring battles of the crosstown rivalry—and viewed by one of its smallest crowds . . . just 58,509 witnesses.

If many of those people found it difficult to believe the Bruins had tied the Trojans—or was it the other way around—don't be alarmed. A Gallup poll of the day revealed that 75 per cent of people surveyed did not believe the U.S. could send a rocket to the moon anytime in the foreseeable future. (Of course, there had been three previous failures.)

Kilmer emerged as the work horse for UCLA, toting the ball 24 times for a net gain of 92 yards. He also punted well and intercepted a key pass late in the game.

The sophomore tailback made a dent on Trojan coach Clark. "Before that boy is finished, he'll become one of UCLA's all-time great backs," he predicted.

Joining Kilmer in the Bruin halo of stars were Norris, Steffen, Parslow and Oglesby.

The tiny scatback, Buford, paced the Trojan charge with 101 yards on 14 carries, while Lou Byrd, Hill and Maudlin were credited with super performances.

Clark defended Maudlin's wild pitchouts: "He is not at his peak, physically. His right shoulder was all taped up, and maybe that bothered him."

But Clark realized the ill-effects of the wayward heaves. "We gave the Bruins both of their touchdowns on pitchouts," he remarked.

The Trojans, however, had eight turnovers in all ... five lost fumbles and three intercepted passes. Only their superior yardage—359 to 148—and ball control—17 first downs to 10—counter-balanced their hand-outs.

USC ended its season at 4-5-1 with a one-touchdown loss to Notre Dame. UCLA was 3-6-1.

Bruin players, exhausted and worn, praised the Trojans, labeling them their toughest opponent of the year. "They really wore us down," was the consensus.

Maybe so. But the record book will forever show a 15-15 tie.

Summary

	USC	UCLA
First Downs	17	10
Yards Rushing	231	130
Yards Passing	128	18
Total Yards	359	148
Passes Attempted	14	15
Passes Completed	6	2
Passes Had Intercepted	3	0
Fumbles Lost	5	1
Punts/Average	2/44.0	9/38.2
Penalties No./Yards	6/60	3/35

Scoring By Quarters:

USC	0	0	7	8	—	15
UCLA	0	0	8	7	—	15

1959
Game 29

The Unbelievers

The powerhouse Southern California Trojans were the second best team in the entire nation, according to *Associated Press* ratings published Saturday morning, November 21st. And by that afternoon of the same day, the Trojans were the second best team in the entire city of Los Angeles.

There are some partisan supporters who will dispute the secondary status of the latter rating, because an aura of controversy did enswathe UCLA's 10-3 upset win over Troy. But there are always two sides to a debate. More on this later.

There was no doubt Southern Cal sported better credentials than did the Bruins. Undefeated, untied, unblemished, unscathed, unbending ... those were the touts of the Trojans. Underdogs, unarmed, unrated, and unbelievers ... those were the traits of the Uclans.

Coach Don Clark's juggernaut was on its way to Troy's first perfect season since 1932, having vanquished eight straight foes: Oregon State, Pittsburgh, Ohio State, Washington, Stanford, California, West Virginia and Baylor.

"We have an unbeaten season within our grasp," admitted Clark, "but we're still 20 per cent away from it."

Up toward Sunset Boulevard, Joe Bruin had not fared so well. Only California, Stanford and North Carolina State had fallen to his paw, while Pittsburgh, Air Force Academy and Washington had

Credit *Los Angeles Times*

The Gridiron Find of the Year!

tamed the critter. Throw in a scoreless tie with Purdue and 3-3-1 is the result.

Statistics further amplified USC's superiority. The Trojans had outscored their opposition, 186-64; the Uclans, 130-105. Troy beat two teams which beat the Ukes. SC was bigger, 11 pounds to the

2 AT GRID LUNCHEON
Scribes Pick SC Over UCLA by 13 Points

man. And tradition was on the side of Troy, which led the series, 15-8-5.

The bookies found few obstacles to keep them from leaning toward Southern Cal, either, fixing the Trojans first as nine point favorites, then nine-and-a-half.

Newspaper scribes assembling for the weekly football writers luncheon were more emphatic. Of 38 scribblers polled, 36 picked USC, and the mean spread was 13 points.

UCLA Coach Bill Barnes didn't dispute the point. "I feel this is SC's finest all-around team," was his appraisal.

But Clark was more cautious. "It's my belief that UCLA has not played it's best game yet this year," he opined.

Other coaches along the coast, in semi-agreement with Clark, found it difficult to settle on the winner.

Braven Dyer, of the *LA Times,* contacted several and here are two typical replies:

"The Trojans are a tremendous team, but the Bruins have come a long way. I think it's a toss-up. But, as in most traditional games, there's the possibility of an upset. I won't be surprised if that happens."–Jim Owens, Washington.

"The Trojans must be rated the outstanding team on the Pacific Coast. But the Bruins are getting better each week. And a traditional game always means danger."–Pete Elliott, California.

Despite their fine slate, the Trojans were actually a young team, with only six seniors among the regulars. But it was a star-studded outfit, boasting such All-America performers as tackles Ron Mix and Dan Ficca, plus the McKeever twins, Marlin and Mike, not to mention the likes of Willie Wood, Garry Finneran and others.

Fifteen seniors dotted the UCLA roster, but the burden of producing points rested on the shoulders of a junior, Bill Kilmer. And this priceless jewel tuned up with an ankle injury the day before the game.

"As of now, I don't believe Bill's injury is serious," said Barnes. "I'm still planning to start him."

But when 85,917 patrons filed into the Coliseum, they saw Kilmer on the bench. And there he remained for the first half.

Southern Cal put a trey of points on the board almost before you could say "Happy Anniversary." (This was the 30th birthday of the big, crosstown rivalry, you know.)

Three plays after the opening kick off, Bruin Gene Gaines fumbled and SC's Wood hopped on the ball on the Bruin 31-yard line. Bob Levingston, Clark Holden and Jerry Traynham obtained a first down to the 12, then Wood and Traynham picked up a yard apiece to the 10. Wood threw incomplete on third down, so little Don Zachik split the uprights from the 17, staking USC to a 3-0 lead.

Southern Cal made inroads on its next possession, too, advancing to UCLA's 21 on six running plays. But the Bruins rudely repulsed Angie Coia on fourth down and took over.

Now the Uclans went on stage, featuring the Bob and Ray Show. Starting from their 20-yard stripe, the Smith boys led a charge that carried all the way to the Trojan four. A penalty set the Bruins back to the nine, and Bob Smith lost two to the 11.

Now in the second quarter, Bob rifled a bullet to Jim Johnson, good for seven yards. His next pass was broken up, so on fourth down, Smith (Bob, that is) crashed over right tackle to the very last grass blade at the goal line. The Bruin players thought they had a touchdown, but the officials disagreed and gave SC the ball on the one-inch line.

The half ended with USC on Westwood's seven yard line and leading, 3-0.

There was no scoring in the third period—although the Trojans, behind Wood and Traynham, hustled from their 18 to the Bruins' six-yard line before giving out of fuel—so the fourth stanza started with SC still leading by three.

With Kilmer now in the game, UCLA took an 87-yard route to tieland, Ivory Jones booting a 31-yarder to knot things at 3-3.

Kilmer, wearing tennis shoes to compensate his ankle injury, was a destructive weapon in sustaining the drive. His passes went to Johnson for 10, to Marv Luster for 11, to Trusse Norris for seven and again to Norris for 16. In between, Kilmer vacated his pocket and eluded would-be tacklers to generate clutch sprints of 17 and 10 yards.

But the Trojans jammed the effort, so Jones came in for his field goal.

Next came the TD jaunt by the Bruins that produced the second—and bigger—controversial issue.

Starting from his 20, Kilmer passed to Johnson on the 43. An-

INSPIRED BRUINS SHOCK TROJANS, 10-3

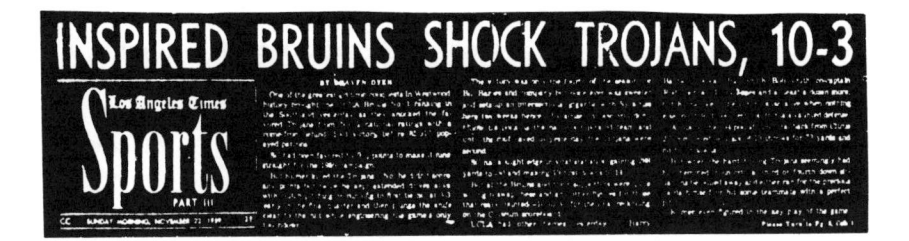

other toss to Norris netted five and R. Smith bulled across midfield to SC's 46. Then Finneran's seven-yard sack of Kilmer set the stage for the "big play".

On second-and-17 from his 47-yard line, Kilmer unleashed a bomb far downfield. Luster was the intended target, but Trojans Wood and Traynham were in bulls-eye range to interrupt the projectory. Wood was successful in intercepting the ball, and he was instantly tackled by Luster.

But wait. Field Judge George Wilson ruled an infraction against Traynham, and handed the ball to the Bruins on the seven, first-and-goal. From there, R. Smith pounded Troy's line three times to rack up the go-ahead points. Jones drilled the PAT to put UCLA up, 10-3, and that's the way it ended.

A lot of people had a lot to say about the pass interference call.

"I was running downfield with Luster," spoke Traynham. "I don't remember whether I grabbed him or not. The next thing I knew an official tapped me on the shoulder and said I interfered with the pass."

Athletic Director Jess Hill of USC was more vehement, reading the riot act to the officials after the game. "The movies had better show it, that's all I've got to say," he admonished.

From Coach Clark came, "No comment. Anyway, I've never seen an official change his mind."

And from Coach Barnes: "I couldn't see what was going on down there. Football is full of hazards, and having penalties called is just one of them."

Barnes drew a comparison to an earlier judgment call that denied his players what they thought was a touchdown (B. Smith's dive to the one-inch line in the second quarter).

If a nutshell summary is desired, it would be that USC manufactured six penetrations and capitalized on just one. UCLA had four opportunities and cashed two.

If a generic summary is desired, review the words of the *Southern Campus,* UCLA's Yearbook: "Mightly Troy Falls. Outsmarted and out-hustled, SC came to the end of the line today as UCLA's magnificent Bruins, led by a wiry, willing line and a crippled tailback, shocked the nation's Number Two ranked team, 10-3."

The tailback alluded to was Kilmer, who completed six passes for 73 yards and ran for 20 more. Other Bruin standouts were Harry Baldwin, Cochran, Jones and both Smiths.

Barnes admitted he was surprised his Bruins allowed the Trojans no touchdowns. "I honestly thought we had a chance to win," he remarked, "but I thought it would take at least three TDs to do it. It was our best overall effort of the year."

To finish out the season, UCLA clubbed Utah, but was slayed by Syracuse, the nation's Number One team. Overall, its record was 5-4-1. The Bruins tied for first place in the newly-formed Athletic Association of Western Universities.

Clark, who was winding up his last season as Troy's coach, felt his team played hard but without the sharpness of earlier games. Even so, the Trojans outgained the winners, 288 to 230, and led in first downs, 19 to 14.

After losing by 10 points to Notre Dame, SC's slate dropped to 8-2-0. Clark's three-year ledger was 13 triumphs, 16 defeats and one tie.

UCLA's stunning upset was a fitting occasion for the unveiling of a plaque at the Coliseum commemorating Henry (Red) Sanders. Inscribed under the plaque is the creed of the late Bruin coach:

Blocking is the essence of offense.
Tackling is the essence of defense.
And spirit is the quintessence of all.

Perhaps that legacy spilled into Blue and Gold hearts battling on the Coliseum turf that autumn day in 1959.

Summary

	UCLA	USC
First Downs	14	19
Yards Rushing	141	214
Yards Passing	89	74
Total Yards	230	288
Passes Attempted	24	16
Passes Completed	9	6
Passes Had Intercepted	0	1
Fumbles Lost	1	1
Punts/Average	4/38	5/33
Penalties No./Yards	4/20	5/51

Scoring by Quarters:

UCLA	0	0	0	10	—	10
USC	3	0	0	0	—	3

1960
Game 30

As the Worm Turns

Here's a twist. UCLA, deviating from valleys of the past, comes in as an overwhelming favorite to sock Southern California. And what happens? Southern California rears its underdog head and slaps a 17-6 UPSET on the Uclans. That's right. The Trojans upset the Bruins.

So regarded with such low esteem were the men of Troy that one Los Angeles writer described them as "hapless". Now, Southern Cal may have an off year now and then — but hapless? Could Joe Louis punch? Could Ted Williams hit? Could Sandy Koufax pitch?

But back to the Bruins. Their role of favorite did have validity in this year of 1960. They were a high-flying pack, anchored by a rugged defense that had allowed only eight points in the last four games . . . zero in the last three. And in Bill Kilmer, they had the Number Four offensive back in the nation.

Pittsburgh, Stanford, North Carolina State, California and Air Force Academy had swayed before the Ukes' fury, while only Washington had withstood their assault. Joe Bruin breezed to a tie with Purdue, so his record on the eve of the SC game was 5-1-1.

Pit that against a 3-5-0 catalogue for Tommy Trojan and UCLA's status as a 12-point favorite comes into focus. The three victories for USC were over Georgia, California and Stanford; the five losses were to Oregon State, TCU, Ohio State, Washington and Baylor. For the eight games, the Trojan offense pumped up an average of less than eight points per event.

UCLA Favored by 12 Over Trojans

60,000 Fans Expected at Game Today

WASHINGTON BEAT SC 34-0

WASHINGTON BEAT UCLA 10-8

SC BEAT CALIFORNIA 27-10

UCLA BEAT CALIFORNIA 28-0

SC BEAT STANFORD 21-6

UCLA BEAT STANFORD 26-8

CROSS TOWN CHAMPIONSHIP

SC BY AN UPSET

UCLA UPSET THE TROJANS IN 1954 — THIS MAY BE SC'S TURN

UCLA BY 12 PTS.

IF THE BRUINS SHUT OUT SC IT WILL BE THE FIRST TIME IN HISTORY UCLA HAS BLANKED FOUR TEAMS IN A ROW FOR A SEASON

Alex Perez

Credit *Los Angeles Times*

Heap on a slew of injuries for Southern Cal, and, well . . . maybe the 12-point spread seemed polite.

"I couldn't say the injury situation at SC has gotten out of hand," wise-cracked John McKay, Troy's new head coach, "but I think we're the only team in collegiate football which practices with a doctor in the huddle and an ambulance on the sideline."

Then, on a serious note ". . . I believe at full strength physically we could take the Bruins, but we're down to rock bottom in respect to boys available for duty. A win will have to be the result of pure desire and dedicated play."

Some of the injured Trojans to whom McKay referred were guard Mike McKeever, end Luther Hayes and tackle Dan Ficca, immobile all, plus Brett Williams and Nick McLean, hobbled but mobile.

So, with every indicator pointing toward Westwood, with the gods of fortune smiling on Westwood, with every chapter in the pre-game book featuring Westwood, Bill Barnes, the amiable Westwood coach comes up with the classic observation, a remark that only a head coach could utter.

"SC is one of the most powerful teams in the country," he stated, adding — now get this — "I don't see how we can stop them."

Not only was Barnes speaking seriously, he issued these statements knowing full well that his wife, Frances, positively planned to wear her lucky blue knit suit to the game — the same lucky blue knit suit she had worn to every Bruin game throughout the season . . . except to the Washington contest, which UCLA lost.

But perhaps the bad practice sessions the Bruins had waded through during the week had more influence on Barnes' prediction than did his wife's choice of wardrobe.

"We've had the worst practice we've had this year," fretted Barnes, "and generally a team plays on Saturday like it practices."

The Southern Cal seniors had never frolicked in the joy that comes with whipping their crosstown rival, not even as freshmen. And their last chance of salvage would be led by a sophomore quarterback, Bill Nelsen. Actually, the seniors were not in bad hands.

Almost 67,000 spectators who ignored a citywide transit strike to come to Memorial Coliseum will vouch for that.

Overshadowing his famous counterpart (Kilmer), Nelsen passed for 87 yards on seven-for-11, including a touchdown, and ran for 58 more yards on 16 carries, all of which was instrumental in helping the Troy seniors relish their first Bruin hide.

Indications pointed quite quickly to the fact that McKay's clan, despite their crutches, meant business. Taking the opening kickoff, the Trojans, with Carl Skvarna and Hal Tobin hoofing the ball, and Nelsen hurling it, constructed a 58-yard maneuver, before UCLA took over on its 22-yard line.

Undaunted by the momentary delay, USC bounced right back to take a 7-0 lead.

Skvarna legged Kilmer's punt 20 yards, back to the Uclan 43. Nelsen orbited an 18-yarder to Jim Bates on the 27. Skvarna zapped for two and the Bruins were penalized 15 yards for unnecessary roughness. From the 12-yard stripe, Jerry Traynham bolted to the seven, but a holding penalty reversed Troy back to the 22.

With some breathing space, the Ukes may have relaxed. For Nelsen found Marlin McKeever open on the two, hit him on the numbers, and the All-American end proceeded into the end zone. Don Zachik kicked the extra point as the first quarter ended.

Hit'em while they're down seemed to be the philosophy of Troy, so four plays after the TD, Traynham plucked a Kilmer aerial from mid-air on the Bruin 40-yard line and jogged to the 14 before being tackled. Twice Tobin sliced the middle to the five and Nelsen maintained control with a first down to the four. On second down, Tobin lunged over center and over the double stripe from three yards out. Zachik's automatic toe lifted USC to a 14-0 advantage.

UCLA's vaunted offense, a sleeping giant since kickoff, yawned and stretched itself with an attack that progressed to SC's four-yard line—but closeness counts only in horseshoes. Kilmer completed three passes on this drive . . . 37 yards to Jim Johnson, 10 to Don Vena and 11 to Chuck Hicks. Skip Smith contributed a 16-yard sprint.

But the Bruins went back to napping in the third period, and the Trojans weren't exactly hyperkinetic, either . . . although they did reach Westwood's 25-yard line on one occasion.

The alarm sounded for UCLA in the final quarter, as Kilmer and Company staged a 66-yard campaign to paydirt.

The drive assumed point possibilities when Kilmer passed 19 yards to Johnson for a sticks-mover on the Trojan 20-yard stripe. Seven plays later (the 18th since the drive started) Kilmer slashed over tackle from three yards out for six points. In quest of two more, the All-American QB tried the same spot, but came up short. Now, SC led, 14-6, with 11 minutes still on the clock.

Southern Cal took the kickoff and when they finally surrendered the ball, there were just two minutes on the clock. And in the process, El Trojan subscribed to an insurance field goal.

The time-consuming escapade covered 79 yards, coming to a detour on UCLA's three-yard chalk strip. So in came little Zachik and his 20-yard FG sealed the SC upset win at 17-6.

Bill Kilmer, UCLA All-American back, 1960.

FIRED-UP TROJANS UPSET BRUINS, 17-6

Los Angeles Times Sports

Not only did the Trojans master the scoreboard, they did the same in the stats: 333 net yards to the Bruins' 171, and 20 first downs to 10.

It was a long afternoon for Kilmer, who ran for only 29 yards, completed only four of 17 passes for 80 yards and suffered three interceptions.

SC's McKay had an explanation.

"Our whole objective was to keep Kilmer from going out to pass or run," he related. "We wanted to wreck that option by making him stop and commit himself. Marlin McKeever was the key. He pushed right at Kilmer."

UCLA Coach Barnes would only say Kilmer had "... an off day". Asked recently to pick the best quarterback he ever coached, Barnes named Kilmer.

Turning to the game, Barnes said, "We were beaten soundly by SC in every phase. We knew they would be up, but I don't think we were overconfident."

The triumph was a big boost for McKay, who in his first year as coach did not have the Troy alumni turning ecstatic cartwheels.

"I think everyone who saw the game will agree it was an all-around team production," spoke the articulate McKay, who then went on to pick out a few individuals: McKeever, Skvarna, Bates and Nelsen.

Even in victory, Nelsen was not altogether satisfied. "We should have scored a couple more times," he commented.

El Rodeo, USC's yearbook, devoted a paragraph to the cool quarterback. "One of McKay's finds during the 1960 season was sophomore Bill Nelsen. Third stringer when the season began, Nelsen took over in Troy's first win (against Georgia) and never gave up the job."

A Trojan who sat on the sideline was awarded the game ball. Co-captain Mike McKeever, convalescing from brain surgery, accepted the ball from co-captain George Van Vliet amid the cheers of his mates.

"This is the greatest team you'll ever see," responded Mike.

Southern Cal still had Notre Dame on its schedule, and perhaps the Trojans left too much of their energy on the Coliseum sod, as they yielded to the Irish, 17-0. McKay, destined for a long and brilliant coaching career, finished his first season at 4-6-0.

Meanwhile, UCLA picked up the pieces of its dismal day, and went on to lace Utah and Duke, giving Barnes a respectable 7-2-1 season.

But the twist had happened. The favorite: UCLA. The winner: USC.

"I told you we would win," McKay told his players.

Summary

	USC	UCLA
First Downs	20	10
Yards Rushing	246	94
Yards Passing	87	77
Total Yards	333	171
Passes Attempted	12	18
Passes Completed	7	5
Passes Had Intercepted	0	3
Punts/Average	3/36	4/37
Penalties No./Yards	2/20	1/15

Scoring by Quarters:

USC	7	7	0	3	—	17
UCLA	0	0	0	6	—	6

**Marlin McKeever, USC
All-America End, 1959-60**

1961
Game 31

Quack, Quack

In a nip and tuck tussle played under a steady downpour of rain, UCLA nipped Southern California, 10-7, and tucked away the championship of the Big Five Conference. With the title came a trip to Pasadena and a spot in the Rose Bowl.

It was the first time since 1952 that the crosstown classic would decide which of the two schools would host the Crown City Classic. The Trojans could go with a win or a tie; the Bruins had to have a win.

The ultimatum of the occasion recently prompted UCLA Coach Bill Barnes to identify the 1961 battle as the most memorable of all his confrontations with USC.

He had other concerns on the eve of the game, however. One was the oddsmakers who tagged the Bruins as the team to beat.

"I see where they've made us a six-point favorite," chortled Barnes. "What a laugh."

Local sportscasters failed to see any merriment in the casting. Polled at their weekly luncheon, the men of the mike picked UCLA to defeat SC by a vote of 16 to eight.

Not surprisingly, one of Barnes' players lined up with the sportscasters. "I think we're ready for USC," said senior guard Frank Macari. (He may have spoken under duress, though, for tough line coach Sam Boghosian was standing within earshot.)

But there was one fellow who simultaneously made Barnes happy and SC Coach John McKay unhappy. Al Wolf, *LA Times* writer

·usually as accurate as William Tell's arrow, selected Southern Cal to emerge victorious by three points. Well, he was right on the spread—he just picked the wrong team. Of the seven *Times* scribes polled, however, four rode the Bruin wagon.

With 13 seniors gracing their roster, the Uclans wheeled into the brawl with a record of 6-3-0. Waylaid along the way were Air Force Academy, Vanderbilt, Pittsburgh, Stanford, California and Texas Christian; while the resistors were Michigan, Ohio State and Washington. Offensively, UCLA had amassed 172 points in these nine engagements.

Southern Cal was playing it down the middle—four wins, four losses, one tie. The Trojans had gotten the better of SMU, California, Illinois and Stanford while yielding to Georgia Tech, Iowa, Notre Dame and Pittsburgh. Washington was a scoreless writeoff. For the nine involvements, McKay's group had generated 143 points.

Both squads glittered with individual performers. Bruin tailback Bobby Smith was the Big Five's scoring leader with 95 points, only four shy of Paul Cameron's modern school record. Smith's 874 yards also paced the league in total offense, and teammate Mike Haffner's 620 rushing yards led that category. Center Ron Hull, an All-American, stabilized the forward wall.

For Southern Cal, Pete Beathard's 39 pass completions were tops in the conference, while Bill Nelsen had the most pass yardage—676. Soph Hal Bedsole had caught 27 passes for 525 yards for the Number One slot in both of those areas. And Ernie Jones was the punter deluxe with a 39.2 yard average.

Neither team crashed *Associated Press'* Top Ten, an elite coterie headed by Missouri and Iowa.

The UCLA-USC conflicts were now embarking on their third decade of altercations, having etched 30 games into the scrolls of history. Attendance during this period totaled 2,242,345, an average of 74,745 per game. Not the highest average in the nation—no, but not many rivalries surpassed it.

But the monsoon that swept across Memorial Coliseum on this, the 31st melee, took its toll as only 57,850 die-hards showed up for the fete champetre.

What they saw was a "three-yards-and-a-shower-of-mud" entanglement in which UCLA came from behind for its three point decision. They also saw Smith register all 10 of the Ukes' points to chalk up a new school modern scoring record—85 points.

Nelsen got the Trojans off to a good start by sloshing 25 yards with the opening kick off. He then rotated with Ken Del Conte and Ben Wilson to paddle the ball to UCLA's 27, but the Bruins ducked

Sunny California? Not for the 1961 mud game.

this threat.

Shortly thereafter, Westwood's Bob Stevens recovered a slippery pigskin that squirted from the grasp of Nelsen on USC's 30 yard line. And although Almose Thompson, Ezell Singleton and Smith splashed to the 10, it was no soap for the Bruins.

In no time, Haffner, Kermit Alexander and Smith mixed runs with a Smith-to-Tom Gutman 13-yard pass to put UCLA in door-knocking territory again. But on fourth down from the 20, Smith's field goal attempt went askew.

After a Trojan punt, Haffner waded through the silt for 61 yards to Troy's eight, before Frank Buncom shouted "Quack, quack" — which on a dry day means "Stop, stop".

"USC guys were falling down all over the place and I just ran by," related Haffner.

The Bruins snorkeled on down to the four, but waved goodbye to this scoring opportunity when on fourth down, Warren Stephenson broke through to spill Smith back on the 12.

But the Trojans didn't have time to catch their breaths. On the first play, Mel Profit whaled the daylights out of Wilson, who coughed up the ball to UCLA's John Walker on Troy's 18-yard stripe.

Thompson waddled to the 13, Smith threw one away, then lost a couple. On fourth down, Smith booted a 31-yard field goal, and UCLA was perched out front, 3-0.

Still in the second quarter, USC, tired of floundering around, opened its flood gates, and sent Beathard storming to a lightning-quick touchdown.

The marker was set up by Jones' 60-yard punt that rolled dead as a mackerel on UCLA's four-yard line. Thompson picked up four, then Keith Jensen quick-kicked from his eight. It was a line drive that Beathard pulled in on his 48, dropped in behind fine blocking, splattered down the sideline, and crossed the goal line with only the brush of a single soggy hand.

Carl Skvarna notched the PAT, staking USC to a 7-3 lead as the teams broke for recess.

Dim was the sky—as was UCLA's hopes—as the third period started, and dim became dark when Troy's Britt Williams jumped on Thompson's fumble at Westwood's 37.

Jim Maples, Wilson, Willie Brown and Beathard splattered to the 23, but Skvarna's field goal attempt just barely missed.

After the Trojan defense dictated a punt, Beathard passed to Phil Hoover on UCLA's 43. Back to throw again, Beathard was rushed by Profit and his slightly altered pass was purloined by Joe Bauwens, who goose-stepped 15 yards to USC's 33-yard line.

"Willie (Brown) was wide open," lamented Beathard. "I don't know where that fellow (Bauwens) came from. I guess I lost it for us." Not really, Pete.

From the 33, Smith plowed to the 18, then rotated with Haffner and Thompson to nudge the ball to SC's eight. Thompson sliced for two, then Smith turned the left corner and slid into the end zone, barely. Completing a one-man point spree, Smith posted the PAT and the Bruin jubilant was sealed at 10-7.

But there was still more than a quarter to play and the Trojans were still fighting like Trojans. And prospects looked bright when Jones punted dead on UCLA's two.

They didn't last long. For the Uclan's Thompson immediately squirmed and zoomed 42 yards to rid his team of any potential hazard.

"I went inside," explained Thompson, "but it was plugged, so I veered out. The end was there, but he wasn't ready."

This may have been the play that muzzled Tommy Trojan, but soaked to the gills, he gave it one more try, starting from his 22. With Wilson, Brown and Tobin grinding out yardage, plus a Nelsen-to-Toby Thurlow pass, SC cruised to UCLA's 33-yard stripe before Chick Hicks and Foster Anderson arose from the mire to impede further progress.

Ten-to-seven . . . that was it; hook, line and sinker.

"Bill Barnes has a good, hard-hitting team," declared SC's McKay. "But they didn't do anything we didn't anticipate—except beat us."

McKay refused to lean on the quagmire field conditions. "I wish I

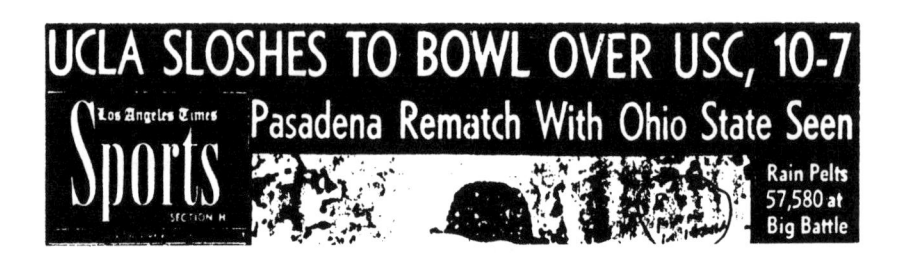

UCLA SLOSHES TO BOWL OVER USC, 10-7
Pasadena Rematch With Ohio State Seen
Rain Pelts 57,580 at Big Battle

Happy Bruins Ready to Play Anyone in Rose Bowl

could use that as an alibi, but I can't," he said. McKay's season ended at 4-5-1.

Across the field, UCLA's Barnes was elated. "This is the biggest game to me that I've ever participated in," he exuded, "and I don't care who we play in the Rose Bowl."

Barnes identified Hull and Profit for playing outstanding games. He also had praise for some of his opponents. "Ben Wilson was awfully strong," he stated. "I also noticed Frank Buncom a lot and that little Warren Stephenson was terrific," Barnes added.

Yearbooks from the two schools came right to the point. USC: "Bruins squish to tight win over valiant USC." UCLA: "We really gave'em hell; victory is so sweet. Homecoming week ended perfectly."

Stat-wise, UCLA led in first downs, 10 to nine, and in yardage, 261 to 148.

UCLA's Thompson led all rushers with 79 yards, followed by mate Haffner's 76. Tops for the Trojans was Wilson, with 72 yards.

The unhappy fact that UCLA lost to Minnesota in the Rose Bowl didn't put a damper on the Bruin season which concluded at 7-4-0, because they could look back to that sloppy day in November. Indeed, it was a rain-drenched afternoon, but it had a rainbow. And all rainbows have a pot of gold. If you don't believe it, ask Joe Bruin.

Summary

	UCLA	USC
First Downs	10	9
Yards Rushing	229	137
Yards Passing	32	11
Total Yards	261	148
Passed Attempted	4	8
Passes Completed	2	2
Passes Had Intercepted	0	1
Fumbles Lost	1	2
Punts/Average	5/36.0	5/42.4
Penalties No./Yards	6/30	3/18

Scoring By Quarters:

UCLA	0	3	7	0	—	10
USC	0	7	0	0	—	7

1962
Game 32

Knockout, In the Fourth

Over at the Sports Arena, 20-year-old Cassius Clay sparred with Archie Moore for three gongs, then rocked the veteran boxer into dreamland with a fourth round KO. Out at Memorial Coliseum, the Southern California Trojans jostled with the UCLA Bruins for three pistol shots, then socked their crosstown rival into submission with a fourth quarter KO.

And that's the way it was supposed to be. Not exactly a fourth period haymaker, mind you, but a Trojan triumph, nonetheless. Because Southern Cal was at the top of the heap in the entire country, rated Number 1 by both wire service polls. So the Trojans beat the Bruins as they were supposed to, but the 14-3 punch was not quite as impressive as most pre-game experts predicted.

In his third year as head mentor, Coach John McKay had led the Cardinal and Gold to eight consecutive victories, running up 180 points along the way. UCLA had lost four of seven games, and wallowed in the hoi polloi of collegiate football.

Few, if any, questioned the Las Vegas line when it proclaimed Southern Cal a 14-point favorite, then later tacked on another half-point. In a poll of 37 Los Angeles writers, 34 rode the Trojan chariot, two sided with the Uclans, and one foresaw a draw.

Both Charlie Park and Al Wolf, *Times* writers, came up with the same score: SC, 21-7. None of which impressed McKay. "I'll go back to 1960," he spate, "when 31 of 32 writers picked UCLA, and we won,

17-6." McKay was surely aware that in this traditional series, the underdog team often finds a way to ridicule the odds-favoring upperdog.

Speaking with Sid Ziff, McKay asked "Do you know UCLA has more experienced men than we have?" Then he answered his question. "They have 21 lettermen back to our 15."

The eight clubs that had felt the Trojan wrath were Duke, SMU, Iowa, California, Illinois, Washington, Stanford and Navy. Athletic Director Jess Hill had an invitation to host the Rose Bowl in his hip pocket, but only he and his coaches knew about it.

Meanwhile, up at Westwood, there had been more thorns than roses. Coach Bill Barnes and his lads had smitten Ohio State, Colorado State and California, but had foozled against Pittsburgh, Stanford, Air Force Academy and Washington.

Then there was the plethora of genuine stars that sparkled the USC roster .. fellows like tenuous Hal Bedsole, the All-American end; dangerous Damon Bame, the All-American linebacker; and Cary Kirner, lineman-of-the-week; not to mention such other heavyweights as Pete Beathard, Willie Brown (496 yards in 67 carries), Ben Wilson . . . the list goes on.

Talk about depth. Senior Bill Nelsen, good enough to be a first-string quarterback on almost any other team in the states, hadn't started a game all season. Here's Troy's total offensive leader for 1960 and '61, and he's second string behind Beathard.

McKay was delighted to have both QBs but leaned toward Beathard because ". . . he has thrown 79 passes, completed over half, and never once thrown an interception. If it takes a run, pass, a good tackle or block Beathard will give it to you."

"Naturally, I'd like to be playing more," Nelsen told Al Wolf, "but winning the national championship is the big thing. And under our three-unit system, everybody gets to play."

Despite the wealth of splendid personnel, McKay could count only nine seniors on his Trojan roster. Sorry about that, Joe.

Now to match the galaxy of lights shining in the Troy skies, UCLA could offer one player worthy of stardom—Kermit Alexander, the All-American tailback. His running-mate-to-be, Mike Haffner, had long before succumbed to injury, leaving a talent void for Mel Profit, Joe Bauwens, Andy Von Sonn and others to fill.

While Barnes was undecided whether to start Carl Jones or Larry Zeno at the Bruin quarterback spot, he was quite sure about the strength of the "total team" he was soon to face. "We realize we're facing what everybody says is the best USC team in years and years. They're loaded."

TROJANS ALMOST TRIP ON WAY TO BOWL
86,740 See Stubborn Bruins Bow in 4th Quarter, 14-3

Get the picture? Well, for 50 minutes the 86,740 fans who bought tickets for the game weren't altogether positive they had come to the right stadium. With a scant 10 minutes to play, that brash bunch from Westwood was clinging precariously to a 3-to-nothing lead. (What's with these Bruins? Didn't they read or listen to the media?) But as you know, might prevailed, the roof caved in, and Master Trojan reaped a come-from-behind, fourth quarter victory, 14-3.

The first half was a rock-and-sock defensive duel, with USC entering Bruin territory only once while the Ukes put together a pair of sustained onslaughts.

Late in the first stanza, Southern Cal concocted a notion to score when Brown, on two lopes, moved the ball from his 27 to his 42. Beathard hurled 26 yards to John Brownwood, and Ken Del Conte, Brown and Beathard added another first down to UCLA's 22. The threat was curtailed when Beathard hit the dirt at the 18 on fourth down.

Midway in the next period, the Bruins' Ezell Singleton filched a Beathard aerial, returning it 27 yards to the Trojan 43-yard line. UCLA sallied forth to the 23, but on fourth-and-four, Zeno missed on a 40-yard field goal attempt.

The Trojans punted out, only to see the Uclans bearing down again. Runs by Jones and Alexander, passes from Jones to Gary Callies and to Alexander, plus a 15-yard penalty assessed on SC, put UCLA menacingly on Troy's 13. At this point, Marv Marinovich and his Trojan mates asserted themselves, forcing Zeno to try another FG. This time, kicking from the 25, his swing was true, awarding the Bruins a 3-0 halftime lead.

What does an 8-0-0 coach tell his kids who are getting beat? Does he deliver a pep talk during intermission? "No," replied McKay, "although I did consider turning on a Knute Rockne record. But we just changed formations and went to our power stuff. We were trying to be too cute in the first half, I guess."

The Trojans went on two rampages in the second half before they finally solved the mystery of lighting the scoreboard.

The first was a 65-yard jaunt. That carried to the Uclans' 20. Here it expired when Bedsole snagged a Beathard pass, but was jarred loose from the ball by a jarring (what else?) tackle by Alexander.

Shortly thereafter, UCLA's Singleton fumbled an Earl Jones punt

Hal Bedsole, USC All-American end in 1962

and Del Conte claimed the ball for SC on Westwood's 21-yard stripe. On short power plays, the Trojans steadily hammered their way to UCLA's three, as the third frame ended.

On fourth down, Wilson plunged toward the goal but was met head-on by Von Sonn. Out came the sticks, revealing the ball to be just inches short of a first down and a yard from a touchdown.

For the measurement, the ball was pointing toward the sideline instead of toward the goal.

"I never saw'em do that before," remarked Wilson, who was later satisfied when McKay explained the rule to him.

Now it was getting late, so SC decided it was now or never. The Bruins had to kick and Brown ran it back 18 yards to UCLA's 26. On fourth down, with things again hairy, Nelsen needled a pass down the middle, which Brown leaped high to make a miraculous reception. He was brought to earth by Al Geverink on the two.

Their appetites now properly whetted, the Trojans sent Wilson crashing into the end zone, and Tom Lupo's PAT put the Bruins four points in arrears at 7-3.

"When I let go, I didn't think he (Brown) was going to catch it," disclosed Nelsen, who then became the recipient of congratulations from Jesse Hill. "You should be talking to Willie about pulling it down from the sky," Nelsen told him. "Whatta' catch."

Even Brown confessed his surprise. "I didn't think I had it until I came down with it."

But UCLA had come too far to fold now. The Bruins manipulated the ball into Troyland, but Beathard despoiled an Alexander heave on the SC 18, and the Bruins had shot their wad.

But El Trojan hadn't. Eighty-two yards they traveled for the game-clinching, conference-clinching, bowl-clinching TD.

Beathard and Wilson pumped early life into the blitzkrieg, moving out to the 46. Then Bedsole took a Beathard toss to cross mid-field, and the Trojans methodically evaporated yardage. From the nine, Wilson boomed to the one, and Beathard slanted off tackle for six points. Lupo finalized the score at 14-3.

"We coaches knew before the game we were going to the Rose Bowl," McKay told the SC rooters, "and our team played like we were already in the darn thing."

Then, more seriously, he added "we played as well as we could today. This is a grudge game and UCLA did real fine."

The Trojans piled up 17 first downs to seven for the Bruins, and led in yardage, 295 to 139. On an individual note, Bedsole nabbed three passes to bring his career mark to 56, a new school record.

UCLA coach Barnes, while disappointed, felt his team played

well. "If we had two more Alexanders—just one more—things might have been different," he commented.

The season was not over for either team. UCLA went on to trip Utah but was trimmed by Syracuse for a 4-6-0 ledger.

USC captured its tenth triumph by lambasting Notre Dame, 25-0, and then prepared for the Rose Bowl.

"I'm glad Wisconsin beat Minnesota, so we can play the Big Ten's best team," remarked McKay.

"USC will have its hands full against Wisconsin," opined Barnes.

Well, the mitts of the Trojans may have been full, but they weren't overflowing. The Badgers came, they saw, and they were conquered, 42-37.

That rounded out an untarnished 11-0-0 season for Southern California. The team was rated National Champions and McKay was selected as Coach of the Year.

Perfect is hard to beat.

Summary

	USC	UCLA
First Downs	17	7
Yards Rushing	203	79
Yards Passing	92	60
Total Yards	295	139
Passes Attempted	18	10
Passes Completed	5	5
Passes Had Intercepted	1	1
Fumbles Lost	2	1
Punts/Average	5/42	8/38
Penalties No./Yards	5/45	2/38

Scoring by Quarters:

| USC | 0 | 0 | 0 | 14 | — | 14 |
| UCLA | 0 | 3 | 0 | 0 | — | 3 |

1963
Game 33

Four Bees and a Gee

Even though the 1963 renewal of the UCLA-Southern California series was postponed a week—from November 23rd to November 30th—it was still a tension-filled affair played under a cimmerian, somber veil of international grief.

We were still a nation in mourning for our slain leader.

The head coaches of both institutions supported the postponement.

"I don't think anyone wants to play football under such circumstances," expressed USC's John McKay. "We were ready to play, but if we're a good football team, the delay shouldn't hurt us."

UCLA's Bill Barnes concurred. "I agree whole-heartedly with the decision," he said. "I'm sure both teams were up for it and will stay up."

Ticket cancellations brought on by the postponement were few in number . . . and the soothsayers who decide in advance which team will win didn't sway in their choice of USC. Twenty-four to seven, Charlie Park; 20-10, Al Wolf; USC by 13½, the line.

Besides having a better record to protect, the Trojans were also flirting with a wee chance to play in the Rose Bowl. But they would have to clobber UCLA, then get an assist from Washington State . . . like beating the Huskies.

Barnes knew the enormity of his task. "We've got to play our very best game yet to beat SC," he posed, "but it can be done. In Willie

BIG FORECAST FOR BIG GAME
Times Experts Agree--USC Over UCLA

Park Calls It 24-7 for Troy
By Charlie Park

Wolf Sees USC Win by 20-10
By Al Wolf

Brown and Mike Garrett, though, USC's got the best two backs on any one team in the country."

Terrific on the field Brown was, but overconfident he was not. "UCLA has just as many good players as we do," he pointed out.

Perhaps. But on paper the Trojans could swagger the name of one All-American—Damon Bame—plus the names of four on the All-Coast wire services teams—Gary Kirner, Brown, Garrett and Bame. The Uclans could match this array only with All-Coast selectee Mel Profit.

Both squads could muster a brace of good quarterbacks. Starting for Troy would be Pete Beathard, considered by pro scouts as the best QB in the west. But the Bruins' Larry Zeno would bring better credentials into the game: running, 123 yards to 84; passing, 855 to 792; and touchdown passes, six to four. Behind Beathard and Zeno were two guys who delighted at putting footballs high into the sky; Craig Fertig for Troy, Steve Sindell for Westwood.

The contest would drop the curtain on the regular season for both schools. Southern Cal had bumped Colorado, Michigan State, Ohio State, California, Stanford and Oregon State, while being curbed by Oklahoma, Notre Dame and Washington; a 6-3-0 manifest.

UCLA had tipped Stanford and upset Washington, but had lost to Pittsburgh, Penn State, Syracuse, Notre Dame, Illinois, California and Air Force Academy; a 2-7-0 slate.

And so, after a week's delay, a shirt-sleeved crowd of 82,460 loyal fans, preoccupied, filed into the Coliseum. Before the kickoff, they stood in silent homage to the memory of the late president.

UCLA had but a single weapon, a passing attack from "Z" to "A" (Zeno to Kurt Altenberg), and this was no match for the "B" boys of Troy (Beathard, Brown, Bame and Hal Bedsole) and the "Big G", Garrett. Result: Southern Cal 26, UCLA 6.

The Uclans took the opening kickoff and drove 50 yards to USC's 24-yard line, but Zeno was short on a long field goal effort.

USC retaliated with a long march, but it, too, was fruitless when the Ukes held for downs on their two.

UCLA punted out and the maroon-clad warriors erased 56 yards in eight plays for the game's first touchdown. Beathard completed a medley of four passes, the clincher being a six-yarder to Bedsole, who shrugged off Bob Richardson in the end zone. Dick Brownell's conversion lifted SC to a 7-0 lead after one quarter of action.

The Uclans soared again, thanks to a long bomb from Zeno to Altenberg, but frittered the ball away on SC's 12.

From there, the Trojans scurried on an 88-yard rampage, scoring another TD in 16 plays. Beathard went to the air waves three times, while Ron Heller and Rich McMahon devoured real estate along the way. At Westwood's two, Beathard rolled out and into the end zone. That put SC up, 13-0, at the halftime break.

Rested, the Bruins mastered an 85-yard assault, spiked by a 53-yard heave from the Z to A pair, that netted a marker in seven plays. The Zeno-to-Altenberg aerial carried to SC's 12, then Zeno passed to Profit for nine more yards. From the three-yard stripe, Zeno faked a flip, and fled into six-point land. It was no dice on the conversion, but UCLA had trimmed SC's lead to 13-6.

That was nice for Bruin fans, while it lasted . . . which wasn't very long. McKay's machine quickly marched 68 yards in six plays for TD No. 3. Garrett accounted for 62 of these yards, including a 46-yard dazzler that carried to the Uclan nine. He and Brown then nudged the ball to the two-yard line, from where Brown did the scoring honors. Tack on Brownell's PAT and you've got a 20-6 Troy lead after three quarters.

The Trojans purchased an insurance marker in the fourth, but not before the Blue and Gold had maneuvered the pigskin 63 yards to USC's 16. The threat sputtered when Tom Lupo intercepted Zeno's pitch in the end zone.

That sort of drained the Bruins, who then allowed the Trojans to sally 80 yards in 10 plays for a tally. Only one pass was completed as Heller and Brown proved able infantrymen. McMahon dived in from one yard out, the score became 26-6, and McKay went to his bench.

Team-wise, USC rolled up 530 total yards while earning 26 first downs; UCLA showed 314 and 16.

Individually, Garrett, named back-of-the-game, amassed 119 yards for the winners, while Beathard completed 14 passes for 152 yards.

"Any time Pete (Beathard) feels as good as he did today, we're a pretty good football team," exclaimed McKay, who also put in good words for Garrett, Bedsole, Bame, Brown, Heller, Hudson Houck and John Thomas.

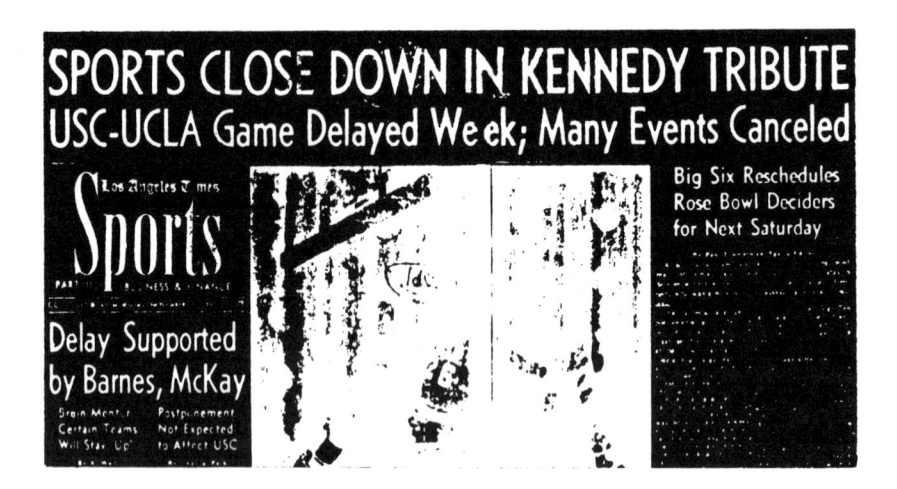

SPORTS CLOSE DOWN IN KENNEDY TRIBUTE
USC-UCLA Game Delayed Week; Many Events Canceled

Los Angeles Times
Sports

Big Six Reschedules Rose Bowl Deciders for Next Saturday

Delay Supported by Barnes, McKay

Anything short of victory never entered the mind of Beathard. "I couldn't believe that the Bruins were a great team like everyone was saying after they beat Washington," he stated, rather frankly, "but I guess maybe their win over Washington wasn't a fluke."

McKay summed up the contest with a somewhat immodest appraisal. "I think we could beat everyone in the country and I always have thought so," he uttered.

Barnes nodded in agreement. "The Trojans are great," he stated, "They're really gifted. When they're at their best, I think they'd beat anybody in the United States. We hung in there with them for nearly three quarters, but we played no better football club all season. I'm convinced, though, we tried hard."

Barnes' passing combo of Zeno to Altenberg amassed 166 yards on eight completions, breaking the UCLA single game record, and earning for the sophomore end lineman-of-the-game honors.

"I think they weren't looking for me," said Altenberg, with prudence.

Barnes, always the good sport, labeled McKay's Trojans as being a well-coached team. "And John (McKay) was a good sport in the late stages," he commented. "He played a lot of people or it could have been worse."

Some observers thought McKay could have strengthened his chances of a trip to Pasadena if he had piled on more points. "I don't think the size of the score would influence the conference vote," he responded. "I know Billy (Barnes) would have done the same thing I did."

Well, Southern Cal didn't get the Rose Bowl invitation — Washington did. Which evoked more talk from talkative Willie

Brown. "I'm not taking anything away from Washington, but I think we're the best team," he averred.

Read now from the pages of *El Rodeo*, USC's yearbook: "Football was the number one topic on campus until that Friday when everybody suddenly forgot about sports. At 11:30 the assassination of President Kennedy was announced. Five hours later AAWU officials postponed the conference schedule a full week. Thus it was on Thanksgiving weekend, that the 33rd biggest game unfolded in the Coliseum. It was an historic occasion. The last time one of the greatest senior groups in school history suited up in Trojan uniforms."

Summary

	USC	UCLA
First Downs	26	16
Yards Rushing	322	76
Yards Passing	208	238
Total Yards	530	314
Passes Attempted	29	30
Passes Completed	19	15
Passes Had Intercepted	1	2
Fumbles Lost	0	1
Punts/Average	1/36	3/35
Penalties No./Yards	5/65	3/25

Scoring by Quarters:

USC	7	6	7	6	—	26
UCLA	0	0	6	0	—	6

1964
Game 34

You Win Some, You Lose Some, You Lose Some, You Lose Some...

For the third straight year, Southern California whomped up on UCLA, riding the chariot of victory into the sunset while leaving its arch rival sprawled on the Coliseum turf. And the 34th encounter bore no semblance of intrigue, no suspense . . . for it wasn't very close, save for a few moments in quarter three. It was, in fact, the most one-sided pelting suffered by the Bruins since 1944. It was 34-13.

For USC to win was no surprise; only the margin by which it did so raised a wrinkle.

The Trojans stole the show with five scenes in four acts, posting one touchdown in each of the first three quarters and two in the fourth. UCLA registered all of its points after intermission.

At the weekly caucus of the Southland football writers, 26 nominated Tommy Trojan, nine hopped on Joe Bruin's bandwagon, and two straddled the fence. The average margin of victory for USC was six points.

Charlie Park of the *Times* thought it would be wider. His predicted score was 27-13. And the morning line said USC was 7½ points better than UCLA.

"The Trojans probably deserve it (the role of favorite) off the records of the two teams this year," Bruin captain Kent Francisco acknowledged, "but we're certainly going out on that Coliseum field figuring we'll win."

Coming into the contest, the machine of Coach John McKay had won five of eight sessions. Troy had closed its gates to Colorado, Oklahoma, Texas A&M, California and Stanford, but its sentry was unguarded against Michigan State, Ohio State and Washington.

It was not quite as rosy for the Uclans, who had gone to the bar nine times and were a five-time loser. Three straight wins over Pittsburgh, Penn State and Stanford were expunged by losses to Syracuse, Notre Dame and Illinois; then a verdict over California preceded unfavorable judgments from Air Force Academy and Washington.

Both clubs were still in contention for a trip to Pasadena, although Oregon State was on the rail, and UCLA was a furlong or so behind USC.

"As far as we're concerned," stated UCLA Coach Bill Barnes, "we feel both teams will be playing for the Rose Bowl—and I'm sure John (McKay) feels the same way about it."

Indeed he did. "I know which team I would rather have go than anybody," spoke McKay. "Ours. But whatever team from the coast that goes will do a real good job."

The Trojans possessed a fine stable of thoroughbreds, and Barnes was duly impressed. "USC, with Mike Garrett, Ron Heller and Homer Williams, can run on anybody," he ventured. "But they've got a well-balanced attack; they can run or pass well."

McKay did not dispute the point. "We'll move the ball, but so will UCLA," he remarked. "They throw the ball well, too, and that's where we have trouble."

Two All-Americans spiced the Trojan roster—guard Bill Fisk and Garrett. In eight games, the gamboling Garrett had accumulated 689 yards on 168 rushes. His admirers numbered many.

"He's great," praised Duffy Daugherty, coach at Michigan State.

"He's outstanding," agreed Coach John Ralston of Stanford.

"Garrett is the best back I've ever coached," exuded McKay. "He's our best blocker, a great faker, and a fine defensive player."

"Garrett is just the best running back in the country," was Bruin Francisco's summation.

Bill Barnes, UCLA Head Coach, 1958-1964

Credit *Los Angeles Times*

nybody Want to Pick One Out?....................By Pete Bentovoja

AAWU had a difficult time picking its queen in 1964. Down to the last week of the season, six entrants still entertained high hopes.

While taking nothing away from the attributes of Garrett, UCLA's Barnes viewed the entire perspective. "You can't key on any one of their players," he warned. "SC has a lot of key breakers, like Craig Fertig, Rod Sherman, Fred Hill, Heller and Williams."

Barnes had Larry Zeno to match the quarterback skills of Fertig, as each held seven gridiron records on their respective campuses. By way of comparison, Fertig had a slight edge in passing—88 completions in 175 attempts for 1322 yards and six touchdowns to Zeno's 87 in 176 for 1255 and 12 TDs. But rushing belonged to Zeno—316 yards to 16.

The Bruins had a top-notch receiver in Kurt Altenberg, and, after a year's absence, again had the services of running back Mike Haffner.

But the 62,108 rooters who streamed into the Coliseum would

USC SMACKS UCLA WITH 34-13 DEFEAT

Troy Runs Up Biggest Score Over Bruins Since 1944 Before 62,108 at Coliseum

witness a match between a team with the best total offense and the best total defense in the AAWU—USC—and a team with the weakest of both catagories—UCLA.

Fertig passed for three touchdowns in the game, and his first was a 31-yard sling to Dave Moton in the first period.

In the second stanza, Sherman broke loose for a 28-yard gainer, setting up Garrett's tally from three yards out. Dick Brownell executed his second PAT, and the 14-0 lead looked like a cakewalk for Troy when the school bands started their halftime exhibitions.

But UCLA opened the third frame with a new-found zest, charging 79 yards for a TD. The final six was a pitch from Zeno to Altenberg. During this assault, Zeno hurled five completions in a stretch of seven plays. And his PAT cut the Uclans' deficit to seven points at 7-14.

Joe Bruin was now fired up and his nostrils flared with the scent of victory. A Trojan retaliation was stalled and UCLA started again from its 38. But as quickly as hope had bloomed, it withered. On third down, Nate Shaw burglarized a Zeno aerial putting USC in control on their 47. Barnes later theorized that this interception was probably the turning point in the game.

Given the opportunity, the Trojans wasted no time. On third down from UCLA's 49, Fertig rifled a strike to Sherman, who pulled in the leather on the 18, shook off Eddie Hutt and Jim Colletto, and pranced into glory-land. Brownell's toe upped USC's lead to 21-7 as air started oozing from UCLA's balloon.

Sherman's marker may have been the key play of the game. And it must have been especially painful for Barnes, since Sherman first enrolled at UCLA before becoming a Trojan.

Quarter Number Four rolled around and the maroon-clad warriors kept right on rolling, too. Heller slammed across the double-stripe from two-yards out and Fertig hit Moton again for a nine-yard tally. Brownell came through again, and now it was 34-7.

One thing about a Barnes-coached team. It doesn't quit. Down but not out, the Bruins finalized the score at 34-13 when Steve Sindall found Altenberg for a five-yard TD.

With reserves now playing, Southern Cal worked its way to Westwood's one-yard line as the final gun sounded.

"Three in a row" chanted the Trojans as they saluted their cheering section after the game.

To the surprise of no one, Garrett topped all runners with 180 yards, and was named back-of-the-game.

"We might have had a chance if it wasn't for Garrett," wailed Barnes.

Moton won lineman-of-the-game honors, and he, along with Garrett, Shaw, Williams, Sherman, Heller, Fertig and Frank Lopez were handed citations for crown performances.

Zeno set two school records for UCLA: 13 TD's in a single season, and 2,857 career yards in passing. Altenberg and Haffner established a campus mark for receptions, each coming up with 31 for the year. And the Bruin leader up front was Francisco.

Haffner, who viewed the 1963 game from the sideline, offered an analysis of USC: "Last year their linemen beat you up. They're not as strong now, but a lot quicker. Then there's Garrett..."

In the stats department, SC ran up 23 first downs to UCLA's 17, and outgained the Bruins, 463 yards to 260.

Barnes took a realistic view, "We tried real hard and did as well as we could," he said, "but USC was too strong. That's all there is to it."

Even though Oregon State nipped Oregon, the AAWU did not immediately choose its representative for the Rose Bowl, which left SC with a glimmer of hope. A victory over Notre Dame the following week would surely clinch it, thought the players.

"We're going after Notre Dame," sounded Fisk.

"We're gonna' be ready for Notre Dame," echoed Sherman.

"We GOTTA beat Notre Dame," blared Garrett.

And that they did, 20-17, putting their season slate at 7-3-0. It was a great game to win, because the Irish were undefeated and untied in nine games. What's more, they led the Trojans, 17-13, with less than two minutes to play. Then Fertig uncorked a 60-yard TD pass to Sherman to pull victory from defeat. Despite the surge that knocked Notre Dame from the collegiate pinnacle, it did not put USC in the Crown City Classic. Oregon State went and was crushed by Michigan.

The 1964 season was the bell-ringer for Bill Barnes at UCLA. The affable coach was at the helm six full seasons and part of another, taking over on an acting basis from George Dickerson after the third game of 1958. Barnes compiled a record of 31 victories, 34 defeats and three ties.

Against USC, he was 2-4-1. For this deficit, *Times* writer Sid Ziff had an explanation. "It takes the horses to win," he wrote, "and UCLA has been playing with ponies."

Summary

	USC	UCLA
First Downs	23	17
Yards Rushing	329	105
Yards Passing	134	155
Total Yards	463	260
Passes Attempted	14	29
Passes Completed	6	16
Passes Had Intercepted	0	2
Fumbles Lost	0	2
Punts/Average	4/36.5	4/38.0
Penalties No./Yards	7/60	2/11

Scoring by Quarters:

USC	7	7	7	13	—	34
UCLA	0	0	7	6	—	13

1965
Game 35

Carnage, In Four Minutes

The misty, gray skies that hung heavily over Memorial Coliseum were an appropriate backdrop for the saturnine and frustrated UCLA Bruins—for 56 minutes. And even though the dark and murky clouds remained solid throughout this late day in autumn, the Uclans—in the last four minutes—found an opening to heaven.

Trailing 16-6 after 56 minutes as a punching-bag, UCLA, on the strong arm of Gary Beban, turned aggressor with two far-reaching touchdown passes to stun the favored Southern California Trojans, 20-16. The dazzling, come-from-behind triumph was an automatic passport to the Rose Bowl.

"It couldn't have been sweeter," exclaimed Tommy Prothro, UCLA's new head coach down from Oregon State. Prothro, who now lives in Memphis, recently adjudged the 1965 game as his most memorable of all scuffles he had against USC.

Both Prothro and USC Coach John McKay had been hampered by inclement weather during the practice week for the game. The Bruins were forced to forsake Spaulding Field for the "Phys Ed" field on one occasion, while the Trojans vacated Bovard for a patch of dry land on North Bovard Field.

And when it came to the game plan, the strategy for Saturday, both mentors had lips of zip.

A Thousand Angles + + + *By Karl Hubenthal*

LOS ANGELES HERALD-EXAMINER Sports

H★   FRIDAY, NOVEMBER 19, 1965   D-1

USC and UCLA: Fastest Guns in the West Shoot It Out Today for a Rose Bowl Bid

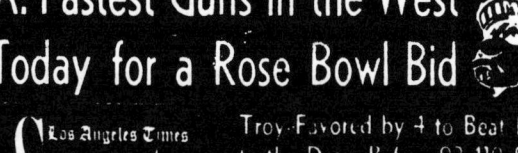

Los Angeles Times Sports

Troy Favored by 4 to Beat Bruins to the Draw Before 93,410 Fans

"Frankly, we don't plan to do anything too much different," said McKay, which could be interpreted as saying, "Our game plan is Mike Garrett."

In previous games, the stocky senior had lugged the ball 20 and 30 times, or more. His average per game was 139.7 yards, a total of 1,118 yards. But the Bruins' defense had previously proved its mettle, limiting Syracuse's All-American Floyd Little to a mere 27 yards.

It was no secret that SC was primarily an infantry club, third best via rushing in the nation, in fact. Besides Garrett, Troy glittered with the speed of flanker Rod Sherman.

But when Troy Winslow, a 57.7 per cent passing quarterback, did put the ball up, SC had some fine receivers in Dave Moton, Sherman and John Thomas.

Then consider that none of these fellows, nor any of their Trojan mates, had ever lost to UCLA. It just wasn't proper, you know.

So, if USC was to take the low road, UCLA would take the high road. For, in Beban, Westwood had a Flying Ace. Though just a sophomore, Beban had completed 57 aerials for 1,079 yards and seven touchdowns. His corps of catchers included such glue-fingered streakers as Kurt Altenberg, Mel Farr, Dick Witcher and Byron Nelson.

"We've probably not faced a passer who can throw the long ball as accurately as Beban does," McKay surmised.

The records of neither team required an apology. The McKay Machine had purred through six teams—Wisconsin, Oregon State, Washington, Stanford, California and Pittsburgh—but had been stalled by a Minnesota tie and a loss to Notre Dame. Six-one-one, no apology.

And the Prothro Pistons could match that, stroke for stroke. Dumped by the wayside were Penn State, Syracuse, California, Air Force Academy, Washington and Stanford. Michigan State was a roadblock and Missouri a draw. Six-one-one, no apology.

Southern Cal was coming off two consecutive shutouts—four in their last five games—and this feat of defense probably tilted the bookies toward the Trojans. Anyway, SC opened a five-point favorite, later dropped to four, and the game-day line was 3½. John Hall of the *LA Times* predicted ". . . USC will turn Cinderella's Superchargers (UCLA) back into a pumpkin by two touchdowns."

And it was an event California Coach John Ralston really wanted to see. "I'd fly down for it if I could," he told Hall. "It's going to be an excellent battle."

Perhaps Ralston envisioned the melee as a performance with many hats, as did cartoonist Karl Hubenthal in the *Los Angeles Herald-Examiner:* USC, best league defense; Garrett, closing in on rushing record; the Bruins, a Cinderella team; Prothro, coach-of-the-year candidate; effects of the weather; and who will pick the roses at Pasadena?

More than 94,000 zealots, ignoring the muggy clouds above, clicked the stadium turnstiles to find answers to these angles.

They didn't have to wait long for one of them, as the Bruins, on their first possession, racked up a six-pointer. It took them eight plays to reach Troy's 49-yard line, from where Beban handed off to Farr, and the speedster shook off Adrian Young and Mike Hunter as he raced into the end zone. Phil Lee blocked Kurt Zimmerman's try for point and the initial quarter ended 6-0, Uclans.

Before it ended, however, the Trojans rampaged 76 yards to UCLA's one-yard stripe, at which point Garrett fumbled and Dallas Grider recovered for the Bruins.

Back again came the Trojans - now in the second period - and this time they made it stick. From UCLA's 47, Troy utilized six plays to reach the 10. From there, Winslow rolled out and hurled the pigskin to Mickey Upton at the goal line. Evading Tim McAfee and Bob Stiles, Upton smashed into paydirt. Tim Rossovich's boot broke the deadlock, enabling USC to lead at recess, 7-6.

The Cardinal-and-Gold generated two more jabs for points in the second frame. Upton bobbled away the first shot on Westwood's 25, and the clock stopped the second with Troy knocking from the Uclans' 14-yard stripe.

At halftime, a large number of Southern Cal's former grid heroes were recognized for their roles in UCLA games, dating back to the days of Russ Saunders and Francis Tappan, carrying through the era of Jim Powers and Elmer Willhoite, and right up to Mike Garrett and Dave Moton of yesteryear.

Turnovers spiced the third stanza. First Beban fumbled, then Garrett bungled again, then Hunter picked off a Beban pass. Then it

Mike Garrett, USC Heisman Trophy winner, 1965.

UCLA BEATS TROY

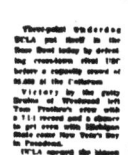

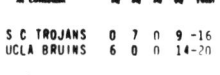

was Sherman's turn to play butterfingers and his mis-play gave Beban an opportunity to pitch another interception... which he did to Young. USC then drove to UCLA's two-yard line from where Stiles stole a Winslow flip for a touchback. All this and no points, so it was still 7-6, SC, after three.

Now the Trojans, aware that a one-point lead was shaky at best, decided it was time to move the ball, at the same time keeping it attached to their bodies. So, 51 yards they moved, and on the tenth play, Winslow hit Sherman with a TD strike from eight yards out. Rossovich's kick wandered, but 13-6 looked rosy for Troy.

Then it seemed even rosier when Gary Fite fled 39 yards to UCLA's 11, setting the stage for Rossovich to toe a 20-yard field goal. Now it was 16-6, El Trojan, the clock was winding down, and many of the impatient were heading for the exits.

They should have stayed. With four minutes to play, SC's Winslow fumbled when hit by Grider and Erwin Dutcher claimed the oval for UCLA just 34 yards from TD territory.

"The ball wasn't slippery," insisted Winslow. "I can't explain the fumble, unless I was trying to get a little more (yardage) than I should."

Joe Bruin, opportunist personified, squandered no time—there was precious little to wither. On the first play, Beban fired a missile over the waving arms of Hunter and into those of Witcher, who stepped in from the one. Beban then tossed a two-pointer at Nelson, and SC's lead was trimmed to two digits, 16-14.

Now it was gambling-time and it paid off for the Bruins. Zimmerman's on-side kickoff was enfolded by Grider on SC's 48-yard line. After gaining a first down, UCLA was thrown back to it's 48, but a few backward steps simply sweetened the cake. Bomb Number Two carried 52 yards, Beban was again the thrower and this time the receiver was Altenberg, who had outdistanced Nate Shaw and Hunter. Beban mis-fired on his attempted two-pointer, but UCLA owned a 20-16 advantage, and the clock looked with disfavor on the Trojans.

"Oh, my God! This is it! Now or never," reeled through the mind of Altenberg as he watched Beban's heave zooming toward him. "I heard everyone on the sideline yelling 'Run, run, run', so I did, and Gary put the ball to me perfectly."

Colorful Pepper Rodgers, assistant coach and later to become head man at UCLA, nutshelled the situation. "I won't say we had given up," he stated, "but we weren't exactly in good shape with the score 16-6, four minutes to go, USC in possession and not scored on in the fourth quarter all year."

Not only had USC goose-egged all opponents in the fourth period; but ironically, the same quarter had been least productive for UCLA's offense. It had totaled only 30 points BBB—Before Beban's Bombs—all season in quarter four.

Two participants came out of the contest with splendid honors awaiting them. Garrett, who piled up 210 yards, was awarded the Heisman Trophy for 1965, the first recipient from Southern California.

And Prothro was named Coach-of-the-Year. Prothro, incidentally, holds the distinction of being the only coach to take two different teams to the Rose Bowl in two straight years—Oregon State and UCLA.

"I anticipated a solid football program when I hired Tommy Prothro, but nothing like this," said UCLA athletic director J. D. Morgan. "He's three or four years ahead of schedule."

Prothro had a reminder. "We did what we have been doing all year, depending on the big play," he remarked. "And we sure got two of 'em there at the finish. The Trojans are a mighty good team—and that Garrett is easily the best all-around runner I've ever seen in college ball."

Garrett was most gracious in defeat. Entering the merry dressing room of the Bruins, he addressed them, "I hate to say it, but you guys are great. I'll be out there yelling for you against Michigan State."

USC outgained the Blue and Gold, 424 yards to 289, and notched 21 first downs to 12, none of which impressed McKay.

"Either you lose or you win," he replied, "and if you lose, you are outplayed. They outplayed us and they beat us."

But until the fourth quarter explosion, USC had completely contained Beban, who had completed only two of eight passes. Also, he had lost 33 yards attempting to run or pass, had thrown two interceptions and lost two fumbles.

"I can't explain it," Beban tried to explain. "I was lousy, but all of a sudden, we were off to the races. But we were lucky the way the breaks went."

Intent on atoning for the upset, the Trojans vented their torment on Wyoming the following week, roping the Cowboys, 56-6. Their season ended at 7-2-1.

Maybe the Uclans suffered a let-down, as they lost to Tennessee, 37-34. George Cafego had scouted UCLA for the Vols and he carried the word on Beban back to Knoxville. "He's even better than the things I've read about him," reported Cafego. "He has more poise than any sophomore I've ever seen."

Then it was a re-match with Michigan State in the Rose Bowl. "Anybody can be beat," confided Beban, so the rest of the Bruins took him at face value. Result: UCLA 14, Michigan State 12. That wrapped up a 8-2-1 ledger and a fourth-place national ranking for the Uclans.

And so, while the Bruins' superb rally over the Trojans in Game 35 was a memorable day for Westwood, it was a bitter pill for the inhabitants of University Park. The USC yearbook considered it blasphemous: "For USC to lose to UCLA after dominating the game is a cardinal and gold sin."

Summary

	UCLA	USC
First Downs	12	21
Yards Rushing	162	345
Yards Passing	127	79
Total Yards	289	424
Passes Attempted	11	9
Passes Completed	5	7
Passes Had Intercepted	2	1
Fumbles Lost	2	5
Punts/Average	5/40.2	2/36.5
Penalties No./Yards	1/15	5/55

Scoring by Quarters:

| UCLA | 6 | 0 | 0 | 14 | — | 20 |
| USC | 0 | 7 | 0 | 9 | — | 16 |

1966

Game 36

The Dow Closes Up

When Gary Beban was felled by a fractured fibula, Coach Tommy Prothro put his UCLA stock in Norman Dow, and the senior quarterback who had never started a collegiate game, and would not start another, turned out to be a blue-chipper.

For it was Dow who stirred from the shadows to a spot in the sun with a bullish performance that enabled the Bruins to shock Southern California, 14-7.

Apprehension prevailed among some observers during the build-up week relative to Dow's ability to take charge, but not among those close to the scene.

"I know one thing," advised Prothro. "Dow will give it everything he's got, plus a little more."

Dow's total playing time in three seasons as a Bruin totaled only 58 minutes, not quite one full game. But backfield coach Pepper Rodgers was well acquainted with his talents. "Dow has always been a great team man," observed Rodgers. "He has always worked hard, he's smart and a real leader."

And from Beban himself: "Norm Dow will be fine. He'll do the job."

So how did the veteran second-stringer feel about the situation?

"Nervous," blurted Dow. Then, in reflection, he added: "When I heard Gary (Beban) was lost, I was sad for him and for our team. I've never even started a game before, and now I'll be starting the most important game of the season. Certainly, there's pressure. But I'm going to do the best I can. I want to go out big. I think I can do it. We can win."

When reminded of Beban's injury at the football writers' meeting, USC Coach John McKay reacted: "We'd prefer to play the Bruins at full strength, but we will not change our defensive plans, now that Dow is at quarterback. I think UCLA is going to use the same plays that got them this far."

Then McKay turned to Prothro and inquired: "You are going to use the same plays, aren't you?"

To which Prothro gave an evasive reply: "For once, I hope the field is 10 inches deep in mud."

And while the Ukes wailed with their Beban-less problem, Southern Cal was not without its personnel troubles, either. Don McCall, called upon to replace Heisman Trophy winner, now-graduated Mike Garrett, had been slowed by a knee injury. His next two replacements, Steve Grady and Wilson Bowie, were also dropped by injuries, and that put McKay down to Jim Lawrence, a very swift sophomore, as a starter.

There would be three All-Americans performing in the fracas; defensive back Nate Shaw and offensive tackle Ron Yary for Troy, and halfback Mel Farr, who had rushed for 742 yards, for Westwood.

The Trojans had ample incentive to win, seeing as how they had lived a year in humiliation on the heels of 1965's set-back.

"I'm tired of hearing we live in Bruin Town," said Ray May to *Times* writer John Hall.

"Losing last year was the biggest disappointment of my life–Saturday means more to me than anything I've ever done," chimed in Adrian Young.

From Troy Winslow: "Nobody is counting on going to the Rose Bowl unless we beat the Bruins."

And from Rod Sherman: "The only way to go in this town is as a winner."

USC, which led the AAWU in defense, had lost only one of eight matches, that to Miami by three points. Taking the ax were Texas, Wisconsin, Oregon State, Washington, Stanford, Clemson and California.

But UCLA's record was a bit better, having lost only one of nine matches, that to Washington by 13 points. Taking the ax were Pittsburgh, Syracuse, Missouri, Rice, Penn State, California, Air Force Academy and Stanford. The Bruins topped the conference in offense.

In wire service polls, Southern Cal was ranked seventh, UCLA eighth. The one-two-three clubs were Notre Dame, Michigan State and Alabama.

Odds for the game opened at 10 in favor of SC, fell to 7½, then firmed at seven. In a poll of writers, 40 picked USC to win, four selected UCLA. (You can imagine the kind of reception the scribes received when they entered the Bruins' dressing quarters after the game.)

Beban snubbed the bookies. "USC hasn't beaten us yet. We'll be right in there," he informed one and all.

But all the talk subsided, and the day of put-up-or-shut-up arrived. The 17 Bruin seniors pledged to "Get the game ball for Gary" and the Trojans promised to "Bust the Bruins" and 81,980 folks came to the Coliseum on a cloudless day to see which vow would be broken.

It first appeared UCLA's would as the Trojans, on their first possession, ripped off 71 yards in seven slashes. Mike Hull bulled for 12, Lawrence sprinted for 39, Hull again for 11—those were the big yard-eaters that put the ball on UCLA's three-yard line, first down.

On two keepers, Winslow got to the one, but then Hull was dropped back on the seven by Mike Roof, later to be named lineman-of-the-game. Rebuking a field goal, Winslow swept his end but Mark Gustafson was in the way and the Uclans took over on their four.

The two squads sparred back and forth, looking for a break. Finally, the Bruins got one when SC's Dick Hough, in punt formation, juggled the snap and lost 14 yards as Vic Lepisto sacked him on USC's 38. Dow then hooked up with Harold Busby down the middle to Troy's 18. But dreams of points vanished when Busby was charged with offensive interference in the end zone, giving USC possession on its 20.

The second period was drawing to a close as McCall cracked for 29 yards, Hull for 10 and 13 and Troy was on Westwood's 15-yard stripe. After three plays gained only 36 inches, Tim Rossovich tried a field goal. It was wide, and shortly thereafter the teams retired to their dressing rooms for halftime lectures. At this point, it was a scoreless tie.

But that changed soon after the playing of the fight songs, the alma mater tearjerkers, and all that halftime jazz.

The Bruin defense, spearheaded by Roof, Terry Donahue, Lepisto and John Richardson, forced the Trojans to punt from their 19, and Ray Armstrong returned Hough's boot to Troy's 42. In seven plays, UCLA entered happy-land, abetted by Dow's 18 yard scamper and a face-mask penalty. From the five, Dow followed the blocks of Rick Purdy, Rich Deakers and Dennis Murphy to cross the goal line, standing up. Kurt Zimmerman found the PAT range and the Bruins found themselves out front, 7-0.

This turn of events must have jolted Tommy Trojan because he came back swinging. Sparked by a 57 yard dilly by Hull, the score was very quickly knotted at 7-7. Dan Scott registered the six-pointer from one yard out, and Rossovich added the one-pointer.

UCLA essayed to unlock the tie as Dow guided a journey to SC's 16, where Zimmerman kicked wide on a field goal attempt.

The Trojan rooters took a new lease on life, but the Bruins foreclosed on short notice. On second-and-27 from his 36-yard line, Dow faded to throw. With Trojan defenders blanketing his targets, Dow set sail on a ducking, dodging, stumbling, baffling excursion of 26 yards, and on the next play, Mike Bergdahl picked up the crucial first down.

"Three guys had Dow," sputtered McKay. "And it was a broken play."

Broken it was, but it also broke the backs of the Trojans. For a few plays later, Dow handed off on a reverse to Cornell Champion on the SC 21 and the halfback scooted into the end zone, putting a neat fake on Shaw at the 10. After Zimmerman upped the score to 14-7, the scoreboard operator took off the rest of the day.

"It's our town! It's our town! And it always will be," shouted Bruin Don Manning from the sideline, his arm in a sling from a third quarter injury. But Champion had just broken the stalemate, and what's a busted shoulder anyway?

Six minutes later, the game ended as Gustafson pilfered a Toby Page pass and ran it back to SC's 10-yard line.

"I'm numb," Prothro uttered. "I don't know how they did it, but they did. Dow was great."

Reserve tackle Tory Matheson knew. "It wasn't luck," he announced. "We carried it to them."

Dow, who accounted for 112 yards running and passing, was named back-of-the-game, and his mates proudly presented him the game ball.

McKay sanctioned both awards. "He's the best quarterback we've faced all season," he stated. "At least, he hurt us the most."

"Norm, you were wonderful," chirped Beban.

All of which drew a simple response from Dow. "It was," he said, "the greatest 60 minutes of my life."

And while one QB was having the fling of his life, another sat in dejection, relegated to the bench by an injury in the second quarter. McKay was asked if the absence of Winslow hurt the Trojans.

"Maybe the loss of Winslow had something to do with it, but I can't say that," answered McKay. "I don't want to take away from their victory."

Mel Farr, UCLA All-American back, 1966.

USC's Hull was the pacemaker for the day, traveling 148 net yards. UCLA's Farr was "held" to 67.

There was still the question of the Rose Bowl nominee. "It's not up to the coaches to say," surmised Prothro, "but offhand, I'd say a team with a 9-1 record (UCLA) deserves it over a 7-2 team (SC)."

Those who decide such things, though, disagreed and dispatched an invitation to Southern Cal, the team with the league's best slate. There may have been some second thoughts several days later, however, as Notre Dame slaughtered Troy in its last regular season engagement.

But the Trojans rebounded to make an admirable showing at Pasadena, losing to Purdue, 14-13. Their final chart read 7-4-0.

UCLA, acclaimed by Prothro as his best team, was ranked fifth best in the nation by both wire services. Much of the credit for that lofty position could be put on the shoulders of a Number Two quarterback . . . who tried harder.

Summary

	UCLA	USC
First Downs	15	10
Yards Rushing	229	243
Yards Passing	30	20
Total Yards	259	263
Passes Attempted	8	6
Passes Completed	2	3
Passes Had Intercepted	0	1
Fumbles Lost	1	2
Punts/Average	5/35.8	5/36.8
Penalties No./Yards	3/27	6/33

Scoring by Quarters:

UCLA	0	0	7	7	—	14
USC	0	0	7	0	—	7

1967
Game 37

Star Trek

Rarely in the annals of collegiate football had there been a game with so much at stake as the Southern California-UCLA meeting of 1967.

Up for grabs was a bid to the Rose Bowl, the AAWU Conference title and a national championship, as well as the Victory Bell and the Los Angeles city crown.

And, in quest of these goals, the two schools would exhibit star players by the dozen to tread the turf of Memorial Coliseum. Just mull over the likes of stellar stars Gary Beban and Don Manning of UCLA; plus Ron Yary, O.J. Simpson, Tim Rossovich and Adrian Young of USC - six All-Americans, not to mention numerous performers of All-Coast calibre.

Want more? Before the year was out, Beban (UCLA) was awarded the coveted Heisman Trophy, and Yary (USC) was honored with the prestigious Outland Trophy. Both players remain unique as the only gridders to ever win these laurels from their respective schools.

These and other stalwarts of the mask had piloted UCLA to the top of the collegiate heap, No. 1 in the nation; with Southern Cal just a shade behind at No. 3. Tennessee was ranked in between.

Joe Bruin had spanked the Vols in his season opener, 20-16. He then went on to paddle Pittsburgh, Washington State, Penn State, California, Stanford and Washington. The only blotch on an otherwise perfect card was a tie with Oregon State.

And those same Beavers were the spoilsports for an otherwise perfect slate of Tommy Trojan. It happened after USC had conquered eight straight foes. And it was 3-0 on a muddy field in Corvallis. Prior to that, the Trojans had trounced Washington State, Texas, Michigan State, Stanford, Notre Dame, Washington, Oregon and California.

So with a galaxy of stars on hand, trophy winners abounding, brilliant records to uphold, classic goals to achieve . . . what happens? One swing of one foot determined all the issues.

Both teams tallied three touchdowns. But sophomore Rikki Aldridge drilled all three of his PAT kicks through the crossbars for Southern Cal, while veteran Zenon Andrusyshyn, UCLA's Super Toe, missed his third attempt. You got it: USC 21, UCLA 20.

And despite the Uclans lofty rating, the SC win was not considered an upset. The Trojans were the choice, first by seven points, but then by three as Saturday approached.

"The spread is four points closer now," analyzed Jimmy (The Greek) Snyder from Las Vegas, "because you take two points away from USC for losing at Oregon State and you give UCLA two points for its strong showing (48-0) against Washington." Understand?

Of course, the presence of Simpson, the nation's top ground gainer with 1,238 yards, was a plus factor in tabbing the Trojans as the team to beat.

"Simpson is the man we fear the most," said UCLA Coach Tommy Prothro. "He's big, fast, agile and nifty."

Conversely, there were certain Bruins on the fear list of USC Coach John McKay, too. "We have to stop Gary Beban, the finest quarterback in college football, and Greg Jones," replied McKay. "Not many people have done that."

Beban had passed for 1041 yards on 68 completions and had run for 395 more.

As usual, when November rolls around, wounded gladiators leave holes in gridiron rosters; such as Mike Hull, Jim Lawrence and Steve Grady for the Cardinal and Gold, plus Rick Purdy and Harold Busby for the Blue and Gold.

And, as usual, the mutual admiration society was again headed by the opposing coaches.

"USC has the best offense and defense we've faced," wailed Prothro. "It is so good at everything and it doesn't have any weakness."

McKay zeroed in on UCLA's kicker. "We've got to keep them outside the 40-yard line because of field goals," he expounded. "When you have a great kicker like Andrusyshyn, the field gets

Gary Beban, UCLA Heisman Trophy winner, 1967.

shorter." He also alluded to the fact that Andrusyshyn led the nation in punting, with a 44.7 average.

The assistant coaches got in the act, too. "The two most important things we've got to do," predicted UCLA's Bob McKittrick, "is to stop Simpson, and also prevent the home-run play."

USC assistant coach Marv Goux was more concerned with pumping up his charges, to make them more hungry. "We've been prisoners in this town for two years," he admonished, "and it's about time we got out of that."

So, with a Rogues' Gallery of assorted headlines and placards adorning Spaulding and Bovard fields—put there, naturally, to incite the spirit and instill hatred for the enemy—the squads readied themselves for this titanic, this "All-Everything" struggle.

Over 90,000 fans saw the Bruins jump to an early 7-0 lead when Jones sliced over from 12 yards out. It was the eighth play of a 47-yard drive, the shortness of which could be traced to a weak 18-yard punt by Aldridge. After an incompletion, Beban found Dave Nuttall for 12 yards, then, on a keeper, darted for 11 to SC's 24. Bill Bolden and Jones moved the pigskin down to the 12 from where Jones carried it over, breaking tackles by Bill Jaroncyk and Mike Battle.

Abruptly, Southern Cal tied it up at 7-all. With third-and-five on his 49-yard stripe, Beban tossed toward Jones in the left flat. Jones never had a chance, as defender Pat Cashman intercepted the ball in full flight on the 45 and jetted 55 yards for a TD.

That TD gnawed on the mind of Prothro. "I made the call on that play," he admitted, "and it was a terrible call."

Before the half frittered away, Troy had taken a 14-7 lead, covering 80 yards in five plays. It started when Earl McCullouch sprinted 52 yards on an end-around play. He fumbled when tackled, but teammate Mike Scarpace fell on the ball to preserve the effort. Steve Sogge then hit McCullouch for 13 yards, USC's only pass completion during the game. Simpson rolled for two, then reeled the Bruins with a 13-yard TD blast.

UCLA failed to endorse two scoring opportunities in the second period. Twice, the Bruins had a first down on SC's 15. The first threat sputtered when Beban's wild pitchback lost eight yards and Andrusyshyn failed on a 33-yard field goal try. The second threat stalled when Beban was dumped for a five-yard loss trying to turn an end.

The Bruins did come through in the third stanza, though, knotting the score at 14-14. It was quick—57 yards in two plays, with the second doing the damage. On second-and-six, Beban rared back and heaved a 53-yard strike to George Farmer, who took the ball over Cashman's head, then outraced Battle to paydirt.

Ron Yary, USC Outland Trophy winner, 1967.

A Change in Plans...An O. J. Run...And Roses!
Trojans Win It All, 21-20, From Bruins, Head for No. 1

Unsatisfied with a tie, UCLA took steps to unravel it in the final frame when Andy Herrera burglarized a Toby Page pass on UCLA's 17 and hoofed it up to his 35. UCLA then marched 65 yards in seven plays for their go-ahead marker. Beban's aerials of 11 yards to Spindler and 16 to Nuttall preceded his TD toss of 20 yards to Nuttall.

Then came the fateful mishap by Andrusyshyn, the swing that hooked and eventually spelled disaster.

"I knew when that kick went wide, it might be a mighty important miss," opined Prothro.

As for the soccer-style-kicking Andrusyshyn, well ... it wasn't one of his better days. Besides the faulty conversion and the second-quarter FG miss, he had two other field goal efforts blocked by the Trojans. He did, however, maintain his 44.7 punting average, on seven boots.

But now the clock was getting low on ticks, less than five minutes to play. The Trojans had possession on their own 34. Two plays gained only two yards. Third-and-eight. QB Page, seeing the UCLA defense go into double coverage on his splitend, called an audible—"23 blast". He took the snap, handed off to Simpson. Tackle Mike Taylor and guard Steve Lehner opened a hole and Simpson slithered through it, picked up blocks from Danny Scott, McCullouch and Ron Drake, then, in his inimitable style, loped 64 yards for the tying touchdown.

Page was lauded for switching plays at the line of scrimmage, and going to Simpson. "It's my biggest thrill," said the redhead.

"It was a great call by Page when he saw that double coverage on Drake," observed McKay.

But now it was clutch-time, separate the men from the boys, and all that. A tie would still send UCLA to Pasadena; USC had to have a win to go. Aldridge knew that as his foot swung true, lifting Southern Cal to a pulsating 21-20 triumph.

"Our team was the difference," remarked the modest sophomore whose boot turned around a whole town. "They just couldn't outplay us today."

It could be said that UCLA took the high road and USC took the low road, and USC got there afore them. For the Trojans gained 292 yards on the ground, only 13 passing; while the Bruins filled the air lanes with 301 yards and only 43 via ground routes.

Bruins Can't Kick This Time

UCLA Dials Z for Zero; O.J. Kills 'Em

"I thought UCLA played a terrific game," McKay commented. "They certainly were comparable to anyone we saw this year."

To which guard Scarpace chimed in with: "It's about time, but I knew we could do it."

As to be expected, the heroes built upon their laurels. Simpson's 177 yards brought him the national rushing crown with 1,415 yards, as well as back-of-the-game.

"I haven't changed my mind. Simpson is the greatest college runner I've ever seen," bragged McKay.

And Beban's 301 passing yards enabled him to pass Terry Baker, Oregon State's recent Heisman winner, as the No. 1 career total yardage man in West Coast history.

Also, UCLA's Nuttall had seven receptions, bringing his season mark to 37, a figure which eclipsed Kurt Altenberg's school record.

Defensive Coach Jerry Long lauded his Bruin defense. "A loss like this can make you sick," he stated, "but I don't feel that way. Our kids were all heart in there."

The Bruins still had one game to play, but it was anti-climactic as they lost to Syracuse. With 7-2-1 credentials, they fell to 10th in the ratings.

And it was on to the Crown City Classic for USC.

"I don't care who we play in the Rose Bowl," announced Simpson. "We're not about to lose, not even there."

Right on, O.J. Southern California 14, Indiana 3. And with the roses, came a bouquet of city champions, conference champions and national champions.

Linebacker Young summed it up. "The jinx is over."

Summary

	USC	UCLA
First Downs	12	17
Yards Rushing	292	43
Yards Passing	13	301
Total Yards	305	344
Passes Attempted	6	27
Passes Completed	1	16
Passes Had Intercepted	1	1
Fumbles Lost	1	0
Punts/Average	9/33.2	7/44.7
Penalties No./Yards	1/5	4/32

Scoring by Quarters:

USC	7	7	0	7	—	21
UCLA	7	0	7	6	—	20

1968
Game 38

OJ, The Trojan Way

As does a ghost from the gray, Southern California tailback O.J. Simpson swirled through the smog and fog shrouding the sod of Memorial Coliseum to pound out 205 yards and three touchdowns, and in so doing, led the way for a 28-16 thumping of rabid rival UCLA in game No. 38.

But the clash was much closer than the score would have you believe. For lack of a yard, it could have gone the other way.

It was a matchup of country club versus YMCA, of Cadillac versus Escort, of aristocrat versus peon, of Park Avenue versus Main Street.

The Bruins had nothing more than three victories to offset six defeats, an image of doing the wrong thing at the wrong time, only five seniors for leadership, and a slew of injured players that would test the dedication of Florence Nightingale.

But the Trojans—ah—they had everything. A perfect 8-0-0 record, momentum, top-ranking in the polls, incentive, the aroma of roses, and two All-Americans—Simpson and Mike Battle.

Small wonder that USC was top dog with the bookies. If you took UCLA, they would give you 14 points.

But John McKay, wily head coach at USC, remained cautious. "It's always tremendously difficult to win this game, no matter how the teams shape up on paper," he warned. "We're not going to be lulled to sleep."

To which Simpson added: "We'll be up, because we'll be going for the national championship."

Habitually, UCLA had been a stubborn first half team, but wilted after intermission. "But unfortunately," reminded UCLA coach Tommy Prothro, "it's a 60-minute game."

Simpson was in hot pursuit of the single-season rushing mark of 1,571 yards held by Mercury Morris of West Texas State. O.J. would enter the game 123 yards shy.

Speaking of The Juice, Don Widmer, UCLA linebacker, remarked: "He reminds me of a mouse. He's always moving in some direction, even sideways, and it's hard to get a shot at him."

Troy's quarterback Steve Sogge was moving in on some records, too, though less prolific. His 79 pass completions for the year and 158 for his career graded him third on campus charts, and a good day would endanger those above him.

Sogge had been instrumental in Trojan whippings of Minnesota, Northwestern, Miami, Stanford, Washington, Oregon, California and Oregon State. No one had tamed the Trojans.

The young Bruins started off with slam-bang swats on Pittsburgh and Washington State, but were zapped by Syracuse, Penn State and California before shading Stanford. Then they were foiled by Tennessee, Oregon State and Washington in their stretch run for USC.

So it was SC at 8-0-0 compared to UCLA at 3-6-0, which evoked Prothro to muse, "You know, we can lose this game if we don't get any breaks."

Of course he was jesting, because he really felt like Larry Agajanian, his huge defensive tackle. "Before every game, I've always felt like we could win," stated the 250-pounder. "I said that before the season, and I still feel the same way."

Mike (Cat) Ballou fell in line with his teammate. "Even if we had lost every game until now," he said, "we'd still be up for this one."

Over in Hollywood, Natalie Wood was starring in the "West Side Story". But the big story at University Park centered around the Rose Bowl. Southern Cal would be going for the third straight year, the only school to ever construct two sets of triple visits. The other trilogy was 1944-45-46.

A crowd of 75,066 was still trying to adjust to the poor visibility when Zenon Andrusyshyn booted a 32-yard field goal to forge the Uclans out front, 3-0. The FG climaxed a 79-yard drive in 13 plays that was featured by runs of nine yards by Rick Purdy, 15 and seven by Bill Bolden, and by two passes from Bolden, one of 13 yards to Purdy, the other 12 yards to Mike Garratt.

O.J. Simpson, USC Heisman Trophy winner, 1968.

The second quarter was a setto of musical chairs as SC jumped ahead 7-3, fell behind at 10-7, then took a 14-10 lead into the halftime break.

But first things first. A 76-yard campaign in 13 plays resulted in Troy's first TD, Simpson going the last four on a pitchout, thanks to a nifty block by Dan Scott. To get there, O.J. had created sprints of 13 and seven yards; Scott had swept for 10; and Sogge had struck through the air with connections to Simpson for 19 and to Bob Chandler for seven and 16. Vic Ayala toed his first of four conversions.

This escapade by the Trojans was kept alive when UCLA was penalized for an illegal substitution, a call that infuriated Prothro.

Bruin cornerback Lee McElroy was injured while tackling Sogge. "We had to put in a man for McElroy in addition to the two substitutions we were allowed to make," Prothro fumed. "I yelled 'injured player' at the official to tell him about the injury sub, but he dropped the handkerchief anyway, said he didn't hear me. He was right most of the time, but wasn't that time."

The call must have riled Mickey Cureton, too, so he decided to get those seven points back for his boss. Fielding a Troy punt on his 15-yard stripe, the flashy halfback criss-crossed the field before being tackled by Chandler on SC's 17-yard line, a 68-yard gem. Seven plays later, Cureton plunged into the end zone from the one. Key play in the short foray was a 10-yard pitch from Jim Nader to Purdy, from the 14 to the four. Andrusyshyn delivered the PAT.

"I thought I could go all the way," said Cureton, who twisted his ankle in the final period, "but I was sure happy to get to the 17."

Just before the halftime festivities, USC regained the lead with a 78-yard, 10 play TD rampage. Sparking the onslaught were darts of 30 and 11 yards by Simpson, plus a nine yard toss from Sogge to Sam Dickerson. The Juice squeezed out the final four that put Southern Cal ahead, 14-10.

After the rest interval, McKay's Machine widened its lead to 21-10. It was a brief drive of only 22 yards, spurred by a 37-yard punt return by Battle. Simpson spurted for six and five yards, Sogge kept for 10, and Scott dived over from the two.

So the Trojan rooters danced in the aisles with visions of sugar-plum roses, while the Bruin fans sat in despair and hoped for a break.

It came early in the fourth quarter when John Young's punt traveled only 25 yards, putting UCLA in business on SC's 37-yard line. In seven plays the Uclans were back in the game at 21-16. Nader threw strikes of 15 yards to Ron Copeland and 10 to Jones before

Cureton eliminated the last nine yards for his second marker. Nadar's two-point conversion mis-fired.

The cloak of victory now seemed within grasp and the Bruins made a jab for it. Employing an unbalanced line for the first time, the Ukes hurtled 74 yards to the very brink of Troy's goal ... only to come away empty-handed.

Moving steadily downfield, UCLA found itself on SC's one-yard line, third down. Nadar, whose rollouts had sustained the desperate drive, slipped and was splattered back on the three. Then on the this-is-it down, Trojan Bob Jensen deflected Nadar's pass intended for Gwen Cooper.

"We really battled about as well as we could," lamented Prothro. "We just couldn't get it in on third-and-one." To which Nadar added: "I got a chance to run, but the turf gave out under my left foot." Concerning the fourth down pass, Nadar explained: "I saw (Jim) Gunn coming across to contain me. Garratt was the primary receiver, but he was covered. Cooper was open, so I threw."

The Bruins received yet another chance, but once again the Trojan defense met the challenge. With just under two minutes to play, Nadar, in Troy territory, hurled a missile toward Garratt, but SC's Bill Redding tipped the ball into the hands of mate Jim Snow.

Apparently, the Trojans had had enough of these dire threats, so, after Snow's interception, Simpson one-manned a 51-yard TD jaunt, erasing 47 on three slices, then four for the hatchet touchdown. Ayala's fourth PAT iced the score at 28-16.

"Simpson gets faster in the fourth quarter, and I get smarter," cracked McKay.

During the contest, Simpson lugged the ball 40 times and averaged better than five yards per carry. These stats brought him back-of-the-game honors and two NCAA season records—most carries at 334, and most yards at 1,654.

But, most importantly, they were stepping stones for college football's highest achievement—the Heisman Trophy. O.J. Simpson became the second Southern California player so honored with this noble award.

Prothro felt his Bruins probably played their best game of the year, adding that the loss joined Oregon State as his "... biggest disappointments" of the season.

UCLA's Widmer, with 16 tackles and four assists, was named lineman-of-the-game. "We seemed to hold them pretty well until the last part of each half," related the big junior, "but I think we had a chance to win it."

McKay put on the finishing touches. "Year after year," he stated, "this is a tough one. UCLA played an awfully fine game. But you must remember, UCLA has some awfully fine players—we tried to recruit a lot of their people, Cureton, Ballou, that Jones boy."

The Trojans still had to worry about Notre Dame before they could think Pasadena. The Irish came through with a 21-21 tie, and then Ohio State draped a 27-16 curtain over SC in the Rose Bowl. So a 9-1-1 seed didn't quite grow the national championship flower, which was plucked by Ohio State.

After 38 brawls of head-to-head knocking, Southern California had walked away with 21 victories, UCLA with 12, and they were even in five. USC had scored 664 points to 449 for the Bruins.

Summary

	USC	UCLA
First Downs	20	15
Yards Rushing	276	140
Yards Passing	70	126
Total Yards	346	266
Passes Attempted	14	19
Passes Completed	7	9
Passes Had Intercepted	1	2
Fumbles Lost	0	1
Punts/Average	7/37.2	5/42.6
Penalties No./Yards	6/49	5/40

Scoring by Quarters:

| USC | 0 | 14 | 7 | 7 | — | 28 |
| UCLA | 3 | 7 | 0 | 6 | — | 16 |

**Mike Battle, USC
All-America DB, 1968**

1969

Game 39

The Cardiac Kids

Being behind in the fourth quarter never seemed to bother the guys who filled out the 1969 roster of Southern California's Trojans. Sure, it added wrinkles to their tutors on the coaching staff, but the players—no sweat.

Even their rooters—those without hypertension, that is—soon learned to take the team's last minute heroics in style, just looking at the deficit on the scoreboard, then winking knowingly at each other.

Why not? In six of their beloved Trojans' nine games, the Cardiac Kids had come from behind in the fourth quarter to win or tie. In the other three games, they didn't need a rally to win.

So no one became hysterical—well, maybe a few—when, with 92 seconds to play against UCLA, quarterback Jimmy Jones stepped back and flung a 32-yard pass which Sam Dickerson flagged in a corner of the end zone to erase a five point shortage and lift USC to another come-from-behind triumph, 14-12. Oh-hum.

"Next season," said SC Coach John McKay, dryly, "I'm going to learn how to get our kids emotionally up for our games. I just might enroll in a psychology class."

The approaching clash shaped up in the same pattern as other great encounters of the past. At stake was, as had become customary, the Rose Bowl, the conference crown and the city, county and state championships.

John Wayne, former USC player, was starring in a movie titled "The Undefeated". And that's just the way UCLA and USC would enter their 39th confrontation, both undefeated, both 8-0-1.

Southern Cal, ranked fifth in the country but called by some as "the worst unbeaten team in the nation" had sailed past Nebraska, Northwestern, Oregon State, Stanford, Georgia Tech, California, Washington State and Washington. The only mar was a 14-14 draw with Notre Dame.

And the only tarnish on the record of the Bruins, who were rated sixth, was a 20-20 stalemate with Stanford. Listed in the "W" column were Oregon State, Pittsburgh, Wisconsin, Northwestern, Washington State, California, Washington and Oregon.

One of the weaknesses of UCLA was a tendency toward errors, particularly fumbles (19 lost), but Coach Tommy Prothro was fielding a veteran team (16 seniors, including All-Americans Mike Ballou and Floyd Reese) and one that had escaped serious injuries during the year. His main asset, though, may have been a junior college transfer now the team leader at quarterback, Dennis Dummit.

Dummit, whose parents attended Southern Cal, was second in the AAWU to Stanford's Jim Plunkett in both passing and total offense. Through his prowess, the Bruins had rolled up 317 points, 80 more than USC.

And the junior QB had already attained two UCLA campus records (most yards passing, 1,710, and most touchdown passes, 14) and was closing in on three more (most completions in a season, most in a single game and most touchdowns rushing).

"I feel pretty much at home running UCLA's offense now," Dummit said. "Each game I think I've learned a little more."

USC's All-American defensive end Jimmy Gunn extolled the virtues of Dummit when he remarked: "He drops back so fast and he's such an accurate passer, very accurate."

Besides Gunn, the Trojans would display three other All-America performers in their lineup: Al Cowlings, Sid Smith and Clarence Davis.

Davis, known for his cloud-of-dust lunges, was filling the void left by the blur-of-lightning known as O.J. Simpson. And doing quite well. Well enough, in fact, to be the nation's No. 1 rusher with 1,238 yards, an average of 4.58 per carry.

The Trojans led the conference in all three defensive catagories; rushing, passing and total defense.

"No team in the country can out-quick our defensive line," bragged Trojan tackle Tody Smith.

And viewing SC in practice, Sid Gillman of the San Diego

Chargers didn't beat around the bush. "Boy, what talent out there," he exclaimed.

True, Sid, but here's a surprise for you. The betting line came out and made USC the underdog, by two points ... the first time since 1961 the Bruins were established as the favorite to win.

But the motivation nodded toward Troy. After all, no school had ever gone to the Rose Bowl four unbroken years.

"You can print this," McKay told *Times* writer Jeff Prugh. "We're gonna' be emotionally up for this one."

Students at the two schools were not exactly bubbling over with enthusiasm for the big game. Some were more interested in watching Charles Conrad and Allan Bean cavort on the moon, some were off demonstrating, some were burning their draft cards, and ... well, it just seemed to many students that football wasn't all that important.

Nevertheless, 90,814 fans streamed into the Coliseum on this fair and cool November afternoon; moon walks, demonstrations and bonfires notwithstanding. They saw a corker.

And, quite early, they saw a halfback pass shoot UCLA out to a 6-0 lead. It was the eighth play of a 75-yard drive and it was executed like this. On third-and-one from the Trojan 14, Dummit pitched out to Greg Jones who faked a sweep, then stopped and lofted a looper to George Farmer who stepped into the end zone, unmolested.

Important plays that set up the TD toss was a nine-yard run by Jones and two passes from Dummit to Mike Garratt, nine and 11 yards. Prothro, aware that a tie would not get his team to Pasadena, opted for a two-pointer after the TD. But Charlie Weaver deflected Dummit's pass and the try went for nought.

In the second quarter, Southern Cal went to the bank three times but endorsed only one trip for points. Jimmy Jones scrambled 30 yards during one jaunt that died on UCLA's 15, and on the next series, the Trojans reached Westwood's 17 before running out of gas.

Finally, Gunn pilfered a Dummit aerial and SC molded a 37-yard touchdown jog in six plays. Along the way, Charles Evans picked up 11 yards on a couple of runs, and Bob Chandler's five-yard gain gave SC a first down on the 15. Then, from the 13, White slashed through the line, broke a tackle, and scored. Vic Ayala's PAT placed USC out front, 7-6, at the half.

Not much happened in the third quarter, although the Trojan defense continued to play with viciousness, wreaking havoc in the Bruin backfield. But the fourth period popped wide open.

SC's Ayala was short on a 50-yard field goal endeavor, so UCLA took possession on its 20-yard line. Dummit passed to Rick Wilkes for 10, to Farmer for 13, then to Brad Lyman for 57, which spotted the ball on SC's 10. The Trojans dug in but to no avail as Dummit, pitching from the seven on third down, hit Gwen Cooper in the end zone for six points. Prothro this time had no choice but to seek two points, but Gunn sacked Dummit before he could throw.

With a 12-7 lead and three minutes to play, Joe Bruin figured he had Tommy Trojan in the bag.

"Yes, I did, too," echoed Prothro.

But the Cardiac Kids decided the time had now arrived for another routine miracle. Starting from their 32, the Trojans traveled 68 yards in nine plays for their all-encompassing touchdown. QB Jones, who had completed only one of 14 passes in 57 minutes, connected with Terry DeKraai for 10 and seven yards, and to Dickerson for eight and 32, the last being the knockout punch. In the huddle, Jones called the play–"64X Post Corner"– and Dickerson knew just where to go.

"We knew they'd have to pass, and we knew they'd go for Dickerson," commented UCLA's Ron Carver, "and we felt we could contain Jones' passing, but SC always ends up with a great play."

McKay wanted to go for two points, but his kicking unit rushed on the field and Ayala kicked the score up to 14-12.

SC's TD drive was greatly enhanced by an interference penalty. It happened on fourth-and-10 from UCLA's 43, turning a bog-down into a pick-up. Jones overthrew Dickerson but Danny Graham made contact before the ball arrived.

"It seems," moaned Graham, "that my whole life just went down the drain."

The play surprised Dickerson. "I knew I couldn't get to the ball," he related. "But he tackled me anyway."

The Uclans made one last stab to pull out a victory, but "miracle" was not in their vocabulary. Dummit was faultless on three passes but faulty on one as Ty Hudson stole his next fling, and the Bruin faithful stole from the stadium out into the darkness.

Dummit was dumped 10 times by Troy's hard-charging line, and its members, along with SC's stunting linebackers, accounted for five interceptions, two fumble recoveries and two deflections.

"Defensively," said McKay, "we couldn't have played any better than we did today." And, referring to another last-gasp episode in the saga of his Cardiac Kids, McKay remarked: "I guess this is our way to go. But we almost won it too early today."

The winning coach had a good word for the losers, too. "That's a tremendous offensive team UCLA has," he stated, pointing out that the Uclans outgained his club, 325 to 229 yards.

So it was on to Pasadena for Southern Cal, an unprecedented fourth consecutive visit. And joyous it was as the Trojans muzzled Michigan, 10-3. But even a 10-0-1 season card didn't bring a national championship, as the prize went to Texas.

But the labor of the Trojans had earned for them a basketful of goodies, the most cherished, probably being the right to live in their home town for another year without the taunts that prick the ears and soul of the loser of the USC-UCLA game. But if the loser was to hang down his head and cry, no one told Bruin Dennis Spurling.

"Sorry about the game," someone consoled Spurling. "Sorry nothing," he retorted. "This is the best team I ever played on. No reason to be sorry."

Summary

	USC	UCLA
First Downs	13	21
Yards Rushing	171	31
Yards Passing	58	294
Total Yards	229	325
Passes Attempted	21	44
Passes Completed	5	22
Passes Had Intercepted	1	5
Fumbles Lost	1	2
Punts/Average	11/39.8	9/39.4
Penalties No./Yards	6/79	8/97

Scoring by Quarters:

USC	0	7	0	7	—	14
UCLA	6	0	0	6	—	12

1970
Game 40

No Joy in Troy

Mudville had no monopoly on grief. Sure, the townfolks were mired in misery after Mighty Casey struck out; but, they were a frolicking, blithesome mob compared to the wretchedness and woe that enveloped the residents of Troyland after their mighty Trojans had been blown into oblivion by a bunch of Bruins from Westwood, 45-20.

It was the most points and the most total yardage—563—ever heaped upon Southern California by UCLA in 40 battles of combat. And it just wasn't supposed to have been that way.

Neither squad was sending its constituents into convulsions with stupendous feats of splendor. No, no one was turning cartwheels over Troy's 5-3-1 performance nor Westwood's 5-4-0. It was only a matter of which school would rule Los Angeles for a year, a "Pride and Character Bowl", so to speak.

Regardless, a bettor riding with UCLA could get seven points, and that seemed like a sham, considering the Bruins were coming off a 61-20 drubbing administered by Washington, while SC in its previous fracas had thrashed Washington State, 70-33.

Also, USC boasted the most productive offense in the Pacific 8 Conference (470 yards a game) and topped the rushing defense (124 per game).

"I really don't think the loss to Washington is going to hurt us against SC," predicted Bob Christiansen, the Bruins' tight end.

While Tommy Prothro, UCLA coach, was worried about the entire Trojan team, his counterpart at USC, John McKay, centered his worries on the Bruin wearing Jersey No. 19—Dennis Dummit.

"USC has a lot of overall ability," pointed out Prothro. "The Trojans are big, fast and agile."

And McKay said, "I was never more impressed with one quarterback than I was with Dummit's performance against Texas."

Supporters for McKay's warriors weren't losing sleep over one big, bad Bruin, though. They knew that, residing in their flock, were All-Americans Charles Weaver and Marv Montgomery, as well as such luminaries as Clarence Davis, Jimmy Jones and Sam Dickerson, among others.

"The records don't mean anything," remarked Dickerson, "and both teams will be up for each other."

McKay voiced likewise: "This is going to be a game between two crippled teams fighting for their self-respect."

In addition to the Washington State lark, Southern Cal had claimed verdicts over Alabama, Iowa, Oregon State and Washington. Its trio of losses were to Stanford, Oregon and California while its deadlock was with Nebraska.

Prothro's proteges, in addition to being humbled by Washington, also dropped decisions to Texas, Oregon and Stanford, while taking home the blue ribbon against Oregon State, Pittsburgh, Northwestern and Washington State.

Similar to the 1969 melee, students at both universities were not agog with excitement. The shots of Kent State and Jackson State had not faded away, and, on the present, muddled scene were Vietnam, Spiro Agnew, Abbie Hoffman and Angela Davis. The Westwood parade, normally a Bruin-week stellar attraction, was canceled; the vigil to guard the Tommy Trojan statue didn't even show up.

But the Big Game was played, in spite of the Big Draft, the Big Bomb, the Big Everything. Over 78,000 big ticket holders would attest to that.

The first quarter . . . indeed, the first half . . . was so hectic that most of the 78,000 were on their feet more than in their seats.

A total of 38 points were posted in the opening stanza, 24 by UCLA. That was the most prolific offensive explosion in a 15-minute span of any UCLA-USC skirmish.

In condensed form, scoring in the affair went like this; first quarter:

—Bruin Rick Wilkes took a six-yard TD toss from Dummit, climaxing a 76-yard, seven play journey. Along the way Reggie Echols

The Incredible Turnabout: UCLA 45, USC 20

trotted 35 yards on a reverse, Marv Kendricks bolted for 16 and Dummit passed to Wilkes for 14. Clayton Record recorded the PAT; 7-0, UCLA.

—Record dribbled a short kickoff which bounced off Trojan Mike Ryan's shoulder and Mike Clayton came up with the ball for UCLA on its 44. Kendrick scooted 15, 10 and 11 yards, Christiansen snagged a 20-yarder from Dummit, and when the assault bogged down after reaching SC's six, Record booted a 20-yard field goal; 10-0, UCLA.

—The Trojans then tallied their first marker, traversing 70 yards in four plays. The payoff was a 51-yard bombshell from Jones to Dickerson who outdistanced Rey Moore. A 15-yard dash by Davis helped set it up. Vic Ayala converted; 10-7, UCLA.

—Make that 17-7, UCLA. On the fifth play of the 74-yard attack, Dummit clicked with Christiansen who fought off Bruce Dyer to eradicate the last 39. The key plays were a 19-yard burst by Echols plus a 15-yard pitch from Dummit to Wilkes. Record again passed the toe test.

—Davis mis-handled the kickoff and Kendricks encircled the errant ball for the Uclans on Troy's 20-yard stripe. Kendricks picked up three, then Dummit nailed Wilkes on the six, after which Kendricks slashed over the goal. Record's kick was true; 24-7, UCLA.

—USC answered that TD with one of its own, moving 44 yards in eight plays. Rod McNeill returned the Ukes' kickoff 36 yards. Davis popped 13 and Jones hurled a hummer of 18 yards to Charles Evans. Those plays helped advance the ball to the one-yard line, from where Davis dived over. Ayala came through and the wooly first quarter finally ended; 24-14, UCLA.

In the second period, the Bruins tacked on 14 more points, like this:

—Starting from SC's 49, UCLA pushed across the double stripe in eight plays. Randy Tyler plunged in from one yard out, but two passes—Dummit to Wilkes for 24 yards and Jim Nader to Clayton for 16—made possible the plunge. Bruce Barnes added loot with his boot; 31-14, UCLA.

Rose Bowl	Sugar Bowl	Orange Bowl	Cotton Bowl
Ohio State Vs. Stanford	Tennessee Vs. Air Force	Nebraska Vs. N.D. or L.S.U.	Arkansas or Texas Vs. N.D. or L.S.U.

Will Big 10 Vote Pac-8 Out Of Bowl?

Melvin Durslag
The Agony And Ecstasy
Bruins Turn Trojans Into Keystone Kops

—One more time, boys. Dummit, with a salvo of bullets, led the Bruins on a 76-yard march that ended in paydirt after 13 plays. Relevant to the TD, which Wilkes registered on a 13-yard heave from Dummit, were other Dummit darts of 17 yards to Wilkes and 12 to Tyler. Barnes' PAT brought a merciful end to the first half; 38-14, UCLA.

"We had trouble with kickoffs," drawled McKay, his understatement referring to mishaps by Ryan and Davis which UCLA capitalized on for points.

So if the banner of the first half was the red flare of rockets with bombs bursting in air, the second was spangled with just two firecrackers. The first was popped by USC in Quarter Three.

—McNeill, on another fine kickoff return, streaked 24 yards to his 48, and the Trojans wiped out the remaining 52 yards in eight plays. It was a case of the Bruins not being able to keep up with Jones. Not only did the junior QB score the TD on a six-yard keeper, he also completed vital passes of 12 yards to Chandler and 30 to Dickerson, the latter being a gutsy call since Tim Osterling had dropped him for a 13-yard loss on the previous play. McNeill pitched in his support of the drive with a nifty 12-yard gallop ... Jones' two-point pass conversion failed; 38-20, UCLA.

—The Uclans came back in the final stanza to wrap up the scoring, the game, and the county of Los Angeles by grinding out 72 yards in 13 plays. Kendricks stepped off 50 of those yards on six handles, the last being a 20-yard waltz into the end zone. After Record's PAT, the final score of 45-20 was in the records.

Oh, a bit later, Ayala did try a 37-yard field goal, but this just wasn't USC's day.

"It's just good to win," exclaimed Prothro.

His assistant, Coach Jerry Long was a little more specific. "I don't think I can ever remember Bruin linemen blocking that well," he stated.

But a Southern Cal player, Greg Slough, came away with Defensive-Player-of-the-Game honors. The 230-pound linebacker was credited with 16 tackles.

Doug Krikorian, writer for the *Herald-Express* asked McKay if this had been his most disappointing season.

"The second one isn't even close," McKay replied. Then turning to the game, he added, "UCLA deserved to win by that margin or better. We weren't lucked out on, we were beaten."

As might be expected in a tussle of such offensive peaks, some records fell by the wayside. Kendricks rushed for 182 yards to overcome Bill Kilmer's UCLA single game mark. And Wilkes caught 11 passes to shatter the Bruins' single game reception record.

"Records are nothing when you measure them against the satisfaction of winning," commented Wilkes. "This team has waited a long time for this."

And then there was Dummit, named Back-of-the-Game. His 19-of-30 for 272 yards brought his career passing yardage to 4,226 and his total offense for a single season to 2,191 yards, both of which waved goodbye to marks held by Gary Beban.

USC assistant coach Marv Goux went to Dummit's locker after the game, shook his hand and told him, "You're quite a man, coming back the way you did after last year."

Perhaps it was this type of sportsmanship that characterized the will and heart of the Trojans. For they arose from the ashes of humility to rousingly swat undefeated Notre Dame the following week, 38-28. This grand slammer gave McKay another winning season at 6-4-1.

UCLA met eighth-ranked Tennessee on the same day, but the Uclans faltered under a 28-17 verdict. Their ledger for the season showed 6-5-0.

There was one touch of sadness that brushed UCLA's superb victory over USC. It was the last crosstown clash for Tommy Prothro, the big genial coach with horn-rimmed glasses, the constant cigarette and a lust for bridge.

Prothro was recently asked to name some of the most outstanding players he had coached, and here are the names he mentioned: offensive lineman, Dave Dalby; running back, Mel Farr; quarterback, Terry Baker or Gary Beban; blocker, Rod Davenport; receiver, Vern

Burke; defensive lineman, Floyd Reese, defensive back; Jim Decker; and linebacker, Donn Moomaw.

During his six years at Westwood, Prothro gathered 41 victories, suffered 18 losses, and had three ties. Against Southern Cal, he was 3-3-0.

And the last meeting, this 45-20 flogging, was certainly a resounding send-off. Don't you imagine, as Prothro bides his time in Lakewood, Ohio, that the joyful shouts of his players still ring in his ears?

"It makes up so much for last year" — Don Carver.

"It's the greatest thing that ever happened to me in sports" — Tim Oesterling.

"It was just plain sweet" — Dennis Dummit.

Summary

	UCLA	USC
First Downs	32	22
Yards Rushing	275	84
Yards Passing	288	285
Total Yards	563	369
Passes Attempted	31	42
Passes Completed	20	16
Passes Had Intercepted	1	1
Fumbles Lost	1	2
Punts/Average	4/34.2	4/32.7
Penalties No./Yards	7/81	5/43

Score by Quarters:

| UCLA | 24 | 14 | 0 | 7 | — | 45 |
| USC | 14 | 0 | 6 | 0 | — | 20 |

Dennis Dummit leads UCLA to victory in 1970.

1971
Game 41

All Things Being Equal...

The Chase Manhattan Bank cut its prime interest rate to seven percent. That has nothing to do with the exciting, pulsating and thrilling aspects of a game called football. Neither did the 41st scuffle in the Southern California–UCLA series.

It seems that each of the 68,426 loyal fans who turned up at the Coliseum on a beautiful autumn day had a one word description of the game ... like dull, prosaic, perfunctory, humdrum. One elderly gentleman, trying to be nice said: lackluster.

And it wasn't that any clever exploitations of the manly art were preconceived. Everyone knew the two teams were mediocre, at best. But perhaps it wasn't quite as, er, lackluster as the old gentleman said. It's just that nobody is satisfied with a tie game, and that's what it was... a 7-7 stalemate.

Except maybe a rookie coach with a 2-7 record going in. "I really feel like we won," spieled Pepper Rodgers, "but we didn't." Rodgers, an animated fellow with a zest for life, had been brought in to fill the big shoes of Tommy Prothro at UCLA.

First off, he inherited a young squad, then had the misfortune to lose 13 quality players through ineligibility or injury, including James McAlister, a potential Heisman Trophy winner.

But frowns from the alumni were peering at Rodgers as his

Bruins dropped decisions to Pittsburgh, Texas, Michigan, Oregon State, California, Washington and Stanford, offering in return a paltry twosome of wins over Washington State and Arizona.

"It's been a long season," said Rodgers, "but at least one good thing has come out of people scrutinizing me—they've finally learned how to spell my name right."

Southern Cal started off with a set-back from Alabama, two whitewash jobs on Rice and Illinois, then three straight losses—Oklahoma, Oregon and Stanford. At that point, from a 2-4 record, the Trojans surged to four consecutive triumphs—Notre Dame, California, Washington State and Washington.

It was this momentum that pronounced SC a two touchdown favorite to lace UCLA. For some inexplicable reason, the odds dropped to 11 points, then closed at 13.

According to Jim Perry, writing in the LA *Herald-Examiner*, a friend, trying to cheer USC Coach John McKay, told him SC would win, 21-10.

"You're crazy," retorted McKay, "we won't score 21 if they don't even show up."

During off years, coaches josh a lot. That distracts the alumni, you know.

Perry: "How did practice go, coach?"

McKay: "The other day we practiced our two-minute offense with no defense on the field and we still had trouble moving the ball. I think we finally scored on an incomplete pass."

Perry, addressing Rodgers: "And how was your practice, coach?"

Rodgers: "Oh, we've had just a wonderful time on the field preparing for this game. Morale is high, and my players all love one another. Now I'm worried we'll love USC too much, too."

Neither would deny, however, that their rosters sparkled with talented jewels. UCLA had an All-American center in Dave Dalby, plus the likes of Bob Christiansen, Marv Kendricks and Fred McNeill.

And leading the Trojan charge were All-Americans John Vella and Willie Hall, ably supported by Jimmy Jones, Mike Pavich, Lou Harris, Sam Cunningham and Lynn Swann.

"There's always incentive in the UCLA game," Vella told *Times* scribe Dwight Chapin, "but this year there's more. We haven't forgotten last year's nightmare."

So, with kickoff time approaching, McKay uttered one last statement: "It is indeed an honor to play in this game."

To which Rodgers added: "It's also frightening. People come looking for you if you lose."

Will ABC Cancel Troy, Bruin

Melvin Durslag

49ers Rise Wasn't Meteoric

In their new enthronement a team described dashingly as a contender, the San Francisco 49ers have come a long piece.

Chances are, minor reversals and all that they are as good as any group in the National Football League.

Their home park is a sellout. Management, in fact, was everyone's money long before the season began.

And, alas, their quarterback restored to good standing last year after a decade or so of derision by the local citizenry, is still on the job, functioning admirably.

It is doubtful that any team in pro football, with the possible exception of the Pittsburgh Steelers, has endured the frustration of the 49ers, who are on the grounds today at the Coliseum with the Rams.

Now in their 22nd year in the NFL, they have never won a title of any kind until last season when they fell only a win short of the Super Bowl.

Their following has been anything but faithful. When the club went flat between 1963 and '70, fans in San Francisco dropped it like a live lobster.

It Then Returned

Not until the fifth game of 1971 did the flock return showing vestiges of the old spirit. As an insight to what used to transpire with San Francisco football...

UCLA Ties Up USC

By BUD FURILLO
Herald Examiner Sports Editor

The student enrollment at UCLA approximates 29,000. An overwhelming majority...

To which literalist Perry suggested a profound compromise: "Well, there can always be a tie."

And, as you learned way back in the third paragraph, that's what it was... a 7-7 draw.

Neither club punctured the end zone in the first quarter, but some activity arose in the second period.

With UCLA on the prowl, Trojan Eddie Johnson filched a pass thrown by Scott Henderson, setting off an 89-yard touchdown drive in eight plays. After several short gainers, Jones passed to Dave Boulware for 12 yards, then sophomore Manfred Moore went on a tear around his end and didn't stop until Jim Bright pulled him to earth on UCLA's three-yard line, a sensational 57-yard spree. Harris cracked for two yards, then crammed over the double-stripe. Mike Rae added the one-pointer.

"It was a 24-power, off tackle play," explained Moore, "and there was a mix-up in the UCLA secondary."

USC drove to the Ukes' 14 after Harris' six-pointer, but was thwarted by a holding penalty, and Rob Scribner intercepted a

Jones pitch from the Bruin 20 to halt another threat.

After intermission, the Trojan offense took the afternoon off, penetrating no deeper than Joe Bruin's 31-yard line.

Meanwhile, the lads from Westwood finally put things together and got themselves a touchdown in the third siesta.

It began when McNeill, the Bruins' defensive end, put a beastly rush on Boulware, who simply wanted to punt the ball away from his 17-yard line. His hurried kick went only 17 yards to the SC 30 and the Uclans leaped all over that opportunity.

Kendricks bulled for 10 yards and Gary Campbell tacked on seven more. Then it was Kendricks for another six as the ball came to rest on the seven-yard stripe. One more handoff to Kendricks and-zoom-Marvelous Marv pounded into the end zone. Pressure abounded on Efren Herrera, but the ace kicker knotted the score at 7-7.

The third quarter ended, and the final quarter ended with both goal lines strongly protected, though Jones was trying to find Swann in Westwood's end zone when the game came to a thud, uh, finish.

"There's no way it should have been that way," lamented Harris whose 118 net yards for the Trojans earned him Offensive-Player-of-the-Game laurels. "A tie is great for UCLA, but we should have won."

Naturally, Kendricks, whose 65 yards led the Bruins, disagreed. "We showed we were superior," he replied. "Getting a tie with SC was like winning."

While McKay stuck with Jones at quarterback most of the game, Rodgers tried Henderson on wishbone attacks and Mike Flores in a shotgun formation. On seven plays from the latter spread, Flores threw three interceptions, two incompletions and was sacked twice.

"I think," reasoned Rodgers, "we're gonna' put the shotgun back in mothballs."

And speaking of his wishbone, Pepper said, "The Trojans didn't contain the wishbone, they contained us."

UCLA's McNeill was rated Lineman-of-the Game honors. His supporting brigade consisted of Pavich, Ed Galigher and Bruce Barnes, who averaged 40.6 on eight punts.

The Trojans were not without their defenders, either . . . guys such as Bob Erickson, John Papadakis, Mike McGirr, Steve Fate and Skip Thomas.

A courageous soul asked McKay why the Trojans didn't score more. "I've got an engagement at seven o'clock," he responded "so I really don't have time to tell you."

The contest lowered the curtain on the season for both teams, but *El Rodeo*, USC's yearbook, refused to permit it to slip into anonymity without one last slur. "The game was a stinking tie, between the team that was picked to win the conference, the team that decisively beat Notre Dame and California against the No. 8 team in the Pac-8," it blared. "It was a game so dull that it put most of the spectators, not to mention the players, to sleep."

And that kind old gentleman just called it "lackluster".

Summary

	USC	UCLA
First Downs	15	12
Yards Rushing	203	158
Yards Passing	92	0
Total Yards	295	158
Passes Attempted	21	8
Passes Completed	10	0
Passes Had Intercepted	1	4
Fumbles Lost	1	0
Punts/Average	9/35.3	8/40.6
Penalties No./Yards	5/54	2/10

Scoring by Quarters:

| USC | 0 | 7 | 0 | 0 | — | 7 |
| UCLA | 0 | 0 | 7 | 0 | — | 7 |

1972
Game 42

A Bone to Pick

Both UCLA and Southern California were high riders in 1972; the Bruins with their celebrated wishbone-T attack, the Trojans with their vaunted I-bone assault.

And each had a bone to pick with the other. That stodgy 7-7 stalemate of the previous year still haunted their thoughts, and only an atonement could eradicate this vile memory.

With an unscarred record of nine straight victories, USC was the No. 1 team in the nation, so acclaimed by both wire services. And the Trojans also owned the country's top-rated defense against the run.

Are you listening? SC defense—best at stopping the run; UCLA offense—wishbone, primarily a running formation. Put the two together and the riddle is solved: Southern Cal 24, UCLA 7.

It wasn't that Bruin Coach Pepper Rodgers went into the game unaware of the strength his opponent could flex. "USC is the best offensive and defensive team we've faced," he cautioned. "But I really don't have to build them up. They're the No. 1 team in the country. It's something they've earned."

In reaching the summit, the Trojans had cast aside Arkansas by 21 points, Oregon State by 45, Illinois by 35, Michigan State by 45, Stanford by nine, California by 28, Washington by 27, Oregon by 18, and Washington State by 41. Their loss column was bone dry.

Bovard Field burnished with the myriad of skilled performers that graced its battered turf ... All-Americans Charles Young, Richard Wood, Sam Cunningham, Pete Adams and John Grant, to name just a few.

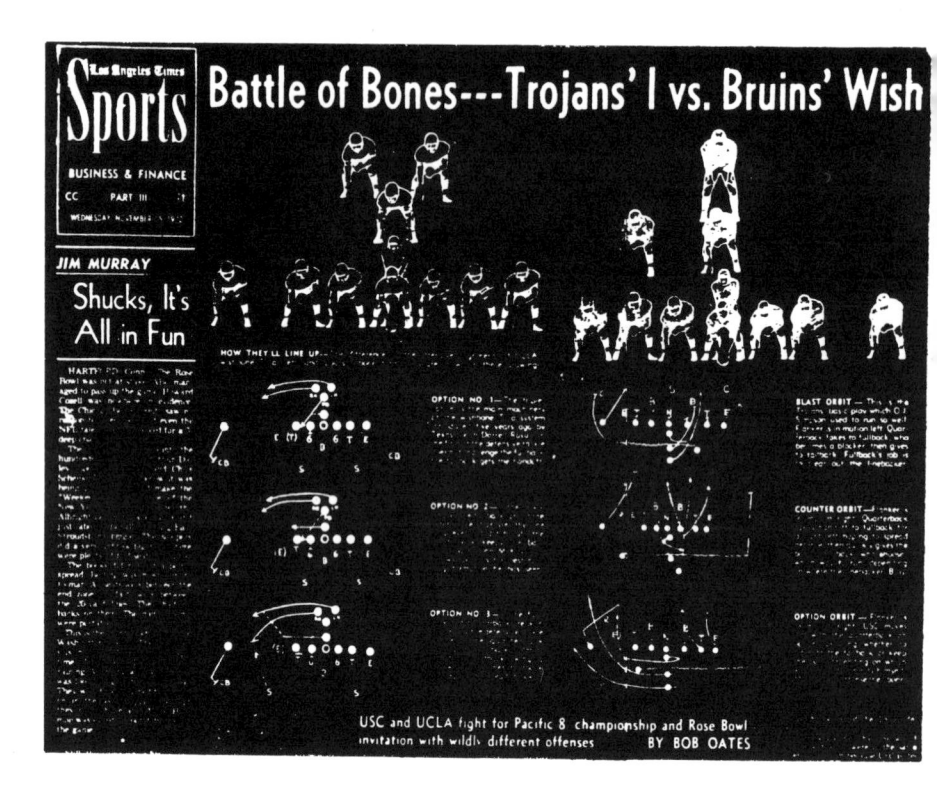

But an all-SC show it was not. UCLA, sporting the second best rushing mark in the states at 361.2 yards per game, was not ready to concede anything to its arch rival from University Park. With an 8-2-0 mark and such runners as Kermit Johnson and James McAlister, no concession was needed. Johnson, in fact, was the PAC-8's leading rusher.

In their opening game, the Uclans upset Nebraska, the top team in the land at that time. Next, they punched Pittsburgh, before bowing to Michigan. Then came six wins in a row—Oregon, Arizona, Oregon State, California, Washington State and Stanford. In their final game before USC, the Ukes were ambushed by Washington.

"In the first half against Washington last week, UCLA had the most devastating offense I've ever seen," USC Coach John McKay said. "Mark Harmon runs the offense extremely well."

Comparing his formation with Rodgers', McKay stated: "Our offense is just like the wishbone, except we overload to one side;

The Trojan Horse celebrates another touchdown.

the wishbone lines up balanced. So you might call our offense the I-bone."

McKay ribbed Rodgers at a Rotary luncheon during the week. "Pepper," he said, winking, "I'll admit our material is not as good this year as it has been. Which, of course, makes me a dammed good coach."

In a ballot of grid writers, 31 selected USC to win, by an average point spread of 11. Four picked UCLA and one predicted a tie. The official line was SC by 13 points.

Marlin McKeever, ex-Trojan and later a Los Angeles Ram, put his former school on the spot. "The Trojans will win by 14 to 21 points," he predicted. "They're the finest college team I've seen in a long, long time."

Rodgers hoped it would rain on the Big Game. "Rain helps the underdog," he explained. However, it was crisp, cool and clear at the shank of the evening as the teams prepared for a 5pm kickoff.

Starting time had been moved from early afternoon to early evening to accommodate the whims of network television. Money talks, you know, and $111,500 was quite vocal.

But 82,929 friends of the institutions took to their little cranny in the Coliseum to see which team would go to the Rose Bowl, which would capture the league title, which would reign over the city. Also, there was the little matter of USC aiming for the national crown, which was surely within its reach.

And the maroon-jersied warriors started out like they wanted it, as Mike Rae toed a 32-yard field goal early in the battle. The boot capped a 60-yard drive that needed seven plays. The biggest was a 34-yard pass from Rae to Lynn Swann, but Anthony Davis chipped in with a 12-yard run plus a nine-yard gain on a swing pass from Rae.

Troy increased its margin to 10-0 when Davis scampered over the double stripe from 22 yards out, and Rae converted. The scoot by Davis was the eighth play of a 76-yard excursion, which sputtered on the Bruins' 38 but was sustained when Rae hit Young for nine yards on a fourth down.

It was still in the first quarter and already the Trojans led by 10. A rout loomed.

But then UCLA's pokes up the middle became effective, and before the quarter ran out, the Bruins marched 75 yards in 17 plays for a TD. Along the way, McAlister streaked for eight, Randy Tyler for 20 and Johnson took a pitchout for nine. McAlister jumped in from the two and Efren Herrera's boot closed the gap at 10-7.

UCLA had a chance to tie the score in the second period. While fielding a punt, SC's Davis fumbled and UCLA's Jack Lassner cov-

Pepper Rodgers, UCLA Head Coach, 1971-1973.

ered the ball in Troy territory. The Uclans moved to Troy's 17-yard line, but the Trojans, led by Charles Hinton, stiffened and Herrera subsequently missed a FG attempt.

"The ball hit my hands and fell to the ground," Davis explained his bobble. "The trouble was my mind was on that open lane I saw, not on catching the ball."

The clock was winding down on the first half when Rod McNeill, brother of UCLA's Fred, crashed over the goal line from one yard out to enrich USC's lead to 17-7 (after Rae's PAT). Runs of nine and 16 yards by Davis, along with a Rae-to-Swann 22-yarder, spiced the 80-yard, 13 play jaunt.

"I don't know if that touchdown or our missed field goal hurt us more," Rodgers contemplated. "Toss a coin."

The fans didn't know it, but most of the offensive fireworks had crackled, as only one touchdown was registered in the second half, and that by USC to seal the outcome.

It happened midway through the third stanza, with the Trojans traveling 96 yards in 13 plays. Similar to their previous trek, the key runs were by Davis (22, 15 and 10 yards) and the key grab was by Swann (15 yards from Rae), although McNeill did contribute nine and eight yard jogs. Rae carried the ball over from UCLA's seven, then drilled the PAT for the final 24-7 score.

"They (USC) were fantastic," extolled Rodgers. "I've never seen anyone better. You can't be too disappointed when someone beats you who is that good."

Davis mulched more real estate than any other runner—178 yards, sufficient to earn Offensive-Player-of-the-Game fame. But he wouldn't claim credit. "I can't say enough about the great blocking I was getting," spoke the soph.

"Anthony Davis played a super game again," praised McKay, "He's like Mike Garrett—lots of ability, tough and durable."

Another SC sophomore, Richard Wood, claimed the Defensive-Player-of-the-Game award, but by his own admission, he had plenty of help from James Sims, Grant, Charles Anthony, Jeff Winans, Dale Mitchell and Hinton. Wood was credited with 13 tackles and five assists. Mike Ryan, Cunningham and Adams caught McKay's eyes for their blocking.

Tyler was tops among Bruin runners with 81 yards, followed by Johnson with 76. UCLA's 198 rushing yards was well below its current average, but was enough to establish a new conference mark for a single season—3,810 yards. The old record was 3,801 set by Southern Cal in 1929.

The Big Game was the last of the year for UCLA, which closed at

8-3-0. "We've got to look forward to next year," said QB Harmon, looking ahead.

But the Trojans still had Notre Dame and the Rose Bowl. No roadblock, though, could stop or even slow down this locomotive welded together by McKay. The Irish were no match, yielding to USC, 45-23. And it was the same in the Rose Bowl with Ohio State, as the Buckeyes fell, 42-17.

With a 12-0-0 slate, the Trojans were a shoo-in for the National Championship. And McKay, for the second time, was named Coach-of-the-Year. What's more, USC rolled up 467 points during the season, the most ever scored in its long and illustrious history.

National champs, Rose Bowl champs, PAC-8 champs, State champs, city champs, best coach, best point-producers . . . oh, it's hard to be humble when you're perfect in every way.

Summary

	USC	UCLA
First Downs	20	15
Yards Rushing	232	198
Yards Passing	129	38
Total Yards	361	236
Passes Attempted	16	9
Passes Completed	9	3
Passes Had Intercepted	0	1
Fumbles Lost	1	0
Punts/Average	4/31.5	7/42.0
Penalties No./Yards	2/10	3/11

Scoring by Quarters:

USC	10	7	7	0	—	24
UCLA	7	0	0	0	—	7

USC's Three-Time All-America Richard Wood, 1972-73-74

1973

Game 43

Bruins Blow Ball, Bell and Bowl

The preceptor of Southern California grid teams, John McKay, had matched wits against his crosstown rival, UCLA, for 13 years. Someone asked him if this, his 14th meeting, would pit him against the best Bruin team yet encountered.

He answered with a monosyllable: "Yes."

UCLA was the No. 1 scoring and rushing team in the nation, averaging 45.7 points and 415.4 yards per outing. Kermit Johnson had racked up 15 touchdowns while rushing for 1,022 yards, a 7.7 per carry average. And when he wasn't intimidating the opposition, James Alexander, Charlie Schuhmann, Mark Harmon or John Sciarra were. By the way, Harmon, the son of movie actress Elise Knox and Michigan's fabled Tom Harmon, is now a popular network television personality.

"I don't think anyone can stop them," stated McKay. "You just try to slow them down."

And USC had the ammunition to do just that. The Trojan defense was ranked as best among Pacific-8 teams, and it had shown a knack for breaking the wishbone, UCLA's bread-and-butter attack.

But the fact that SC had shut down the wishbone offense of Arkansas and Nebraska didn't seem to faze Bruins Johnson nor McAlister.

Said Johnson: "I don't see how USC is going to defense us, or how they can stop us."

And said McAlister: "We were afraid against USC last year, but not anymore. USC is in trouble. They're going to get theirs."

Bold words, for sure. But the Trojans weren't biting.

"I've read what they've said," reacted Monte Doris. "All I care to say is Kermit Johnson and James McAlister are fine running backs and UCLA has a good team."

To which Charles Anthony added, "We'll find out after the dust settles."

Mal Florence, *LA Times* writer, put the struggle in proper focus when he wrote, "It will be UCLA's runaway wishbone offense against USC's wishbone-breaking defense."

"If we expect to win, our defense will have to take the ball away from USC enough times to give our offense a chance," visualized Pepper Rodgers, UCLA's head coach.

McKay put the same thought in different terms: "We have to have our offense control the ball, both by running and passing, and not give it away in scoring areas."

While much attention had dwelled on the Ukes' offense and the Trojans' defense, their counterparts on both teams were certainly not without their Saturday Heroes.

The deft hands of Anthony Davis, Lynn Swann, Pat Haden and Rod McNeill put magic into the ball for USC, while UCLA had a stout defense built around Fulton Kuykendall, Jimmy Allen, Fred McNeill, James Bright, John Nanoski and Cal Peterson.

"Southern Cal's backs are a little bit better than any we've seen," observed Kuykendall, "and their line is a lot more physical."

UCLA, ranked eighth by both wire services, was mauled by Nebraska in its season opener, then rattled off nine victories in a row — Iowa, Michigan State, Utah, Stanford, Washington State, California, Washington, Oregon and Oregon State. None stopped the slashing wishbone, as the Uclans amassed 457 points.

Southern Cal was rated one notch behind the Bruins, having compiled an 8-1-1 chart. That old plunderer, Notre Dame, had removed Troy from the ranks of the undefeated in the seventh game and Oklahoma had escaped with a tie in the third. Otherwise, it was clear sailing against Arkansas, Georgia Tech, Oregon State, Washington State, Oregon, California, Stanford and Washington.

In contrast to the usual rule, UCLA opened as a 3½ point favorite to win, dropping to three on the morning line. And the consensus of area sports scribes was that UCLA would win by a score of 25-11.

Noting the odds, McKay quipped, "I always go with the favorite.

Kermit Johnson, UCLA All-American back, 1973.

But, really, I have no idea how the game will turn out."

The day of the game broke cold and overcast, but it didn't dampen the zeal of autograph seekers among the crowd of 88,037 who revolved the Coliseum turnstiles. With 10 All-Americans romping on the turf, pen and pads had a field day.

AA stars on display for Southern Cal were Richard Wood, Swann, Booker Brown, Artimus Parker and Steve Riley. And cavorting for UCLA were Allen, Johnson, McAlister, McNeill and Efren Herrera.

Statistics in the game were nearly equal. Both teams had 19 first downs, and the Bruins advantage in total yardage was slight, 331 to 316. So the story of the game had to be—turnovers. And the unfortunates were the Bruins. Six times they gift-wrapped the ball for the Trojans, and no team does that and wins. In a mild upset, Southern Cal 23, UCLA 13.

A reporter asked Rodgers if turnovers was the difference between the two teams. "Yeah," nodded Rodgers, "we made six, they didn't make any."

The Trojans were first to activate the scoreboard, composing a 68-yard entourage in 15 plays. During the stretch, Haden pitched 18 yards to Jake McKay, son of SC's coach, and to Swann for six. The trek appeared to fizzle on UCLA's 27, but, on fourth-and-three, Davis loped for five yards. A few plays later, he stepped into pay-dirt from four yards out, as Manfred Moore cleared the way. Chris Limahelu hammered the PAT; 7-0, USC.

Late in the initial quarter, UCLA's Herrera slammed through the uprights a 42-yard field goal, closing the gap to 7-3. It was the culmination of a 67-yard spree in 11 plays, most notable of which was a 13-yard burst by McAlister and a six-yarder by Johnson.

The point mill continued to grind in the second period, producing 10 points for USC and seven for UCLA.

The Trojans were first, staging an 80-yard pigskin parade that crossed Westwood's goal in a dozen plays. Haden was ringmaster of an aerial circus, throwing 13, 10 and 14 yards to Jim Obradovich, then 16, while scrambling, to McKay for the six-pointer. The Bruins were putting double-coverage on Swann, opening lanes for Haden's other receivers. The PAT by Limahelu raised SC's lead to 14-3.

UCLA then mastered the science of touchdown precision, putting together an impressive 84-yard drive in nine plays. Johnson took a pitchout and rambled 29 yards to highlight the movement. He also had an 11-yard sprint before scoring the TD from four yards out. McAlister's 10-yard dash also aided the cause, and Herrera's conversion put the Bruins back in the battle at 14-10.

Scoring in the first half ended when SC's Limahelu served up a 35-

Fulton Kuykendall, named Most Outstanding Defensive Player against USC, 1973.

yard field goal, terminating a 92-yard campaign that took only eight plays. Davis ripped off a fancy 48-yard gallop, McNeill swished for 10 and snagged a 12-yard pass from Haden to put the Trojans in range for Limahelu; 17-10, USC.

UCLA was on the move in the third quarter, but McAlister was separated from the ball on a fierce tackle by Doris, and Art Riley pounced on the ball for SC on the Bruin 47.

That led to another field goal by Limahelu, who drove home a 32-yarder on the ninth play. Davis consumed 16 of the 47 yards on three carries; 20-10, USC.

On the ensuing kickoff, Johnson made a spectacular return of 51 yards to SC's 44-yard line. But, on second down, Troy's Anthony collided with Russel Charles, causing a fumble which Danny Reece enfolded for the Trojans.

In the fourth stanza, Sciarra fumbled and was intercepted, but the Bruins still managed to slip in a 27-yard field goal by Herrera. The approach covered 61 yards and required 12 plays. McAlister accounted for 27 on five carries, Johnson for 14 on four, and Jones for 10 on a pass from Sciarra; 20-13, USC.

With just over three minutes to play, the Bruins were pushing for a tie, which would escort them to Pasadena. But Sciarra was blindsided by Sims at midfield, and Dale Mitchell popped up with the ball for SC.

If, by then, the issue was not fully settled, it was when Limahelu rammed through his third field goal, a 28-yarder that put on the finishing touch to an 18-yard drive, as well as to the Bruins. The FG was set up by Ted Roberson's interception of Sciarra's toss; 23-13, USC.

"We played well in the second half," reflected Rodgers, "but then . . . well, we had those turnovers."

"This had to be our best all-around game," exclaimed Doris, who accumulated 18 tackles. "UCLA had run up all sorts of points, but it hadn't done it in a game like this."

Once again, Davis led the Trojan charge with 145 net yards on 27 carries. That lifted his season yardage to 1,038, the second straight year he had exceeded the four-figure mark. Among Trojan runners, only O.J. Simpson could make the same claim.

Referring to pre-game remarks uttered by Bruins Johnson and McAlister, Davis said, "I admire confidence. And I have nothing against Kermit or James. They're my friends. But what they said before the game riled up our defense."

Rodgers had reservations about judgement calls that resulted in

Lynn Swann, USC flanker, 1971-72-73.

two of his team's six turnovers.

On Roberson's interception, Rodgers contended Sciarra stepped out of bounds before his release; and on Sciarra's fourth quarter fumble, Rodgers maintained the QB had started forward motion with his arm when smacked by Sims. Sciarra agreed. "I didn't think it should have been ruled a fumble," he said. "I was just starting to throw."

Sims disagreed. "I was blitzing and got to Sciarra just as he was starting to throw."

The list of Trojan warhorses for the game was almost endless... Haden, Davis, McKay, Moore, Doris, Anthony, Wood, Sims, Brown, Roberson and even a freshman, Gary Jeter.

"This was our best game of the season," commented McKay, "and it obviously wasn't their's because of mistakes."

And while UCLA waded under the cumber of turnovers, USC cruised through a near-faultless enactment. McKay was beside himself. "We didn't jump offsides but once," he jostled. "My coaching was outstanding."

The Rose Bowl was next for Southern Cal. "It doesn't matter who we play," shouted Sims. "Just bring 'em on."

The opponent turned out to be Ohio State, the Big-10 champ which was seeking revenge for the lashing it took in the previous Rose Bowl from USC. The Buckeyes got it, 42-32 . . . shaping the Trojan's year at 9-2-1.

For UCLA, the USC game spelled finis to its 9-2-0 season, and to Rodgers' regime at Westwood. The colorful Pepper heeded a call from his alma mater, and would return to Georgia Tech.

His three year slate at UCLA was 19 triumphs, 12 defeats and one tie. But he would leave behind a legacy of Pacific-8 offensive records: most yards total offense in one season (5,177, snapping USC's 1970 mark of 4,956) and most yards rushing (4,403, breaking UCLA's figure of 3,810 established in 1972). Also, Rodgers' last team scored 470 points, the most any UCLA team had ever amassed.

Summary

	USC	UCLA
First Downs	19	19
Yards Rushing	222	249
Yards Passing	94	82
Total Yards	316	331
Passes Attempted	15	10
Passes Completed	8	5
Passes Had Intercepted	0	2
Fumbles Lost	0	4
Punts/Average	4/37.5	1/39
Penalties No./Yards	4/28	3/25

Scoring by Quarters:

USC	7	10	3	3	—	23
UCLA	3	7	0	3	—	13

1974
Game 44

1974, A.D.

To some people, A.D. means Anno Domini, in the year of the Lord. But ask anyone along Exposition or Hoover or Jefferson or Vermont Streets and you'll get a different translation. A.D. stands for Anthony Davis . . . they'll all tell you that.

And, if you ask, they'll tell you how the senior scatback strutted and squirmed for 195 yards and a touchdown on the afternoon of November 23rd, a clear, warm day, to guide Southern California to a convincing 34-9 pasting of arch rival UCLA. Don't ask—they'll bend your ear, anyway.

The outcome of the debacle was no startling surprise; the margin was.

Siding with the Bruins would get you 15 points, and you'd have to go back a long way to find a USC-UCLA contest with a spread that huge.

"I'll be disappointed if it's a 15-point game," said Dick Vermeil, UCLA's new head coach, "disappointed for our kids. They have pride. They'll be ready to play."

The area sports writers went along with the odds, and then some. Their margin was 17 points, with USC receiving 21 of 23 votes polled.

As usual, USC head coach John McKay came to the point. "Based on comparative teams we've played, the point spread is out of line," he stated.

But gamboleers along Spring Street had a reason, two reasons in fact, for setting the wide 15-point spread: quarterback John Sciarra,

UCLA's total offense leader, and running back Wendell Tyler, tops among Bruin rushers. Neither would play, due to injuries.

Alluding to Sciarra, McKay sympathized, "Anytime a coach loses a guy he has picked for No. 1, it's got to hurt. Sciarra is solid."

But Sciarra had confidence that his mates would excel under the mantle of underdog. "The odds won't change our attitude at all," he expounded. "We'll give 100 per cent, and if we're fired up enough, we can best them."

Sports editors of the school newspapers joined the hassle, too.

"Everybody has kind of taken it for granted that we'll beat the Bruins"—Loren Ledlin of the *Daily Trojan*.

"I'd like to be optimistic, but I just can't be"—Marc Dellins, of the *Daily Bruin*.

Southern Cal was dumped by Arkansas in its curtain-lifter, then rode roughshod over Pittsburgh, Iowa, Washington State, Oregon and Oregon State before California drew a draw. Then the Trojans clipped Stanford and Washington, all of which etched a 7-1-1 slate and a seventh spot national ranking, with UCLA upcoming.

The Uclans were a step or two behind with a 6-2-2 ledger. Vermeil's victims were Michigan State, Utah, Washington State, California, Oregon and Oregon State; his conquerors were Iowa and Washington; his equals were Tennessee and Stanford.

UCLA would enter three players—Norm Anderson, Gene Clark and Fulton Kuykendall—of All-Coast calibre into combat but USC would counter that with five of All-America stature—Richard Wood, Davis, Charles Phillips, Bill Bain and Jim Obradovich.

Replacing Sciarra at QB for the Ukes would be sophomore Jeff Dankworth. "I really feel confident I can do the job," he stated.

Vermeil's switch from a wishbone-T to a veer-T didn't seem to ruffle McKay. "There's not much difference," he pointed out.

So the rookie coach, the new kid on the block, the brash upstart had stacked his blocks and was in readiness to put them on the line in the Big Game with the veteran coach, the holder of three national championships, seven Rose Bowl appearances, eight conference titles, two Coach-of-the-Year awards, and 24 consecutive PAC-8 games without a loss.

"USC is the best team in the nation when it wants to be," commented Vermeil.

Over 82,000 zealots arrived at Memorial Coliseum to see for themselves just how good USC wanted to be.

They saw Davis dart through a gaping hole for 16 yards on his first carry, a scamper that broke O.J. Simpson's Pacific-8 career rushing record.

Pat Haden, USC quarterback and Bob McCaffrey, center, 1972-73-74.

On the same drive, Davis ran for another 16-yarder, David Farmer swept for 13, and from his 47-yard line, Pat Haden drilled a bullet to John McKay, son of the coach, that carried to UCLA's 39. The 70-yard march came to a TD conclusion on the ninth play when Haden scored on a rollout from eight yards out. Chris Limahelu converted; 7-0, USC.

Early in the second quarter, Limahelu padded SC's lead to 10-0 with a 20-yard field goal. It was the 14th play of a 68-yard journey that was spiced by dashes of 11 and nine yards by Haden and seven by Allen Carter.

Just as it seemed USC was going to stash the Bruins under the stadium, UCLA managed to crack the scoreboard. True, it was just a 24-yard field goal by Brett White, but 10-3 looked much better to Bruin fans than did a 10-point margin. The FG culminated a 60-yard, 10-play drive highlighted by gallops of 16 and 12 yards by Dankworth.

But the Trojans roared back. In eight plays, they erased 77 yards and, in the process, marked up another tally. The payoff was a spectacular 17-yard pitch from Haden which McKay snared with a backhanded twist, evaded Kent Pearce and Phil Kimble, and sped into the end zone. Earlier, Haden had sustained the jaunt by scrambling for 20 yards on third-and-13 from his 20-yard line. But the heartbeat of this movement was a brilliant 46-yard sprint by Davis, all the way to UCLA's 11. Limahelu was true; 17-3, USC.

Still, Joe Bruin would not play dead. Just before the first half ended, Dankworth teamed with his tight end, Gene Bleymaier, for a seven-yard touchdown toss, the fifth play of a 69-yard trek. Russel Charles skipped 37 yards and Dankworth hurled 14 yards to Norm Anderson to spotlight the excursion. Wood crashed through to block White's PAT attempt; so the clubs broke for recess with SC ahead, 17-9.

Whatever hope for victory that burned within the Uclans' chests was snuffed in the third period when McKay's marauders latched on to 10 more points, the first six of which were posted by Davis on an eight yard burst. It was the 12th play of an 81-yard foray that saw Haden pass to McKay for 11 and 14 yards. Limahelu's swing escalated USC's lead to 24-9.

SC's Danny Reece then intercepted Dankworth's heave intended for Steve Monahan. That led to Limahelu's record-breaking 50-yard field goal, the fourth play of a 35-yard push.

Moments later, Trojan Dennis Thurman, a freshman, plucked Charlie Schuhmann's fumble out of mid-air and breezed 80 yards to paydirt. Little Limahelu's conversion finalized the score at 34-9.

Aerial view of the UCLA campus, mid-1970s. Drake Stadium is in upper center.

"I was only thinking 'goal line' as I was running down the sideline," exuded Thurman, who also made two interceptions. "It's the kind of thing you dream about."

Not surprisingly, Davis was voted Player-of-the-Game. His 195 rushing yards inflated his season to 1,306 yards and his career to 3,609, surpassing Simpson's 3,423. "It's a great honor to be in the same category with O.J., but I didn't want the record if I couldn't have the win," said Davis.

"UCLA played well, we played well, we won," McKay summed up. "But I don't think it was our best game."

Trojan defenders most responsible for harassing Joe Bruin included Gary Jeter, Otha Bradley, Art Riley, Reece, Kevin Bruce and Wood, named Defensive-Player-of-the-Game.

Charles, with 81 yards, paced the Bruin ground attack. Dankworth netted 66 and passed for an additional 188 (12 for 25).

Vermeil told reporters USC was so good it might have won if UCLA had played its best game, praised Davis, and said he hoped the Trojans would "play like hell" on New Year's Day.

Bruins cited for outstanding defensive work were Rick Kukuliea, Gene Settles, Herschel Ramsey, Dale Curry and Fulton Kuykendall.

"We knew what they were going to do, exactly," remarked Kuykendall. "We went into the game thinking we could stop them. But they're just such a terrific offensive team."

The Uclans finished third in the PAC-8 and their overall mark was 6-3-2.

The Trojans were rolling now and it seemed nothing could stop them—not even Notre Dame. In a memorable comeback, USC bulldozed the Irish, 55-24. And that set the stage for their third straight meeting with Ohio State in the Rose Bowl.

'We're going home, baby, we're going home to the bowl," center Bob McCaffrey had shouted after the win over UCLA.

Southern Cal won in 1972, the Buckeyes in '73, so this would be the rubber game. It would also place "A.D." on the same field with the player who beat him for the Heisman Trophy, junior Archie Griffin.

But Ohio State found themselves cast in the same role as Notre Dame and UCLA... the role of loser. It was close, but USC prevailed, 18-17. The Trojans' card of 10-1-1 was good but not quite good enough, as Oklahoma was crowned national champions.

Summary

	USC	UCLA
First Downs	20	24
Yards Rushing	287	182
Yards Passing	56	188
Total Yards	343	370
Passes Attempted	8	25
Passes Completed	4	12
Passes Had Intercepted	0	3
Fumbles Lost	0	2
Punts/Average	5/35.8	3/37.6
Penalties No./Yards	9/128	8/66

Scoring by Quarters:

| USC | 7 | 10 | 10 | 7 | — | 34 |
| UCLA | 0 | 9 | 0 | 0 | — | 9 |

1975
Game 45

For Bobble or For Worse

Bold Joe Bruin stumbled nine times on his way to the altar, gulped to overcome his awkwardness, then deftly slipped a leather-encrusted ring on the dainty finger of Miss Victoria Bell. After the ceremony, the happy couple departed for a honeymoon in Pasadena, where it is said they spent a most delightful New Year's Day. The hand of the bride was given by Tommy Trojan, and the best man was Dick Vermeil.

That introduction was for the discreet who revel in the high brow of society. Now for the sports addicts: The bruising UCLA Bruins committed nine turnovers, regrouped to shed their mis-doings, then rammed the football down the throats of Southern California's Trojans, 25-22, to earn a trip to the Rose Bowl, where they baffled Ohio State. Neither team used a "shotgun" offense.

The 45th meeting of UCLA and USC, staunch rivals to the core, presented an intriguing sidelight. It would be the last Big Game for both head coaches. Vermeil, after only two years as UCLA's boss man, and John McKay, a legend after 16 years at the helm for USC, would both move into the ranks of professional tutoring. The bright Vermeil was headed for the Philadelphia Eagles (although not yet announced), the crafty McKay would tackle the job of cultivating the newly-spawned franchise at Tampa Bay.

Until McKay announced his plans to relocate, SC had powered past Duke, Oregon State, Purdue, Iowa, Washington State, Oregon and Notre Dame . . . unmarred in seven games. After the revelation, the Trojans were winless against California, Stanford and Washington. That was their seal . . . 7-3-0, with UCLA on the horizon.

Naturally, the abrupt about-face hurt McKay. "For one thing, you don't expect to lose," he said. "For another, your fans do not expect you to lose."

According to *Associated Press* rankings, UCLA had the 14th best team in the nation; the *United Press* poll revealed them 16th best. (Among the Top 20, USC was nowhere in sight.)

The Bruins' rating was penned in a 7-2-1 ledger. In black ink were entered the names of Iowa State, Tennessee, Stanford, Washington State, California, Oregon and Oregon State; in red ink were Ohio State and Washington; and scribbled in pencil was a tie with Air Force.

Consider the facts. The Bruins: a slightly better record, an aroma of roses tickling their palate, a PAC-8 title theirs for the taking, an explosive offense, a team on the perk. The Trojans: indecisiveness at quarterback, a lame duck coach, a dutiful date in the Liberty Bowl, a potent defense, a team on the skid.

To the surprise of no one, UCLA was installed as the favorite to win, the spread set at two points.

"I sincerely feel," ventured Vermeil, "that if we play our best football of the year, we can win." That's playing it cool, Dick.

McKay was more specific: "We know UCLA will probably score two or three times, so if we're going to have a chance, we'll have to do the same thing."

Each squad sported a running back with imposing talents, juniors both. UCLA's Wendell Tyler would need only 44 yards to snap Kermit Johnson's school rushing record of 1,129 yards for a single season. But USC had the country's leading rusher in All-American Ricky Bell, and he could break the NCAA record held by Cornell's Ed Marinaro by getting 143 yards in the Big Game.

"Nobody can really stop Bell," Vermeil observed. "What we must do is keep USC in such field position that he must run a long way."

Besides Bell, SC would line-up with another All-American, offensive tackle Marvin Powell. But UCLA could off-set that pair with a trio of AA's—Randy Cross, Cliff Frazier and John Sciarra.

Though a senior, Sciarra had never started a game against USC. But he had the respect of McKay. "Anytime you face a quarterback who can run as well as Sciarra," he stated, "you have an extra

Dick Vermeil, UCLA Head Coach, 1974 to 1975.

burden on your defense."

It was a cold, blustery night, the last Friday in November, that greeted a crowd of 80,927 hearty souls as they filed into the Coliseum. The "John, we love you" badges adorning the lapels and jackets of many USC fans were flashed through video tape cameras into living rooms across the land, as McKay, stolid and drawn, dispatched his Trojans onto the Coliseum turf for the last time.

Pick up the action, first quarter. The Trojans took the opening kickoff and conducted a 71-yard maneuver that paid off with the battle's first touchdown. On the 11th play, Bell lunged over from one yard out. He had helped locate the ball in scoring position with runs of eight and 16 yards, along with an eight yard dash by Vince Evans and an aerial from Evans to Randy Simmrin, good for 13. Glen Walker's PAT was good; 7-0, USC.

UCLA retaliated by traveling 80 yards in 13 plays. Along the way, Sciarra kept twice for 16 yards. Tyler added 11 and Eddie Ayers tacked on eight before scoring the TD from the five-yard line. Brett White's kick failed; 7-6, USC.

Early in the second period, Evans swept four yards into paydirt on a keeper as Southern Cal pulled away to a 14-6 advantage. It was a drive made of Evans, as the strong-armed QB threw twice to Simmrin for 17 and 18 yards, and sprinted once for 15. Walker again kicked the PAT.

The marker jolted the Bruins, who then traveled a quick 80 yards in just four plays. Sciarra sped for 19 yards and Tyler skipped and skittered for 57, which was all he needed to cross the double stripe. The Uclans tried for two points, to no avail; 14-12, USC.

Loving the taste of SC's end zone, the Bruins went back for more. Starting from its 14-yard line, UCLA tallied in 10 plays to go ahead for the first time at 18-14, which was the score at intermission. Sciarra pitched 18 yards to Dan Pederson for the six-pointer. Key plays in the trip were jogs of 13 and 16 yards by Sciarra, and 18 by Ayers. The run for two points was short.

Early in the third period, Harold Hardin wrapped himself around a Mosi Tatupi fumble on Troy's 19-yard stripe and - zap - the Bruins tallied in one all-consuming play. Again, it was the Sciarra-to-Pederson combination that clicked. The Bruins finally converted, thanks to White's kick, so UCLA led, 25-14.

Turn-around is fair play, so UCLA bungled the ball back to USC in the final stanza, as Ayers lost the handle and Kevin Bruce found it on Westwood's 12-yard line. On the third play, Bell scampered into the end zone from three yards out. He then repeated the feat for a two-pointer, which brought the scoring to a close at 25-22, UCLA.

John McKay, USC Head Coach, 1960 to 1975.

UCLA DROPS BALL BUT HOLDS ROSES
USC Loses in McKay's Farewell, 25-22

Unable to stand prosperity, the Bruins thereafter enacted several attempts to situate the game on a silver platter and present it to USC.

Sciarra flung an interception to Reece; White missed a 44-yard FG attempt; Tyler committed his fourth bobble, but Cliff Frazier and Dale Curry forced the Trojans to try a long field goal, which Art Sorce missed; White dropped a wide snap on punt formation, but, after Rod Martin recovered for SC, the Bruin defense held again; Kenny Lee lost fumble No. 8 for the Bruins; and finally, in desperation, Sciarra just fell to earth with the ball to let the final ticks tock away. On the bright side, the Uclans mishandled no kicks . . . since they didn't punt a single time.

The conflict was fraught with negatives. UCLA's eight abandoned balls (11 total fumbles) set a new PAC-8 record; it was the first time Southern Cal had dropped four consecutive conference games since joining the league in 1922; and Bell, with 136 yards on 36 totes, fell six yards shy of the NCAA record.

On the positive side, it was UCLA's first conference title and subsequent trip to the Rose Bowl in 10 years, as well as its first victory over the Trojans since 1970.

As heralded as was the Bruins' offense, it may have been their defense that preserved their hides.

"I've been waiting for this moment," shouted UCLA's Frazier, with pride. "Now I can say it. Our defense is great, we showed the nation."

Sciarra agreed. "What about that defense? Weren't they something?"

In the understatement of the night, Vermeil suggested, "That's the hard way to win. If we hadn't turned it over so much, it probably would have been an entirely different ball game. We were just fortunate to win."

The Bruins' total yardage amounted to 414, of which Tyler claimed 130 on 17 rushes. That soared his season to 1,256 yards, enabling him to mold a new campus record. Sciarra rushed for 85 yards and passed for 86.

Speaking for the offense, senior guard Phil McKinnely remarked "We were confident we could move the ball. Our line is a solid, fine unit."

Coach Dick Vermeil and Jeff Smith, Cliff Frazier and John Sciarra take possession of the Victory Bell, 1975.

Some of the Trojans weren't overly impressed with the decorum of certain Bruins during the heat of the battle.

"Don't talk to me about UCLA. They got no class," muttered Harold Steele. Bruce joined in, though perhaps with more elocution. "John Sciarra and some of the other guys on that team have a lot of class; most of the others, I wouldn't let in my house." Bruce did wish the Bruins well in the Rose Bowl, though.

McKay, as expected, was his usual, erudite self: "Well, they just outplayed us and won."

So, with a game of bob-bob-bobbling, of bungling, fumbling and rumbling, of crossfire between blunder and brilliance, and a game difficult to distinguish between fact and fantasy, the two institutions regrouped their troops for invasions of bowls.

Southern Cal, participating in a bowl other than the Rose for the first time, journeyed to the banks of the wide Mississippi to take on Texas A&M in the Liberty Bowl. After four straight humiliations, a cop-out would have been the easy way. But that's not the Southern Cal way. It's a monument to the players that SC pulled itself together and flattened the Aggies, 20-0, sending the legendary McKay to the pros with a game to remember.

"John McKay is a winner," said Vermeil, "He can coach any team and still win."

Of equal import was the manner in which UCLA turned the tables on Ohio State, making its fourth straight appearance in the Rose Bowl. Earlier in the season, the Buckeyes had blistered the Bruins, 41-20.

"There's no question that we're a much better team now than when we played Ohio State," commented Vermeil, whose two-year record at UCLA was 15-5-3.

Either he was right, or there was some deterioration back east, for the Uclans staggered the Big-10 champs, 23-10, moving to fifth on the national chart on the strength of a 9-2-1 slate.

So the season ended, Vermeil was leaving and McKay was gone. Some of USC's great stars had stopped by to pay their respects to the cunning veteran . . . O.J. Simpson, Mike Garrett, Anthony Davis, and others.

"Well, they've been the happiest days of my life," reflected McKay, sedately.

Summary

	UCLA	USC
First Downs	23	16
Yards Rushing	328	175
Yards Passing	86	111
Total Yards	414	286
Passes Attempted	9	24
Passes Completed	3	7
Passes Had Intercepted	1	0
Fumbles Lost	8	1
Punts/Average	0	5/45.6
Penalties No./Yards	2/10	5/45

Scoring by Quarters:

| UCLA | 6 | 12 | 7 | 0 | — | 25 |
| USC | 7 | 7 | 0 | 8 | — | 22 |

1976
Game 46

The Low Down on High Ranks

Not since 1952 had UCLA and USC brought such majestic rankings to the arena for their annual bash with each other. The Bruins, with a 9-0-1 chart, were the No. 2 rated team in the nation; the Trojans were just a step behind at No. 3, thanks to an 8-1-0 slate.

UCLA was the second best scoring team in the land with an average point production of 37.1 per game; the Trojans were just a step behind at No. 3, thanks to a 36.8 average.

Southern California led the nation in total offense, averaging 455.9 yards a game; UCLA was just two steps behind in third place, thanks to a 446 average.

UCLA was the second best team in the country in rushing offense, averaging 361.5 yards per outing; USC was just a few paces behind in seventh position, thanks to a 293.3 average.

And all this with rookie coaches doing the high jinks for both clubs; Terry Donahue at Westwood, John Robinson at Troy.

Donahue's Demons had achieved their offensive blue ribbons with a devastating veer-T formation; Robinson's Raiders with a power-I attack.

"Down through the years," said Robinson, "most of football's great teams have been power teams."

Donahue explained the basic difference: "On a veer play we stretch the defense until we see a crack, then use one of three options to attack there. The I-formation principle tries to pound a hole open."

Besides the concern for his offense, both coaches had a nagging problem: injuries to their bread-and-butter runners. USC's Ricky Bell, whose 3,431 yards spotted him as No. 2 among Pacific-8 league career rushers, and UCLA's Wendell Tyler, whose 3,070 yards was the leader among Bruin all-time rushers, were both hobbled.

And if Robinson was plagued with Bell's readiness, Bell was fretting about UCLA. "They have a quick, strong, aggressive defense that moves to the ball really well in pursuit," he stated.

Both squads sported outstanding quarterbacks. Jeff Dankworth had 1,359 total yards while completing 55.1 per cent of his Bruin passes; Vince Evans had 1,074 yards with 52 per cent for SC.

"USC is very strong at the point of attack," observed Dankworth. "They seem more disciplined than last year."

Dankworth was one of three All-Americans UCLA would depend upon for direction, the other two being Oscar Edwards and Jerry Robinson. But four AA's would trot onto the field for USC; Bell, Dennis Thurman, Marvin Powell and Gary Jeter.

Picking the favorite was difficult, but UCLA got the nod—by two points. Certain head coaches and players up and down the coast, however, didn't agree.

In a poll conducted by Skip Bayless of the *LA Times*, coaches Jackie Sherrill of Washington State and Craig Fertig of Oregon State, jumped on the Trojan chariot, while Jack Christiansen of Stanford, Don James of Washington, Don Reed of Oregon and Mike White of California, all said, in effect, flip a coin. Of the players polled, seven joined the Trojan bandwagon while only one, Oregon QB Jack Henderson, felt UCLA would win.

The Bruins leaped to a good start, lacing Arizona State, Arizona and Air Force before hitting a 10-10 snag with Ohio State. UCLA then reeled off six conquests in a row—Stanford, Washington State, California, Washington, Oregon and Oregon State.

Some of the Trojans thought they were overconfident when they fell to Missouri in the lid-opener. If so, it was good medicine as Troy spooned a dose of victories over Oregon, Purdue, Iowa, Washington State, Oregon State, California, Stanford and Washington.

At stake was the Rose Bowl (UCLA could get there with a tie), the league championship (for the 19th time in the crosstown series), state and city crowns, plus a possible shot at national champion.

With freshmen enthusiasm, the two coaches respected each

THURMAN GIVES USC A GAME BALL...
...Trojans Take It to Pasadena, 24-14

other's ability, and both stood in awe at the magnitude commanded by the series.

"The USC game is something very special," observed Donahue. "The players run harder, hit harder and, on Sunday, hurt more."

Robinson knew how much the game meant to the players. "I think if somebody from UCLA called us and said the game was set for midnight on Thursday, both teams would be there," he opined.

But it was set for Saturday afternoon and, not only the players, but 95,019 fans as well, showed up for the confab at the Coliseum on a warm, sunny day.

Goal lines were untarnished in the first quarter, but in the second, the ball squirted from the hands of UCLA's Theotis Brown, SC's Thurman snatched it in mid-air and fled 47 yards for the game's first touchdown.

"It was just a poor exchange," brooded Brown, "but it cost us the game."

The play was reminiscent of a similar pick-off by the same Thurman the previous year. "That '74 game flashed through my mind when the ball came to me," exuded Thurman. "The ball just squirted out of his hands into mine."

Glen Walker booted the extra point, staking Southern Cal to a 7-0 halftime lead.

That became 10-0 in the third period when Walker slammed thru a 43-yard field goal, climaxing a 72-yard thrust in a dozen plays. To reach Walker's range, Bell hauled leather for 14, nine, eight and six yards, and Dave Farmer snared an eight-yard pass from Evans.

Methodically pulling away, the Trojans tallied early in the fourth stanza and then again just a few moments later, to escalate the scene to 24-0.

Bell pushed over the first TD on a one-yard buck that culminated a 61-yard jaunt, and Evans seared the Bruin defense with a dazzling 36-yard burst for the second.

Bell's marker was accomplished with the taint of a controversial pass interference call—Levi Armstrong on (or near) Randy Simmrin—that left the Trojans needing just a yard, which Bell got.

"All I know is that we both went for the ball and there was a collision," said Simmrin.

Vince Evans led USC to an 11-1 record, 1976.

Evans' nifty scamper was made possible when Rod Martin despoiled a Dankworth toss on his 47-yard line and hot-footed 17 yards with the ball. Walker converted after both TDs.

"I think they thought I was going to pass when I took this half-rollout," pointed out Evans.

Meanwhile, the Bruins were a study in placid immobility, failing to reach midfield in two quarters. Their deepest penetration had been to USC's 34-yard stripe.

But with the shocking prospect of a lambasting in the making, UCLA finally lit up the scoreboard in the last four minutes of the game, twice.

For the first, Brown capped a 60-yard trip in nine plays, slashing over the goal from nine yards out. The biggest gainer was Dankworth's 10-yard pitch to Wally Henry. The Bruins made good on a two-pointer, Dankworth to Rick Walker, but trailed 24-8.

Frank Corral dribbled an on-sides kickoff and Michael Moline squatted on the ball for UCLA at SC's 47. On the fifth play, Dankworth dodged in for six-points. His 32-yard aerial to James Sarpy featured the drive. The two-pointer failed, but the Uclans came right back with another on-sides try on the kickoff. It, too, failed, and along with it, UCLA's chance for a comeback of reward. Final score: USC 24, UCLA 14.

The game could be capsuled into three basic components: the Trojans squelched the Bruins with its defense, pulverized them with their offense, and consistently got the break on close plays and judgment calls that could have gone either way.

Robinson focused on the first item listed above, heaping credit on "... (Coach) Marv Goux, who heads our defense."

But to list Trojans noteworthy of defensive praise would be simply to scan the roster... Jeter, Clint Strozier, Thurman, Ricky Odom, Eric Williams, Walt Underwood, Ron Bush, David Lewis, Harold Steele, Rich Dimler, Vinny Van Dyke, Clay Matthews, Garry Cobb and, probably, the water boy.

The fellows who carry the ball weren't overlooked by Robinson, either... Bell, who netted 167 yards, Evans, Farmer and Mosi Tatupu.

Then to make sure he had touched all bases, Robinson added, "I just can't say enough about our offensive line." (Anybody left out?)

Brown's 63 yards was tops for the Bruins, followed by Tyler with 52. Dankworth ran for 25 yards and threw for 90.

"SC won today because they outplayed us," Donahue conceded, then quickly added, "On this particular day."

But now it was time to go bowling and off to Memphis went the Bruins, there to hopefully sandbag the Crimson Tide of Alabama in the Liberty Bowl. Coach Bear Bryant's 'Bama boys had other notions, though, and dispatched Joe Bruin back to Westwood on the short end of a 36-6 sheet. Donahue's first show in the big time finished 9-2-1.

Pasadena awaited the Trojans, primed with Robinson's Rose Bowl acceptance outburst, "We're back where we belong." It was a close battle, but Southern Cal knocked off Michigan, 14-6, for its 11th conquest in a row. Still, there was no room at the top, as Pittsburgh wore the tiara of national champions.

Forty-seven years had now sifted into the sands of time since

Southern California and UCLA lined up for their first kickoff. Tempus fugit. Since that memorable date, the Trojans had carted away 26 wins, the Bruins 14, and six were tied. USC had scored 832 points, UCLA 581.

Summary

	USC	UCLA
First Downs	25	15
Yards Rushing	266	140
Yards Passing	79	90
Total Yards	345	230
Passes Attempted	13	17
Passes Completed	7	8
Passes Had Intercepted	1	1
Fumbles Lost	0	1
Punts/Average	5/32.4	7/44.5
Penalties No./Yards	8/100	3/42

Scoring by Quarters:

USC	0	7	3	14	—	24
UCLA	0	0	0	14	—	14

UCLA's Jeff Dankworth, All-America, 1976

1977
Game 47

Bruins Short, by a Foot

Southern California was without any time-outs as it drove relentlessly toward UCLA's goal, trailing by one point, and the clock grinding mercilessly toward its double zeroes in the fourth quarter.

From the Bruin 40-yard line, SC quarterback Rob Hertel fired 17 yards to Randy Simmrin. Dwight Ford plunged to the 19-yard stripe and Hertel pitched out of bounds to halt the clock at 22 seconds.The Uclans, fighting for their lives, jammed a full-back drive by Mosi Tatupu for no gain. With Big Ben ticking away, the Trojans hurriedly lined up for a do-or-die field goal effort.

A stocky junior took his stance and, with two seconds remaining, drilled his kick on dead center through the uprights for three points. Frank Jordan was the hero of USC's nail-biting 29-27 victory over UCLA.

And if Jordan was the fair-haired boy, UCLA safetyman Johnny Lynn may have been the goat. For it was his pass interference infraction on Kevin Williams—controversial though it may have been—that pumped new life into the Trojan movement when it was about to expire at mid-field on third-and-10. After the penalty was assessed to UCLA's 40, USC clamored on for its game-winning FG.

Oddly, Lynn did not know the interference call was on him until he reached the locker room. "I was hurt on the play and came out, that's why," divulged Lynn. "But I don't feel I hit him. I dove out in front of him and hit the ball with my right hand. When I hit the ground, I hurt my knee."

Head linesman F. E. Conley didn't see it that way and threw a flag. USC Coach John Robinson backed up the official ("definitely was pass interference"), as did receiver-to-be Williams ("definitely was"). But UCLA Coach Terry Donahue refused to comment, explaining he did not have a vantage position.

The season had been one of disappointment in the land of Troy as their warriors, a pre-season nominee for laurels, limped into the Big Game with six victories, four losses and a wilted rose on each hip pad.

USC had been prone to err, its own worst enemy, so to speak. "If we had played error-free football on offense, we could have and probably should have won all our games," said Robinson. "Those errors have destroyed us."

The Trojans clipped Missouri, Oregon State, TCU and Washington State, were nipped by Alabama, drubbed Oregon, were thumped by Notre Dame and California, blanked Stanford and bowed to Washington.

But Donahue knew the brawn that lay beneath the bosom of this ungainly giant. "USC physically is one of the best teams in the nation," he remarked, "and we'll have to play our best to stand a chance."

The bookmakers didn't think too soundly of the Bruins chance, making them a six-point underdog, despite a superior 7-3-0 record. UCLA had licked Kansas, Iowa, Washington State, California, Washington, Oregon and Oregon State while being soaked by Houston, Minnesota and Stanford.

There were three All-Americans on the field; Dennis Thurman and Clay Matthews for USC, Jerry Robinson for UCLA, but both clubs were treading the season with new, untested quarterbacks—astute Rob Hertel at USC, and Rick Bashore at UCLA. Bashore, a man of few words, was recuperating from a broken rib and a collapsed lung, so Steve Bukich was standing in the wings.

Hertel, a senior but a one-year starter, had set an infamous Trojan record by having 16 of his passes intercepted.

"Because of my inexperience, little things have gone wrong," stated Hertel. "My biggest disappointment is throwing so many interceptions. But I don't think any team we lost to is better than we are."

Over 86,000 fans packed Memorial Coliseum on a warm Friday night late in November to see which would prevail—the physical power of the Trojans or the motivation of the Bruins. That's right, motivation. A triumph by the Uclans would embark them to the Rose Bowl.

Ricky Bell, USC Heisman Trophy Runner-up

Well, after Frank Corral boomed a 52-yard field goal to terminate a Bruin 86-yard journey, that ol' nemesis called "mistake" reared its ugly head to bedevil the Trojans. Charles White fumbled on his three-yard line and Mike Molina recovered for UCLA. It took four plays, but Theotis Brown crashed over from the one, Corral converted, and UCLA led, 10-0.

That was the first quarter. The second belonged to Southern Cal, which tallied a field goal and two touchdowns for a 17-10 lead at intermission.

Jordan kicked the FG, a 25-yarder, after Hertel hurled passes of 13 and 21 yards to Simmrin, 16 to Ford and scrambled for six himself. It was a 71-yard drive.

Both touchdowns were shot from the arm of Hertel, too . . . 20 yards to Bill Gay and 40 to Williams, to tap off 70 and 52-yard movements. Jordan missed the first conversion, but Hertel tossed to Gay for two digits on the second.

The halftime break didn't cool the verve of Hertel, who came right back with a 27-yard TD strike to Williams to cap a 53-yard trek. Jordan again was wide on the PAT, but the diminutive kicker compensated for the miscue by hitting a 36-yard field goal, lifting USC to a 26-10 advantage. Ed Gutierrez had recovered Bashore's fumble on UCLA's 41 to set the drive in motion.

Finally, after 26 unanswered points, the Bruins revived their offense. Brown returned the ensuing kickoff 29 yards, and UCLA scored in five plays. The TD came when Bashore drifted to his right, stopped, and fired a crossfield missile to James Owens, all alone in the end zone. Corral kicked true, and the third frame ended with USC ahead, 26-17.

UCLA's Bryan Baggott then pilfered a Hertel heave on USC's 48, which led to a Corral 20-yard field goal and a 26-20 composite.

Now the game was boiling, a genuine sizzler on the brew. With time becoming a factor, the Bruins marched 80 yards in 16 plays, the last of which was a play-action, one-yard pass from Bashore to Don Pederson for a TD on fourth down. Key plays along the way were aerials from Bashore of 14 yards to Pederson and 19 to Owens, plus runs of 10 by Owens and 13 by Bashore.

The score was knotted, but Corral's talented toe unraveled it as UCLA forged ahead, 27-26, with less than three minutes to play. Roses began to bloom.

But then came Southern Cal's fatal 63-yard drive, the 13th play being Jordan's pressure-packed, game-winning field goal. The roses withered.

"It all happened so quick," expounded Jordan, "I didn't have time

Cheers turn to tears as USC's Frank Jordan kicks a winning field goal on the last play of the game, 1977.

to think about it. I didn't even know if it went through or not, but I could soon tell by how they were jumping on me."

Robinson gave the sideline view. "I called the block play for the field goal rush," he said "And that's all I remember. I looked up and saw the ball go through the uprights."

Someone, meaning well of course, asked Donahue if there was a tougher way to lose a game. There was a long pause as Donahue fought to maintain his composure.

"No," he replied in a low tone. "But what kind of question is that? Ask me something I can answer."

Hertel, the year-long whipping boy for the Trojans, vindicated himself by throwing for three touchdowns, setting a school single season record of 15. For the game, he completed 15 of 24 for 254 yards, and was named the game's top offensive player.

"Rob did an absolutely brilliant job," praised Robinson.

Bashore, busted rib and all, completed 11 of 18 passes for 136 yards, and trotted for 51 more. "We'll be back next year," vowed Bashore. His teammate, linebacker Robinson was selected top defender of the game, with 23 tackles.

"I guess this shows this is the best rivalry in the nation," observed tight end Pederson. "Every year, it seems the game is like this."

The season had come to an abrupt and unhappy end for UCLA, but USC, by tipping the Bruins, won a berth in the Bluebonnet Bowl at Houston. There they met and trounced Texas A&M, 47-28.

So, with two verdicts at season's-end forming an 8-4-0 record, the Trojans found some redemption. The Bruins finished 7-4-0, but that last, heartbreaking loss overshadowed the other 10 games. Truly, it was as UCLA's *Southern Campus* yearbook read, "... a game of cheers and tears".

Note: Due to violations in recruiting, UCLA was forced to forfeit every game it had won during the year. Officially, the Bruins were 0-11-0.

Summary

	USC	UCLA
First Downs	20	18
Yards Rushing	140	174
Yards Passing	254	136
Total Yards	394	310
Passes Attempted	24	18
Passes Completed	15	11
Passes Had Intercepted	2	1
Fumbles Lost	1	1
Punts/Average	3/46.3	4/37.0
Penalties No./Yards	7/41	4/35

Scoring By Quarters:

USC	0	17	9	3	—	29
UCLA	10	0	7	10	—	27

1978
Game 48

A Game Divided

The late Ed Danforth, erstwhile sports editor of the Atlanta *Journal,* had a way of equalizing things. One autumn day, some visiting team squashed Georgia Tech, 37-7; the winners scoring all 37 of their points in the first half, while the Jackets got their skimpy seven in the second half.

Addressing Tech Coach Bobby Dodd, Danforth drawled in his gravel tone, "Well, Robert, they won the first half and we won the second half, and in my books, that's a tie."

UCLA Coach Terry Donahue would buy that.

In the 48th clash of UCLA and Southern California, the Trojans won the first half with 17 points, while the Bruins won the second half with 10. As halves go, that may be a tie, but the official result of the game will forever more be indelibled as a 17-10 victory for USC. Sorry about that, Terry.

Over the years, Southern Cal had been stereotyped as the "big, strong Trojans" and UCLA as the "gutty, little Bruins". Deservedly or not, these were the syndromes that each would carry into the 48th battle.

"Nothing has changed," said Donahue.

Based on a record of eight wins and one loss, plus fifth spot in the national rankings, USC was installed a seven point favorite. The Trojans led the Pacific-10 conference in total defense, rushing defense, scoring defense and total offense.

Compiling its fine slate, SC bowled over Texas Tech, Oregon, Alabama, Michigan State, Oregon State, California, Stanford and Washington. Arizona State, its fifth opponent, was the splotch.

In the PAC-10 listings, the Uclans were second in rushing offense and in scoring and fifth in total defense. They tendered 8-2-0 credentials, respectable by any standard. Washington, Tennessee, Minnesota, Stanford, Washington State, California, Arizona and Oregon were mauled by Joe Bruin, but Kansas and Oregon State escaped his mitts.

Not many gridirons throughout the land would offer defensive stalwarts to compare with USC's Dennis Thurman or UCLA's Kenny Easley and Jerry Robinson, All-Americans all.

Robinson, in fact, was a three-time selectee, the first player to accomplish this feat since Doak Walker in the late forties.

"He's the guy who holds it all together," California Coach Roger Theder told *Times* writer Terry Shepard.

"You feel he's going to be a factor no matter what you do," added USC Coach John Robinson. "He has great range, intensity and intelligence."

So, surprisingly, a few eyebrows were raised when Foster Andersen, ex-Bruin player, ex-Trojan coach and ex-Ram coach, said: "If I had to pick one athlete off either team to start my own team, I'd pick Easley. That's right, I'd pick him over Jerry Robinson, Charles White or anyone you can name."

The White he mentioned was the nation's fifth best runner, averaging 139.8 yards per outing for SC. His 3,594 career yards placed him third (behind Ricky Bell and Anthony Davis) among all-time PAC-10 rushers. During the current season, he had gained 1,258 yards, thanks in no small degree to the excellent blocking of Lynn Cain.

Theotis Brown was UCLA's answer to White. Brown had accumulated 2,812 career yards, second only to Wendell Tyler's school mark. But Brown was not in A-1 condition for the impending scuffle.

The Bruins' Rick Bashore was billed as a better running quarterback than Paul McDonald, but the Trojan QB was the superior passer, having flung for 1,289 yards and 14 touchdowns.

The Trojans' forward wall that protected McDonald was spearheaded by All-American Pat Howell.

Fruits of the contest matched those of many previous conflicts: Rose Bowl, PAC-10 title, city champs, bragging rights, etc.

On the eve of the game, Donahue put it in perspective. "This represents what college football is all about," he stated. "A great game between two outstanding schools. It's the only rivalry of its

Theotis Brown rushed for 2,914 career yards at UCLA, 1976-77-78.

kind in the nation."

Over 90,000 people felt the same way and came out to the Coliseum under a clear sky to witness the melee.

As previously stated, USC monopolized first half scoring, stepping out front, 3-0, when Frank Jordan toed a 21-yard field goal in the first quarter. Cain's dodging, elusive dash of 26 yards helped to set it up.

The Trojans increased their lead to 17-0 in the second period, then turned the matter of preserving the lead over to its defense. It was the strong arm of McDonald that accounted for both markers.

On TD No. 1, McDonald found Bobby Hosea 36 yards away in the end zone, despite being hit on a vicious tackle by Bruin Brad Plemmons. Prior to the TD toss, McDonald threw strikes to Calvin Sweeney and Vic Rakhshani, 10 yards on each.

"I didn't think the pass would get there," related McDonald. "It's fortunate he (Plemmons) hit me from my right side." (McDonald was a portside flinger).

UCLA gave the Trojans an assist for their second touchdown. On the first play after the kickoff, Brown fumbled and Gary Cobb adopted the wayward ball for SC on UCLA's 17. It was a short trip made long by three penalties, but from the 10-yard line, McDonald spotted Kevin Williams slanting across the end zone and hit him in the numbers. Jordan's second PAT boosted Troy's lead to 17-0.

The most notable effort concocted by UCLA in the first half was interrupted when Herb Ward stole Bashore's pass on SC's 17-yard stripe. But the Bruins, behind Freeman McNeil's 14-yard gallop and Bashore's 19-yard aerial to Ken Brisbin, had fashioned a noteworthy drive before the interception.

In the third period, Bruin Manu Tuiasosopo stripped Cain from the ball deep in Trojan territory, Don Jackson recovered, and UCLA was in business on the six-yard line. From the two, James Owens plowed over the goal line, but there were 12 Bruins on the field, nullifying the TD.

Encouraged, the Trojans stiffened and UCLA had to settle for a field goal, a 22-yarder by Peter Boermeester. But the Bruins were on the board and now trailed, 17-3.

Westwood's only touchdown struck like lightening in the final frame. From his 19-yard line, Bashore bombed a rocket downfield which Severn Reece pulled down on SC's 37 and outran Tim Lavender to the goal line. Boermeester brought the final score to 17-10.

It was a game of few surprises, one that was played by the book and in line with forecasts.

"There's no doubt the Trojans were the superior team," remarked

Jerry Robinson (Nr 84), UCLA All-American linebacker, 1976, 1977 and 1978.

USC Fullback Lynn Cain (Nr 21) Blocks for Charles White.

Donahue. "Yes, they're the best team we've faced all year."

Southern Cal's defense restricted UCLA's rushing attack to 62 yards, far below its accustomed 264-yard average.

The ringleaders were Ty Sperling, Rich Dimler, Dennis Smith, Myron Lapka, Ron Lott, Garry Cobb, Dennis Johnson and Riki Gray.

"We held Brown, McNeil and Owens to under 100 yards, so our defense has to be congratulated," lauded Robinson. "They gave us a tremendous effort."

Leading the Bruin defense were Robinson with 21 tackes, Easley, Tuiasosopo and Jeff Muro.

"We've taken it down to the fourth quarter for two straight years," lamented Robinson. "It's rough."

But if things were rough on Robinson, the sailing was smooth for White. The junior All-American tailback rushed for 145 yards, escalating his career level to 3,739, best ever in the PAC-10.

The spurt that gained the pinnacle was an 11-yarder late in the fray. "I looked at the board after that run and knew I had it," exclaimed White. "I embraced everyone on our offensive team that made it possible."

White's coach, Robinson, was speechless. "I've run out of words to describe him."

All was not lost in the Big Game for the Uclan clan, though. The folks in Arizona invited them to the sprightly Fiesta Bowl, along with Arkansas. That evolved into a 10-10 draw, ending UCLA's season at 8-3-1.

But it appeared Southern Cal was just getting started. After UCLA came Notre Dame and that was a Trojan squeaker by two points. Then, after a romp over Hawaii, USC was ready for the Rose Bowl and Michigan. Mark that one up for the Trojans, too . . . 17-10.

Twelve triumphs and one defeat for the Robinson express—but Alabama, a 10-point loser to SC back in September—wound up as national champions.

Even Mr. Danforth might find it difficult to rationalize that.

Summary

	USC	UCLA
First Downs	16	9
Yards Rushing	213	62
Yards Passing	97	154
Total Yards	310	216
Passes Attempted	10	16
Passes Completed	7	8
Passes Had Intercepted	0	1
Fumbles Lost	1	1
Punts/Average	6/40.2	9/38.3
Penalties No./Yards	7/56	4/40

Scoring By Quarters:

| USC | 3 | 14 | 0 | 0 | — | 17 |
| UCLA | 0 | 0 | 3 | 7 | — | 10 |

1979
Game 49

A Lott of White

Southern California's All-American Charles White scored four touchdowns and Ron Lott posted one in the 49th renewal of the USC-UCLA annual brawl . . . and that was just in the first half. These early shenanigans led to a Trojan lead of 35-0 after two quarters— the widest halftime margin in the history of the series, including the 1929 rout.

It is moot to report that the warriors from Troy went on to capture the contest, unless the labor of fact demands completeness. If so, for the record, it was 49-14, and for a sidelight, that was the worst shellacking painted on a UCLA team by USC since the days of Howard Jones. (Gasoline was 20 cents a gallon then.)

The great majority of pre-game observers believed—no, they knew—that the fourth ranked, 9-0-1 Trojans would hang the unranked, 5-5-0 Bruins by their heels, they just didn't think the Trojans would cut the rope.

Dissident bettors, the brave few, were taking UCLA and 15 points, but in the end, it was they who were taken.

Still, USC Coach Robinson waxed caution on the inconsistent Bruins. "Those up-and-down teams are great when you catch them down," he said, "but when you catch them up, it gets kinda' scary."

Many UCLA-USC games in the past had determined which school would host the Rose Bowl; this would be the first to decide the host after the fact.

To explain that: USC had apparently clinched the Pacific-10 crown when it tumbled Washington, but Arizona State used ineligible players and had to forfeit all of its victories. That converted a Washington loss to the Sun Devils into a win, which scrambled the standings and put the Huskies back in contention.

So, realizing that life is no bed of roses, the Trojans had to prove themselves again to get some.

"We're not approaching this game as a spoiler—the idea of 'Let's knock USC out of the Rose Bowl'," remarked UCLA Coach Terry Donahue. "It's an opportunity for us to move up a notch in the conference and finish with a winning record."

After 48 engagements, the Bruins had trotted off the field in the attire of victor only 14 times. Sheila Moran, *Times* writer, wondered if this dominance by the Trojans might have a psychological effect on the Uclans, a mental block, so to speak.

Dr. Thomas Tutko, San Jose State psychologist, told her that "... being consistent losers is a UCLA liability in a way, as the players carry into the game that frame of reference".

But USC's Robinson remained leery of the Blue and Gold wearers. "We feel that UCLA's talent is among the best in the country," he said. "I know they've had some struggles for whatever reason this year, but I still think they're in the top six or eight teams in their ability." Then, acknowledging the ruling inherent to his shibboleth, he added, "Football is played on the field, not in the classroom."

In addition to White, Southern Cal had gleaned three other All-Americans in Brad Budde, Dennis Johnson and Paul McDonald. Kenny Easley was UCLA's lone selectee.

But the match-up attracting attention was that between tailbacks White and UCLA's Freeman McNeil. White had been churning ground at the rate of 178 yards a game, tops in the nation. On 258 carries he had gained 1,609 yards for the season, tops in the nation. And for his career, his 5,464 yards was second only to Tony Dorsett in NCAA history. The Heisman Trophy seemed a certainty.

White had even made a dent on that grizzly veteran down Alabama-way, Coach Bear Bryant. "I don't ever remember playing against a tailback that can run like that White," he observed.

And while not quite as imposing, McNeil needed no alibi for his stats: 1,276 yards on 241 rushes, third best in the nation, and closing in on the UCLA school record.

At quarterback, Donahue would start a freshman, Tom Ramsey; while Robinson would counter with McDonald, a left-handed senior. McDonald was the third best passer in the land, completing 63 percent of his passes for 1,790 yards and 16 touchdowns.

Brad Budde, USC Lombardi Award winner, 1979.

THE CRUSH OF '79: USC 49, UCLA 14
Trojans Turn It Into a Rout for the Roses as White Gets 4 TDs

Only Stanford had managed so much as a tie with Southern Cal, which had bottled Texas Tech, Oregon State, Minnesota, LSU, Washington State, Notre Dame, California, Arizona and Washington.

Things were more topsy-turvy at Westwood where the Bruins had bumped Purdue, Wisconsin, California, Arizona State and Oregon, but had submitted to Houston, Ohio State, Stanford, Washington State and Washington.

So, on a Saturday afternoon in late November, USC—the PAC-10 leader in total offense—took the field against UCLA before 88,214 fans at Memorial Coliseum.

White racked up his first half touchdowns on runs of two, one, 26 and two yards, capping USC drives of 78, 68, 26 and 67 yards. His third tally was set up when Larry McGrew recovered McNeil's errant lateral on UCLA's 26-yard line; the other three simply tailed long sustained drives.

During the four movements, the longest single gain from scrimmage (other than White's 26-yard TD run) was by Marcus Allen—20 yards. And McDonald's passes led to White's second marker, the senior lefty hooking up with White for 13 yards, to Dan Garcia for 10, to Ray Butler for 17 and to Vic Rakhshani for another 17.

In between White's mad dashes, Lott intercepted a Ramsey pitch on the Uclans' 30 and breezed across the double stripe, easily.

Eric Hipp converted five times and that's the way it was in the first half... 35-0, USC.

Bruin QB Ramsey, the yearling, had found rough going (three completions in 13 attempts, two interceptions), in the first half, so spectators were not too surprised to see veteran Rick Bashore warming up for the third quarter.

"I didn't think taking Ramsey out in the first half would be good for his future development," said Donahue. "The only really bad pass he threw was that first interception. It's easy to say 'yank him', but you've got to consider what he's done (in the past)."

Bashore got UCLA on the scoreboard on its first possession in the third period, connecting with Jojo Townsell for an electrifying 79-yard scoring pass moments after Tom Sullivan pilfered a McDonald pitch in the end zone. Pete Boermeester's PAT notched the score at 35-7.

But the Trojans canceled the effects of UCLA's TD when Mike Hayes returned the kickoff 40 yards, igniting a 55-yard jaunt to paydirt. The clincher was a five yard flip from McDonald to Rakhshani, and Hipp's kick made it 42-7, after three quarters.

Bashore found Townsell open again and delivered a five-yard touchdown strike to him, terminating a short trek born of a fumble. USC's Allen lost the ball and UCLA's Mike Barbee found it on Troy's 31-yard stripe. That made it 42-14 after Boermeester split the bars.

The official scorekeeper was haggard and worn when Hayes broke clear and skittered 54 yards for the final six-pointer of the skirmish. And the Bruins were haggard and worn when Rob Kerr booted the final one-pointer: USC 49, UCLA 14.

"We've got licked by a vastly superior team," acknowledged Donahue, "one that is extremely well-coached. I won't say this is the best USC team I've faced, but this is the weakest UCLA team I ever had going into an SC game."

Alan Greenberg reported in the *Times* that some thoughtless person asked Donahue if his team was dejected over the thrashing it took.

"If they weren't," snapped Donahue, "they better get over to the UCLA Medical Center and have a blood transfusion, their pulse taken and their heartbeat checked to see if they're still alive."

There was one bright item for the Uclans. McNeil gained 120 yards, raising his season mark to 1,396, a figure which exceeded Wendell Tyler's UCLA record.

But the main man was White: 194 yards on 35 carries, four pass receptions for 35 more, and four touchdowns (giving him 52 for his career).

The aura of confidence was a trademark of White. When he was a green-behind-the-ears freshman, he strode into Heritage Hall, pointed to the Heisman Trophies won by Mike Garrett and O. J. Simpson, and blurted, "I'm gonna' win me one or two of those."

Brashness, you can overlook. Talent, you cannot. White did win himself a Heisman Trophy, which is now on display alongside those of Garrett and Simpson.

As spectacular as were the feats of White, the heroics of McDonald were not far behind. Behind near-flawless protection, Mc-

Charles White, USC Heisman Trophy winner, 1979.

Donald completed 17 of 23 passes for 199 yards (one touchdown) and ran for 18 yards (one carry). Up front, Budde turned in an outstanding performance, another step which led to his winning the Lombardi Award.

UCLA's season was over at 5-6-0, but it was on to Pasadena for Southern Cal, its 10th visit in 14 years.

Feeling they had to twice win the PAC-10 title, Robinson, with a touch of sarcasm, said: "It might be premature to accept this Rose Bowl bid; there might be another (PAC-10) council meeting. But we're happy to accept it."

And the Trojans went on to justify their selection by nudging Ohio State, 17-16. It sealed another fabulous year for Southern Cal: 11 victories, no defeats, one tie. But guess who was the national champion? Alabama.

Summary

	USC	UCLA
First Downs	27	16
Yards Rushing	340	135
Yards Passing	199	258
Total Yards	539	393
Passes Attempted	23	30
Passes Completed	17	12
Passes Had Intercepted	1	3
Fumbles Lost	3	2
Punts/Average	3/42	5/36
Penalties No./Yards	4/29	4/40

Scoring By Quarters:

| USC | 14 | 21 | 7 | 7 | — | 49 |
| UCLA | 0 | 0 | 7 | 7 | — | 14 |

# 1980
Game 50

Tip in History

It's obvious none of the players on UCLA's 1980 football roster were history majors. So they were blameless for not knowing that fate was dressed in Cardinal and Gold anytime the outcome of a gridiron battle against Southern California came down to the wire. Somehow, someway, it was Lady Luck, or some sort of legerdemain, or just plain old-fashioned ability, that, with the clock ticking away in do-or-die situations, the resourceful Trojans would emerge in glory.

But the Bruins, not being history majors, didn't know that. All they knew, all they were concerned with was forever erasing the humiliation bestowed upon them by USC with that 49-14 thrashing 12 months previous. Revenge.

So it all seemed perfectly natural when, with just over two minutes left in the game and the Bruins in arrears by three points, that a Trojan defender should tip a pass into the arms of a Bruin receiver who would simply stroll for the winning touchdown. Revenge sought, revenge gained.

It happened sort of like that but more like this: two minutes, seven seconds to play. UCLA's ball on its 42-yard line, trailing 17-14. Reserve quarterback Jay Schroeder stepped back and threw long toward Freeman McNeil. Cornerback Jeff Fisher leaped high and deflected the ball into the eager arms of McNeil, who raced by safety Dennis Smith on his way to a 58-yard touchdown. Final score: UCLA 20, USC 17. Fate had changed her dress to Blue and Gold.

As the USC yearbook *El Rodeo* put it: "Trojans give Bruins a winning tip".

The game was billed as the "Probation Bowl", since neither UCLA nor USC were eligible for participation in any bowl, or to win the Pacific-10 title. Seems there was some violation of conference academic rules . . . hence, a wrist-slapper. Since 1971, one or both teams had played for the Rose Bowl . . . but not this time.

"I don't think the rivalry depends on the Rose Bowl," said UCLA Coach Terry Donahue. "There are many incentives and the Rose Bowl is just another added one. The game itself causes a great deal of excitement, anticipation and anxiousness."

Both clubs brought impressive records into the fracas; USC, 7-1-1 and UCLA 7-2-0. That slight edge made the Trojans a one point favorite to win.

Strewn in the ashes of Troy were Tennessee, South Carolina, Minnesota, Arizona State, Arizona, California and Stanford. Oregon pulled a tie from the fire, and Washington burned the Trojans.

The whizzes of Westwood captured six straight—Colorado, Purdue, Wisconsin, Ohio State, Stanford and California—before yielding to Arizona and Oregon. Then came a decision over Arizona State, and the Uclans were ready for the Trojans.

"I've grown up with a lot of these USC guys," stated Bruin Tim Wrightman. "That's what makes it so big for me. Coming out of that tunnel and getting hit with all that Blue and Gold on one side, Cardinal and Gold on the other—I can't describe it."

Trojan Kenny Moore summed it up: "This is the crosstown rivalry, the city championship. This is the biggest game of the season."

Junior Marcus Allen had stepped into the all-important tailback position, the workhorse spot in Southern Cal's assault. And, in the tradition of Trojan tailbacks, his 1,491 rushing yards was leading the nation.

USC would place three All-Americans on the field: Ronnie Lott, Keith Van Horne and Roy Foster. UCLA would counter with McNeil and Kenny Easley.

Both McNeil and Easley were banged up, but were determined to play. But Southern Cal's starting quarterback, Gordon Adams, had undergone a knee operation and would not play.

That left the signal-calling spot to Scott Tinsley, a sophomore of negligible experience but supreme confidence. "Shucks, this is why I came to USC," he drawled, "to play in front of 95,000 in the Coliseum."

Well, not quite that many folks showed up—83,491 to be exact—but what's a few thousand throats when you're making your first

Kenny Easley, UCLA All-American safety, 1978-79-80.

start in the Big Game? Especially after you've just directed your team 48 yards to a field goal?

Eric Hipp kicked it—a 32-yarder—after Steve Busick gave USC possession with an interception of a Tom Ramsey pass and a 20-yard runback.

UCLA forged ahead with an 80-yard, 11-play drive, highlighted by Jairo Penaranda's 20-yard scamper, Schroeder's 15-yard pitch to Michael Brant, and McNeil's six-yard touchdown blast. Norm Johnson's PAT lifted UCLA to a 7-3 halftime lead.

The score see-sawed again in the third period, with USC first regaining the lead at 10-7. Lott pounced on a McNeil fumble on the Ukes' 33-yard line, and on the fifth play, Tinsley passed 12 yards to Jeff Simmons for six-points. The key play on the brief trip was Tinsley's 24-yard toss to Kevin Williams. Hipp converted.

Then it was UCLA's turn, and the Bruins marched 80 yards in just six plays, Schroeder hurling the last 25 to Brant for a touchdown. Along the way, the relief QB hit Wrightman for 15 yards and Jojo Townsell for 17, while McNeil contributed a 19-yard gainer. Johnson again divided the uprights and quarter three ended with UCLA ahead, 14-10.

Before three minutes had evaporated in the fourth stanza, the Trojans were back on top at 17-14. It was a 43-yard journey that took 10 plays with Allen, on fourth down, plunging in from one yard out. Kevin Williams streaked 16 yards on a reverse to aid the cause, and Hipp tacked on the PAT.

That led to Schroeder's flip, Fisher's tip and McNeil's trip, the alley-oop play that brought Joe Bruin a long-awaited conquest of the Trojans . . . five years, for the record.

It was " . . . an act of God," sighed Donahue.

"I thought," revealed Southern Cal Coach John Robinson, "UCLA's tipped pass had an element of fortune in it."

And from Fisher, the man whose tip rewrote the chapter on cliffhanger finishes in the crosstown series: "I didn't see Freeman make the catch. I guess I misjudged the ball."

After the shocker, USC formulated one last stab at salvaging the contest, reaching UCLA's 29-yard line with seconds to play. A 46-yard field goal would tie the score, and Hipp had booted a 47-yarder against Tennessee. Instead, Tinsley went for Williams in the end zone, it didn't click, and the game ended.

"There was no way we were going for a tie," said Robinson.

Before the idea is assumed that only happy songs comprised the Bruins' repertoire, let it be known there were some tragic arias, too:

Freeman McNeil, UCLA All-American back, 1980.

two lost fumbles, two interceptions, two roughing-the-punter penalties and an illegal substitution call.

"We had some bad luck," Donahue reflected.

Donahue had installed a new defensive alignment, an eight man front, and it succeeded in holding Allen, who had been averaging 165 yards a game, to only 72 yards on 37 carries, less than two yards per push.

"UCLA did a good job on defense," Allen admitted. "They stacked on us, knowing we would be predictable with Gordon (Adams) out."

UCLA's McNeil was the top rusher with 111 yards on 24 handles, but the surprise of the game was the unsung Schroeder, who came off the bench and completed nine of 11 passes for 165 yards and two touchdowns.

"I was impressed with UCLA's offense," said Robinson. "They're a fine team and they came back. That was the name of today's game, coming back."

Both schools still had another team on their schedule. For Southern Cal, it was Notre Dame, and the Trojans bounced back from the UCLA loss to whip the Irish, 20-3. That gave USC an 8-2-1 record for the year, and, over the past three years, a fantastic 31-3-3 slate.

The Bruins traveled all the way to Tokyo for their curtain-dropper, and they found easy sailing over Oregon State, 34-3. The season was sweet at 9-2-0 and the win over USC stood tall over the others.

As Easley exclaimed, speaking for the 18 seniors and all the other Bruins, "There was no way we were gonna' lay down and die for USC."

The storied crossfire between USC and UCLA had now reached its half-century mark. The Trojans had won 29 times, UCLA 15 and they had fought six times to a tie. The soldiers from Troy led in points scored, 944 to 652.

Summary

	UCLA	USC
First Downs	18	18
Yards Rushing	164	109
Yards Passing	165	146
Total Yards	329	255
Passes Attempted	14	27
Passes Completed	9	15
Passes Had Intercepted	2	1
Fumbles Lost	2	0
Punts/Average	3/39.7	5/41.0
Penalties No./Yards	6/90	4/36

Scoring By Quarters:

UCLA	0	7	7	6	—	20
USC	3	0	7	7	—	17

1981
Game 51

A Rose by Any Other Name

There were four seconds to play when UCLA broke its huddle and went into field goal formation, the line of scrimmage at Southern California's 29-yard line. The Trojans, clinging tenaciously to a one point lead, spat, and dug their cleats in defiance.

Rich Newheisel spotted the snap on the 36, Norm Johnson swung his foot and the ball started its projectory toward the uprights. It never arrived. Up front, Trojans Dennis Edwards and Charles Ussery split Bruins Steve Williams and Russell Rowell, allowing nose guard George Achica, fresh off the bench, to charge through the tiny crack and slam the ball to earth, blocking UCLA's path to victory and to the Rose Bowl. USC, though out of the running for Pasadena, had preserved a 22-21 triumph.

"If we weren't going," Edwards said, "they weren't going for sure."

So, since neither team made it to the Rose Bowl, both were receptive to invitations from other bowls; the Trojans to the Fiesta, the Uclans to the Bluebonnet. It was the first time both institutions had gone to bowls outside the state the same year.

The story of the 1981 Trojans was Marcus Allen, All-American. Through 10 games, the senior tailback had rushed for 2,123 yards, the first college player ever to crack the elusive 2,000 mark barrier.

Behind the slashing darts of Allen, USC had compiled an 8-2-0 record, but both losses were to Pacific-10 competitors—Arizona and Washington. The eight verdicts were gained at the expense of Tennessee, Indiana, Oklahoma, Oregon State, Stanford, Notre Dame, Washington State and California.

Because of Allen's proclivity to run, Coach John Robinson had not acquired the balanced attack to which he aspired. Too, USC was operating behind a sophomore quarterback... John Mazur, the first to start since Jimmy Jones in 1969. Mazur's statistics were mediocre—73 completions in 149 attempts for 940 yards and seven touchdowns.

"Sometimes I wish I had more of a role to play," said Mazur.

UCLA's answer to Allen was tailback Kevin Nelson, and his 771 yards rushing did not exactly constitute a yell. But the Bruins did have more experience at quarterback in junior Tom Ramsey, whose stats showed 110 completions in 180 efforts for 1,477 yards and 13 touchdowns, second best overall efficiency rating in the conference.

"Consistency is what I have been shooting for," Ramsey remarked.

Tim Wrightman, UCLA leading receiver, 1981.

A few players of All-America calibre were sprinkled among the rosters . . . Allen, Chip Banks, Achica, Roy Foster for Southern Cal; Tim Wrightman for UCLA.

The Bruins, going into the Big Game, were 7-2-1. Iowa and Stanford were the spoilsports and Washington State got a tie, but UCLA stashed away Arizona, Wisconsin, Colorado, California, Oregon, Washington and Arizona State.

The Bruins of Coach Terry Donahue had earned a reputation of being an alert and opportunist bunch, having converted 19 of 38 turnovers into 113 points. On the other hand, the Trojans led the PAC-10 in scoring defense, and this was one factor that influenced the oddsmakers to favor USC by 3½ points.

It was with the attitude expressed by former Trojan Marvin Powell, later with the NFL Jets, who told *Times* scribe Mal Florence..."You just have to win this game for the city championship, if nothing else," that UCLA and USC squared off for the 51st time before 89,432 avid fans in Memorial Coliseum on a brisk Saturday afternoon in late November.

USC got the first break when Banks recovered Jojo Townsell's fumble on the Ukes' 29-yard line. Allen slithered for 12, nine and five yards but an offensive interference penalty against Jeff Simmons stalled the endeavor, so Steve Jordan drilled a 38-yard field goal; 3-0, USC.

Turn about is fair play, so SC's Allen bobbled the ball back to UCLA's Mike Durden on Troy's 11. In two plays, Nelson was in the end zone, and Johnson's PAT made it 7-3, UCLA.

Second quarter—busy, busy, busy. Jordan toed a 44-yard FG and Allen notched a TD on a seven-yard burst, and those two antics vaulted USC into a 12-7 lead.

Jordan's three-pointer capped a 54-yard exertion in which Allen had key runs of 12, seven and 14 yards; while Allen's six-pointer culminated an 80-yard journey. Todd Spencer donated a 15-yard pick-up, but the heart of the drive was a reverse from Allen to Timmy White who hurled 48 yards to Simmons, down to UCLA's seven. After Allen's TD, a pass for two points failed.

Then it was UCLA's turn to light the board with a TD and an FG. Troy's Joey Browner muffed a punt, and Westwood's Luis Sharpe put his mitts on it at SC's 48. There were six plays in the drive but only three of note. Ramsey raced for 14, went topside to Ricky Coffman for 17, then to Coffman for a 23-yard touchdown. For the two-point conversion, Ramsey hooked up with Coffman again.

SC's Allen was enjoying a field day, but he wasn't always carrying the ball with him. His second fumble (he had three during the game)

John Robinson, USC Head Coach, 1976-1982 and 1993-

Terry Donahue, UCLA Head Coach.

found its way into the arms of UCLA's Gene Mewborn, which led to Johnson's 32-yard field goal. The clubs broke for recess with UCLA leading, 18-12.

That was raised to 21-12 at the end of three periods, as Johnson kicked a 28-yard field goal to climax a 69-yard push in 13 plays. Along the way, Frank Bruno bolted for 12 yards, and Ramsey threw 17 and 16 yard strikes to Townsell.

But the fourth stanza was a song of Troy. First, the Trojans staged a 77-yard movement that produced a 22-yard field goal by Jordan on the 12th play. The quaver-like feet of Allen banged out dashes of seven, eight, six, 10 and 13 yards, while the duo of Mazur and Simmons played pitch and catch for 16 yards. USC had narrowed the gap to 21-15.

Then with two minutes and 14 seconds showing on Big Ben, Allen stepped across the Uclan's goal, standing up, from five yards out. That locked the score and Jordan's clutch PAT shoved USC out front, 22-21. The go-ahead marker was made possible when Troy West sniped a Ramsey aerial on UCLA's 44 and returned it to the 39. The jaunt took six plays, the longest of which were Spencer's eight and nine yard blasts.

Starting from their 20, the Bruins sallied forth on their last ditch, gasping maneuver, the stadium clock blinking an unfriendly countdown. Shoulder to shoulder, the stouthearted Bruins left behind the shadow of their goal posts as they approached mid-field. Suddenly, with 79 seconds left, all was lost . . . or so it seemed. Trojan Joe Turner swiped a Ramsey pass—but August Curley drew a flag for roughing the passer, and the subsequent penalty gave the Bruins a first down at Troy's 44.

The Uclans advanced to the 29, then called upon Johnson to deliver a game-winning field goal. What happened is history, filed under "A", for Achica.

"We looked at a lot of their field goal diagrams," said Achica, "and we noticed the weak guard gave us a little gap, so we took it."

There were 29 seconds to play when UCLA reached SC's 29-yard line, and the Bruins had one time-out remaining. Armchair quarterbacks wondered why UCLA didn't run one more play, try to get a little closer, then try the field goal. Instead, they permitted the clock to run down to four seconds, then used their time out. Was there confusion on the field?

"Why run another play?" asked Donahue. "We'd risk taking another sack. Quite frankly, that's within Norm's range, and we had the ball in the most advantageous position as it was."

Of course, the strategy didn't call for Johnson's boot to be

NG George Achica Blocked UCLA's Last-Second Field Goal Attempt to Preserve a 22-21 USC Victory, 1981

blocked. "Our guard is supposed to step down and close the gap off," stated UCLA assistant coach Jim Colleto. "Obviously, nobody closed it off."

It was a thrilling finish to a thrilling battle, but it didn't upstage the game-long and season-long accomplishments of Allen. His 40 rushes produced 219 yards, upping his season to 2,342, tops, by far, in the nation. It was the 11th time in his career that he had exceeded 200 yards in a game, and that, too, set a record. Per game rushing average of 219.9 yards? The best. Per carry rushing average of 5.81 yards? The best.

Small wonder, with such astonishing performances, that Allen was awarded the Heisman Trophy, the fourth Southern California player so honored.

Marcus Allen, USC Heisman Trophy winner, 1981.

The heroics of Allen and the game in general left Robinson flush of face. "This is one of the most memorable games since I've been here," he commented. "This game showed our courage and that's something special all USC players have. UCLA is an opportunistic team, and we gave them a lot of opportunities."

So, with both teams singing "California, here we go", UCLA and Southern Cal departed their native soil for bowl encounters elsewhere.

Joe Bruin steered toward Texas where he was corraled by Michigan, 33-14, in the Bluebonnet. And Tommy Trojan fared no better, as Penn State had all the fun in the Fiesta Bowl. Allen was ineffective in the 26-10 loss.

Summary

	USC	UCLA
First Downs	25	15
Yards Rushing	310	98
Yards Passing	113	154
Total Yards	423	252
Passes Attempted	23	25
Passes Completed	10	12
Passes Had Intercepted	1	2
Fumbles Lost	5	1
Punts/Average	3/43.3	6/44.0
Penalties No./Yards	8/86	4/51

Scoring By Quarters:

| USC | 3 | 9 | 0 | 10 | — | 22 |
| UCLA | 7 | 11 | 3 | 0 | — | 21 |

USC Blocks UCLA From Rose Bowl, 22-21
Achica Thwarts Bruins' Shot at Game-Winning Field Goal on the Last Play of the Game

Change of Venue

A 53-year old marriage of the UCLA-USC football program to Memorial Coliseum ended in divorce in July, 1982... with Joe Bruin filing the papers.

Some purveyors of tidings said the change of domicile to the Rose Bowl in Pasadena was traceable to volatile Al Davis who, after lengthy litigation with the brass of the National Football League, was moving his Raiders from Oakland to the Coliseum, there to set up housekeeping under a bevy of fashionable concessions.

Maybe yes, maybe no.

"We had determined that under appropriate circumstances, we could co-habitat the Coliseum with the Raiders," said Chancellor Charles Young. "But the new agreement with the Coliseum would have created many long-range problems for us. The move really had to do with our relationship with the Coliseum on one hand, and our relationship with the Raiders on the other."

The lease of the Westwood school with the Coliseum expired at the end of the 1981 season. The new arrangement at Pasadena extended through 1986, then was renewed.

"The future of UCLA football and UCLA is going to be much better at the Rose Bowl," concluded the chancellor.

Of course, the Bruins will still play in the Los Angeles Coliseum once every other year... when they meet the Trojans of Southern California. But they'll come as visitors.

1982

Game 52

Sack of Roses

All or nothing or all. The daring Trojans knew it... as they lined up for a two-point conversion attempt with double zeroes on the clock and trailing by a point. The defiant Bruins knew it... as they wiped gritty sweat from their brows and braced their bodies for one last laborious defense.

All or nothing at all. The 95,763 fans who jammed the innards of Pasadena's Rose Bowl knew it. Certainly the coaches knew it... Terry Donahue who had prepared his Bruins for just such a situation, and who could now only watch, and hope, for execution. And John Robinson, intense and unshakable, who had seen his Trojans drive too far and too hard to turn back. Perhaps Robinson knew something, too, that few others did: this would be his last opportunity to whip his tart crosstown rival from Westwood.

With slightly more than five minutes to play and in arrears by seven points, the troops of Troy had marched 66 yards to a fourth-down touchdown as the clock expired. Now it was 20-19, UCLA... and a time for reckoning.

"A tie was an alternative," pondered Robinson, "but not an acceptable one. We came here to win."

The plucky Bruins took their stance, the just-uttered challenge of Donahue ringing loudly in their ears: "You've played hard all day and given it your best shot. Now give it your best shot for just one more play."

SPORTS

Did Morgan Deliver Roses to UCLA in a Sack?

Disdaining a rollout, Scott Tinsley dropped straight back, looking, looking. He hesitated, cocked his arm, still looking. Suddenly a giant, blue-shirted mountain rose above and smothered him to the turf. The name of the mountain was Karl Morgan, and he was assisted on the sack by Eugene Leoni.

The battle was over, UCLA was a 20-19 victor, and still in the running for host team in the Rose Bowl.

"When I broke through, I saw Tinsley start to raise his arm," explained Morgan. "I stopped. But when he lifted again, I hit him."

Donahue recalled the 1981 contest which USC won on the last play of the game by blocking a field goal effort. "That (the sack) makes up for last year and alleviates some of the pain," he commented.

Robinson was a tad philosophical. "If you're going to lose, that's the way to lose it, on their goal line, passing to put the game away," he remarked.

As in all previous USC-UCLA clashes, there would be a plethora of bona-fide stars on the field. Nine were named to the AP All-PAC team: Carmac Carney and Morgan for UCLA; Tony Slaton, Bruce Matthews, Don Mosebar, George Achica, Jack Del Rio and Joey Browner for USC. Tom Ramsey of the Bruins was tabbed in a tie for quarterback with Stanford's John Elway, a decision with which USC's Robinson was not in full accord.

"Tom Ramsey is the best quarterback in the country," stated Robinson. "He deserves to be called that." (The media did not agree, later hyping Elway into the top choice in the NFL draft, despite Ramsey's nation-leading 21 touchdown passes and 2,824 passing yards.)

Matthews, Mosebar and Achica were consensus All-Americans, while Carney, whose 108 pass receptions set a new Westwood career record, earned a spot on the Academic All-America team.

And of course, the new site cast an overtone to the atmosphere of the conflict. For the first time since the initial meeting in 1929, the clubs did not play in Memorial Coliseum.

"The people playing in the game don't care where it is played," intoned Robinson. "They just want to win, and it could be played in a parking lot."

Mosebar, USC's All-America Tackle   Bruce Matthews, USC's All-America Guard

Tom Ramsey, UCLA's Record-Breaking Quarterback,
With Coach Terry Donahue

UCLA was designated as the home team, but Donahue deemed that as unimportant. "We've never played them there before, so I can't say for sure that we'll have a true home-field advantage."

Donahue was more concerned with the condition of the turf, soft from heavy rains and chopped up by a Friday night prep doubleheader, and with his injury report. Morgan had sprained an ankle in the previous game, joining Ron Butler, Tom Sullivan and Don Mahlstedt on the hobble list.

But the single-most critical casualty may have belonged to Southern Cal, which would again play without Sean Salisbury, leaving the QB duties to journeyman Tinsley. (John Mazur had long-since departed for Texas A&M.) Others wounded for the Trojans were Todd Spencer, Neil Hope, Fred Crutcher and John Kamana.

The encounter was billed as UCLA's offensive strength versus USC's defensive prowess, ironic indeed, as the eventual outcome turned in opposite directions.

But if the Trojans possessed a weakness anywhere, Donahue feigned ignorance of it. "This might be the best defense I've ever seen at USC," he praised. "It's the best offensive line in college football," he added. "They're all gifted, without a weakness."

Naturally, Robinson couldn't let all of those exultations go unanswered. "I would imagine UCLA is the most explosive team we've seen," he responded. "They throw the ball well and appear to be improving as a running team."

Because of probationary inflictions, Southern Cal was ineligible for post-season activity. UCLA was assured of a bowl bid, the only question being which: the Aloha, Fiesta, Sun... or, with a miracle or two, the Rose.

The Uclans brought a better record (8-1-1) into the fray; triumphs over Long Beach State, Wisconsin, Michigan, Colorado, Washington State, California, Oregon and Stanford, a tie with Arizona and a loss to Washington.

The Trojans were just a shade below that with a 7-2-0 slate. Victims of the Cardinal and Gold were Indiana, Oklahoma, Oregon, Stanford, Oregon State, California and Arizona, with only Florida and Arizona State claiming the upper hand.

So the stage was set for the 52nd engagement of this, another battle of crosstown crossfire between Joe Bruin and Tommy Trojan.

UCLA wasted no time getting on the scoreboard, erasing 80 yards in eight plays on its first possession. The payoff pitch was an eight-yarder from Ramsey to Harper Howell, but the drive was patched by runs of 19 yards by Danny Andrews and 14 by Kevin

Nelson plus a 20-yard peg from Ramsey to Andrews. John Lee booted the PAT after Rick Neuheisel improvised a futile two-point effort. But SC was offsides, giving UCLA a reprieve for the Lee kick. Neuheisel's reward? A dislocated shoulder.

The visitors from Vermont Avenue closed the gap to 7-3, moving 53 yards in 10 plays for Steve Jordan to drill a 44-yard field goal. The invasion was sparked by sprints of 11 yards by Kennedy Pola and eight by Tinsley, as well as Tinsley tosses of 17 yards to Jeff Simmons and 13 to Fred Cornwell.

The Uclans came right back, ignited by a 40-yard kickoff return by Dokie Williams. Ramsey heaved nine yards to Nelson, then 14 to Carney before Andrews hit a hole opened by Chris Yelich and Irv Eatman and dashed 23 yards to paydirt, concluding a 60-yard journey in nine plays. Lee's conversion changed the score to 14-3 as the first quarter ended.

"I sure didn't expect to score from the 23," said Andrews, "but when I hit the hole, all I saw was endzone."

UCLA stretched its bulge to 17-3 when Lee split the uprights on a 45-yard FG, made possible when Don Rogers snitched a Tinsley flip and ran back seven yards to Troy's 28.

Later, Ramsey was separated from the ball by John Harvey, and it was claimed by Keith Browner to put the Trojans in business on the Westwood 15-yard stripe. Spencer bolted for seven yards, then on his fifth carry, crashed over from the three. Jordan added the PAT, and the clubs departed for halftime lectures with UCLA out front, 17-10. It could have been wider as a late drive by the Bruins was stymied when Nelson fumbled and Tony Brewer recovered.

Only three points were posted in the third frame, those from a 42-yard FG by Bruin Lee. It was the product of a slender five-yard trek in three plays to SC's 25 after Mark Walen pounced on Tinsley's bobble.

"Our defensive team was absolutely spectacular," exuded Donahue. "Defensively, we were at our very, very best."

But his defensive stalwarts who wouldn't bend in the third began to break in the fourth quarter as the Trojans racked up nine points... and tried for two more. First came a 22-yard field goal by Jordan, born of a 55-yard invasion in a dozen plays and nourished by scurries of eight, five, 12 and eight yards by Anthony Gibson.

Even so, some of the fans of little faith started jostling for their car keys as the clock began its impartial countdown with UCLA leading, 20-13. After a Bruin punt, the Trojans took over on their 34-yard line with 5:28 to play.

Tinsley threw 17 yards to Simmons, 15 to Timmie White, 13 to Pat McCool, seven to White, and USC was soon perched on the Uclan four, with first down.

Gibson took a handoff and was stopped on the one by Blanchard Montgomery, whose left shoulder popped out with the jolting impact. Stunned, but refusing to leave the battle, Montgomery halted Gibson on his second-down dive over right tackle. On third down, Gibson swung right and once again was pulled down by Montgomery for no gain. Having seen enough of the senior linebacker, Tinsley rolled right and lofted a touchdown pass to Mark Boyer, setting the scene for the dramatic two-point attempt, which failed when Morgan sacked Tinsley.

"I had enough time," said a dejected Tinsley. "I should have gotten rid of the ball."

Despite the decisive sack, Tinsley was awarded the UCLA Game Trophy for his offensive contributions. Browner was the defensive recipient.

Donahue was ecstatic. "We were at our best today, and had to be to win," he exclaimed. Named as his best on offense were Dan Dufour, Blake Wingle and Andrews; on defense, Neal Dellocono, Mike Durden and Montgomery.

Even in the despair of defeat, Robinson kept high his head. "I've never been more proud of a team than this one," he pronounced.

It would be 11 years until he would coach a USC team against UCLA again. For, three days later, Robinson resigned to become a senior vice-president for university relations at Southern California. He was replaced by Ted Tollner, the Trojans' offensive coordinator.

Robinson, however, never assumed the task of veep at USC, switching instead to head coach of the Los Angeles Rams in the NFL. Later, he entered the broadcast booth as a network color analyst; then returned as head coach at USC in 1993.

But the Trojans had one more game on their schedule, always-tough Notre Dame. In a spirit of "...win one for the coach", USC thumped the Irish, 17-13, presenting Robinson with a farewell gift and an 8-3-0 finale. He attained an incredible 67-14-2 record during his tenure at USC, and was 5-2-0 against UCLA.

The win over Troy ended UCLA's regular season at 9-1-1. And the sack that preserved their victory over USC was part of a bizarre trilogy that catapulted the Uclans into the Rose Bowl. For, lo and behold, Washington State upset Washington and Arizona upset Arizona State, thrusting PAC-10 laurels and a Rose Bowl invitation upon the glad-to-oblige Bruins.

Buoyed by the turn of events, UCLA decked Michigan, 24-14, in the Pasadena Classic, its second conquest of the year over the

Wolverines. The win earned the Bruins a fifth-place ranking in both wire service polls.

The *Sporting News* magazine recently released its evaluation of the four top college football rivalries in the nation (not in order): Army-Navy, Texas-Oklahoma, Michigan-Ohio State, USC-UCLA. Have you ever known the bible of sports to be wrong?

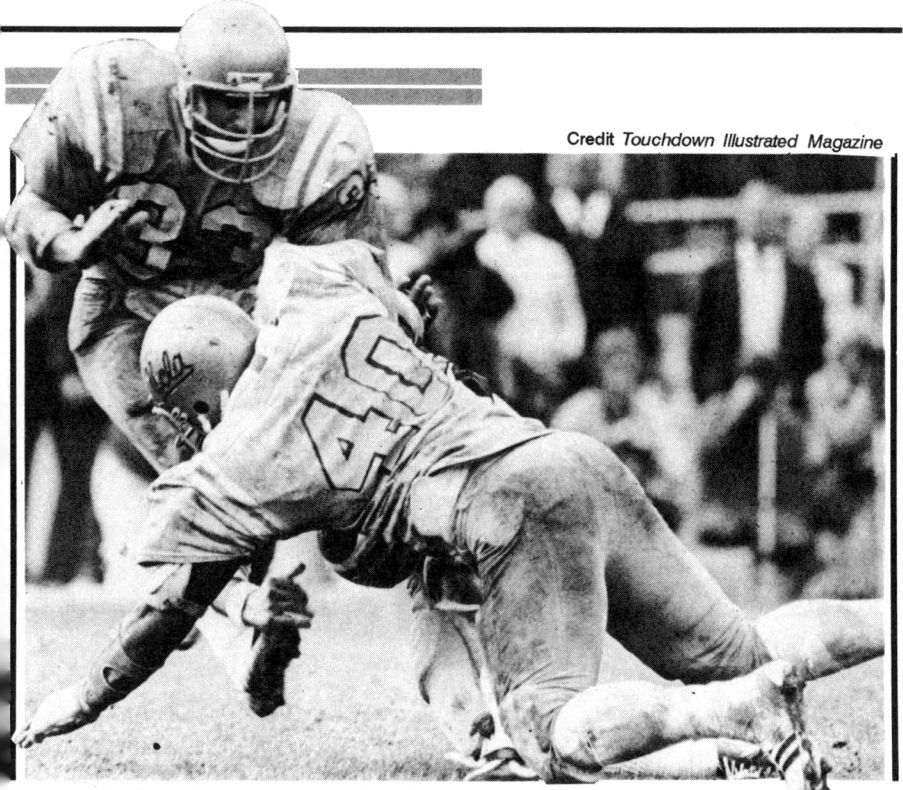

Credit *Touchdown Illustrated Magazine*

UCLA's Karl Morgan (40) with help from Eugene Leoni Sacks Scott Tinsley (obscured) to preserve a 20-19 win over USC

Scoring by Quarters:

USC   3   7   0   9   -   19
UCLA   14   3   3   0   -   20

1983
Game 53

Tumbletown

An epic confrontation it wasn't. But an epic confrontation no one expected. Here's why: UCLA and Southern California entered their 53rd engagement with a combined record of 9-9-2, the worst since 1971.

Only four of those nine victories belonged to Southern Cal, and its 4-5-1 ledger was the poorest it would bring into a UCLA game since 1960. What's more, to compound the negative, the Trojans had been denied any points by Washington the previous week, the first time in 187 games the men of Troy had failed to score. Yes, an NCAA record was snapped.

The Bruins had lost the previous week, too, but five straight wins prior to that had formulated a 5-4-1 record. And that was ample reason to establish them a four point favorite to kick USC.

The oddsmakers picked correctly on the winner and they weren't too distant on the spread, as UCLA used a potent third quarter to drop Southern Cal, 27-17.

The blemish ended a disappointing season for the Trojans, a preseason pick of ninth in the nation by *Sporting News*. At that time, their new head coach, Ted Tollner, agreed and disagreed.

"I think we're very talented," he said, "but we're also very inexperienced." To support that, Tollner noted a return of only 11 starters.

Bruins Get a Magic Message

After Donahue Tells Them Huskies Are Losing at Seattle, They Proceed to Explode in Third Quarter at the Coliseum

Absent from last year's 8-3-0 slate were three All-Americans: Don Mosebar, Bruce Matthews and George Achica, as well as stalwarts Joey Browner, Riki Gray and Jeff Simmons.

But if Tollner had some gaping cavities to fill, Coach Terry Donahue had similar problems up at Westwood. Gone were QB Tom Ramsey, Irv Eatman, Carmac Carney, JoJo Townsell, Dokie Williams, Karl Morgan, Dan Dufour, Blake Wingle... blue-chippers who had led the Bruins to a 10-1-1 season in 1982.

On the bright side, Donahue could point to a bevy of quality athletes to anchor his '83 vessel, most notable of whom were defensive backs Don Rogers and Lupe Sanchez and tight end Paul Bergmann.

Viewing the upcoming tussle with USC, Bergmann observed: "Actually, it's very simple. We're playing USC. Whatever we have done or failed to do so far becomes immaterial. Whether you are 0-10 or 10-0, the USC game is always important."

Others returning to the Bruin den included backs Kevin Nelson, Danny Andrews and Frank Cephus, plus Harper Howell, Duval Love and Chris Yelich on offense; Lee Knowles and Ron Butler on defense, along with place-kicker John Lee.

While Southern California had lost three All-Americans, three AA candidates were ready in the wings. They were center Jack Slaton and linebackers Jack Del Rio and Keith Browner. Quarterback Sean Salisbury would return, too, as would running backs Michael Harper, Todd Spencer, Fred Crutcher, Fred Kamana and Kennedy Pola, tight end Fred Cornwell and place-kicker Steve Jordan.

"When I was recruited by USC, one of the first things that came to mind was that I would get a chance to play against UCLA," said Salisbury, who sat out last year's skirmish. "My chance has finally come."

Salisbury would look to such defensive specialists as Brian Luft, Jeff Brown and Neil Hope to stop the Bruins and put the ball into his hands.

As previously stated, Tommy Trojan could boast of only four triumphs going into the UCLA contest. They were over Oregon State, Washington State, California and Stanford. Kansas, South

Carolina, Arizona State, Notre Dame and Washington dealt defeats to USC while Florida earned a tie.

And, as previously indicated, Joe Bruin started slow, losing in the rain to Georgia, tying Arizona State, then falling to Nebraska and Brigham Young before reeling off wins over Stanford, Washington State, California, Washington and Oregon. A three-point loss to Arizona preceded the USC game.

While Tollner was a yearling as a head coach in the storied USC-UCLA rivalry, Donahue had been through more than a dozen of these crosstown crossfires.

"I could use all the usual cliches about throwing out records and past history not meaning a thing," he reflected, "but it's all true. It's impossible for any other game to have as much intensity, drama and color. There's a lot of pride at both schools," Donahue concluded.

Such was the tone as 83,763 fans crammed into the Coliseum for a battle billed as UCLA's offense against USC's defense.

And for two quarters, the defense of the Trojans appeared superior, as the teams split for intermission with USC atop, 10-6.

It could have been a larger lead, but SC's Jordan missed a 44-yard field goal attempt in the first period and UCLA's Knowles purloined a Salisbury pass in the endzone, wasting a 73-yard drive in the second.

Seizing their opportunities, the Bruins were first on the scoreboard, posting a pair of field goals by Lee. His first was a 25-yarder which capped a 65-yard drive and featured passes by Rick Neuheisel of 17 yards to Mike Young, 14 to Karl Dorrell and 10 to Nelson.

Lee's next field goal, from 20 yards out, was set up by Joe Gasser's sprint of 28 yards to the USC 32 after stealing a Salisbury aerial. To place Lee in position, Neuheisel connected for 11 yards to Nelson and 12 to Bergmann. UCLA led, 6-0.

Midway the second period, the Trojans stormed back, putting together a 70-yard jaunt in just seven plays. Spencer plunged over after Salisbury and Cormier played pitch-and-run for a 32-yard gain to the one-yard line. Other key plays: Salisbury to Cornwell, 20 yards; Spencer, 11-yard run. A true kick by Jordan gave USC a one point lead.

This stretched to four points when Tony Brewer pilfered Neuheisel's pass and returned it 19 yards, Spencer garnered 22 yards on three carries, and Jordan booted a 30-yard field goal just 16 seconds before intermission.

In the locker room, the Bruins learned that Washington State was in the process of whipping favored Washington, and they

Don Rogers, UCLA's
All-America Safety

Lupe Sanchez, UCLA's
All-Coast Cornerback

Ted Tollner, USC Head Coach
1983-1986

knew a Cougar upset was their opportunity for a return trip to the Rose Bowl.

"I have to give USC credit for dominating the first half," stated Donahue, "but that Washington State score really motivated us at halftime. That helped us blow open the third quarter."

Did it ever?

Taking the second half kickoff, UCLA drove 80 yards in 11 plays to go up, 13-10, a lead it would not surrender. The clincher was a seven-yard toss from Neuheisel to Dorrell, who also grabbed a 13-yarder along the way. A 20-yard gallop by Nelson helped spark the trip, which ended with Lee's PAT.

Then Sanchez returned a Troy Richardson punt 39 yards to USC's 21-yard line, from which point Nelson crossed the goal line from 12 yards out on third down. The score became 20-10 after Lee's point-after.

Still in the third stanza, the lads from Hilgard Avenue added an insurance TD. To set it in motion, Jeff Chaffin recovered a fumble by Harper on SC's 26-yard stripe.

"I took my eyes off the ball before I had it," wailed Harper.

The Trojans pushed the Bruins back to the 31, but on third down, Neuheisel passed 24 yards to Bergmann. USC's Tommy Haynes sacked Neuheisel for a 10-yard loss, but Bryan Wiley reclaimed those 10 plus seven more for a touchdown. Lee's kick upped the lead to 27-10 with just over a quarter to play.

"In the third quarter we just exploded," exuded Nelson, the Bruins senior tailback. "When we get going, we can do that."

The Trojans closed the gap to 27-17 and still had 10:35 to catch the Bruins, but Donahue's Uclans would not cooperate, burning the next six minutes off the clock with clutch running and, according to Trojan Brown, favorable spots from the officials.

"A couple of those spots were questionable," he observed, "but I have to admit we had some defensive breakdowns."

Anyway, score one final touchdown the Trojans did. It resulted from a 68-yard, 12-play drive that culminated when Spencer eradicated the final seven yards. Key plays were flings from Salisbury of 11 yards to Malcom Moore and 10 to Cormier plus a 10-yard burst by Spencer. Jordan's PAT finalized the score at 27-17, UCLA.

"I am proud of my team and I know Ted Tollner is proud of his," remarked an elated Donahue.

Proud, perhaps... but it was secondary to disappointment, which shrouded the headmaster of Troy. "It hurts, it hurts," lamented Tollner. "Our guys played extremely hard and really wanted to win. I just cannot explain that third quarter.'

Tony Slaton, USC's All-America Center

Del Rio concurred. "It's disappointing to lose to your crosstown rival because you have to put up with those people for a year."

Joy resided across the field. Bergmann sat alone on the bench, tears in eyes that focused on the scoreboard. "I just wanted to take a moment to let it all soak in," he said. "It was a moment I will always remember."

Also gazing at the scoreboard, a fifth-year walk-on named Neuheisel summed up his years of grit and patience: "It's the prettiest sight I've ever seen."

During the affair, Neuheisel completed 13 of 19 passes for 154 yards; for the losers, Salisbury was 19 of 25 for 218 yards. USC's Harper led all foot soldiers, rushing for 120 yards on 27 carries.

Ironically, Southern Cal made more first downs than did the Bruins, as well as out-rushing and out-passing them.

So it was on to the Rose Bowl for UCLA, its first time ever for back-to--back appearances.

"I knew all week we could end up in the Rose Bowl, and we are definitely going to represent the PAC-10 well," noted Rogers, "but I also knew we had to concentrate on beating SC first."

That done in fine fashion, UCLA added to its laurels with a sweeping 45-9 smash over Illinois, bringing its season to a respectable 7-4-1 record, adequate for a No. 17 ranking by the AP and No. 13 by UPI.

Southern Cal wound up at 4-6-1, its first losing season in 22 years. But the Trojans boasted a consensus All-American: center Tony Slaton. Not to be outdone, UCLA had a consensus AA, too: safety Don Rogers.

Earlier in this chapter, it was pointed out that Southern Cal's NCAA record of scoring in 186 consecutive games was broken in 1983. Well, guess who took over as the new NCAA leader? UCLA.

Scoring by Quarters:

UCLA   3   3 21   0 - 27
USC   0 10   0   7 - 17

1984

Game 54

Blundering Herd

Apparently, when a team is already in the Rose Bowl it's difficult for it to play in the Rose Bowl. Such was the puzzling mishap when Southern California, already assured of meeting the Big-10 champion in the Rose Bowl on New Year's Day, squared off against unranked UCLA in the Pasadena stadium on November 17th... and lost.

Coming off a stunning upset of No. 1 Washington the previous week, the Trojans, with an 8-1-0 record, ranked No. 7 in the land and were listed by various bookies as a four-to-11 point favorite. One national tout service based in Boston, called USC "...a lock to win." Why not? UCLA's modest 7-3-0 credentials were unworthy of a spot in the Top-25.

But the Bruins did, indeed, possess a few assets in their portfolio... two consecutive wins over the Trojans, a position of perhaps being "overlooked" by the lofty visitors, and an unbridled statement by Tim Green, USC's quarterback, as a motivating spur.

"The Trojans will hand UCLA a serious whuppin' this weekend," boasted Green, who had replaced an injured Sean Salisbury earlier in the season.

Closer to the mark was Steve Horn, a writer for the Los Angeles *Herald-Examiner:* "When USC plays UCLA, you can throw pointspreads out the window. Throw in the fact that the Trojans will be suffering a big letdown from last week, and we like the Bruins to cover the points at the Rose Bowl."

SPORTS

You see, L.A. belongs to Bruins

USC thrashed in Rose Bowl en route to the Rose Bowl

Trojans not taking 'em one game at a time

But even a better prophet was Steve Bono, UCLA's quarterback: "We have a good chance to win. I know a lot of people have been saying UCLA isn't very good. We'll prove a few people wrong on Saturday."

Give the last word to Bono. Capitalizing on five USC turnovers and inspired by the sturdy right leg of John Lee, it was Joe Bruin who spanked Tommy Trojan with a "serious whuppin'", 29-10. It was the most points yielded all season by SC's vaunted defense, and it was only the second time since the series started in 1929 that UCLA had won three games in a row.

But if preseason ratings and expectations have any merit, UCLA's victory was an item of order. For the Bruins were tabbed as the fifth best team in the country; the Trojans weren't in the Top-20 on Labor Day.

Veterans galore graced the Westwood campus. In addition to Bono and Lee, Coach Terry Donahue would count on stellar performers such as Mike Sherrard, Mike Young, Danny Andrews, Jim McCullough, Bryan Wiley, Duval Love, as well as Ron Pitts, Lee Knowles, Chris Block, David Randle, Joe Gasser, Herb Welch, Dave Baran and Neal Dellocono.

Dellocono, a linebacker who hailed from Baton Rouge, Louisiana, would be starting his 35th straight game for Donahue.

"A lot of people back home were unhappy when I chose UCLA over LSU," said Dellocono, "but going to two straight Rose Bowls took the pressure off. People now say I made the right choice.'

344

Instrumental in those Rose Bowl visits but now departed were such sterling Bruins as Don Rogers and Lupe Sanchez on defense; Rick Neuheisel, Kevin Nelson, Frank Cephus, Paul Bergmann and Harper Howell on offense.

Precariously, a teetering question mark hung over the walls of Heritage Hall, but in reality, ardent Trojan fans could not foresee another losing season.

"I was disappointed as anyone else about last fall," commented Coach Ted Tollner, "but we're coming back with a vengeance."

Give Tollner credit. From alumni and supporters, the ultimatum was to "...shape up or ship out", and he uttered his "we're coming back" declaration knowing full well he would line up minus such stars as Tony Slaton, Keith Browner, Jeff Brown, Fred Cornwell, Michael Harper and Todd Spencer.

But Tollner also knew the quality of his holdovers: Kennedy Pola, Salisbury, Fred Crutcher, Joe Cormier, Hank Norman, Tommie Ware, Ken Ruettgers, Jeff Bregel, James Fitzpatrick, Tom Hallock on offense; plus Duane Bickett, Jerome Tyler, Neil Hope, Tommy Haynes and Jack Del Rio on defense, as well as place-kicker Steve Jordan.

Of Del Rio, Tollner observed: "He is the most aggressive, intense player I've ever been around."

It took Southern Cal one week into the season to find a slot in the Top-20, appearing at No. 17 after decimating Utah State, 42-7. A decision over Arizona State moved Troy to No. 15, but an embarrassing 20-point loss to unranked Louisiana State quelled the upward surge.

Regrouping was in order, however, as the Trojans vanquished Washington State, Oregon, Arizona, California, Stanford and Washington to crest at No. 7 prior to the battle with UCLA.

As stated, the Bruins opened the season at No. 5, but when verdicts over San Diego State, Long Beach State and Colorado failed to impress the voting writers as much as did losses to Nebraska and Stanford, UCLA disappeared from the polls. They remained in oblivion, despite the fact that wins over Washington State, California, Arizona State and Oregon State overshadowed a lone setback to Oregon.

More than 90,000 zealots clicked the turnstiles of the Rose Bowl for the 54th confab of UCLA-USC, with half of them anticipating an easy romp and the other half simply heirs of hope.

But hope can turn dreams into reality. And such was the scenario when the underdog Bruins carved a 3-0 lead, and later roared into the halftime break atop a resounding 19-3 margin.

**Jack Del Rio (L) and Duane Bickett,
USC's All-America Linebackers, 1984**

Six of the Bruins' seven scores came from bungles by the Blundering Herd, so aptly coined by Allan Malamud, of the Los Angeles *Herald.*

The first mistake came in the initial quarter when Craig Rutledge pilfered a heave by Green. A clipping penalty stalled the Bruin drive, so Lee came in and nailed a 46-yard field goal.

Their dander aroused, Southern Cal engineered a six minute drive from its 20-yard line to UCLA's three... where it became fourth-down-and-a-foot. Shunning an almost-automatic field goal for a tie, Tollner sent Crutcher off left tackle where he was met head-on by linebacker Tony Phillips for no gain.

"That's how you judge a defense," said UCLA's defensive line coach, Greg Robinson. "This defense makes plays when it has to."

Undaunted, the Trojans stormed back. But in character for this day, a bolt of thunder interrupted their storm. An erratic handoff from Green to freshman Ryan Knight resulted in a fumble which Dellocono pounced upon. Subsequently, Lee knocked through a 29-yard FG and UCLA led, 6-0.

USC's Jordan and UCLA's Lee exchanged field goals on the next two possessions, Jordan from 45 yards out, Lee from 43.

To this point, the battle had been a string of field goals and there was yet another to come, a 37-yarder by Lee. It was ignited when Green passed over the middle to Cormier who was jolted by Ron Butler, jarring loose the ball. On a bounce, it cuddled into the anxious arms of safety James Washington. The drive stalled on the 20, however, so in entered Lee. UCLA, 12-3.

Finally, after five field goals, the fans were treated to a touchdown - though those of Cardinal and Gold descent would just as soon not have seen it. It was a 51-yard UCLA journey that featured two huge plays: a 13-yard completion from Bono to Sherrard and a 28-yard scamper down the sideline by freshman Gaston Green (playing for the injured Andrews) to SC's five-yard line. Actually, there were three important plays: Sherrard eluded Del Rio and gathered in a scoring pass from Bono. Lee's PAT increased the Uclan lead to 19-3 as the teams, one bewildered, the other blissful, left the sod for intermission.

Not content with a 16-point advantage, UCLA posted another touchdown about 10 minutes into the third quarter. Green's errant pass intended for Cormier was picked off by substitute Dennis Price who, getting a key block from Washington, raced 63 yards to paydirt. Lee's point-after was true.

Now trailing by 23 points, it was crunch time for Troy. A touchdown they needed and a touchdown they got, just three minutes after UCLA's marker. The key play was a 36-yard over-the-head snag by Ware of a Green fling down to UCLA's one-yard line. On second down, Green crossed the double-stripe from two yards out, and Jordan's PAT was accurate.

USC still had 17 minutes to erase its 16-point deficit, but UCLA had different notions. Welch intercepted Green to stymie one Trojan effort, and another soiree ended with a shanked punt by Paul Green, setting up the Bruins on the Trojan 40. Three plays later, the ball rested on USC's 32, from which point Lee slammed a 49-yard field goal, removing all doubts about the game's outcome, as well as setting two NCAA records for himself: most field goals in a single game, five; most field goals in a season, 29.

Said Lee: "I was fortunate the offense gave me so many chances. I was really nervous before the last kick, but now I feel honored to have these records." For his heroics, Lee was named to several All-America teams.

In a way, the contest was a carbon of the 1983 affair: USC made more first downs and gained more total yardage, but fell shy on the scoreboard... where it counts.

"They whipped us in every phase of the game," moaned Tollner, apparently unaware of the statistics. "But, when you play a good team like UCLA, you can't turn the ball over. I thought we were ready to play but, obviously, they were more ready."

As usual, Donahue was gracious in victory. "To beat a school like USC three times in a row is a real accomplishment," he said. "Our players have been disappointed at times this year, but today we came out an aggressive, hungry football team."

Top rusher in the game was UCLA's Green, garnering 134 yards on 18 carries. USC's Crutcher picked up only 34 yards, but that was sufficient to put him over the 1000-yard mark, the first Trojan to exceed this figure since Marcus Allen in 1981.

Southern Cal displayed one consensus All-American... linebacker Del Rio. And his linebacking mate, Bickett, was selected on four AA teams.

For the Bruins, the regular season was over, but a date in the Fiesta Bowl remained. A 39-37 shade over Miami-F closed UCLA's slate at 9-3-0 and earned a No. 9 rank.

This rating was superior to USC, which finished at No. 10 with a similar 9-3-0 ledger, which was achieved after a loss in the mud to Notre Dame and a triumph over Ohio State in the Rose Bowl.

Scoring by Quarters:

USC   0   3   7   0   -   10
UCLA 3   16 7   3   -   29

1985

Game 55

Tollner Rolls Dice

Get the picture: Southern California, in arrears by three points, had moved the ball 50 yards, where it rested on UCLA's six-yard line. But time and downs were impatient enemies, for only 3:30 remained in the game and the sideline marker flashed fourth down. The Trojans needed two yards to gain a new series of downs... two long yards.

The reliable foot of Don Shafer could almost certainly guarantee a tie for USC. But Coach Ted Tollner did not waver from a pre-game decision he had made. Shafer and the bench remained companions.

Instead, redshirt freshman quarterback Rodney Peete rolled out for three yards and a precious first down. Grudgingly, the Bruins yielded the coveted terrain that could preserve their lead, but on fourth down - and a repeat decision by Tollner - Peete sneaked the last few inches with 73 seconds on the clock to claim a 17-13 upset win for Southern Cal.

It was the first triumph for Tollner over his intracity adversary, and it was his gut decisions that probably earned it.

"I made the decision before the game," explained Tollner. "Our objective was not to take UCLA out of the Rose Bowl with a tie. Our objective was to win."

And for the third straight year the winner was the improbable choice. For sweeping into the meeting with high-flying laurels was UCLA, ranked as the 8th best team in the USA with an 8-1-1 record. Compare that with USC, which limped into the arena unranked with a mere four victories in nine games. No wonder the Bruins were a seven-point favorite on the morning line.

For sure, it wasn't the type of autumn the fans of Troy had envisioned. For back in August, wire service polls rated Southern Cal at No. 6, and the Trojans were selected by one and all to run away with the PAC-10 title. This rosy outlook prevailed despite the departure of such potent performers as Jack Del Rio, Duane Bickett, Neil Hope, Tommy Haynes and Steve Jordan.

SPORTS

Bruins Go From the Ruins to the Roses

Jim Murray Tollner

USC Is Victor but Not Quite Spoiler, 17-13

But the offense, which had sputtered in '84, was returning seven starters. This fold included Fred Crutcher, James Fitzpatrick, Hank Norman, Joe Cormier and Jeff Bregel, whom Tollner described as "...strong, fast and nasty." Also greeted by Tollner were Tom Cox, Tom Hallock, Kennedy Pola, Ryan Knight, Zeph Lee, as well as Tony Colorito, Tim McDonald, Jerome Tyler and Brent Moore. QB Sean Salisbury would try another season, too, having sat out most of the previous year with an injury.

"We re-established our credibility last year," said Tollner. "Now we have to continue to improve."

As the season unfolded, it appeared Tollner should have worn dark-hued spectacles. It started out okay with a win over No. 10 Illinois, but Baylor stunned the Trojans and Arizona State blanked them. The next six games were split, victories over Oregon State, Stanford and Washington State; losses to Notre Dame, California and Washington. Yes, there were scars on the battered torso of Tommy Trojan in what was expected to be his year of excellence.

While gloom did not hover over the village of Westwood, aspirations didn't quite equate lofty peaks, either. Preseason pollsters didn't foresee much, barely slipping in the Bruins at No. 20.

Gone from last year's 9-3-0 squad were such dynamos as Danny Andrews, Neal Dellocono, Ron Pitts, Herb Welch, Bryan Wiley,

Dave Baran, Duval Love, Mark Mannon and Karl Dorrell (although an injury idled him for most of '84, anyway).

A solid corps of returnees included Tommy Taylor, Mike Sherrard, Gaston Green, James Washington, Jim McCullough, Mark Walen, Joe Gasser and Korean-born John Lee, place-kicker deluxe.

Coach Terry Donahue's troops marched off on the right foot by upsetting Brigham Young, the defending national champion. Then came a knot with Tennessee, a rout of San Diego State and a submission to Washington. The Bruins then subdued six straight opponents - Arizona State, Stanford, Washington State, California, Arizona and Oregon State, thus earning their No. 8 rank and their role as favorite over Southern California.

On days leading up to the conflict, supporters and former players alike shared their sentiments about the game and the USC-UCLA rivalry in general.

Marc Dellins, UCLA SID: "In any given year, both teams feel like they can go out there and win the game. This year is no different."

Pat Haden, USC QB 1972-74: "Kids go to USC because they want to go to the Rose Bowl, and to do that, you have to beat UCLA."

Norm Anderson, UCLA WR 1973-75: "It's the most special week in a Bruin's career."

Terry Ragan, USC TB 1945-47: "There are two games that I always want USC to win - UCLA and Notre Dame."

Patt Troutman, UCLA SI Office: "USC is the team you really want to beat."

But maybe Sam Anno, USC's linebacker, summed it up best: "War! That's the way I look at it. War!"

War, or whatever, Donahue was cautious as the teams prepared for an afternoon kickoff before 90,064 boosters in the Coliseum. "USC is a very, very good team that has had some misfortunes," he pointed out.

It was UCLA, however, that Lady Luck deserted on this late November day, as a total of five turnovers would attest.

Early on came the first. Receiving the opening kickoff, the Bruins shredded Troy's defense with the arm of David Norrie and the legs of Green, soon arriving in the shadow of USC's goalpost. Then, on second-and-four from the 20, Mel Farr Jr. was divorced from the ball and a Trojan recovered.

Misfortune could rule just so long, however, and the Uclans mastered their next possession to success. It was a 63-yard drive in nine plays, highlighted by passes of 17 and 19 yards from Norrie

Jeff Bregel, (L) USC All-America Guard, 1985-86;
John Lee, UCLA All-America Place-kicker, 1984-85

to Dorrell, the latter reaching SC's one-yard line. From there, Eric Ball ploughed over, Lee added the extra point, and UCLA led, 7-0.

But the sleeping giant from Troy to whom Donahue alluded rose to its haunches and knotted the score at 7-all, moving 80 yards in 11 plays as the first frame expired. Along the way, Cormier pulled down flings of 14 and nine yards from Peete, and Peete gained 17 yards on a quarterback draw. The clincher came when Peete abandoned his pocket and found Cormier open near the sideline. Cormier dodged Washington and streaked down the side to complete a 34-yard scoring play. Shafer converted.

A slender six points posted by the Bruins belied their dominance of the second quarter. After advancing 51 yards in nine plays, UCLA faced a fourth-down-and-inches at USC's six-yard line. Donahue opted for a 22-yard field goal, Lee responded, and UCLA led, 10-7. Green's 21-yard scamper spotlighted the drive.

Some Monday-morning quarterbacks questioned Donahue's decision to forgo a shot at moving the sticks, pointing out that the Bruins needed fewer than 12 inches.

"I had absolutely no second thoughts," said Donahue. "We have the best field-goal kicker in America and we went ahead at halftime."

His lead at halftime was actually 13-7 as Lee added a 34-yard FG, his 79th career boot. Washington intercepted a Peete pass on UCLA's 21-yard line to make No. 79 possible.

The Bruins' margin could have been wider, but Green fumbled away the ball on third down at the USC 12-yard line just before the halftime buzzer.

Fireworks were dim in the third period but the Trojans inched a tad closer on a 38-yard field goal by Shafer. Peete rolled out for 19 yards and passed for 12 and 11 yards to Cormier as the Trojans eradicated 67 yards on eight plays. So, entering the fourth quarter, UCLA led, but only by 13-10.

Shortly thereafter, the Bruins muffed another opportunity to salt away the game. From the one-yard line, Ball essayed a dive into the endzone. While airborne, he lost its handle and SC's Marcus Cotton plucked the oval from the air and wrangled his way out to the 12.

"I was thinking touchdown," grinned Cotton, shy though he was by 88 yards.

The Trojans were forced to punt and the Bruins forced to punt back, thereby starting the winning 56-yard drive by Southern Cal.

Knight chalked up runs of 21 and 11 yards and Peete netted 11 on a quarterback draw, casting Tollner on center stage for his "Go for it" decision on fourth-and-two from the six. Peete's subsequent

TD sneak was, of course, for the marbles, but of secondary importance was Shafer's conversion because it lifted the Trojans to a more comfortable four-point lead.

"There wasn't any doubt I'd lead the team to a touchdown," exuded Peete, who started in lieu of senior Salisbury.

The game, however, wasn't finished at this point, so USC kicked off. But shortly thereafter, it was over. Because whatever chance UCLA had was squelched when McDonald filched a second-down pass from Norrie, intended for Sherrard.

Naturally, Tollner was beaming. "Our guys made the play when they had to," he uttered. "It was a courageous effort."

Donahue felt Peete was a big factor in the downfall of his gladiators. "His running kept USC alive with several key long runs," noted the Westwood taskmaster. "He hung in there when he had to."

Peete completed only eight passes and Cormier was on the receiving end of all.

"UCLA was trying to stop Hank (Norman), and that left me open," explained Cormier. For the record, Norman had become USC's all-time leading receiver with 113, and Peete would, in time, become the school's passing leader.

Each team had rushers that exceeded 100 yards: SC's Knight with 147, UCLA's Green with two yards fewer.

And once again, statistics-wise, the contest mirrored the previous year in that the loser tabulated more first downs and gained more yardage than did the winner.

UCLA rebounded from the USC upset with a solid triumph over Iowa in the Rose Bowl, its fourth straight bowl win in as many years. That provided the Uclans with a 9-2-1 slate and a final rank of No. 7. Lee repeated as an All-American, this time, however, as a consensus pick.

Southern Cal still had Oregon on its menu and the Ducks waddled away on the short end of a 20-6 score. That win brought the Trojans to a 6-5-0 record, which was adequate for an invitation to the Aloha Bowl. Alabama was the foe and the victor.

Matching UCLA in the glitter arena, USC, too, displayed a consensus All-American: offensive guard Bregel. Defensive back McDonald was listed for some AA accolades.

Scoring by Quarters:

UCLA 7 6 0 0 - 13
USC 7 0 3 7 - 17

//
1986
Game 56

A Green Blowout

Abashment, frustration, embarrassment... whatever. These emotions and more reflected in the heart and soul of each Trojan who dared to look at the scoreboard early in the fourth quarter. Through misty eyes, the brave ones who did look saw: UCLA 38, Southern California 0.

The 56th tussle of these titans of the turf didn't end quite so lopsided, however, as benevolent Coach Terry Donahue, having seen enough, pulled his front-line troops and instructed his reserves not to rush the USC passer. The Trojans responded to these gestures with three fourth-quarter touchdowns, thereby retaining a morsel of dignity in their 45-25 defeat. But it was still their third-worst loss in the history of the intracity series.

The surprise factor in Joe Bruin's romp was that bookies viewed the game as virtually a toss-up, a slight tilt, possibly, toward Westwood. Because season records were just about similar: UCLA, 6-3-1; Southern Cal, 7-2-0. And rankings weren't too far apart: USC, 10th; UCLA, 18th.

The Trojans had achieved this late-season status in dire dispute to preseason polls which did not include them in the Top-20. And, back in August, an air of uncertainty clouded the tenure of Coach

Ted Tollner, now embarking on his fourth season draped in rumblings and grumblings from disgruntled fans and alumni.

Appearing in the L. A. *Times* was a letter from a citizen in Orange County: "Keep Ted. Keep Ted. Keep Ted. But don't mind me, I'm a UCLA fan."

That was part of the disenchantment for Tollner: his inability to beat UCLA. And, overall, an anemic 19 victories and a tie in 37 games was far shy of Trojan standards.

In perspective, Tollner was apprehensive, even slightly optimistic. "Obviously, we're disappointed about not having as big of a year as we expected last season," he noted, "but that's behind us."

For his showdown season, Tollner welcomed back 42 lettermen, but only a dozen were starters, not a deep well from which to draw. Of these veterans, however, there were several aces, spearheaded by All-Americans Jeff Bregel and Tim McDonald. This duo was supported by David Cadigan, Marcus Cotton, Junior Thurman, Ryan Knight, Aaron Emanuel, Erik McKee, Sam Anno, Keith Davis, Lou Brock and QB Rodney Peete, though much would depend on his recovery from a torn Achilles tendon.

But Tollner would also play sans 26 lettermen, prominent names such as Hank Norman, Joe Cormier, James Fitzpatrick, Tom Hallock, Tom Cox, Brent Moore, Tony Colorito, Kennedy Pola, Fred Crutcher, Jerome Tyler, Sean Salisbury and Gaylord Kuamoo, plus a couple of Matts - Johnson and Koart.

If there were dark clouds hanging over the Cardinal and Gold of Tollner, conversely, there were rays of sunshine beaming on the Blue and Gold of Donahue. For his Bruins were predicted as a "can't miss" for PAC-10 laurels. And, although preseason polls placed the Uclans no higher than 16th, some prognosticators envisioned them as contenders for the national title.

No doubt, this was influenced by the return of 51 lettermen, including a stable of running backs - Gaston Green, Eric Ball, Mel Farr, James Primus - that any college would be hard pressed to match. Other standouts returning to the fold: Karl Dorrell, Marcus Greenwood, Terry Tumey, Matt Stevens, Derek Tennell, Chuckie Miller, Joe Grebel, Ken Norton, James Washington, Craig Rutledge and Frank Batchkoff.

Donahue's most piercing loss may have been place-kicker of renown John Lee, but the astute coach could point to the departures of Tommy Taylor, Rob Cox, Mike Sherrard, Mark Walen, Jim McCullough, Mike Hartmeier and Steve Jarecki, too.

No. 1 rated Oklahoma appeared first on the Bruin schedule, and the Sooners justified their reputation by slaughtering UCLA, 38-3. So it was back to the drawing board for the Bruins, who then trounced San Diego State and Long Beach State, dropped a decision to Arizona State, conquered Arizona, California, Washington State, Oregon State, fell victim to Stanford and locked even with Washington. Next up: Southern California.

The Trojans broke quickly from the gate and racked up four straight triumphs - Illinois, Baylor, Washington and Oregon. But, while basking in the sunlight of a No. 9 ranking, rain drops suddenly fell in the form of reversals from the forces of Washington State and Arizona State. Then, Stanford, Arizona and California returned the radiance to the Trojan camp. Next up: UCLA.

Regardless of the game's outcome, neither school would represent the conference in the Rose Bowl. Instead, UCLA flirted with the strong possibility of playing in the nearby Freedom Bowl at Anaheim, while USC would definitely participate in the more coveted Citrus Bowl way across the land in Florida.

That arrangement didn't sit too well with Bruin linebacker Norton. "I'm not really sure why the Citrus folks chose USC," he muttered. "We're just going to beat USC so bad Saturday, I think they will know we should have been there."

Donahue, however, played the cards he was dealt. "If you can't go to a major bowl," he reasoned, "it's still nice to be asked to the dance."

Turning his attention to the battle at hand, Donahue added: "Just because the Rose Bowl isn't at stake against USC doesn't alter the flavor of this game. We've both got exactly the same things to play for, and the pride of the city."

UCLA's strong safety Rutledge agreed with his coach. "Either team could be 0-10 or 10-0 and it wouldn't make a bit of difference," he said. "This game is like a season within a season."

As did most bookmakers, Tollner viewed the conflict "...as a tossup."

But his defensive coordinator, Artie Gigantino, was more specific. "Gaston Green is the best tailback we've played against. It's going to take a monumental effort to stop him," he warned.

Apparently, even a monumental effort was insufficient as Green tallied four touchdowns while rolling up 224 yards, the most ever amassed by one runner in one game against Southern California. Green also joined an exclusive coterie of only four players in UCLA history who had rushed for more than 1,000 yards in a single season (Freeman McNeil, Theotis Brown, Wendall Tyler, Kermit Johnson).

**Tim McDonald (L) USC All-America, 1985-86;
Gaston Green, UCLA All-America, 1987**

So, on a windswept afternoon, a gathering of 98,370 spectators at Pasadena looked on with mild surprise as, midway the first quarter, Green broke off tackle from the USC 46, avoided McDaniel and Brock, then raced down the sideline for a touchdown. David Franey's PAT capped the 58-yard drive and staked UCLA to a 7-0 lead.

Late in the same period, the Bruins moved 67 yards in seven plays for their second TD with Green erasing the final 27, thanks to a clearing block by Onno Zwaneveld. A prelude to the score was a 20-yard toss from Stevens to Flipper Anderson.

Franey converted, then early in the second frame, added a 23-yard field goal. Again, a pass from Stevens to Anderson - a 25-yarder - sustained the 63-yard drive. Dismay was brewing among Trojan rooters, but they figured a 17-point deficit wasn't insurmountable.

But what about a 24-point spread? That's what it became shortly thereafter as UCLA mixed the running of Green with the passing of Stevens to eradicate 80 yards in 14 plays. Green scored from the two and Franey split the uprights.

Now dismay had turned into despair for Trojan fans, and a play that ended the first half would bring on despondency. It was a so-called "Hail Mary" episode, and here's how Thomas Bonk described it in the L.A. *Times:* "With only nine seconds left in the first half, on second-and-nine from the USC 39, Stevens launched a pass that had the trajectory of a rainbow and was aimed for the endzone.

"Three USC defenders leaped, and so did the intended receiver, Flipper Anderson. The ball was tipped into the air, where it was finally reeled in by Karl Dorrell with no time left on the clock. Touchdown, UCLA. Also, 31-0, UCLA."

Dorrell was ecstatic, albeit honest. "It was a fluke," he cracked.

Fluke or not, Tollner wouldn't focus on that single play. "The whole first half was kind of a shock," he observed.

Regardless of Tollner's summation, that throw-it-up-for-grabs heave may have been the blow that crumbled the walls of Troy. For the Trojans were still in a daze as the Bruins opened the third stanza by proceeding 80 yards in 10 plays to increase their lead to 38-0. Green sped the final yard on a pitchout, but it was a 33-yard pass from Dorrell, a flanker, to Anderson that kept alive the march.

Finally, with the setting sun matching the spirits of the Trojans, Ol' Sol cast a teasing ray of brightness on the bewildered visitors. It came in the form of a 78-yard drive that SC consumed in seven plays and which was sealed with Knight bolting over the goal line from one yard out. The key play was a 34-yard sling from Peete to Paul Green. Don Shafer's conversion marked the score at 38-7.

Hospitable, however, the host Bruins were not... at least, not at this stage of the game. With Green still pounding out yardage and Stevens connecting with Joe Pickert for 25 yards, UCLA covered 77 yards in 10 plays. On the 11th, Stevens drilled a 3-yard TD pass to Greenwood, and Franey's PAT brought the third quarter to a close with UCLA soaring, 45-7.

Whether it was charity from UCLA or never-say-die courage from Southern Cal is uncertain; however, regardless of the nature, the fourth quarter belonged to the Trojans.

Knight accounted for USC's second touchdown on a one-yard carry, and Randy Tanner pulled down pitches of 13 and 15 yards from Peete to rack up TD numbers three and four. Two-point conversion attempts after each score all failed.

Knight's marker was the 14th play of an 80-yard journey that included important passes from Peete to Lonnie White for 19 yards and to Ken Henry for 23.

Dan Owens enfolded a Stevens' fumble on UCLA's 13-yard line which led to Tanner's first score, and the second was abetted by flings of 13, 18 and nine yards from Peete to White. Final score: UCLA 45, Southern Cal 25.

But if the final period belonged to Troy, it might be said the entire contest belonged to the officials. For the lads in stripes dropped their hankies 21 times, assessing USC for 105 yards and UCLA for 114. Yes, that created a new high mark for infractions in the series.

Tollner's overview of the skirmish was brief: "We were whipped in every phase of the game, especially in the first half."

His defensive ace, McDonald, was more expressive. "I'm very disappointed," he uttered. "I'm upset the way we played defense. We just didn't play aggressively and I don't know why. The game was embarrassing."

Donahue didn't lack for verbiage, either, though his was naturally upbeat.

"It was a very important, very crucial win for us because it allowed us to salvage the season," he stated. "The difference in points could have been even greater, but the key was not to beat USC by 20 points, the key was to beat USC." Then he added: "This was one of the brightest moments in UCLA history. And I don't know what to say about our offensive line except they were great."

So it was merrily on to the Freedom Bowl for the Bruins where they found a cooperative foe in Brigham Young, a final victory that posted an 8-3-1 season and a national rank of No. 14.

SPORTS

Green and UCLA Make It a Runaway, 45-25

Tailback Helps Rout USC With 224 Yards, 4 TDs; Bruins Add Hail-Matt Pass

Southern Cal still had unranked Notre Dame on its schedule and the affair was a heartbreaker... for the Trojans. With two seconds to play, ND's John Carney slammed a 19-yard field goal to edge USC by a single point. Then a loss to Auburn in the Citrus Bowl framed an unpretentious season of 7-5-0 for USC.

The Trojans, however, took pride in having two consensus All-Americans - Bregel and McDonald - but their performances, along with their mates, could not save Tollner from dismissal as SC's head coach. In four autumns, Tollner won 26 games, lost 20 and tied one. In eight square-offs against chief rivals UCLA and Notre Dame, Tollner registered one-and-seven.

In short, that was simply not acceptable to the people of Troy or to the standards that envelop Heritage Hall.

Scoring by Quarters:

USC	0	0	7	18	-	25
UCLA	14	17	14	0	-	45

1987
Game 57

An Ungroovy Win

Over at Hollywood Park, a 4-year-old colt named Groovy was upset by a filly in the Sprint event of the Breeders' Cup. But at the Coliseum, the manner in which Southern California, a nine-point underdog, upset the University of California-Los Angeles was anything but groovy. For, as Jim Murray, of the L.A. *Times,* summed up the game: "USC had to beat USC Saturday before it could beat UCLA." His reference was to touchdowns that were nullified, goal line fumbles, endzone interceptions, untimely penalties, and other failed opportunities.

"Obviously, we wanted to win more than they did," said Marcus Cotton, USC's brilliant linebacker. And win the Trojans did, 17-13.

As implied above, they weren't supposed to finish on the tall side. UCLA entered the melee with 9-1-0 credentials, purring on eight consecutive conquests, and an *Associated Press* ranking of No. 5.

Under new head coach Larry Smith, imported from the arid land of Arizona, Southern Cal brought a 7-3-0 record, including three straight victories, but ignored in AP's Top-20.

Those stats were in line with fortune-tellers who utilize preseason crystal balls. Those Merlins of August envisioned UCLA as the third best, the fourth best, the sixth best or the seventh best squad in the land, depending on which a reader chose to believe. Accord was present on one prediction, though: the PAC-10 tiara could adorn Joe Bruin's head for the asking.

SPORTS

Trojans Go for Juggler, Beat UCLA, 17-13

Affholter Is in Bounds; USC Is in Rose Bowl

Southern Cal's place in the national picture ranged in slots near the bottom of the Totem Pole: as high as 13th, as low as 19th. But one survey named the Trojans as conference runners-up to UCLA.

Certainly, logic supported the prophets who were so enamored with UCLA's chances. For, heading a list of 56 returning lettermen were tailback Gaston Green and linebacker Ken Norton, both All-Americans-to-be. Add Eric Ball, Mel Farr, James Primus, Willie Anderson, Paco Craig, Joe Pickett, Russ Warnick and John Kidder to offensive returnees, plus Terry Tumey, Jeff Glasser, Carnell Lake, Jim Wahler, Eric Smith, James Washington and Dennis Price on defense and what is the result? Answer: a wide grin on the face of Coach Terry Donahue.

Make that a wide, wide, wide grin. Donahue also had two prize transfers in his camp - Troy Aikman from Oklahoma and David Richards from SMU.

True, the wily one from Westwood had some huge plugs to fill... 26 lettermen, including such veterans as Matt Stevens, Karl Dorrell, Derek Tennell, Chuckie Miller, Craig Rutledge, Joe Goebel, Eric Rogers, Jim Alexander and Onno Zwaneveld.

At USC, incoming-coach Smith lost only 16 lettermen, but the group included Tim McDonald, Jeff Bregel, Lou Brock and James Thurman, as well as Todd Steele, Erik McKee, Ron Brown and Bruce Parks.

Heading an array of 45 returning lettermen were offensive tackle Dave Cadigan, destined for consensus All-America honors, and quarterback Rodney Peete. Supporting this pair were Ryan Knight, Steve Webster, Ken Henry, Randy Tanner, Paul Green, Erik Affholter and John Katnik. Aaron Emanuel was due to return but was suspended for the entire year for disciplinary reasons.

Cotton was the main man among defensive returnees, but help was present in the forms of Rex Moore, Keith Davis, Tim Ryan, Greg Coauette and Dan Owens.

**USC's Erik Affholter Makes Catch
That Beats UCLA in 1987**

As Trojans scrimmaged on practice fields, Smith - a martinet, he - was getting a lot of unsolicited advice from former players, alums and fans in general. But Smith listened.

"I want to get these people back with what we're doing, so they can feel a part of it," he remarked. "We need to get some re-direction in our program."

So the season opened... but on a sour note, as Michigan State dumped the Smithmen. Not to worry. The Trojans bounced back to capture seven of their next nine games, bowing only to Oregon and No. 10 Notre Dame, while buffing Boston College, California, Oregon State, Washington, Washington State, Stanford and Arizona, the school just abandoned by Coach Smith.

UCLA opened with an easy win over San Diego State, but faltered the next week against No. 2 Nebraska. That was the lone stumble, however, as the Bruins reeled off impressive victories over Fresno State, Arizona, Stanford, Oregon, California, Arizona State, Oregon State and Washington.

The usual hoopla engulfed the days leading up to USC-UCLA's 57th clash... toga parties at Troy, street dances in Westwood Village, verbiage freely offered by one and all.

USC Coach Smith: "It's the best UCLA team I've seen since I've been in the PAC-10 (eight years). They're big, fast and have an excellent defense. We'll have to play our best game by far to win."

UCLA Coach Donahue: "I'd much rather be playing a passing team instead of getting into a street fight we'll be getting into. I'm sure they'll remember last year's game and will be anxious to make sure it isn't a repeat."

USC's Peete: "I can hardly wait. We can't help but think about how badly we got beat last year."

Stanford Coach Jack Elway: "USC has a potent offense because it can throw and run. UCLA can do the same. Overall, I think UCLA has the better team."

Foster Andersen, mighty Bruin of yore, was a bit philosophical: "The number of times the underdog rises to the occasion in this game far outweighs the times I've been able to predict who has the better team."

But not Mike Downey. Despite the odds, the *Times* columnist boldly tabbed Southern Cal as a 24-20 victor. He picked the winner and the four-point margin.

Unlike the previous eight games, the winner of this encounter would also get the nod as host team in the Rose Bowl. The Bruins had a cushion, though, as a mere tie could send them packing for Pasadena, whereas a win was a must for the Trojans.

**Dave Cadigan, USC
All-America OL, 1987**

**Larry Smith, USC
Head Coach, 1987-92**

"All the marbles are on the line," announced Smith at a Tuesday luncheon.

And all the faithful from both institutions - 92,516 - were on hand at the Coliseum to see firsthand who would pick up the marbles.

At first, it seemed the choice of the bookies would, as the Uclans built a 13-0 lead while watching the Trojans shoot themselves in their collective feet, time and time again.

Midway through the first period, UCLA constructed a 72-yard drive, and the 11th play was a 6-yard touchdown dash by Green, who eluded Dwayne Garner to reach the corner. Green contributed a 20-yard scamper, too, and Aikman passed 19 yards to Anderson to sustain the campaign. Alfredo Velasco's PAT firmed the score at 7-0, UCLA.

Receiving the ensuing kickoff, USC steadily moved downfield. But a 21-yard pass from Peete to John Jackson to UCLA's 18 went for naught because of a holding penalty. Undaunted, the Trojans struck again on the same drive... a 34-yard touchdown pass from Peete to Henry. Scratch that, too. The TD was nullified due to a delay-of-game penalty.

Now the Bruins figured they could play that routine, too. Aikman hurled 10 yards to Anderson and 10 to Craig, then tossed a 15-yard scoring pass to Mike Farr which was, naturally, wiped out by a holding penalty. But Joe Bruin didn't come away empty as did Tommy Trojan after his misfortune. One play after the TD-killing penalty, Velasco delivered a 32-yard field goal.

Trailing 10-0 in the second stanza, the Thundering Herd rolled downfield again, driving to the Uclan's one-yard line... to no avail. On a confused fourth down, Knight took a handoff from Peete, slammed into the line - and fumbled. UCLA recovered.

Not to matter, chorused the Trojans. So downfield they marched again, all the way to UCLA's four-yard line. On first down, Peete drifted back and fired toward the left corner of the endzone. The ball was tipped by Bruin Marcus Patton and deflected into the bosom of teammate Eric Turner, who set sail in high gear for the opposite endzone, six points dancing gleefully in his head.

He even had blockers ready to protect his sideline avenue. But Peete, the fellow who threw the interception, suddenly appeared in hot pursuit. Doggedly, he chased Turner and finally brought him to earth after an 89-yard pursuit that terminated at SC's 11-yard line as the half ended. Instead of being behind by 17 points, the Trojans were in arrears by just 10.

"I really thought I could catch him, but I didn't know when," declared Peete. "'Don't let him score' is all that went through my mind."

Of course, Turner was down on himself. "I thought I was gonna' go all the way," he lamented. "I don't have blazing speed, but I'm 4.56 in the 40."

To which Mr. Peete replied: "I'm 4.50."

Did six-hundredths of a second prevent six points?

Or, did failure by the officials to call a face mask penalty on Peete save the Trojans? Turner claimed, and Peete admitted, the infraction.

"Yup, I got it (face mask), too," acknowledged Peete. "I'm glad the ref didn't see it." If "the ref" had seen the infraction, UCLA would have had one shot to score... from USC's six-yard line.

Regardless, UCLA owned the points at intermission, but it seemed USC owned the confidence.

"We knew once we cut out mistakes, we'd put it in the endzone," noted Trojan Tanner. "It wasn't like they were stopping us, it was what we were doing to ourselves."

But the gift bag from Southern California was not empty. Early in the third period, Chris Sperle's punt traveled a short 18 yards, setting up UCLA just 27 yards away from paydirt. A touchdown did not materialize, but a field goal did... a 32-yard swing by Velasco. UCLA, 13-0.

Still in the third frame, USC finally put some digits on the board, albeit only a trey. Spirited by passes of 19 and 15 yards from Peete to Affholter, the Trojans churned 62 yards in nine plays, setting up a field goal of 26 yards by Quin Rodriguez.

Now, USC was free of mistakes, right? Nope. From UCLA's 23-yard line, Trojan Ricky Ervins' bobble was picked up by Peete, who drilled a touchdown pass to Tanner. But, once again... no cigar. The TD was called back because of an ineligible receiver downfield.

Unbroken in spirit, the intrepid Trojans fought back. This time, they were not to be denied. The Peete-to-Affholter combination clicked for gains of 16 and 19 yards before Peete, from the six, found Tanner in the middle of the endzone to seal a 76-yard, 13-play drive. After Rodriguez' PAT, Southern Cal had pulled to within three points.

But, unaccustomed to prosperity, the Trojans couldn't shed the yoke of errors. As the fourth quarter unfolded, USC's Mark Carrier intercepted an Aikman pass and ran it back 72 yards for a touchdown, but that score, too, was nullified by an illegal block penalty.

Had the bars of justice forsaken the land of Troy? Not quite, because even after the washed-out TD by Carrier, the Trojans were in good field position, just 42 yards away from UCLA's goal, and more than half-a-quarter to do something about it. Mixed in with a penalty, Leroy Holt bolted for eight yards and Peete hit Tanner for 10. On the sixth play of the abbreviated drive, the bedeviled Trojans pulled ahead for the first time. The vehicle was a 33-yard scoring pass from Peete to Affholter, who beat cornerback Marcus Turner, momentarily juggled the ball, but pulled it to his chest while barely keeping his feet in bounds.

"The pass wasn't designed to come my way," said Affholter. "I was supposed to clear out with the tight end getting the ball underneath. I just saw the ball at the last minute and pulled it down."

With Aikman in the saddle, the Bruins still had time to stage a comeback, even starting from their own five-yard line following a 47-yard punt by Sperles. But, a few plays later, their dream of New Year's Day roses was snuffed when Carrier filched a pass by Aikman. It was the fourth turnover by UCLA in the second half. Final score: USC 17, UCLA 13.

Three All-Americans played in the game: Cadigan for USC, Green and Norton for UCLA.

Afterwards, there were no excuses by Donahue. "USC played a great game," he praised. "They did the things they needed to win and they were the better team today."

Winning-coach Smith was emotionally charged: "I've been associated with many teams, but never one that had as much fight, drive and desire. This team truly earned its championship. I'm not a great coach, but they're a great team."

Great, perhaps, but not invincible, as proved by Michigan State in the Rose Bowl. The three-point loss to the Spartans framed the Trojan season at eight victories and four defeats, adequate for a final rank of No. 18 by AP.

Though beaten by USC, the Bruins notched a higher national rank, coming in at No. 9. This was based on a 10-2-0 record, the 10th win achieved in the Aloha Bowl over Florida.

Scoring by Quarters:

UCLA	7	3	3	0	-	13
USC	0	0	3	14	-	17

Ken Norton, UCLA All-America, 1987

1988

Game 58

A Peete Repeat

Anticipation, reward, revenge, honor, intrigue, controversy... the 58th wrangle between Southern California and UCLA refined these elements, and more.

The anticipation belonged to the Trojans, who approached the skirmish on the unblemished plateau of perfection - nine victories in nine games. A win over the Bruins, followed up by a likewise verdict over Notre Dame, would bring a national championship to the hallowed halls of Heritage.

The reward belonged to both schools. For the winning team would vault into the Rose Bowl on New Year's Day. Actually, Southern Cal could qualify with a tie, and Coach Larry Smith wouldn't hedge at the thought. "If that decision rose, I'd go for the tie," he pondered, "because a tie would put us in the Rose Bowl."

The revenge belonged to UCLA which was upset the previous year in a strange game that most experts deemed "...could have gone either way."

The honor - that of having a Heisman Trophy winner - could possibly anoint either the Ackerman Union Quad or the Exposition Park Campus. For Troy Aikman, UCLA's stone-faced quarterback, and USC's Rodney Peete, he of the infectious grin, were the leading candidates for the Big H.

The intrigue? Well, that belonged to Tommy Trojan through the personage of Mr. Peete, who not only had an infectious grin, but

What Separates Aikman and Peete?
Saturday's Game Should Go a Long Way in Providing an Answer to That

also had succumbed to an infectious case of measles several days before the game.

Would he play? If so, would he start?

"He's under a doctor's care," acknowledged Smith on Wednesday, four days prior to kickoff.

"Coach, don't worry about it. I'll be there," responded Peete.

And the controversy? Well, not Peete nor anyone else would play if heed were given to Dr. Lawrence Ross, an infectious disease control specialist who was concerned with the spreading attack of the virus at both universities.

"A two-week postponement of the game would be appropriate," he suggested. "It would be in the best interest of everyone - fans, players, everyone."

Not surprisingly, the measles bug became the talk of the town. Can I catch it? Have I had it? The unfunny bug even gave rise to a bit of humor, too. Unable to attend the traditional Rotary Club football luncheon on Friday, UCLA Coach Terry Donahue sent quarterbacks coach Rick Neuheisel to represent him. When asked of Donahue's whereabouts, Neuheisel replied: "He's over on campus standing in a long line at a pay phone, waiting to call his mom to find out if he's had the measles."

USC's Smith did attend the luncheon, and he joined in the frivolity by "...wishing UCLA the best of luck - in whichever bowl it chooses to play in."

But students, players and coaches were immunized, Peete - at the sound of the whistle - miraculously recovered, and the game was indeed carried out on schedule, much to the chagrin of Joe Bruin. For the No. 2 Trojans battered the No. 6 Bruins and remained undefeated and untied after 10 games. The score: 31-22.

It was no easy feat, it being only the second loss of the season for UCLA, which entered the contest with nine triumphs, too.

Before the season started, the sports media bracketed the two teams just about equal. *Associated Press* foresaw USC as No. 8, UCLA as No. 9. Sage Don Heinrich placed UCLA at No. 6, USC No. 9. One magazine tabbed USC as No. 1 in the PAC-10 race with UCLA No. 2; another reversed the order.

"I'm anxious to see how this UCLA team develops," stated Donahue. "It's going to be interesting. We have the best quarterback we could possibly have. But people don't want to accept the fact that this is a rebuilding year for us."

He didn't need to identify the quarterback by name. "Aikman" was not only a household word around Morgan Center but equally as well in the world of sports, and his reputation had already caught the eyes of professional scouts.

Tex Schramm, then-president of the NFL Dallas Cowboys, was asked if he thought Aikman would look good wearing a helmet with a blue star. "I'm thinking of Troy Aikman," he quipped. "I cannot tell a lie."

And the rebuilding to which Donahue referred? Well, 14 starters hailed farewell to Westwood... among them Gaston Green, Willie Anderson, Paco Craig, Mel Farr, John Kidder, David Richards and Russ Wamick on offense; Terry Tumey, Jeff Glasser, Alan Dial, Melvin Jackson, Ken Norton, Dennis Price on defense.

Overshadowing these departures was the return of 56 lettermen. In addition to Aikman, Donahue would count on offensive stars such as Charles Arbuckle, Frank Cornish, Rick Meyer and Eric Ball, as well as place-kicker Alfredo Velasco. Punter Harold Barkate was back, too, along with Darryl Henley, Chance Johnson, Carnell Lake and Jim Wahler on defense.

"Last year we were able to reload," observed Donahue, "but this year we're trying to replace a lot of senior leadership. I hope we can reload again."

Optimism was in full sway at Southern Cal, and Smith rode the wave in stride. "I knew we'd be picked high," he said. "But if we get everybody back that we have on paper, we could be quite a bit better than last year. And that, quite frankly, is our goal."

Indeed, a wealth of talent roamed the halls of Troy as Smith prepared for his second autumn. Greeting the soph coach were 51 lettermen... radiant offensive stars such as Peete, who as a junior set a dozen school career, season and game records; tailback Steve Webster, the league rushing champ; leading receiver Erik Affholter, plus Paul Green, Scott Galbrath, John Guerrero, Leroy Holt, Brent Parkinson, Mark Tucker and Aaron Emanuel, back after a year of suspension.

But "...on defense, we could be a rock," predicted Smith, casting an admiring eye on the gifts possessed by Mark Carrier, Cleveland Colter, Tim Ryan, Chris Hale, Don Gibson, Dan Owens, Scott Ross and Delmar Chesley.

Eligibility had expired for a slim but quality-laden bunch of Trojans. Gone were Dave Cadigan and Randy Tanner on offense,

The Southern California Tradition Began With These Trojans in 1888

Trojan All-Americans Rodney Peete (L) and Cleveland Colter

along with Greg Coauette, Marcus Cotton, Keith Davis, John Katnik and Bill Stokes on defense.

Although Webster and Green showed up with severe knee injuries, the Trojans were indomitable as foe after foe wilted under their assault. First victim was Boston College, followed by Stanford, No. 3 Oklahoma, Arizona, Oregon, Washington, Oregon State, California and Arizona State... nine games, nine wins. Now ready for UCLA, the Trojans would fare as the second best team in the nation, according to the AP poll.

What's more, save for a four-point upset setback to Washington State, the Bruins would have entered the USC fray undefeated and untied, too. Prior to the shocker by the Cougars, UCLA had snuffed San Diego State, No. 2 Nebraska, Long Beach State, Washington, Oregon State, California and Arizona. Afterwards, the Bruins bounced back with decisions over Oregon and Stanford. Not bad: 9-1-0, No. 6, and now poised for the Troy invasion.

Focal point of the brawl centered on the quarterbacks. Peete, in leading USC to its near-pinnacle, had thrown for 2,240 yards and 17 touchdowns. Aikman had passed for 2,282 yards and 21 TDs.

"But I've got to play better than I have in the past two weeks; in fact, everyone must play better," surmised Aikman.

Neither squad was without key injuries. Hobbled Bruins included Ball, Wahler, David Keating, Scott Spalding, Steve Mehr and Brad Bryson. Crippled Trojans included Colter, Webster, Green and, of course, the infirm Peete.

Because of uncertainty surrounding the status of Peete, betting odds dropped from UCLA-plus-3 on Monday to UCLA-plus-1 on Saturday.

Odds notwithstanding, Giles Pellerin was in the Rose Bowl Stadium ready to witness the 58th bout of the crosstown rivals. But unlike the other 100,740 spectators in attendance, it would be the 676th Southern California game in a row that he had seen. Mr. Pellerin, whose age reached four score and one, hadn't missed a USC game, home or away, since 1926.

His loyalty was rewarded, though his beloved Trojans first spotted the other team to a three-point lead. Receiving the opening kickoff, UCLA drove to USC's 29-yard line in 10 plays, four of them pass completions by Aikman. On third-and-three, Aikman's pass aimed at Keating was batted down by cornerback Hale, so Velasco booted a 46-yard field goal. That was the only time the Trojans trailed.

Scott Lockwood's 21-yard return of a booming Barkate punt put USC in business at the Uclan 36. Spiced by a 17-yard strike from Peete to Affholter, the Trojans scored in seven plays, Emanuel erasing the final four. After Rodriguez' conversion, Southern Cal led, 7-3.

In the second quarter, Peete guided the Trojans from their own 33-yard line to UCLA's 29, flavored by passes of 13 yards to Jackson and 15 to Affholter. On third down, Peete found Affholter near the sideline. After making the catch, Affholter evaded cornerbacks Eric Turner and Henley and raced into the endzone. Rodriguez added the point-after. USC, 14-3.

The Bruins retaliated, unfurling a 57-yard movement on the strength of passes from Aikman to Mike Farr for 13 yards and to Shawn Wills for 11 and 10. On third down from USC's nine-yard line, Reggie Moore failed on a diving effort to snare Aikman's throw, so Velasco trotted in to drill a 27-yard FG.

It seemed UCLA's only weapon was the reliable foot of Velasco, as the junior pumped through a third field goal to narrow USC's margin to 14-9. It was a 25-yarder that capped a 38-yard trek in eight plays. Brian Brown donated a 28-yard dash to make possible the FG.

UCLA couldn't register a touchdown and it was a mystery to Aikman. "That's been the story with us pretty much for the last four or five weeks," he shrugged.

Now feeling on his shoulders the escalating breath of Joe Bruin, Tommy Trojan hoisted his arches and answered the surge with a put-down marker of his own.

Ricky Ervins returned the ensuing kickoff 60 yards, after which USC eradicated 39 more in eight plays. Peete tossed 14 yards to John Jackson, 13 to Green, then sneaked over the double stripe from the one. Enter Rodriguez, enter score of 21-9, USC.

There's a never-say-die spirit among the lads of Donahue, and this quality rose to the fore in the last minute of the first half as the Bruins racked up their first touchdown. It was born of a 70-yard march that required just seven plays, and the curtain dropped with a 10-yard bullet from Aikman to Moore. Preceding the TD, Moore had garnered passes of 15 and 11 yards, Farr snagged one for 12 and Larry Burkley pulled in a 16-yarder... all from Aikman. With Velasco's point-after, the clubs broke for intermission with USC atop, 21-16.

In the hearts of the Trojans, that differential was insufficient. So, after stopping UCLA's first possession in the third period, USC stormed 51 yards in seven plays. Emanuel went up the middle and over from three yards out, but it was a 30-yard sling from Peete to Green that spiked the attack. Rodriguez' toe was true.

UCLA generated two stabs at scoring in the third frame, but Earnest Spears intercepted an Aikman heave to halt one effort, and Ryan sacked Aikman to effectively stymie the other.

Scoring was sparse in the fourth quarter, but one of the game's turning points came early on. With fourth-and-inches on his own 33-yard line, USC's Smith decided not to punt. Instead, Peete hit the line, spun outside, and moved the sticks.

"In a game like this, you've got to go for it, be aggressive," related Smith.

Later, USC tacked on a 21-yard field goal by Rodriguez, thanks to a botched reverse by UCLA. Fielding Chris Sperle's punt, Henley attempted a handoff to Marcus Turner but, while doing so, was creamed by SC's Hale, and fumbled. Mike Serpa recovered for Troy.

The FG upped USC's lead to 31-16, but UCLA was not ready for the showers. Hurling missiles of 17 yards to Farr and 11 to Brendan McCracken, Aikman led the Bruins 60 yards downfield, signing off with a 26-yard TD strike to McCracken. His 2-point conversion fling to Farr fell incomplete. Final score: USC , 31-22.

Statistically, Peete was upstaged by Aikman in the QB duel. The Trojan senior connected on 16 of 28 passes for 184 yards with one touchdown, and scored a TD himself. The Bruin senior was 32 of 48 for 317 yards and two touchdowns.

"It wasn't good enough," said Aikman, glancing at the scoreboard. "USC has a good football team, but I don't think they really stopped us, except for a few critical times."

Smith was ecstatic in his praise of Peete. "Rodney's performance today was one of the greatest I've ever seen," he acclaimed. "It was a superhuman effort." So, to the surprise of only a few, Peete - measles and all - was named "Player of the Game".

But if the task of spanking UCLA was difficult, even a more challenging hurdle loomed ahead for the Trojans: No. 1 Notre Dame in a quarrel for the national championship. Unfortunately, it was not the gridders from the West Coast who would wear the crown as the Irish spoiled Southern Cal's perfect record with a 27-10 lacing. And the stigma of defeat remained with the Trojans as Michigan prevailed in the Rose Bowl game. But it was still an excellent season for Smith and his gladiators from Troy: 10 wins, two losses, a No. 7 national rank, and a bevy of All-Americans - Affholter, Carrier, Peete, Colter and Ryan.

Not to be far outdone, four All-Americans resided in the Westwood camp - Aikman and Henley, both consensus, plus Lake and Arbuckle.

UCLA met and defeated Arkansas in the Cotton Bowl, earning a final rank of No. 6 on the girth of a 10-2-0 season. By the way, conquest of the Razorbacks marked the seventh consecutive bowl victory for the Bruins in as many years.

Oh... so who was awarded the Heisman Trophy? Well, neither Mr. Aikman nor Mr. Peete. Ever heard of a tailback from Oklahoma State named Mr. Barry Sanders?

Scoring by Quarters:

USC	7	14	7	3	-	31
UCLA	3	13	0	6	-	22

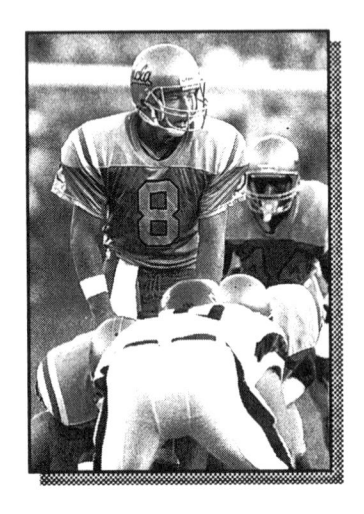

**A Trio of
Bruin All-Americans:
Troy Aikman (UL)
Carnell Lake (UR)
Darryl Henley (LR)**

1989
Game 59

Crossbar Folly

As the clock flashed 2:02 to play, Southern California's Brent Parkinson fell to his knees. He may have prayed. For the offensive tackle had just seen teammate Leroy Holt fumble on UCLA's 12-yard line... just as his highly-favored, but highly-struggling Trojans were on the verge of breaking a 10-10 tie. With further disbelief, he watched UCLA's Rocen Keeton pounce on the loose ball.

Now on the sideline, Parkinson cringed as Bruin QB Bret Johnson sailed a bomb over cornerback Dwayne Garner and into the outstretched arms of Scott Miller for a 52-yard gain, all the way to USC's 36. Shawn Wills earned a yard and Johnson kept the pigskin for another.

"We were just trying to get to the 32," explained UCLA Coach Terry Donahue, "because we thought he (Alfredo Velasco) could kick a field goal from there."

Perhaps he could have, but on third down, Wills, going wide, was flattened by Cleveland Colter for a three-yard loss, back to the 37.

"Wills didn't run where the play was meant to go," said Donahue.

Now, a hoped-for-49-yard FG effort became in reality a 54-yard attempt... with two seconds to play.

Breathlessly and helplessly, Parkinson and his sideline mates watched as Velasco lined up for his long-distance kick, the trajectory of which would either crush the Trojans or bring delirium to the Bruins.

It's a Win From 53, but a Tie From 54

A 54-yard field goal attempt by UCLA's Alfredo Velasco hits the crossbar on the final play of the game Saturday. Photo was taken from ABC television replay.

The crowd of 86,672 fans in the Coliseum, somewhat pale by usual gates, was stone quiet, and none was seated. It was akin to a priest reading the Gospel - all eyes centered on the deliverer, in this case a smallish fellow wearing jersey No. 25.

Up, up, up, the flight was true. Then... thud. The ball hit the crossbar, bounced up agonizingly, then fell innocently onto the endzone turf. There was no miracle for UCLA, only the faint satisfaction of a 10-10 tie against a team rated vastly superior as a 17-point favorite.

"I smacked it about as good as I could and I really thought it was going through," moaned Velasco.

And while many Bruins stretched out on the war-zone ground in agony, deep down they knew they had achieved a victory of morale.

Because entering the game, Southern Cal was ranked No. 8 in the land, having lost only two of ten games played. UCLA was unranked, having lost seven of ten games played.

At the outset of the season, both teams were highly regarded, but only USC had justified its billing.

Preseason dopesters spotted Southern Cal as low as No. 3, while the *Associated Press* placed Troy at No. 5. The PAC-10 gold medal was a foregone conclusion - Southern California all the way.

This bright outlook was influenced by the loss of only a handful of key players: Erik Affholter, Rodney Peete, John Guerrero on offense; Chris Hale and punter Chris Sperle on defense.

The number returning was impressive: 47 lettermen. Offensive names included Mark Tucker, Aaron Emanuel, John Jackson, Holt, Brad Leggett, Scott Galbraith, Marlon Washington, Parkinson, Dan Barnes and place-kicker Quin Rodriguez.

"But defense will be the strength of our team," predicted Coach Larry Smith, scanning a roster that embraced Mark Carrier, Colter,

Tim Ryan, Scott Ross, Junior Seau, Don Gibson, Delmar Chesley, Dan Owens, Earnest Spears and Mike Williams.

If, however, the future appeared rosy around the environs of Heritage Hall, there were likewise no thorns adorning Royce Hall. For soothsayers envisioned the Bruins as low as No. 6, with AP listing them at No. 9. And UCLA was picked as runner-up in the conference derby.

True, the Uclans lost such offensive stalwarts as Troy Aikman, Eric Ball, Bobby Menifield, plus such defensive stick-outs as Carnell Lake, Jim Wahler, Darryl Henley, Chance Johnson, Eric Smith and Marcus Turner.

But 57 lettermen returned, headed by Charles Arbuckle and Frank Cornish. They were joined on offense by Brian Brown, Wills, Reggie Moore, Mike Farr, Rick Meyer, Mark Estwick, Bill Paige, Lance Zeno and Velasco. Defensive veterans included Matt Darby, Mike Lodish, Craig Davis, Eric Turner, Bryan Wilcox and Punter Kirk Maggio.

"We lost some very special performers from last year's team," observed Donahue, "but I look forward to the 1989 season with a great deal of optimism."

Where aces performed at the quarterback position for both schools last year, now there was uncertainty for both. At Troy, Pat O'Hara edged out redshirt freshman Todd Marinovich in the spring, but eventually became second fiddle. At Westwood, it was a battle between redshirts Johnson and Jimmy Bonds, with the former getting the call.

But as the season slipped underway, the path to glory became rocky for Joe Bruin. San Diego State, California and Arizona State were gobbled up in the second, fourth and fifth games of his schedule, but the others - Tennessee, Michigan, Arizona, Oregon State, Washington, Stanford and Oregon - all enjoyed a feast of bear meat. Five of these banquets in straight order preceded the combat with USC.

Speculation centered on several reasons for UCLA's fall from grace: loss of seven players to the NFL, including Aikman; coaching changes; loss of six players through suspension or academics; and a plethora of injuries.

One person who understood the plight of Donahue was genial Dick Vermeil, former UCLA and Philadelphia Eagles head coach, now a network television analyst. "The one thing you get coaching at UCLA or USC is that you never get conditioned to handling the adversity of losing," he offered. "When it does happen, it hurts more than if you were used to it."

**Three More All-America Stars at USC:
Mark Tucker (75), Mark Carrier (7), Junior Seau (55)**

To open the season, Southern Cal's road to renown was supposed to lead it to Moscow to meet Illinois in the Glasnost Bowl. The arrangement crumbled, and the Trojans did likewise... in Los Angeles. The only other defeat was administered by Notre Dame in the seventh game. Sandwiched around the Irish were victories over Utah State, Ohio State, Washington State, Washington (the 600th USC win), California, Stanford, Oregon State and Arizona.

Notre Dame's four-point verdict over USC did not impress Vermeil. "Southern Cal is the best team in the country," he opined.

But even that accolade did not impress UCLA linebacker Marvcus Patton: "We know we can beat SC if we play the best game we've ever played."

Cautious about USC's apparent dominance was a former Trojan quarterback named James Jones: "If USC is not ready to play a hard game," he admonished, "it could be a sorrowful one. The most embarrassing thing is to lose to a team you are supposed to beat."

And certainly, USC was supposed to clobber UCLA, even though nothing was at stake, except pride and the city crown. Win, lose or draw, the Trojans had already clinched the Rose Bowl bid and, regardless of the outcome, the Bruins had no travel plans for the holidays.

"This is a game for pride," remarked Smith, "and tradition, and just the fact that it's SC-UCLA week."

Pride, tradition, bragging rights, whatever... both squads showed up at the Coliseum for a mid-day kickoff in late November.

As expected, USC blazed away at the opening gun, Marinovich hitting Gary Wellman for a 39-yard pickup on his first play from scrimmage. The Trojan QB then connected with Ricky Ervins for 11 yards and with Galbraith for another 11. On the ninth play of the 79-yard tour, Marinovich spotted Wellman at the edge of the endzone, barely ahead of defender Carlton Gray. From the 13-yard line, Marinovich lofted the ball and down with it came Wellman. The official ruled he was in bounds and awarded the Trojans six points.

"I was step for step with him," said Gray. "It was a perfect throw, but I still think he was out of bounds. But I don't blame the ref. He called it like he saw it."

In bounds or not, USC owned a 7-0 lead after Rodriguez made good the point-after.

Surprisingly, UCLA bounced back, refusing for the moment to let USC rest on its reputation. It started when Turner pilfered a pass from Marinovich and lugged it back six yards, setting up the Uclans

49 yards from paydirt. They quashed those in seven plays, the payoff being a pitchout to Kevin Williams from three yards out. Instrumental in reaching the three were Johnson passes of 13 yards to Farr, 15 to Miller and 15 to Arbuckle. Velasco knotted the score at 7-all with his PAT.

On the final play of the first half, Rodriguez forged USC into a 10-7 advantage with a 40-yard field goal. Ironically, in contrast to Velasco's last-second FG try which bonked the crossbar and fell back, Rodriguez' kick also hit the crossbar... but bounced through. Carrier enveloped a fumble by Williams to put the field-goal drive in motion, and it was accelerated by Marinovich flings of 13 yards to Ervins, 11 to Jackson and 22 to Joel Scott.

Both teams gave the scoreboard a rest in the third quarter, but - surprise again - UCLA evened the score at 10-10 early in the fourth. On third-and-six from the USC 45, a pitchout from Marinovich to Ervins was bobbled, and UCLA's Meech Shaw was Johnny-on-the-spot. Abetted by an unsportsmanlike conduct penalty after Seau sacked Johnson, the Bruins moved to USC's 32-yard line, from whence Velasco jetted a 49-yard three-pointer.

The quarter was young and Southern Cal was poised to reclaim the lead, marching to the shadow of UCLA's goal... only to incur Holt's fumble and the Bruins' subsequent drive that preceded Velasco's dramatic near-hit field-goal effort at the buzzer.

Holt told reporters the fumble was his first ever... in high school, in college. "But it was totally my fault," he admitted.

If any contest ever swung on two last-second field goals, this one was the model. To understand, balance USC's shot that bounced over the crossbar on the final play of the first half against UCLA's shot that bounced back from the crossbar on the final play of the game. One succeeds, one fails.

Even with these breaks, Donahue gleaned a rainbow among the clouds. "We've been in a lot of these games," he expounded, "and I'm not sure any UCLA team has played harder or with more pride and spirit."

Senior linebacker Patton agreed with his coach's evaluation, but felt the Bruins should have won. "I feel like we did win the game," he muttered. "That touchdown they gave USC in the first quarter was ridiculous. He (Wellman) wasn't anywhere near inbounds. Ridiculous."

Though not losers, some Trojans reacted as if they were.

Ervins: "This loss hurts."

Carrier: "It almost feels like a loss. Right now, there's just a numb feeling."

Ryan: "It was very dis-satisfying."

Smith: "That last kick (missed) was lucky for us, because it kept us from defeat."

Overall, the conflict was classified by many observers as ugly and poorly executed. The Trojans had six turnovers and were penalized nine times; the Bruins had three turnovers and were flagged seven times.

Of course, the season was over for UCLA, which finished 3-7-1, but recognition awaited two Bruin players: Cornish and Maggio, both named consensus All-America.

The honor store was flush with Trojans, too. Ryan was a consensus All-American, Carrier a unanimous AA as well as recipient of the Thorpe Award, while Seau and Tucker were listed as All-America, too.

Rapidly, the wounds of the inglorious tie with UCLA healed, and the Trojans regrouped to earn a victory over Michigan in the Rose Bowl. That settled their season with nine wins, two losses, one tie and a national rank of No. 8.

But, thanks to a fickle crossbar... it could have been worse.

Scoring by Quarters:

UCLA	0	7	0	3	-	10
USC	7	3	0	0	-	10

**Frank Cornish, UCLA
All-America Center, 1989**

1990

Game 60

Point Parade

Todd Marinovich, Southern California's beleaguered-turned-hero quarterback, didn't see the play that whipped UCLA. He was flat on his back, belted into that prone position by Bruin Roman Phifer. It didn't matter.

The football he had just arched into the air with 16 seconds to play out-paced the chase of safety Michael Williams and landed securely into the bosom of redshirt freshman Johnnie Morton in the left corner of the endzone.

Southern California 45, UCLA 42.

Right - just another nail-biting, hair-raising, cliff-hanging finish to which fanatics of these West Coast giants have become accustomed. But it was unique in one aspect: the 87 total points were the most ever amassed in the 60-year crossfire series between these fierce crosstown rivals.

And while Mike Downey, L.A. *Times* columnist, didn't foretell the volume of points, he was pin-point accurate with his prediction: "In Saturday's big Troy-Donahue battle, I'll go with the Trojans by a couple of points," he wrote, "but I could be wrong. Could be three." (Remember last year? Downey picked 17-point underdog UCLA to upset USC - it was a tie.)

Forecasts for the year 1990 paralleled 1989: the experts again tapped USC as best in the west, with UCLA shuffling along somewhere between maybe-good and mediocre.

SPORTS
Los Angeles Times

USC Gets In Last Gasp, 45-42

If only numbers were the criteria, however, these evaluations would not compute. For USC lost 23 lettermen and brought back 46, while UCLA lost two fewer and welcomed back 10 more.

"We have a lot of pluses," noted USC Coach Larry Smith, "but the combination of inexperience and our demanding schedule makes this the toughest coaching challenge of my career."

Part of this challenge was finding replacements for offensive leaders such as John Jackson and Leroy Holt. But his bigger task was rebuilding the defense, which had been depleted by the expected departures of Cleveland Colter, Dan Owens, Tim Ryan, Mike Williams and Earnest Spears, as well as the premature exit of Mark Carrier and Junior Seau, who entered the NFL draft as juniors.

Smith may have spoken with tongue-in-cheek. Take a gander at the sterling calibre of those returning: Ricky Ervins, Marinovich, Pat Harlow, Gary Wellman, Mike Moody, Pat O'Hara, Quin Rodriguez and, after missing '89, Scott Lockwood on offense; Scott Ross, Don Gibson, Kurt Barber, Brian Tuliau, Craig Hartsuyker, Marcus Hopkins on defense. Perhaps it was the quality of these athletes that sparked a No. 12 preseason ranking by *Associated Press*.

Though unheralded, UCLA had only a few important holes to fill. Most notable were Charles Arbuckle, Frank Cornish and Alfredo Velasco on offense; Mike Lodish, Marvcus Patton and punter Kirk Maggio on defense. But replacements with potential were abundant.

"We have several talented youngsters," acknowledged Coach Terry Donahue, "but they're going to have to mature and assume some major responsibilities."

Quarterback position seemed to be solid with the return of Bret Johnson and Jim Bonds. Then Johnson transferred to Michigan State, but waiting in the wings was a redshirt-freshman gem named Tommy Maddox, who would emerge as top banana. Offensive support would come from Brian Brown, Shawn Wills,

Kevin Williams, Reggie Moore, Lance Zeno, Randy Austin, Scott Spalding and Corwin Anthony.

On defense, Donahue would rely on veterans such as Matt Darby, Eric Turner, Recon Keeton, Carlton Gray, Siitupe Tuala, Dion Lambert, Brian Kelly and Phifer, who missed the '89 season. What's more, two transfers would add depth and talent: Arnold Ale from Notre Dame and Mike Chalenski from Pittsburgh.

As the season progressed, the Bruins, if nothing else, were consistent, losing and winning every other game: Oklahoma, Michigan, Arizona, California and Oregon dropped UCLA; while on alternate weeks, Stanford, Washington State, San Diego State, Oregon State and No. 2 Washington fell victims to the paw. To maintain the pattern, UCLA was doomed to lose to Southern Cal, which it did.

There was no similar regimen as the USC schedule unfolded. First came a deuce of wins, Syracuse and Penn State; a loss to Washington; then a trey of victories, Ohio State, Washington State, Stanford; another setback, Arizona; a conquest, Arizona State; a tie, California; and finally victim No. Seven, Oregon State. With 7-2-1 credentials, the Trojans were ranked No. 19 by AP.

A couple of weeks before the battle, USC was rated a substantial favorite to win. But the odds tumbled to "slight favorite" after UCLA shocked Rose Bowl-bound Washington in its tuneup for the Trojans.

Smith concurred with the newly-found status of the Bruins. "UCLA is a steadily improving team," he commented. "They hit their peak against Washington last week. They played excellent and found a way to beat the league champion. No one else has done it."

While perhaps flattered, Donahue wasn't buying the pedestal on which Smith aspired to place his Bruins.

"USC has a big offensive line and is a very good rushing team," he countered. "They've also got some real weapons offensively, and Wellman is a major player."

So now it was time for Bobby April, USC's defensive back coach, to augment the concerns of his head coach, and April's support dwelt on Bruin QB Maddox.

"Maddox is as good as anybody we've faced - maybe better," expounded April. "He's tremendous, and on the verge of being one of the great players in the country."

Donahue wouldn't argue with that, so he turned the back-and-forth dialogue into a banner of jest at the Rotary Club luncheon.

From the floor: "Terry, in your pregame chalk talk, what special strategy will you have, what will you tell your players?"

**Tim Ryan, DT (99) Celebrates With Scott Ross, ILB (35)...
Both All-Americans at Southern California**

Donahue: "I'm going to tell them to stay out of the way of that damn horse."

That was wise advice that needed only adherence. For the game was in its infant seconds when Gibson rushed Maddox, causing the Bruin QB to rush his throw. Steve Pace intercepted the lob and raced 27 yards for a Trojan touchdown, setting Traveler, USC's white horse mascot, off on a spirited gallop around the gridiron. The point-after failed when O'Hara didn't handle the snap.

"We knew they would come out throwing," said Pace, who had moved out of his normal free safety spot.

Most of the 98,088 boosters were now seated in the Rose Bowl stands when UCLA nudged into a 7-6 lead. It resulted from a 77-yard escapade, capped by Maddox' nine-yard TD run on the 11th play. Passes of 12 and 26 yards from Maddox to Moore, 12 to Miller, and an 18-yard dash by Brown enriched the journey, which was cloaked by Brad Daluiso's PAT.

Southern Cal regained the lead, obliterating 84 yards in a dozen plays. Mazio Royster went the final seven, but needed aid from a Marinovich to Larry Wallace connection for 20 yards plus a personal foul penalty against Turner. Marinovich's conversion toss to Lockwood was successful. USC, 14-7.

The Bruins retaliated in the second quarter when Brown bolted for 12 yards and Maddox kept for 11 before launching a 47-yard TD grenade to Sean LaChapelle, closing a 76-yard, six-play trek. Daluiso drilled the PAT, and the score was locked at 14-apiece.

Late in the first half, Maddox lost the handle on the ball and it was grasped by Gibson, just 29 yards shy of point heaven. Royster ran for 12 yards and Marinovich sneaked over the goal line from one yard out on the fifth play. Rodriguez kicked his first PAT, giving USC a 21-14 halftime edge.

The Trojan senior then knocked through a 20-yard field goal in the third period, topping a 68-yard campaign. The key gain was a 14-yard aerial from Marinovich to Bob Crane.

Before the quarter ended, Maddox riveted the Trojan secondary with completions of 10 yards to Brown, 12 to Wills and 42 to Miller. From the five-yard stripe, Brown scored to end a 73-yard drive in just six plays. Daluiso, up and through.

Both teams tallied 21 points in the fourth frame. USC registered the first when a pass from Maddox intended for Moore was tipped by Pace and claimed by Jason Oliver, who scampered 34 yards to glory land. USC held a 10-point advantage after the PAT by Rodriguez.

Revving up his arm, Maddox then threw two touchdowns to Miller, the first for 29 yards, the second for 38. Wills returned

USC's kickoff 35 yards to ignite the first TD, which finished off an abbreviated 39-yard drive. Lambert recovered a fumble by Lockwood on Troy's 38-yard line to make possible Miller's second touchdown, which came on the first play. Daluiso kicked true after both scores, shoving UCLA into a 35-31 lead.

Still playing musical chairs, Southern Cal reclaimed the lead by three points when Morton pulled in a 21-yard scoring strike from Marinovich. The brace also played pitch-and-catch for 14 yards, the fuel in the 47-yard, eight-play sojourn. Rodriguez tacked on USC's 38th point.

It was not a knockout blow, however, as Kevin Smith dived over from one yard out with 79 seconds to play and Daluiso converted to put UCLA in the driver's seat, 42-38. To earn this lead, the Bruins hammered out 75 yards in seven plays, the best of which were flings of 29 yards from Maddox to Miller, 14 to Moore, nine to LaChapelle, plus an 11-yard rollout by Maddox.

With just over a minute to play, the Trojans found themselves 75 yards away from UCLA's goal, and in dire need of a touchdown. Marinovich expunged most of these with completions of 27 and 22 yards to Wellman. Then, on the fifth play and from UCLA's 23-yard line, the aforementioned game-winning heave exploded... that ended with Marinovich on his back and Morton with the ball in the endzone. Rodriguez' kick finalized the high-scoring affair at 45-42, USC on top.

"I was supposed to run a comeback route," said Morton, "but versus their coverage, we adjusted to a post corner route. Todd made such a perfect pass that I couldn't have missed it."

Marinovich didn't see Morton's catch "...but I looked up and saw our crowd jump up and felt about 10 players jump on top of me, so I knew it was good."

It was a scintillating bit of action that delivered jubilation to Troy, but simultaneously negated a magnificent performance by Maddox, who set UCLA records by passing for 409 yards and 445 yards in total offense.

"To be up with just over a minute to play... to have that taken away, it hurts worse than I can explain to anybody," wailed Maddox, belittling his record-setting heroics.

Donahue was sympathetic, but more realistic. "You've got to stop them with 1:19 left," he stated. "But it was a classic. Both teams played hard, neither would quit. From their standpoint, it was a great victory; from ours, a real tragedy."

Smith was just happy to see the last pass by Maddox fall incomplete, ending the parade of points. "For a pure game, it was the best I've ever been associated with," he chirped.

**UCLA Displays a Couple of All-Americans:
Roman Phifer (40), Eric Turner (29)**

Even though his Trojans yielded the following week to Notre Dame, USC was still tapped for the John Hancock Bowl. But it, too, was spoiled by Michigan State, so the season was drawn at 8-4-1, barely adequate for a No. 20 final rank. Ross earned All-America honors.

For the Bruins, the year closed with the USC mischance, and their final 5-6-0 slate was their second straight losing season. One bright side: Turner and Phifer were listed as All-America.

The crosstown crossfire had now engaged in 60 clashes since Goliath Southern California first met David UCLA in 1929. The Trojans had captured 34 games, the Bruins 19, and seven were stalemates. USC led in total points scored, 1,157 to 894.

Scoring by Quarters:

USC	14	7	3	21	-	45
UCLA	7	7	7	21	-	42

1991

Game 61

A Sparkling Ale

Monday morning quarterbacks were asking: which play stood uppermost in UCLA's hard-earned 24-21 conquest of Southern California in the 61st conflict of the intracity schools? The controversial touchdown scored - or not scored, according to allegiance - by Bruin Brian Allen in the second quarter? Or the uncontroversial sack administered by UCLA's Arnold Ale on QB Reggie Perry to snuff the Trojans' desperate endeavor to pull victory from the pit at game's-end?

Maybe the answer was academic, because regardless of the impact of either, the result of UCLA's triumph was three-fold: it enabled the Bruins to snap a four-year drought of winless years against Troy; it chiseled a six-game losing streak into Southern Cal's record book, the most ever; and it wrapped up the Trojans' season at 3-8-0, the most woeful in 35 years.

To be sure, it had been a brutal term for the warriors of Troy... the tone of which was set when tempestuous quarterback Todd Marinovich opted for professional status after his sophomore season, and punctuated quite emphatically when Memphis State (not to be confused with Notre Dame òr Michigan) humbled the Trojans in their curtain-raising game.

Few, if any, wise men expected Southern Cal to scale heights of supremacy, but neither did they envision a courtship with

UCLA All-America Matt Darby Gets Help From Jamir Miller To Bring Down USC's Reggie Perry

wretchedness. The *Associated Press* did, however, place USC at No. 16 on its preseason poll.

In addition to Marinovich, Coach Larry Smith would see no more of offensive masters such as Ricky Ervins, Gary Wellman, Pat Harlow, Mark Tucker and place-kicker Quin Rodriguez; nor defensive jewels such as Scott Ross, Don Gibson, Brian Tuliau, Craig Hartsuyker and Marcus Hopkins.

Sophomore Perry, with scant game experience, was bequeathed the quarterback role, and he was supported by the return of 49 lettermen. Offensive weapons included Mazio Royster, Johnnie Morton, Scott Lockwood, Derrick Deese, Tony Boselli, Michael Moody, Craig Gibson, Curtis Conway, Travis Hannah and Larry Wallace. And, to anchor his defense, Smith would depend on Kurt Barber, Calvin Holmes, Terry McDaniels, Jason Oliver, Matt Willig, Stephon Pace, Matt Gee and punter Ron Dale.

But if a mist of dankness shrouded University Park, so did an atmosphere of uncertainty prevail over Pauley Pavilion. There, however, Coach Terry Donahue would greet the return of 47 lettermen, most notable of whom was a tall sophomore quarterback from Texas named Tommy Maddox.

Harken verbiage from Marc Dellins' media guide: "With normal progress, Maddox will develop into the finest quarterback in UCLA history. With Maddox at the controls, the sky is the limit for the Bruin offense."

Maddox would team with Sean LaChapelle, Shawn Wills, Kevin Smith, Vaughn Parker, Scott Spalding, Marc Wilder, Kevin Williams, Craig Novitsky and Paul Richardson to fuel the offense.

Donahue's defense would display a ringleader, too: Matt Darby. And ample assistance would come from Carlton Gray, Ale, Dion Lambert, Mike Chalenski, Brian Kelly and James Malone. Not overly impressed with this array, AP's preseason poll spotted UCLA at No. 23.

Going into the USC fracas, the Bruins counted success over Brigham Young, San Diego State, Arizona, Oregon State, Washington State and Oregon, but counted failure against Tennessee, California and Stanford. The 7-3-0 card barely slipped the Uclans in AP's poll at No. 25.

But that was superior to USC, which was unlisted in the Top-25. Of course, that was logical... since El Trojan could brandish a mere three wins in 10 encounters. One of the victories was a doozy, though - over No. 5 Penn State. Oregon and Washington State also felt the sword of Tommy Trojan but, in addition to the Tigers from Memphis, Arizona State, Stanford, Notre Dame, California, Washington and Arizona also kicked his derriere. And yes - that's right - USC lumbered into the UCLA engagement on a dead roll of five consecutive losses, traceable in part to unrest among some of the players. Or so said some armchair know-it-alls.

Even Smith did not view the opportunity to whip UCLA as a chance to salvage his season. "One game doesn't make a season," he noted, "but it can enable us to finish on a good note."

Ignoring the odds which staked UCLA as a five-point favorite, Donahue was more concerned with uncovering the blanket of four years without possession of the Victory Bell. "I'd like to hope that our team would be capable of not going another year without beating Southern Cal," he hankered.

With few plums to pick, the yearly pride of bragging rights to the city notwithstanding, the mid-afternoon brawl attracted fewer than 84,700 people. Naturally, one of them was 85-year-old Giles Pellerin, who was attending his 724th consecutive USC game.

Even the fervid loyalty of Mr. Pellerin must have been tested in the first half, as UCLA piled up a 17-0 lead before giving up a marker to the Trojans in the last 46 seconds.

The scoring started on UCLA's second possession with a 41-yard field goal by Louis Perez. It was a 49-yard drive, sustained by a 27-yard pass from Maddox to LaChapelle and a 12-yard pickup by Williams.

Later in the first quarter, Williams, on a first-down option play, bolted 72 yards for a touchdown which, after Perez' PAT, lifted the Bruins to a 10-0 lead.

After stopping the Trojans, the Bruins conducted another drive, starting from their 10-yard line. Sixteen plays later, UCLA was on SC's one-yard stripe, thanks to completions from Maddox to LaChapelle for 15 yards, to Bryan Adams for nine, to Michael Moore for 14 and to Maury Toy for 13.

On third down, Toy plunged into the line, seeking to wipe out the remaining 36 inches. Somewhere between the handoff and the goal line and a ferocious hit by McDaniels and the endzone, the ball spurted from his grasp. About a ton of beef formed a human pyramid as the elusive pigskin disappeared under the mass. Or did it? Seconds of eternity ticked off as the officials unpiled the gridders. But where was the ball? Why - there it was nestled in the welcome hands of Bruin Brian Allen, standing apart in the endzone.

So, as the old adage admonishes, the "...ref may or may not be right, but he's final." It was indeed a touchdown and, after Perez' point-after, a 17-0 bulge for UCLA.

Some of the Trojans disagreed with the brain trust in zebra shirts.

SPORTS
Los Angeles Times

UCLA Deep-Sixes USC, 24-21

McDaniels: "I had him down shy of the goal. He never crossed it. But I never even saw him fumble."

Willig: "He was tackled short of the goal, the whistle blew it dead, then he let go of the ball, but the officials seemed to have no inkling he had fumbled."

Gee: "He never even got a good handle on it. It was a bad handoff, and the ball rolled into the endzone. Jason (Oliver, Trojan DB) got the ball when we all were jumping for it, but the ref didn't seem to see that. Then the whistle blew and the UCLA guy took the ball away after that."

Hmmm. Counterpoint, Mr. Allen?

"Maury ran up the middle and got in. I'm sure he got in. On the way down, he fumbled and a whole bunch of Trojans jumped on it. I knew he had scored, but when I saw all those Trojans go after it, I just reached into the pile and pulled it out."

And you, Mr. Toy?

"Well, we didn't have far to go. I remember looking down and seeing my head and torso over the line. Then, with all the tugging and pushing going on, I made the mistake of reaching out with the ball away from my body to stretch it over the goal, and it was there it got knocked loose."

Okay, whatever... the decision must have raised the ire of the Trojans, who took the ensuing kickoff and stormed 67 yards in seven plays for a touchdown. Estrus Crayton ran for seven yards, Perry kept for eight, then threw for 11 to Conway and 30 to Wallace before touching off the comeback with a 13-yard TD fling to Conway. J.J. Dudum added the PAT, enabling USC to await halftime lectures on the short end of a 17-7 score.

"That was a big play for them," said UCLA's Ale, alluding to Conway's catch.

Both teams collected seven points in the third period, the Trojans getting theirs' first on a 58-yard, six-play trip. Perry consumed the last yard after connecting with Morton for 11 yards and Wallace for 34. Dudum booted true.

That brought USC to within three points of UCLA. but that gap would never close; in fact, temporarily, it widened again.

Sensing a threat, Maddox completed five-of-six passes during a 73-yard cruise that docked with Toy burning Gee and grabbing a 17-yard scoring toss on the 11th play. Toy also had an eight-yard reception, while Ricky Davis claimed one for 17 yards and LaChapelle one for 21, all sailing from the arm of Maddox. A conversion by Perez became UCLA's 24th digit of the game.

Now trailing by 10 points with time in the third frame running out, Southern Cal started a 69-yard expedition that ended on the first play of the fourth quarter with a six-yard scoring strike from Perry to Yonnie Jackson. Big plays in the drive were a 20-yard sprint by Crayton and a 38-yard bomb from Perry to Crayton. After Dudum's PAT, the Trojans were behind, 24-21, but they had 14 minutes and 56 seconds to alter that measley deficit.

The Bruin defense stiffened, however, and, as the clock wound relentlessly toward its double zeroes, the score remained unchanged. Suddenly, the Trojans found themselves 96 yards away from the Bruins' goal with a do-or-die challenge facing their situation.

Momentum increased as USC moved downfield. Perry connected with Hannah for a 23-yard gain to UCLA's 42. Then, with just over two minutes to play, fate smiled on the Trojans when Perry's pass slipped through the hands of Bruin Randy Cole.

"I blew a big opportunity," Cole admitted.

Reprieved, Crayton advanced the ball to the 37, where it became fourth-and-five.

"We weren't sure it was going to be a pass, but the pressure of the game kind of dictated a pass there," said Donahue.

The mentor guessed right, but Perry's pitch never became airborne. He was belted by Ale, the ball squirted free and UCLA's Chalenski enfolded it. Too bad, too, because Morton, streaking up the right sideline, had beaten his defender.

Smith concluded that some Trojan had missed his assignment, allowing Ale to reach Perry unimpeded.

Ale viewed his sack somewhat differently. "I had the tackle man on man," he related. "Then I saw a hole inside so big, and started to take it. But I knew Perry could scramble, so I faked inside, the lineman bit, and I went outside."

Regardless of how it happened... "Our team is thrilled," exclaimed Donahue, hugging his wife, Andrea, and their three daughters in shadows of the vesper light. "We needed a win over USC very badly," he added.

At the moment he may not have been aware that two of his gridders had just established school records: Gray with his 10th interception; LaChapelle with his 68th reception for 987 yards.

UCLA had a date in the Hancock Bowl with Illinois providing the opposition. The Bruins were slim victors, bundling up their season with a 9-3-0 ledger, which was sufficient for a final rank of No. 19. Darby was the only player selected to the All-America squad.

Southern Cal was through for the year and the merciless curtain couldn't have dropped too soon. Trojan supporters were not accustomed to eight spankings in 11 games.

Scoring by Quarters:

UCLA	10	7	7	0	-	24
USC	0	7	7	7	-	21

All-Americans
Tony Boselli (71) USC
and Tommy Maddox, UCLA;
Plus Top Receiver
Sean LaChapelle, UCLA

1992
Game 62

Paw Robs Rob

Three score and three years ago, mighty Southern California condescended to play run, block and tackle against UCLA, an upstart neighbor accustomed to knocking heads with such compatible opponents as Whittier, Pomona and Redlands. Since that momentous event in 1929, the intracity institutions have engaged in many skirmishes that unraveled - one way or another - at the buzzer with an electrical finish. Such was the excitement that engulfed Game No. 62.

Trojan quarterback Rob Johnson sneaked over the goal line with 41 seconds to play, bringing his team to within a point of the Bruins, 37-38. The dependable leg of place-kicker Louis Perez was charged and ready to tie the contest.

Coach Larry Smith never considered that avenue. He knew Southern Cal needed a two-point conversion, because only a victory would earn a share of the PAC-10 title and send his squad into some post-season bowl. Smith called a timeout to select the two-point conversion play. Then UCLA coordinator Bob Field called a timeout to adjust his defense.

Credit Field with the proper alignment. For linebacker Nkosi Littleton rose to the occasion by knocking down Johnson's pass intended for Yonnie Jackson in the left corner of the endzone, thereby preserving UCLA's one-point win, touching off a wild celebration among Bruin fans, and depriving USC of a major bowl.

The agonizing defeat was another arrow that unhappy Trojan supporters could hurl toward the embattled Smith, now closing his fifth year as head coach.

Worn by the distressed, a popular T-shirt laced the USC campus. "Top 10 reasons why Larry Smith should be fired," it emblazoned.

Upon questioning, some of the unrest stemmed from: Smith's bowl record, three losses in four games; lack of success against Notre Dame, winless in five games; inability to recruit top California prepsters; falling attendance; and failure to get a bowl spot in 1991, the first omission since 1983.

"But it's not just wins and losses," rationalized a prominent booster. "It's attitude, atmosphere. There's no spark now, no real USC feeling."

Justified or not, Smith expressed optimism at the outset of the season.

"We'll come back this year," he predicted, alluding to the horrendous 3-8-0 fiasco in '91. "We'll go out and compete with intensity. We'll stress fundamentals. But the keys to our success will be our character, our competitiveness, and our confidence."

Well, the talent was in camp to support Smith's sentiments: 42 returning lettermen, including 18 starters (nine on each side of the line).

Heading the offensive array were Tony Boselli and Curtis Conway, but they were amply backed by Johnnie Morton, Jackson, Wes Bender, Deon Strother, Estrus Crayton, Craig Gibson and Kris Pollack.

"Tony (Boselli) is the key to our offensive line," Smith told USC's sports information director, Tim Tessalone. "We'll build our line around him."

There were plaudits for Conway, too. "Curtis is one of the premier receivers and returners in the nation," added Smith.

Reggie Perry was the returning starter at quarterback, but Johnson, a young sophomore, was pushing hard for No. 1 status.

While no player of All-America calibre loomed on defense, a stable of solid performers were gunning for practice on Howard Jones Field: David Webb, Willie McGinest, Lamont Hollinquest, Jason Oliver, Stephon Pace, Mike Salmon, Mike Hinz and Terry McDaniels, to name a few.

Naturally, eligibility had expired for some Trojans. These included Mazio Royster, Michael Moody, Scott Lockwood and Derrick Deese on offense; Matt Gee, Calvin Holmes, Kurt Barber, Matt Willig and punter Ron Dale on defense.

SPORTS
Los Angeles Times

Bruins Win a Barnes Burner

■ **Game:** Barnes connects with Stokes for 90-yard touchdown. Trojans later miss two-point try for victory, 38-37.

By CHRIS BAKER
TIMES STAFF WRITER

After USC's thrilling 45-42 victory over UCLA in 1990 at the Rose Bowl, many fans called it the most extraordinary game in the history of the rivalry, which began in 1929.

However, UCLA's 38-37 victory over USC Saturday before 80,568 at the Rose Bowl provided almost as much drama.

Trailing, 38-31, after UCLA quarterback John Barnes combined with wide receiver J.J. Stokes on a 90-yard touchdown

■ **HE WALKED ON**
In John Barnes, the Bruins again find their hero in unusual circumstances. C8
■ **HE BARELY MISSED**
Rob Johnson drove USC to the final touchdown, but two-point conversion failed. C8

pass play with 3:08 remaining in the game, the Trojans' Rob Johnson scored on a one-yard quarterback sneak with 41 seconds left to cap a 69-yard, 11-play drive.

USC, which needed a victory to earn a share of the Pacific 10 co-championship with Washington, which lost to Washington State, and Stanford, which defeated California, called a timeout to design a play for the two-point conversion.

After watching the Trojans line up, UCLA called a timeout to design a defense to stop the conversion attempt.

And the defense that UCLA

UCLA's J.J. Stokes straight-arms USC's Jerald Henry to set up the tying touchdown and also scored the game-winner on a 90-yard play.

It Was a Night to Remember

Big Games
A look at some other rivalries that were renewed Saturday:

Folks matriculate at UCLA, too. And chief among those departed were Matt Darby, Dion Lambert, Brian Kelly and James Malone on defense; Shawn Wills, Kevin Smith, Scott Spalding, Marc Wilder, Maury Toy and Paul Richardson on offense.

But Coach Terry Donahue's most crippling blow came from one not graduated, but rather who chose to forsake Westwood after his sophomore year and enter the professional ranks in Denver. That defector, of course, was dazzling Tommy Maddox, quarterback elite.

"Obviously, we lost some valuable players from last year's team," remarked Donahue, " however, I am optimistic about the upcoming season."

Perhaps Donahue's cheerful outlook was based on the return of 56 lettermen, including 12 starters. The offense flashed such bright names as Sean LaChapelle, Rick Daly, Vaughn Parker, Kevin Williams, Craig Novitsky, Brian Allen, Ricky Davis, Kaleaph Carter and place-kicker Perez.

And, not to be outdone, the guys who tackle and stunt and knock down passes were meritorious, too, paced by Carlton Gray. Behind him were Mike Chalenski, Othello Henderson, Bruce Walker, Carl Greenwood, Garrett Greedy and Arnold Ale.

"In Arnold Ale, we have one of the nation's top linebackers," said Donahue. "He is strong and quick and always seems to know where to find the football."

But coach, who is the heir to Mr. Maddox at quarterback? Well, Marc Dellins' media guide listed seldom-used Wayne Cook as heir apparent, with redshirt freshman Rob Walker his backup... plus an unknown senior walk-on named John Barnes somewhere in the rotation.

Cook opened the schedule as the starting signal-caller, but waived to Walker in the second game. When Walker surrendered to an ankle injury in the sixth contest, in stepped Barnes.

UCLA captured its first three games - over Fullerton, Brigham Young and San Diego State - then hit a skid of five straight setbacks, bowing to Arizona, Stanford, Washington State, Arizona State and California. However, prior to the USC tussle, the Bruins rallied to dispose of both PAC-10 universities in Oregon, which brought them to the .500 mark at 5-5-0.

Southern Cal's record was better: six wins, two defeats, one tie - not great, but sufficient for an AP ranking of No. 15. Lightweight San Diego State muffed two opportunities in the final minute to upset the Trojans, then settled for a tie. After that, USC posted victories over Oklahoma, Oregon, California, Washington State, Arizona State and Arizona, interspersed with put-downs from Washington and Stanford.

Oddsmakers listed USC as a nine- point favorite, but Smith was cautious in the role.

"We have a lot to play for," he answered. "We don't have anything wrapped up yet. We've got to continue fighting to get as much as we can get."

While Donahue was wavering on his starting quarterback - Barnes or the now-recovered Walker - no comparable mystery existed at Southern Cal. The nod was to Johnson, whose brother, Bret, played briefly at UCLA before transferring to Michigan State.

Biased or not, Johnson's distaste for UCLA ran deeper than the normally intense rivalry between the two schools.

"It's a very important game to me," said Johnson. "It's something I've looked forward to ever since Bret left."

However, the pure tone of the upcoming battle was set by UCLA's Chalenski, who transferred from Pittsburgh after playing as a freshman in 1988 for the Panthers.

UCLA Coach Terry Donahue and QB John Barnes
Celebrate Victory Over Southern California

USC All-America Carlton Gray Chats With Bob Hope

"I thought Pitt-Penn State was a big rivalry," mused Chalenski. "When we played at Penn State, people would throw beer bottles at us. But UCLA-USC is an even bigger rivalry. I mean, people live or die by this game out here."

Kickoff was set for 4:30pm in the Rose Bowl, and zealots who would live or die clicked the gates by the thousands - 80,658 to be exact.

Both teams scored 10 points in the first quarter, and they notched seven apiece in the second, so the half ended at 17-all.

Southern Call drew first blood with a 36-yard low, razor-close field goal by Cole Ford. The FG finalized a 47-yard drive, highlighted by a 14-yard fling from Johnson to Travis Hannah.

Williams played a major role as UCLA forged ahead, 7-3. He not only scored the TD on an 18-yard dash, but also fetched a 19-yard pass from Barnes and recovered a fumble by teammate J.J. Stokes to sustain the movement. UCLA used 13 plays to erase 80 yards as Barnes connected with Kevin Jordan for 10 yards, to Daly for another 10, and to Stokes for 14.

Perez converted, then shortly thereafter, drilled a 47-yard three-pointer that was in the realm of a "near-gift." Here's why: in an attempt to keep the ball away from Conway, UCLA kicked off high and short. The ball struck the ground in front of Gray and then did a backspin. It was recovered by Bruin Don Gallatin on USC's 32.

Still in the first period, the Trojans knotted the score with a little trickery when flanker Conway hurled 36 yards to QB Johnson, completing a 61-yard trip in just four plays. Ford added the PAT.

Midway through Quarter Two, UCLA broke the tie with a 57-yard pass-and-run execution from Barnes to Stokes, which capped a 72-yard drive. Along the way, Barnes also found LaChapelle for an 11-yard gain. Perez kicked the point-after.

Troy retaliated, putting together a 67-yard drive and scoring on the ninth play, a one-yard plunge by Johnson. Before that, Johnson kept for 13 yards and Crayton sprinted for 31. The score was again even after Ford's PAT.

Donahue put the second half in perspective. "The last two quarters in this unique game were totally different," he stated. "USC totally dominated the third quarter and UCLA totally dominated the fourth."

Okay, third quarter, Southern Cal, go: Zuri Hector blocked a Bruin punt and Bruce Luzzi sprawled on the bounding oval in the endzone. Next - the warriors of Troy marched 80 yards in 10 plays with Crayton racing the final 32. Other than Crayton's run, only one play gained double-digit yardage - a 14-yard heave from Johnson to Conway. Ford kicked true after both tallies, giving USC a 31-17 lead.

Okay, fourth quarter, UCLA, go: Stokes gathered in a 29-yard scoring strike from Barnes to abate a 69-yard journey which was assisted by a 15-yard Williams' run and a 15-yard penalty against USC. Next - Stokes snagged passes of 59 and 14 yards from Barnes, enabling Williams to seal an 80-yard trek with a one-yard scoring buck. Next - Barnes, from his 10-yard line, threw to Stokes in stride at the 25 and the soph whiz broke to the middle of the field, outrunning cornerback Jerald Henry to paydirt. That put the dot on a 98-yard drive that consisted of only three plays. Perez converted after each TD as UCLA leaped ahead, 38-31.

"He (Barnes) put it right in front of me and I was just worried about getting into the endzone," said Stokes. "But with our preparation, I felt I could get open on anybody."

The Trojans still had three minutes to redeem their breakdown, and Johnson issued a gallant effort. Starting from their 31-yard stripe, downfield roared the Trojans, lifted by a 39-yard gain from Johnson to Morton on a fourth-down gamble. On the 10th play of the surge, Johnson scrambled 12 yards to the one-yard line, then sneaked over on the 11th play.

Now it was crunch time, the Trojans a single point in arrears. The play selected for the two-point conversion was a pass to Jackson.

"We tried to sneak our tight end (Jackson) over there," said Smith.

Although Johnson had hoped for an option call, he tried to force the ball into Jackson's hands, but was thwarted when the paws of Bruin Littleton knocked the ball to earth. The battle was over and UCLA was the surprise and perhaps stunned victor, 38-37.

Reaction from Troy was bitter disappointment.

"I wanted to win this game real bad," wailed Johnson. "When you're up by 14 and then lose to UCLA just kills me."

"I'm angry," Smith exploded. "I'm very angry. We had a shot at it, and we blew it. We have nobody to be mad at but ourselves." Later, he calmed down. "But it was a game of big plays and gambling and they got the best of us," Smith conceded. "UCLA won and we lost. It's that simple."

UCLA's unsung and unlikely hero - Barnes - was naturally on Cloud Nine. "You dream about days like this," he beamed. "This was by far the best win of the season."

Said Donahue: "He (Barnes) came up with the game of his life." Barnes was 16 of 28 for 385 yards for three touchdowns and no interceptions.

Henderson led the Uclan defense with a game-topping 13 tackles, followed by Jamir Miller with 10. By grabbing five passes, LaChapelle brought his career total to 142 and became UCLA's all-time leading receiver. But, more importantly, the improbable squeeze over USC elevated UCLA to a winning season: 6-5-0.

Johnson completed 16 of 32 passes and scored thrice while Crayton carried for 140 yards to pace USC's offense. Jason Sehorn had a dozen tackles.

Each school boasted a brace of All-America performers: Parker and Gray for Westwood; Boselli and Conway for Troy.

Perhaps still in mild shock, Southern Cal wilted before No. 5 Notre Dame the following week, then was mortified by unranked Fresno State in the Freedom Bowl. The three season-ending losses translated into a 6-5-1 slate which, teamed with other items, translated into the dismissal of Smith as head coach.

Scoring by Quarters:

USC	10	7	14	6	-	37
UCLA	10	7	0	21	-	38

Southern California's Curtis Conway, All-America Flanker

407

1993
GAME 63

Deja Vu

Once again - for the 22nd time - the foray between UCLA and Southern California would determine the host school in the Rose Bowl come New Year's Day. USC had won 15 of these clashes, including the last 10 in a row. But not this time. Yes, after 10 straight losses in Rose Bowl-deciding games, the Bruins were victors, 27-21.

What a rude, intracity welcome for John Robinson, returning to Southern Cal as head coach after a hiatus of 10 years!

"But it's an honor for me to return to USC," mused Robinson. "This is a great university and I'm excited about being a part of its future."

Robinson wasn't directing shots from the sideline in 1992, but his first re-match against the Bruins was, at game's end... well, deja vu. To that, Trojan QB Rob Johnson would attest.

Last year, UCLA's Knosi Littleton batted down in the endzone Johnson's game-ending pass that preserved a Bruin victory. This year, UCLA's Marvin Goodwin intercepted in the endzone Johnson's aerial in the final minute, again preserving a Bruin win. Both years, USC stood on the brink of glory... only to be denied.

That was not the manner in which the 1993 script was written, not precisely.

For, even though UCLA was ranked No. 16 with a 7-3-0 record and USC was graded No. 22 with a 7-4-0 register, the morning line listed the Trojans as a two-point favorite to win.

Perhaps the prophets were flashing back to August, when preseason polls ignored the Bruins and pegged the Trojans in a range of No. 11 to No. 18.

There were valid reasons to justify these expectations, too, as Robinson inherited a wad of experience. Returning to the fold in Troyland were 17 starters, eight on offense, nine across the line. Tony Boselli and Johnnie Morton were highly respected offensive performers, and they were backed by Kris Pollack, Len Gorecki, Craig Gibson, Bradford Banta, Joel Crisman, Deon Strother and Johnson.

Speaking of Morton, Robinson felt "...Johnnie will be among the best receivers in the nation, and he could earn All-America honors."

Ruling the defensive unit were Willie McGinest and Jason Sehorn, with bountiful support from Brian Williams, Jeff Kopp, Mike Salmon, Shannon Jones, Jason Oliver, Jerald Henry, Mike Hinz and Terry McDaniels. Also, former quarterback Reggie Perry was shifted to safety.

On the minus side was the offensive loss of Curtis Conway, who defected to the NFL as a junior. Wes Bender, Yonnie Jackson and Estrus Crayton would be missed on the offensive unit, too; along with Stephon Pace, David Webb and Lamont Hollinquest on defense.

Major names no longer on the Westwood campus included Kevin Williams, Sean LaChapelle, Kaleaph Carter, Rick Daly, Cinderella-QB John Barnes and place-kicker Louis Perez from the offense; Mike Chalenski, Carlton Gray, Othello Henderson and Arnold Ale from the defense.

But 14 starters from last year would salute Terry Donahue as he entered his 18th season as head coach at UCLA.

"I feel we will have a very exciting offensive unit this year," the veteran coach surmised, visions of J.J. Stokes, Mike Nguyen, Craig Novitsky, Jonathan Ogden, Derek Stevens, Vaughn Parker,

GAMES / EVENTS / PEOPLE

SPORTS

Los Angeles

A Very Good Win for Bruins

■ **College football:** Goodwin's end-zone interception in final min puts UCLA in the Rose Bowl, 27-2

By EARL GUSTKEY
TIMES STAFF WRITER

UCLA beat back a furious USC assault on line in the final minute Saturday at the C defeating the Trojans, 27-21, and securing trip to the Rose Bowl game since Jan. 1, 1986
UCLA strong safety Marvin Goodwin int a Rob Johnson pass in the end zone with 5 remaining, after Johnson had taken the Trojans 79 yards to the UCLA two-yard line. Most of it came on a 43-yard pass play that put USC on UCLA's three with 1:16 to go.
USC gained little on two Shawn Walters running plays, then Johnson threw a ball into a crowd of three Bruins, trying to find tight end Tyler but Goodwin was there.
Jubilant Bruin players bounded onto the launched an early Rose Bowl celebration.
And when UCLA quarterback Wayne Co ed the ball three times to make it official, started all over again.
The Bruins' victory, before 93,458, 10-game losing streak to USC when the Ro on the line for both schools.
The Trojans trailed, 17-0, at the half, made it interesting with two quick touchdo in the third quarter to make the score 17-1
UCLA pounded USC all afternoon wit

■ **ANALYSIS**
UCLA's imaginati selection kept US fense on the run. C
■ **THE LAST STAND**
On the critical pla game. The Bruin saw what was com
■ **TROJANS**
John Robinson di the send-off he for his senior play

Please see B

JIM MURRAY

He Steals Sho After Five Ye

It was the start of the fourth quarter Trojan horse threw his helmeted, swo rider.
It was a bad omen for the Trojans, a again that the original Trojan horse was ba those earlier Trojans.
So was this one.
This Trojan team got unseated, too.
The original Trojan horse was full of G one was full of enemies, too. Bruins.
Here was the picture: With one minu these Trojans had the ball on the UCLA line, first down and trailing by only six po
Game's over, right? Four plays to go thr No trick at all for Tailback U., Student F and the Thundering Herd, right?
Forget it. Howard Jones probably w believe it, but these Trojans could move (f one yard in two plays. In fact, they mov

Please see ML

KEN LEVINE / For The Times
Of his game-saving interception, UCLA's Marvin Goodwin said: "We knew it was coming. We had it all the way."

Ricky Davis, Brian Kelly, Rob Walker and injury-healed Wayne Cook dancing in his thoughts.

And the defense? "Defensively, we have the nucleus of another aggressive unit returning," answered Donahue. That nucleus would embrace Jamir Miller, Matt Werner, Bruce Walker, Littleton, Carl Greenwood, Carrick O'Quinn, Donnie Edwards, Goodwin, Garrett Greedy and Sale Isaia.

The first two games of the season were heartbreakers for UCLA; a two-point loss to California and a one-point demise to powerful Nebraska.

"The Nebraska game was very important because it showed us we could play with a nationally-ranked team," said Donahue. "Once we got through it, it seemed we took off like a rocket."

With jet fuel now burning, the Bruins then clicked off seven consecutive wins: Stanford, San Diego State, BYU, Washington, Oregon State, Arizona and Washington State. Then, with QB Cook sidelined with an injury, UCLA dropped a decision to Arizona State by six points. So, with Southern Cal on the horizon, the Bruins had skidded in three games by a total of just nine points while cruising in seven with a whopping 156-point spread.

Southern California had an early date for Robinson to commence his second term, August 29th in the Pigskin Classic. The classic turned into an ambush as the Tar Heels of North Carolina rolled to a 31-9 conquest.

The rest of the schedule revealed victories over Houston, Washington State, Oregon, Oregon State, California, Stanford and Washington, with setbacks at the hands of Penn State, Arizona and Notre Dame.

Each team could display a marquee receiver for the matchup. Morton, a USC senior, had caught 74 passes for 1,278 yards and 12 touchdowns; Stokes, a UCLA junior, had 62 for 952 yards and 16 touchdowns.

"I think we both run good routes," opined Stokes. "We both understand defenses, we both make things happen - no, it doesn't bother me if I'm compared with him, even if SC and UCLA don't like each other."

USC's McGinest compiled 16 sacks in 1992, which tied him for the conference lead. But the senior linebacker downgraded his achievements. "I'd give away all my sacks, all my stats, if it meant we'd beat UCLA this Saturday," he offered.

Robinson, on the eve of his renewal encounter against UCLA, echoed the sentiments of McGinest. "We're not playing for the Rose Bowl," he remarked. "We're playing to win the game. Sure, the Rose Bowl is involved, but you play to win the game.'

Alas, the heart was strong, the muscle a shade weak, maybe due to an inability to overcome a 17-point first-half deficit.

With 93,458 fans watching in the Coliseum, the Bruins tallied touchdowns on their first two possessions, each using 11 plays. The first was a 66-yard drive, the second a 79-yard journey.

Cook capped the first sojourn with a five-yard keeper, after completing short passes to Ken Grace, Stokes and Nguyen. Davis donated to the effort, too, picking up 29 yards on four carries.

Then Cook riddled the Trojan secondary with completions of 15 yards to Nguyen, 12 to Stokes and 14 to Allen before Skip Hicks pranced into the endzone from four yards out. Redshirt freshman Bjorn Merten converted both PATs.

Merten's 47-yard field goal was the only scoreboard activity in the second quarter. It was a 27-yard trek and elevated the Bruins to a seemingly unshakable 17-0 lead at halftime.

But rushing from their dressing room came the Trojans, their fiery eyes focused on one objective: shake the unshakable. Which they did on their first possession of the third period.

Johnson rifled a 52-yard bullet to Grace and, from the one-yard line, Shawn Walters dived over the goal as USC mowed 57 yards of turf in just three plays.

UCLA handed the ball back to USC when Bryan Adams bobbled a punt and Erroll Small claimed the prize for the Trojans a scant 11 yards from paydirt. On third down from the nine, Johnson connected with Johnny McWilliams for a TD. Cole Ford converted both markers, closing UCLA's gap to 17-14.

Now ruffled, the Bruins retaliated. Adams returned John Stonehouse's 50-yard punt 32 yards down to USC's 36-yard line. Four plays later from the 17, Cook threw from the shotgun to Stokes in the endzone. Merten added the point-after, stretching the lead of UCLA to 10 points.

Southern Cal fought back, starting a 72-yard drive in the third period and dotting it early in the fourth frame with a six-yard scoring dart from Johnson to Banta on the eighth play. Key gainers included passes of 15 yards to Banta, 25 to Walters and 12 to Morton, all from Johnson. Ford's PAT again drew the Trojans to within three points at 21-24.

Touching off the next score and providing insurance for the Bruins was Merten's 20-yard field goal, which ended a 70-yard drive in eight plays. Big asset in the assault was a 53-yard pass from Cook to Kevin Jordan. Now it was UCLA up, 27-21.

That set the scenario for Southern Cal's gritty endeavor to snatch victory from defeat.

**Southern Cal's All-America Johnnie Morton (80);
UCLA's Brilliant Redshirt Freshman Place-kicker Bjorn Merten (middle);
UCLA's All-America J.J. Stokes (18) and '93 Game Hero, George Goodwin**

Down by six points with two-and-a-half minutes on the clock, the Trojans started from their 19-yard line. Quickly, Johnson hit passes of 33 yards to Morton and 43 to Grace. Suddenly, the Bruins were backed up to their three-yard line, facing 1:16 to play and with first down coming up for the Trojans.

After a timeout, Walters' dive was halted by George Kase for no gain. Then Miller aborted Walters' plunge at the two.

"The coaches told us that when USC gets into a first-and-goal situation, they like to run on first and second down and then throw," said UCLA's Goodwin.

Good advice. On third down, Johnson drifted back with 50 seconds remaining, spotted Tyler Cashman in the endzone and projected the ball in his direction. But a completion it was not, for in stepped Goodwin with his dramatic steal, effectively sealing doom for USC and bliss for UCLA. Ironically, it was the only interception of the entire game.

"We knew it was coming," exclaimed the jubilant free safety. "We had it all the way."

Naturally, Johnson's calculations did not include an abrupt intervention by Goodwin. "It was basically a one-man route and I threw it to him," he flatly stated.

Speaking of flatly, that was the repugnant position in which Johnson found himself during the game... seven times. Bruins Donovan Gallatin was credited with three sacks, Miller with two, Kase and Werner with one each. In fact, so fierce was the UCLA defense that it yielded only 26 total yards to all Trojan carriers.

Davis, UCLA's lightly-used tailback, amassed almost six times that many yards... carrying for 153 yards on 26 efforts.

"He's a fifth-year senior and he was fourth on our depth chart a few weeks ago," said Donahue. "But he was hot today, so we let him play."

So it was a 27-21 mastery for UCLA and a ticket to the Rose Bowl, its first New Year's visit in eight years.

"This is a changing world," Donahue shouted amid a boisterous celebration in the Bruins' locker room. "The Berlin Wall has come down and now UCLA has won with the Rose Bowl on the line."

Across the way, Robinson heaped praise on his gladiators, calling up first his seniors... Sehorn, Salmon, Morton, McGinest, and on and on.

"Salmon is one of the most competitive guys I've ever had... Morton, one of the best receivers ever... McGinest, a hell of a Trojan..." the plaudits continued.

Robinson's positive attitude carried over for the Trojans into the Holiday Bowl, in which Johnson passed for 345 yards and Morton was on the receiving end of 10 pitches, sparking a 28-21 decision over Utah. Johnson became the first Trojan to exceed 3,000 yards passing in a single season, and Morton ended his career as Troy's all-time reception leader with 201. Had Tailback U become Air Robinson?

Unfortunately, UCLA did not fare as well in its bowl game, bowing to Wisconsin. The defeat framed the Uclans' season at 8-4-0 and slotted them at No. 18 on AP's ranking chart. USC finished with an 8-5-0 slate, and lumbered in at No. 26.

No surprise here: most All-America rosters included the names of Stokes and Morton. And, while it was a huge surprise for a freshman to appear on AP's AA list, one did: UCLA's Merten.

While on the topic of surprises, here's another: columnist Allan Malamud, of the Los Angeles *Times,* made a near-perfect prediction of the '93 game - UCLA 24, USC 21, he wrote.

But neither Mr. Malamud nor anyone else could have predicted the standing of the two universities at the end of 63 clashes on the gridiron. For the record, Southern California had won 34 times, UCLA 22, and there were seven ties. Points scored: USC 1,236; UCLA 983.

Finally, a surprise but unwanted shocker: during a devastating earthquake on January 17th, 1994, Memorial Coliseum - home of the Trojans - was severely damaged with gaping cracks in the seat structure. Repairs were estimated at 35-million dollars.

...Some say, however, it will take more than a 6.7 scale shaker to interrupt the crosstown crossfire between the University of California-Los Angeles and the University of Southern California. *Just play around that ravine on the 40-yard line, guys.*

Scoring by Quarters:

UCLA	14	3	7	3	-	27
USC	0	0	14	7	-	21

Reflections

Even though I had a very short tenure at UCLA in comparison to the other head coaches that worked at Westwood, I think I can fully appreciate the dynamics of such a great rivalry.

Rivalries exist all through the country, but I doubt very much any two competitors are closer in geographical location and more intense in a desire to win. The football game actually goes far beyond the athletic competition itself. The alumni representing both schools badger each other back and forth all through the year in hopes they will be able to boast about a win rather than define a loss. I have had many people tell me that a win for either alumni group directly affects the work efficiency and enthusiasm of the winning alumni.

Pro football is big and the rivalry is intense, but it doesn't match the level that develops through a year's build-up when the Bruins and Trojans play. USC is leading in the series, but the games are normally very, very competitive and usually go down to the final seconds regardless of the performance of either team leading up to the game.

Having coached in the game and lost, I think I have experienced the lows that exist. Having coached the game and won, I know I have had the opportunity to experience the highs. There was no other win that gave me the same feeling of satisfaction within conference play as the win over Southern Cal.

You hate them in preparation, you hate them the day you play them, but when it is all over, regardless if you win or lose, you have tremendous respect for their program. One of the highlights of my career was having been given the opportunity to lead a UCLA football team in the Coliseum against those Trojans.

- **Dick Vermeil**
Network Television Football Analyst
Former Head Coach, UCLA Bruins & Philadelphia Eagles

APPENDIX
RECORDS SECTION
THE CROSSFIRE

Game	Year	Winner	Score	Standings USC	UCLA	TIE	Cumulative USC	Points UCLA
1	1929	USC	76-0	1	0	0	76	0
2	1930	USC	52-0	2	0	0	128	0
3	1936	-	7-7	2	0	1	135	7
4	1937	USC	19-13	3	0	1	154	20
5	1938	USC	42-7	4	0	1	196	27
6	1939	-	0-0	4	0	2	196	27
7	1940	USC	28-12	5	0	2	224	39
8	1941	-	7-7	5	0	3	231	46
9	1942	UCLA	14-7	5	1	3	238	60
10	1943	USC	20-0	6	1	3	258	60
11	1943	USC	26-13	7	1	3	284	73
12	1944	-	13-13	7	1	4	297	86
13	1944	USC	40-13	8	1	4	337	99
14	1945	USC	13-6	9	1	4	350	105
15	1945	USC	26-15	10	1	4	376	120
16	1946	UCLA	13-6	10	2	4	382	133
17	1947	USC	6-0	11	2	4	388	133
18	1948	USC	20-13	12	2	4	408	146
19	1949	USC	21-7	13	2	4	429	153
20	1950	UCLA	39-0	13	3	4	429	192
21	1951	UCLA	21-7	13	4	4	436	213
22	1952	USC	14-12	14	4	4	450	225
23	1953	UCLA	13-0	14	5	4	450	238
24	1954	UCLA	34-0	14	6	4	450	272
25	1955	UCLA	17-7	14	7	4	457	289
26	1956	USC	10-7	15	7	4	467	296

27	1957	UCLA	20-9	15	8	4	476	316
28	1958	-	15-15	15	8	5	491	331
29	1959	UCLA	10-3	15	9	5	494	341
30	1960	USC	17-6	16	9	5	511	347
31	1961	UCLA	10-7	16	10	5	518	357
32	1962	USC	14-3	17	10	5	532	360
33	1963	USC	26-6	18	10	5	558	366
34	1964	USC	34-13	19	10	5	592	379
35	1965	UCLA	20-16	19	11	5	608	399
36	1966	UCLA	14-7	19	12	5	615	413
37	1967	USC	21-20	20	12	5	636	433
38	1968	USC	28-16	21	12	5	664	449
39	1969	USC	14-12	22	12	5	678	461
40	1970	UCLA	45-20	22	13	5	698	506
41	1971	-	7-7	22	13	6	705	513
42	1972	USC	24-7	23	13	6	729	520
43	1973	USC	23-13	24	13	6	752	533
44	1974	USC	34-9	25	13	6	786	542
45	1975	UCLA	25-22	25	14	6	808	567
46	1976	USC	24-14	26	14	6	832	581
47	1977	USC	29-27	27	14	6	801	608
48	1978	USC	17-10	28	14	6	878	618
49	1979	USC	49-14	29	14	6	927	632
50	1980	UCLA	20-17	29	15	6	944	652
51	1981	USC	22-21	30	15	6	966	673
52	1982	UCLA	20-19	30	16	6	985	693
53	1983	UCLA	27-17	30	17	6	1002	720
54	1984	UCLA	29-10	30	18	6	1012	749
55	1985	USC	17-13	31	18	6	1029	762
56	1986	UCLA	45-25	31	19	6	1054	807
57	1987	USC	17-13	32	19	6	1071	820
58	1988	USC	31-22	33	19	6	1102	842
59	1989	-	10-10	33	19	7	1112	852
60	1990	USC	45-42	34	19	7	1157	894
61	1991	UCLA	24-21	34	20	7	1178	918
62	1992	UCLA	38-27	34	21	7	1215	956
63	1993	UCLA	27-21	34	22	7	1236	983

COMPOSITE OF 63 GAMES

	USC	UCLA
First Downs...	1042	869
Yards Rushing...	12719	8542
Yards Passing...	6921	8185
Total Yards...	19640	16727
Passes Attempted...	1175	1170
Passes Completed...	558	567
* Passes Had Intercepted...	71	92
Fumbles Lost...	107	81
# Penalties/Yards...	2703	2507

* 62 Games Only
# 60 Games Only

Scoring By Quarters:

	1	2	3	4	TOTAL
USC	202	379	287	368	1236
UCLA	234	228	208	313	983

419

UCLA Coaches Versus USC

Name	Years			Won	Lost	Tied	Pct
William H. Spaulding	1929	-	1938*	0	4	1	.100
Edwin C. Horrell	1939	-	1944**	1	4	3	.313
Bert LaBrucherie	1945	-	1948**	1	4	0	.200
Red Sanders	1949	-	1957	6	3	0	.667
Bill Barnes	1958	-	1964	2	4	1	.357
Tommy Prothro	1965	-	1970	3	3	0	.500
Pepper Rodgers	1971	-	1973	0	2	1	.167
Dick Vermeil	1974	-	1975	1	1	0	.500
Terry Donahue	1976	-	1993	8	9	1	.472
Totals				22	34	7	.405

USC Coaches Versus UCLA

Name	Years			Won	Lost	Tied	Pct
Howard Jones	1929	-	1940*	5	0	2	.857
Sam Barry	1941	-	1941	0	0	1	.500
Jeff Cravath	1942	-	1950**	8	3	1	.708
Jesse Hill	1951	-	1956	2	4	0	.333
Don Clark	1957	-	1959	0	2	1	.167
John McKay	1960	-	1975	10	5	1	.656
John Robinson	1976-82	+	1993	5	3	0	.625
Ted Tollner	1983	-	1986	1	3	0	.250
Larry Smith	1987	-	1992	3	2	1	.583
Totals				34	22	7	.595

* No Games 1931 thru 1935
** Two Games 1943-44-45

Southern California Award To Players Contributing the Most During the UCLA Game

1952 - Bill Hattig
1953 - Dick Petty
1954 - Orlando Ferrante
1955 - Gordon Duvall
1956 - Bob Voiles
1957 - Bob Voiles
1958 - Lou Byrd
1959 - Al Bansavage
1960 - Marlin McKeever
1961 - Frank Buncom
1962 - Marv Marinovich
1963 - Pete Beathard
1964 - Mike Garrett
1965 - Mike Garrett
1966 - Mike Hull
1967 - O.J. Simpson
1968 - O.J. Simpson
1969 - Al Cowlings
1970 - Sam Dickerson
1971 - Lou Harris
1972 - Richard Wood
1973 - Monte Doris
1974 - Anthony Davis
1975 - Ricky Bell (off.)
        Walt Underwood (def.)
1976 - Ricky Bell
1977 - Rob Hertel
1978 - Charles White (off.)
        Ty Sperling (def.)
1979 - Charles White (off.)
        Ronnie Lott (def.)
1980 - Keith Van Horne (off.)
        Ronnie Lott (def.)
1981 - Marcus Allen (off.)
        George Achica (def.)
1982 - Scott Tinsley (off.)
        Joey Browner (def.)
1983 - Michael Harper (off.)
        Tommy Haynes (def.)
1984 - Hank Norman (off.)
        Jack Del Rio (def.)
1985 - Joe Cormier (off.)
        Matt Koart (def.)
1986 - Rodney Peete (off.)
        Rex Moore (def.)
1987 - Rodney Peete and
        Erik Affholter (off.)
        Mark Carrier (def.)
1988 - Rodney Peete and
        Aaron Emanuel and
        John Guerrero (off.)
        Tim Ryan and
        Don Gibson (def.)
1989 - Ricky Ervins (off.)
        Mark Carrier (def.)
1990 - Mazio Royster (off.)
        Stephon Pace (def.)
1991 - Estrus Crayton (off.)
        Calvin Holmes (def.)
1992 - Rob Johnson (off.)
        Stephon Pace (def.)
1993 - Rob Johnson

UCLA Awards to Outstanding Players in Southern Cal Game

OFFENSE

1972 - Bruce Walton
1973 - Steve Klosterman
1974 - Randy Cross
1975 - Randy Cross
1976 - Rick Walker
1977 - Jim Main
1978 - Max Montoya
1979 - Jojo Townsell
1980 - Freeman McNeil
1981 - Ricky Coffman
1982 - Danny Andrews, Blake Wingle, Dan Dufour
1983 - Paul Bergmann
1984 - Duval Love
1985 - Gaston Green, Karl Dorrell
1986 - Gaston Green
1987 - Gaston Green
1988 - Troy Aikman, Bill Paige
1989 - Charles Arbuckle
1990 - Scott Miller
1991 - Kevin Williams, Tommy Maddox, Maury Toy
1992 - Kevin Williams, John Barnes, J.J. Stokes
1993 - Wayne Cook, Ricky Davis

DEFENSE

1972 - Allan Ellis
1973 - Fulton Kuykendall
1974 - Dale Curry
1975 - Oscar Edwards
1976 - Manu Tuiasosopo
1977 - Dave Morton
1978 - Manu Tuiasosopo
1979 - Kenny Easley
1980 - Lupe Sanchez
1981 - Tom Sullivan
1982 - B. Montgomery, Neal Dellocono, Mike Durden
1983 - Don Rogers
1984 - Den.Price, Tom Taylor
1985 - Norton, J.Washington
1986 - Ken Norton
1987 - C.Johnson, Jim Wahler
1988 - Chance Johnson
1989 - Eric Turner
1990 - A.Ale, Matt Darby
1991 - Arnold Ale, Stacy Argo, Mike Chalenski
1992 - Carlton Gray, Carrick O'Quinn, O.Henderson
1993 - Marvin Goodwin, Jamir Miller, Donovan Gallatin

This and That
...Since 1929

If you're just entering the UCLA football program, don't ask for jersey number 5 or 13 or 16 or 34 or 38 or 80 or 84. You won't get it. For those numbers have all been retired... in honor of Kenny Easley, Kenny Washington, Gary Beban, Paul Cameron, Burr Baldwin, Donn Moomaw and Jerry Robinson.

Pickings are not so slim at Southern California, where only four numbers have been removed. Charles White, Mike Garrett, O.J. Simpson and Marcus Allen have put jersey numbers 12, 20, 32 and 33 on the shelf.

Your best bet for achieving All-America honors at USC is to request jersey number 16 or 42 or 66 or 78. Each of these numbers were worn by four Trojan All-Americans. And three wore numbers 17, 28, 71, 77 and 89.

Laurels have found their way to University Park in greater volume than to Westwood. Since 1929, Southern Cal has had 112 players named to All-America status, as well as four Heisman Trophy winners, an Outland Trophy winner, a Lombardi Award winner, and a Thorpe Award recipient.

The Bruins have had 60 players named to AA status, one Heisman winner, and one Davey O'Brien Award recipient.

UCLA has had two players selected as All-Americans three consecutive years: Jerry Robinson and Kenny Easley. One from Troy duplicated this feat: Richard Wood.

Since the two schools opened fire upon each other 65 years ago, Southern Cal has enjoyed three undefeated and untied seasons: 1932 (10-0-0), 1962 (11-0-0) and 1972 (12-0-0). The Trojans were unbeaten - but tied - in four other years: 1939, 1944, 1969 and 1979. USC has been tapped conditional national champion 11 times during the period of UCLA combat.

The Bruins flashed a 9-0-0 perfect record in 1954, were undefeated - but tied - in 1939 and were crowned national champ by UPI in 1954.

As might be expected, Southern Cal boasts a superior bowl record. Since 1929, the Trojans have hosted the Rose Bowl 26 times, winning 18. In all post-season affairs, SC has credentials of 22 wins and 13 losses.

UCLA claims five victories in 11 Rose Bowl appearances. And its overall bowl slate is 10 wins, eight setbacks, and a tie.

Of the 63 games played, the team that led or was even at halftime went on to win or tie the contest 53 times. Southern Cal made second-half comebacks to win after trailing at the break six times; UCLA, four times.

The longest unbeaten string of games was molded by USC between 1978-1980: 28. UCLA's best streak was 14 put together between 1975-1976.

Los Angeles, the City of *Braggin' Rights* for Which USC and UCLA Engage in Annual Crossfire

USC Football Lettermen, 1929-1993

Abram, Fabian 55-56
Abrams, Andre 92
Achica, George 79-80-81-82
Adams, Gordon 80
Adams, Pete 70-71-72
Adams, William 67
Adelman, Harry 41-42
Adolph, Robyn 73-74
Affholter, Erik 85-86-87-88
Aquirre, John 41-45
Aldridge, Charles 67
Alexander, Del 93
Allen, Marcus 78-79-80-81
Allmon, Richard 67-68
Allred, John 93
Anderson, Brad 81
Andersor, Charles 60-61
Anderson, William 37-38-40-41
Ane, Charles Jr. 51-52
Anno, Sam 83-84-85-86
Anthony, Charles 71-72-73
Anthony, Frank 27-28-29
Antle, Ken 56-57-58
Antles, Russ 44-45-46
Apolskis, David 90-92-93
Apsit, Marger 28-29-30
Arbelbide, Garrett 29-30-31
Archuleta, Bobby 87
Arnest, Henry 61
Arnett, Bob 57-58
Arnett, Jon 54-55-56
Arrington, Gene 88
Arrivey, Jim 82
Arrobio, Charles 63-64-65
Artenian, Mickey 52-53
Ashcraft, Walt 49-52
Atanasoff, Alex 37
Audet, Earl 43
Ayala, Vic 68-69-70

B -
Baccitich, John 66
Bain, William 73-74

Bain, Marvin 64-65
Baker, John 29-30-31
Baldock, Al 49-50-53
Bame, Damon 62-63
Banks, Chip 78-79-80-81
Bansavage, Albert 59
Banta, Bradford 90-91-92-93
Banta, Jack 38-39-40
Barber, Kurt 88-89-90-91
Barber, Richard 31-32
Bardin, Oliver 32-33
Barnes, Dan 87-88-89
Barnes, Mercer 49-50
Barnum, Terry 92-93
Baroncelli, Andy 84
Barragar, Nathan 27-28-29
Barry, Allen 52
Barry, Joe 92-93
Barry, Nelson 30
Barry, Stephen 65-66
Bastian, Bob 46-47-48
Bates, James 60-61
Battle, Art 46-48-49
Battle, Mike 66-67-68
Beard, Fran 32-33-34
Beard, Gregory 75
Beathard, Pete 61-62-63
Beatty, Blanch. 30-31
Beatty, Homer 34-35-36
Beck, Eugene 48-49-50
Becker, Henry 29
Bedsole; Hal 61-62-63
Beeson, Bob 40
Belko, Max 34-35-36
Bell, Joseph 43
Bell, Ricky 73-74-75-76
Belotti, George 54-55-56
Beloud, Bret 93
Bender, Wes 91-92
Bennett, Frank 39
Benson, Carl 39-40
Benson, Jeff 85
Berry, John 81-83
Berry, Michael 69-70
Berryman, Richard 36
Berryman, Robert 39-40
Betz, Bill 47

Bescos, Julius 32-33-34
Bethel, Gary 75-76-77
Bettinger, George 35
Bianchi, Steve 41
Bickett, Duane 82-83-84
Biggers, Keith 83-84
Biggs, Henry 30-31-32
Bird, Jim 47-48-49
Black, Rupert 30
Blanche, John 66-68
Blecksmith, Ed 64-65
Bledsoe, Leo 41
Bledsoe, William 40-41
Bleeker, Mel 40-41-42
Bohlinger, Tom 72-73
Boies, Herbert 49
Boies, Larry 57-58
Bond, Ward 28-29-30
Bordier, Warner 54-55
Born, Dennis 67
Boselli, Tony 91-92-93
Bothelho, Rod 58
Boulware, Dave 71-72-73
Bowers, William 50
Bowie, Wilson 68
Bowlin, Brandon 86-87-88
Bowman, Charles 39
Boyer, Mark 82-83-84
Bozanic, George 51-52-53
Bradford, Joe 45
Bradley, Otha 73-74
Brady, Greg 81
Brandt, Harvey 34
Braziel, Larry 77-78
Breeland, Garrett 84-85
Bregel, Jeff 83-84-85-86
Brennan, Scott 85-86-87-88
Brenner, Hoby 78-79-80
Brewer, Tony 82-83
Bright, Kenneth 32-33
Brock, Louis 84-85-86
Boskovich, Martin 93
Brooks, Bruce 77
Bronson, Richard 57
Brouse, Willard 31
Brousseau, Raphael 35-36-37
Brown, Booker 72-73

Brown, David 70-71-72
Brown, Everett 28-29-30
Brown, George 34
Brown, Jeff H. 86-87-88
Brown, Jeff L. 80-81-82-83
Brown, Marcel 90
Brown, Ray 30-31-32
Brown, Ronald 54-55
Brown, Ron 85-86
Brown, Rory 90-92-93
Brown, Willie 61-62-63
Brownell, Richard 64
Browner, Joey 79-80-81-82
Browner, Keith 80-81-82-83
Browning, Ward 32-33-34
Brownwood, John 62-63-64
Bruce, Kevin 73-74-75
Brummett, Mike 83
Budde, Brad 76-77-78-79
Buckley, Robert 51-52-53
Buford, Don 57-58
Bukich, Rudy 51-52
Buncom, Frank 60-61
Bundra, Mike 59-60-61
Bundy, Bill 39-40-41
Burchard, Gerald 33-34-35
Burke, Don 48
Butkus, Matt 93
Burns, Dan 76-77
Burns, DeChon 89
Burns, Michael 75-76
Busby, Marvin 34
Busby, Stuart 61
Busch, Ernie 47
Busick, Steve 78-79-80
Bush, Ron 74-75-76
Butcher, Ron 61-62
Butler, Ray 78-79
Butts, Tracy 85-86-87-88
Byrd, Glenn 72
Byrd, MacArthur 62-63-64

Byrd, Louis 57-58

C -
Cadigan, Dave 85-86-87
Cahill, Ray 66
Cain, Lynn 77-78
Calabria, Ronald 54
Callanan, George 43
Callanan, Howard 42
Callanan, James 44-45 46
Cameron, Rodney 33 34-35
Campbell, Jack 78
Cannamela, Pat 50-51
Cantor, Al 48
Cantwell, John 74
Carey, Mike 76-77
Carmichael, Al 50-51 52
Carpenter, Ken 34-37
Carrier, Mark 87-88-89
Carter, Allen 72-73-74
Carter, Kent 70-71
Caruthers, Gerald 93
Cashman, Tyler 93
Cashman, Pat 66-67
Catoe, Ed 76-77
Celotto, Mario 74-75 76-77
Chambers, Mahlon 27-28-29
Champlain, Jay 81
Chandler, Robert 68 69-70
Chaney, Chris 72
Chantilles, Tom 41
Charles, Ben 59-60
Chavez, Sal 88
Chesley, Delmar 86 87-88-89
Chesley, J.R. 90
Chesley, Martin 85-88
Chuha, Joe 57
Clark, Kevin 93
Clark, Don 42-46-47
Clark, Gordon 31-32 33
Clark, Jack 35
Clark, Jay 62-63
Clark, Monte 56-57-58
Clark, Roger 60-61
Clarke, Eugene 30-31
Clarke, Leon 53-54-55
Clayton, Franklin 52 53-54
Cleary, Paul 46-47

Clemons, Calvin Jr. 32-33-34
Coauette, Greg 84 85-86-87
Cobb, Garry 76-77-78
Cobb, Marvin 72-73-74
Coia, Angelo 58-59
Colley, Tom 48
Collins, Pat 73
Colorito, Tony 83-84 85
Colter, Cleveland 86 87-88-89
Conde, John 49-50-51
Connors, Rod 77
Conroy, James 56-57 59
Conroy, Jerome 65
Contratto, Jim 53-54-55
Conway, Curtis 90-91 92
Cook, Brian 82
Coones, Ken 59
Cordell, Michael 73 74-75
Cormier, Joe 83-84-85
Cornwell, Fred 81-82 83
Corsinotti, Dave 81
Cotton, Marcus 84-85 86-87
Coughlin, Alvie 32-33 34
Covington, Humphrey 68-69
Cowlings, Allen 68-69
Cox, Robert 51-52
Cox, Tom 84-85
Cramer, Stanley 47
Crane, Bob 89-90-91
Crane, Dennis 67
Crawford, Willie 77-78
Crayton, Estrus 91-92
Crisman, Joel 90-91 92-93
Crittenden, Wallace 44
Crow, Lindon 52-53-54
Crowthers, Jim 41
Crutcher, Fred 81-83 84-85
Culbreath, Cliff 72
Cunnigan, Donn 91 92-93
Cunningham, Sam 70 71-72
Curley, August 80-81 82

Curry, Edsel 43-46-47
Curtis, Louis 44
Cutri, Cosimo 50-51

D -
Dabasinskas, Tom 87-88-89
Dale, Ron 88-89-90-91
Dandoy, Aramis 52 53-54
Danehe, Richard 41
Darby, Byron 79-80 81-82
DaRe, Mario 52-53-54
Davis, Anthony 72 73-74
Davis, Clarence 69-70
Davis, David 34-35-36
Davis, George 44-47 49
Davis, George 34
Davis, Joe 40-41-42
Davis, Joe E. 73-74-75
Davis, Keith 84-85-86 87
Davis, Michael 81
Day, Oliver 37-38
Debovsky, Philip 57
Decker, George 29-30
Decker, James 53-54 56
Deese, Derrick 90-91
Dehetre, John 34-37
DeKraai, Terry 68-69
Delaney, Gary 60
deLauer, Bob 39-40-41
Del Conte, Kenneth 60-61-62
Del Rio, Jack 81-82 83-84
Demirjian, Ed 50
Dempsey, Edward 38 39-40
Denvir, John 85
Deranian, Vaughn 28 29-30
Diaz, Rigo 88
Dickerson, Samuel 68-69-70
Diggs, Shelton 73 74-75-76
Dill, Dean 47
DiLulo, Paul 78-80
Dimler, Richard 75 76-77-78
Dittberner, Art 33 34-35

Doll, Don 44-46-47-48
Dominis, John 43
Doris, Monte 72-73
Dotson, David 93
Douglas, Don 57-58
Downs, Bob 50
Drake, Ron 66-67
Dreblow, Milford 43-44-45-46
Duboski, Phillip 36
Dudum, J.J. 91
Duff, Clinton 49 50-51
Duffield, Marshall 28 29-30
Dunaway, Warren 34
Dunn, Coye 36
Dunning, Corwin 32
Durkee, Harvey 28 29-31
Durko, Sandy 68-69
Duvall, Gordon 53 54-55
Dye, George 29
Dye, John 31-32-33
Dye, William 33-34
Dyer, Bruce 70-71

E -
Ebertin, Chuck 87-88
Eddy, Andy 85
Edelson, Harry 27 28-29
Edwards, Dennis 78 79-80-81
Edwards, Robert 58 59
Elliott, Ian 41
Emanuel, Aaron 85 86-88-89
Engle, Roy 37-38-39
Enright, Richard 54 55
Eriksen, Bob 71
Erskine, Robert 31 32-33
Ervin, Anthony 85
Ervins, Ricky 87-88 89-90
Essick, Douglas 41 42-46
Evans, Charles 69-70
Evans, John 43
Evans, Vincent 74 75-76
Exley, Landon 52-53

F -
Failor, Walt 70
Farmer, David 74-75-76
Fassell, Jim 69
Fate, Steve 71-72
Fay, Ken 31-32-33
Ferguson, James 66
Ferrante, Orlando 53-54-55
Ferraro, John 43-44-46-47
Fertig, Craig 62-63-64
Ficca, Dan 58-59-60
Fields, Scott 92-93
Finneran, Gary 57-58-59
Finney, Hal 42
Fiorentino, Frank 56-57-58
Fisher, Jeff 79-80
Fisher, Robert 36-37-38
Fisk, Bill 37-38-39
Fisk, William Jr. 62-63-64
Fite, Gary 65
FitzPatrick, James 83-84-85
Fletcher, Oliver 48
Fletcher, Ronald 54-55-56
Flood, Jeff 73-75
Floro, Robert 60
Foley, Shane 89-90
Follett, George 71-72
Foote, Chris 77-78-79
Ford, Cole 91-92-93
Ford, Dwight 74-75-77-78
Foster, Roy 78-79-80-81
Fouch, Edward 52-53-54
Fouch, John 49-50
Fraser, Scott 77-79
Freier, Scott 87-88-89
French, Martin 85
Fruge, Gene 87-88-89-90
Fuhrer, Bob 32-33-34
Fuhrman, Seymour 42

G -
Gachett, Derrick 86-88
Gage, Stuart 93

Gaisford, Bill 35-36
Galbraith, Scott 86-87-88-89
Gale, Michael 61-62
Gallaher, Allen 70-71-72
Gallaway, Darren 91-92-93
Galli, George 53-54-55
Galloway, Clark 27-28-29
Galvin, Glen 36-37-39
Garcia, Dan 78-79
Garlin, Donald 44-46-47-48
Garner, Dwayne 86-87-88-89
Garrett, Michael 63-64-65
Garrison, Edesel 71-72
Garzoni, Mike 43-44-45-46
Gaskill, Lynn 59-60-61
Gaspar, Phil 37-38-39
Gay, William 75-76-77
Gaytan, Michael 91
Garrido, Norberto 93
Gee, Doug 45
Gee, Matt 88-89-90-91
Gelker, Benjamin 43
Gentry, Byron 30-31-32
George, Ray 36-37-38
Ketz, Bob 32
Gibson, Anthony 80-82
Gibson, Craig 90-91-92-93
Gibson, Don 87-88-89-90
Giers, Michael 63-64
Gifford, Frank 49-50-51
Gill, William 34-35
Givehand, James 72
Goller, Winston 50-51
Gonta, Stanley 62
Gorecki, Len 92
Gorrell, Walter 56
Goux, Marv 52-54-55
Gowder, Robert 27-28-29
Gracin, Jerry 34
Grady, Stephen 66-67

Graf, Allan 70-71-72
Grant, Jon 70-71-72
Gray, Gordon 43-44-46-47
Gray, Ken 72-73-74
Gray, Riki 78-79-80-82
Gray, William 43
Grace, Ken 93
Green, Brad 79
Green, Max 40
Green, Paul 84-86-87-88
Green, Tim 83-84
Greenwood, C.D. 52-53-54
Griffin, Frank 88-89-90
Griffith, Charles 54
Griffith, Homer 31-32-33
Grissum, James 68-70
Guerrero, John 85-87-88
Gunn, James 67-68-69
Gurasich, Walt 56-57
Gutierrez, Ed 76-77

H -
Haas, Brian 92-93
Haas, Earl 36
Hachten, Boyd 48
Haden, Pat 72-73-74
Hale, Chris 87-88
Hall, Frank 54-55-56
Hall, Robert 29-30-31
Hall, William 33-34
Hall, Willie 70-71
Hallock, Tom 83-84-85
Haluchak, Mike 68-69-70
Halvorsen, Ray 36
Hamilton, Tom 48
Hammack, Harold 29-30-31
Hampton, Clint 81-82
Hand, Harold 52-53
Hancock, Mike 72-73
Hannah, Travis 89-90-91-92
Hansell, Ellis 81
Hansen, Owen 35-36-37
Hardy, Don 43-44-46
Hardy, Jim 42-43-44

Harlan, David 32-33
Harlow, Pat 87-88-89-90
Harper, Hueston 32-33-34
Harper, Michael 80-82-83
Harris, Lou 70-71
Hart, Speedy 80
Hartsuyker, Craig 87-88-89-90
Hartwig, Carter 76-77-78
Harvey, Clarence 45
Harvey, John 81-82
Hatfield, Hal 48-49-50
Hattabaugh, Clay 91-92
Hattig, Bill 50-51-52
Hawkins, William 30
Hawthorne, Addison 52-53
Hayes, Jim 52-53
Hayes, Luther 58-59-60
Hayes, Michael 77-79
Hayhoe, Jerry 64-66
Hayhoe, William 67-68
Haynes, Tommy 83-84
Headley, Blake 44
Hector, Zuri 89-90-91-92
Heinberg, Sylvester 45
Heller, Ron 62-63-64
Henderson, Deryl 85-86
Henderson, James 35-36
Hendren, Robert 46-47-48
Henke, Edgar 48
Henry, Jerald 91-92-93
Henry, Ken 85-86-87
Henry, Michael 56-57-58
Herpin, John 92-93
Hertel, Robert 75-76-77
Hervay, Edward 93
Haywood, Ralph 41-42-43
Hibbs, Gene 35-36-37
Hickman, Don 55-56-57
Hickman, Donnie 74-75-76
Higgins, Clark 44
Hill, Fred 62-63-64
Hill, Gary 62-63-64

Hill, Hilliard 56-58
Hill, Jesse 28-29
Hindley, Lewis 40
Hinton, Charles 71-72
Hinz, Mike 90-91-92 93
Hipp, Eric 79-80
Hoff, Cecil 27-28-29
Hoffman, Robert 37 38-39
Hogan, Douglas 73 74-75
Hogue, Jeremy 93
Holden, Clark 57 58-59
Holden, Dave 84
Holland, Bill 70-71
Holland, Thomas 91 92-93
Hollinquest, Lamont 88-89-91-92
Holmes, Calvin 88 89-90-91
Holt, Leroy 86-87-88 89
Homan, James 65-66
Hooks, Robert 51-52
Hooks, Roger 54
Hoover, Philip 61-62
Hope, Neil 81-82-83 84
Hopkins, Marcus 88 89-90
Hopper, Darrel 82 83-84
Hopper, Tarriel 93
Hoard, Randy 88-89
Houck, Hudson 63
Houlgate, Jack 33
Howard, Bill 57
Howard, William 33 34-35
Howell, Mike 75
Howell, Pat 76-77-78
Hubby, Lindsy 56-57
Hudson, Tyrone 69-70
Hughes, Don 44-47-49
Hull, Michael 65-66-67
Hull, Warren 34-35
Humenuik, Rod 56 57-58
Hunt, Loran 61-62-63
Hunter, Floyd III 65
Hunter, James 78-79 80
Hurst, Joe 33-34

I -
Ingle, Ray 43
Isaacson, Robert 55-56
Isherwood, Ed 56 57

J -
Jackson, Duaine 81 82-83-84
Jackson, John 86-87 88-89
Jackson, Melvin 74-75
Jackson, Vic 76
Jackson, Yonnie 89 90-91-92
Jacobsmeyer, Walt 42
Jamison, Dick 42
Jaroncyk, William 66-67
Jensen, Robert 30
Jensen, Robert A. 68-69
Jesse, John 36-37-38
Jessup, Bill 48-50
Jeter, Gary 73-74-75 76
Johnson, Dennis 77 78-79
Johnson, Eddie 71-72
Johnson, Gary 60-61
Johnson, Matt 82-83 84-85
Johnson, Paul 64-65
Johnson, Rob 91-92-93
Johnson, Ricky 77-79
Johnson, Tom 62-63
Johnston, Rex 56-57 58
Jones, Bob 39-40-41
Jones, Don 80
Jones, Ernie 61-62-63
Jones, James 36-37-38
Jones, James A. 69 70-71
Jones, James R. 62
Jones, Michael 91-92
Jones, Shannon 90 92-93
Jordan, Frank 77-78
Jordan, Steve 81-82 83-84
Jorgenson, Ellwood 32-34-35
Joslin, J.Howard 29 30-31

Jurich, Anthony 29-30

K -
Kalinich, Pete 39
Kamana, John 80-81 82-83
Kasten, Donald 58
Katnik, John 86-87
Keehn, Ludwig 56
Keiderling, Jason 93
Keller, Donald 36-37
Keller, John T. 35
Kemp, Rockwell 27 28-29
Keneley, Matt 93
Kerr, Rob 77-78-79
Khasigian, Harry 67 68-69
Kidder, Allan 34-35
King, Eddie 63-65-66
King, Marty 77-78
Kirby, Jack 46-47-48
Kirkland, Al 52
Kirner, Gary 62-63
Kissinger, Ellsworth 54-55-56
Klein, Gary 84-85
Klein, Robert 66-67 68
Klenk, Quenton, 39 40
Knight, Ryan 84-85 86-87
Knight, Sammy 93
Knutson, Steven C. 73-74
Koart, Matt 82-83 84-85
Koch, Desmond D. 51-52-53
Kopp, Jeff 91-92-93
Kordich, John 48
Kovac, Pete 34
Kraintz, Rudy 34
Kranz, Doug 55-56
Kreiger, Wm. Karl 27-28-29
Kroll, Darrell 42
Krueger, Al 38-39-40
Kuamoo, Gaylord 84-85
Kubas, John 57
Kuhn, Gil 34-35-36
Kurlak, Wayne 54-56

L -
Lamb, Mike 83

Lady, George 32-33 34
Langley, Lawrence 35-36
Langlois, Dave 82
Lansdell, Grenville 37-38-39
Lapka, Myron 77-78 79
Lardizabel, Ben D. 55-56-57
Larrabee, Duane 33-34
Lavender, Tim 78
Lavin, Tim 90-91
Lawrence, James 66-67-68
Lawryk, Eugene 76
LeDue, William 36
Lee, James 72
Lee, Junior 74-75
Lee, Phillip 64-65-66
Lee, Zephrini 82-85
Lenderman, Ryan 93
Leggett, Brad 87-88 89
Lehmer, Steven M. 67-68-69
Leimbach, Charles 54-55-56
Leimbach, Joe 80-81 82-83
Leon, Richard 66
Levingston, Robert 59-60
Levy, Dexter 86
Lewis, David R. 74 75-76
Lewis, Mike 58
Lillywhite, Verl 45 46-47
Limahelu, Chris 73 74
Lincoln, Irwin 92-93
Linehan, Tony 46-47 49
Lingenfelter, Dean 73
Littlejohn, Leroy 42
Lloyd, Dave 44-47-48
Lockwood, John 64 65
Lockwood, Scott 87 88-90-91
Logie, Dale 74-75
Lopez, Frank 64-65
Lorch, Karl 72
Lowell, Russell 47

Lott, Ronnie 77-78 79-80
Love, Robert 32-33
Lowery, Willie 93
Loya, Robert 92-93
Lubisich, Peter 61 62-63
Lucas, James 74
Luft, Brian 81-82 83-84
Luizzi, Bruce 89-90 91-92
Lupo, Thomas L. 62-63-64
Lynch, Ford 34-35 36

M -
MacKenzie, Doug 80-81
MacPhail, Peter 41 42-43
McArthur, Gary 69
McCaffrey, Robert 72-73-74
McCall, Don 65-66
McCall, Fred 41-42 46-47
McCardle, Mickey 42-43-46-47
McClanahan, Bob 80-81
McConnell, Stephen 68
McCool, Pat 80-81-82
McCormick, Walt 45 46-47
McCowan, Howard 90
McCullouch, Earl 67
McDade, Jack 86
McDaniels, Terry 90 91-92-93
McDonald, Mike 76 77-78-79
McDonald, Paul 77 78-79
McDonald, Tim 83 84-85-86
McFadden, Dwight 92
McFarland, Don 54-55
McGarvin, Tom 40
McGee, Bob 50
McGinest, Willie 90 91-92-93

McGinley, Francis 31-32-34
McGinn, John 44-45
McGirr, Mike 71-73
McGrew, Larry 77 78-79
McKay, John K. 72-73-74
McKee, Erik 84-85-86
McKeever, Marlin 58 59-60
McKeever, Mike 58 59-60
McKinney, Harry 44 45-46-47
McLean, Kevin 84 85-86-87
McMahon, Richard 61-62-63
McMoore, Robert 35
McMurty, Paul 49-50
McNeil, Don 36-37-38
McNeill, Rod 70-72-73
McNeish, Bob 31-32 33
McNeish, George 34 35-36
McPartland, Kevin 76
McWilliams, John 93
Maddux, James 55
Magner, Gary 65-66-67
Mahone, Elick 90-91 92
Malley, Duane 41
Mallory, Tom 29-30-31
Maloney, Al 30
Manning, Dick 41
Maples, Jim 59-60-61
Marderian, Gregory 71-73-74
Maree, Jeff 85-86-87
Marincovich, Andy 43
Marinovich, Marvin 59-61-62
Marinovich, Todd 89-90
Marshall, Derrell 88
Martin, Rod 75-76
Martin, William 48
Matthews, Bruce 80-81-82
Matthews, Clay 74 75-76-77
Matthews, Garland 32-33-34
Mazur, John 81

Matthews, Robert 38 39-40-42
Mattson, Don 56-57
Maudlin, Tom 57-58
May, Reg 65-66
Mena, Sal 38-39-40
Merk, Ernest 54-55
Mietz, Roger 58-59 60
Miller, John 53-54-55
Miller, Rick 76
Miller, Robert R. 66 67-68
Miller, Ron 51-52-53
Minkoff, Cliff 91
Mitchell, Dale 72-73 74
Mitchell, Marc 80
Mix, Ron 57-58-59
Mohler, Orville 30 31-32
Moi, Junior 91-92
Mollett, Gerald 59
Moloney, Jerry 50
Monson, Jim 48
Montgomery, Marv. 69-70
Moody, Michael 88 89-90-91
Mooney, Mike 90-92
Moore, Brent 83-84-85
Moore, Darryl 81-82
Moore, James 65-66
Moore, Kenney 78-79 80
Moore, Malcolm 80 81-83
Moore, Manfred 71 72-73
Moore, Rex 84-85-86 87
Morgan, Boyd F. 36 37-38
Morgan, David J. 59 60-61
Morgan, Michael 70 71
Morill, Charles 38 39-40
Morovick, Dan 79
Morris, Patrick 75
Morris, Robert 44
Morrison, Robert 32
Mortensen, Jesse 28-29
Morton, Johnnie 90 91-92-93

Mosebar, Don 79-80 81-82
Moses, Charlie 78
Moses, Don 27-28-29
Moton, Dave 63-64-65
Moyer, Steve 80
Mullins, Gerald B. 69-70
Munch, Arlo 34
Munoz, Anthony 76 77-78-79
Murphy, George 44 46-47-48
Murray, Joe 82
Murray, Thomas 34
Murrell, Gidion 90 91-92-93
Musick, Billie 41
Musick, Bob 41-42-45
Musick, James 29-30 31
Musick, John E. 44 45-46

N -
Naumu, Johnny 46
Naumu, Sol 50
Nave, Doyle 37-38-39
Neidhardt, David 29
Nelsen, William 60 61-62
Nickoloff, Thomas 51-52-53
Nix, Jack 48
Noble, Bill 41-42
Noor, Dennis 36-37
Nordstrom, Ron 51
Norene, George 30-31
Norman, Hank 82-83 84-85
Norris, Neil 30-31-32
Norton, Miles 36-37
Nunis, Dick 51-52
Nunnally, Lawrence 75

O -
Obbema, Joseph 68
Obradovich, James 73-74
Obradovich, Steve 76
O'Brovac, Nick 50
Odom, Ricky 76-77
Oestreich, Newell 46
O'Grady, Steve 77
O'Hara, Pat 88-90
Olivarria, Tony 79

Oliver, Jason 90-91 92-93
Oliver, Ralph 66-67
O'Malley, John 68
Ortega, Anthony 56 57-58
Orcutt, Gary 69
Ossowski, Ted 43
Ostling, Gerald 33-34
Owens, Dan 86-87 88-89
Owens, James 31-32

P -
Pace, Stephon 89-90 91-92
Packard, David 32
Page, Charles 43
Page, John 86-87
Page, Mike 57
Page, Otis 76-77-78
Page, Toby 66-67
Palmer, Ford 30-31 32-33
Papadakis, John 70-71
Pappas, Nick 35-36-37
Parker, Artimus 71 72-73
Parkinson, Brent 86 87-88-89
Parks, Bruce 85-86
Parsons, Earle 43
Patapoff, William 43
Patrick, Doug 64-65
Pavich, Frank 52-53 54
Peccianti, Angelo 36 38
Peete, Rodney 85-86 87-88
Pehar, John 44
Pekarcik, Al 72
Peoples, Robert 38 39-40
Perrin, Jay 47
Perry, John 80
Perry, Reggie 91-92 93
Persinger, Gerald 58
Peters, Ray 78
Peters, Volney 48-50
Peterson, Chuck 48
Petrill, Larry 65-66
Petty, Dick 52-53
Peviani, Bob 50-51-52
Phillips, Charles 72

73-74
Phillips, Floyd 38 39-40
Phillips, Jim 83
Phillips, Micah 92-93
Piersen, Mel 47
Pinckert, Erny 29-30 31
Pivaroff, Ivan 60-61
Plaehn, Alfred 30 31-32
Pola, Kennedy 82 83-84-85
Pollack, Kris 91-92 93
Pollard, Marvin 88 89-90-91
Porter, Don 92
Porter, Vincent 42
Potter, Gary 62
Poulsen, Alfred 33
Powell, Edward 72 73-74
Powell, Marvin 74 75-76
Powers, Jim 47-48-49
Powers, Russell 34
Pranevicius, John 40-41
Preininger, Joe 34 35-36
Preston, Marc 88-89
Preston, Rob 78-79
Preston, Ron 70
Prindle, Bill 85
Probst, Cliff 33-34-35
Prukop, Al 58-59-60
Pryor, Dave 79-80 81-82
Psaltis, David 51-52
Pucci, Ed 51-52-53
Pucci, Ralph 48-49-50
Pugh, Allen 77-78-80
Pultorak, Steven 70
Purling, Dave 82-83-84
Pye, Ernest 62-63-64

R -
Raab, Marc 90-91
Radovich, Bill 35-36-37
Rakhshani, Vic 78-79 80
Rae, Michael 70-71-72
Ramey, Theron 30
Ramsay, Kian 89
Ramsay, Kyle 92-93
Randle, Ken 73-75-76

Ransom, Walt 78
Ratliff, John 61-62-63
Ray, Terrel 68
Rea, John 45-46-47
Reade, Lynn 62
Reagan, Pat 56-57
Reboin, Al 32-33-34
Redding, William 68-69
Reece, Dan 73-74-75
Reed, Dick 45
Reed, Robert 36-37
Renison, William 64
Rhames, Timothy 73 74-75
Richardson, Troy 83 84-85
Richman, Dennis 64
Riddle, William 51 52-53
Ridings, Gene 31 32-33
Riley, Arthur 87
Riley, Steve 72-73
Ritchey, Bart 28-30
Roberson, Theodore 73-74-75
Roberts, C.R. 55-56
Roberts, Gene 35
Robertson, Robert 39-40-41
Robertson, Wilbur 49
Robinson, Mike 76
Rodeen, Don 34-35
Rodgers, Marc 88
Rodriguez, Fran 83
Rodriguez, Quin 87 88-89-90
Rodriguez, Ray 72-73
Rogers, Don 48
Rogers, Ed 34
Rollinson, Bruce 71
Romer, Marshall 43 44-46
Roquet, Russel 40
Rorison, James 34 35-36
Rose, Mason 35
Rosenberg, Aaron 31-32-33
Rosendahl, Robert 56
Rosin, Benjamin 59 60-61
Ross, Scott 87-88 89-90
Rossetto, John 46

Rossovich, Timothy 65-66-67
Roth, Mike 82
Roundy, Jay 47-48-49
Royster, Mazio 90-91
Rubke, Karl 55-56
Ruettgers, Ken 82 83-84
Runnerstrum, Grant 89-90
Ruppert, Richard 70
Russell, Lynman 36 37
Ryan, Mike 70-71-72
Ryan, Tim 86-87-88-89

S -
Saenz, Edwin 43
Sager, Mark 86-87-88
Sagouspe, Larry 62-63
Salapa, Paul 44-46-47
Salisbury, Sean 82-83 85
Salmon, Mike 90-91 92-93
Salness, Ty 64-66-67
Sampson, Ben 50-51 52
Sampson, Vernon 53 54-55
Samuels, James 60
Sanbrano, Al 50-51
Sanchez, Armando 62-63
Sanders, Robert 34 35-36
Sangster, William 37-38-39
Sargent, Hugh 41
Saunders, Russell 27-28-29
Scarpace, Michael 65 66-67
Schindler, Ambrose 36-37-39
Schmidt, Dennis 62
Schmidt, Henry 55
Schneider, Dean 49-51
Schuhmacher, John 76-77
Schultz, Bill 89
Schutte, George 46 47-48
Scoggins, Eric 77 78-79-80
Scott, Joe 60

Scott, Dan 66-67-68
Scott, Joel 89-90-91-92
Scott, Will 67-68-69
Sears, James 50-51-52
Seau, Junior 88-89
Sehorn, Jason 92-93
Seitz, William 28-29
Seixas, John 32-33
Seixas, William 42
Sellers, Leon 51-52-53
Serpa, Mike 85-86-87-88
Shafer, Don 85-86
Shannon, Ken 32-33
Shannon, Tim 80
Shaputis, Bob 73
Shaver, Gaius 29-30-31
Shaw, Gerald 67-68-69
Shaw, Jesse 28-29-30
Shaw, Nathaniel 64-65-66
Shea, Pat 60-61
Shell, Joe 37-38-39
Sherman, Rodney 64-65-66
Sherman, Thomas 31
Shields, Alan 59-60
Shipp, Joe 77
Shuey, Edward 35
Simmons, Jeff 80-81-82
Simmrin, Randall 75-76-77
Simpson, O.J. 67-68
Sims, James 72-73
Skiles, John 70-71
Skvarna, Carl 60-61
Slaton, Tony 81-82-83
Slatter, James 37-38-39
Slough, Greg 69-70
Small, Errol 93
Smedley, Ron 61-62
Smith, Corby 92
Smith, Dennis 77-78-79-80
Smith, Ernest 30-31-32
Smith, Harry 37-38-39
Smith, Jeff 64-65
Smith, Michael 73-74
Smith, Robert 34
Smith, Roy 54
Smith, Sidney 68-69
Smith, Stanley 32
Smith, Tody 69-70
Snow, James 66-67-68

Snyder, Ed 37
Snyder, James 47
Sogge, Steve 67-68
Sohn, Ben 38-39-40
Sovers, Glenn 50
Sparling, Raymond 30-31-32
Spears, Ernest 86-87-88-89
Spears, Raoul 90-91
Spector, Irwin 53-54
Spencer, Todd 81-82-83
Sperle, Chris 85-86-87-88
Sperling, Ty 77-78-79
Spraggins, Ed 34
Stall, Joseph 46
Stanley, Ralph 36-37-38
Steele, Hal 75-76
Steele, Todd 83-84-85-86
Stephens, Barry 29-30-31
Stephenson, Warren 60-61
Steponovich, Tony 27-28-29
Stevens, Lawrence 31-32-33
Stevenson, Ed 36
Stewart, George 73-74
Stillwell, Bob 47-48-49
Stillwell, Don 50-51-52
Stirling, Robert 70-71
Stoecker, Howard 37-38-39
Stokes, Bill 86-87
Stonebraker, John 38-39
Stonehouse, John 92-93
Streelman, Brad 78-79
Strother, Deon 90-91-92-93
Strozier, Clint 75-76
Studdard, Howard 77
Sullivan, J.P. 87-89
Sullivan, Tim 81-82

Sutherland, James 31-32
34-35-36
Svihus, Robert 62-63-64
Swann, Lynn 71-72-73
Swanson, Robert 67
Sweeney, Cal 77-78
Sweeney, Cordell 88-89
Swirles, Frank 39
Swope, Jess 49

T -
Tancredy, Tom 49-50
Tannehill, Ted 45-46-47
Tanner, Randy 84-85-86-87
Tappaan, Francis 27-28-29
Tarver, Bernard 76
Tatsch, Herbert 31-33-34
Tatupu, Mosi 74-75-76-77
Taylor, Michael 66-67
Taylor, Paul 41
Templeton, George 27-28-29
Terry, Tony 69
Theier, Jack 58-59-60
Thiede, Cliff 29
Thomas, Alonzo 71
Thomas, John 63-64-65
Thomas, Kelly 81-82
Thomas, Ronald 40-41-42
Thomassin, John 37-38-39
Thompson, Kenneth 51-52-53
Thompson, Rod 30-31
Thurlow, Leavitt 34-35-36
Thurlow, Leavitt 62
Thurman, Dennis 74-75-76-77
Thurman, Junior 85-86
Timberlake, George 52-53
Timmons, Curt 71
Tinsley, Scott 80-81-83
Tipton, Howard 30

Tobin, Harold 60-61
Tolman, Ernie 47
Tonelli, Amerigo 36-37-38
Traynham, Jerry 58-59-60
Truher, James 28-29
Tsagalakis, Sam 52-53-54
Tucker, Mark 87-88-89-90
Tuiasosopo, Titus 90-91-92
Tuliau, Brian 87-88-89-90
Turner, Joe 80-81
Tyler, Jerome 82-83-84-85

U -
Uhl, Jason 90-91-93
Underwood, Walter 75-76-77
Upton, Gary 65
Ussery, Charles 80-81

V -
Vaca, Vic 83
Van Doren, Robert 50-51-52
Van Dyke, Vinny 76-77
Van Horne, Keith 77-78-79-80
Van Vliet, George 58-59-60
Vasicek, Vic 45
Vella, Chris 71-72
Vella, John 69-70-71
Vellone, James 64-65
Verry, D.Norman 41-42-43
Viltz, Theophile 64-65
Voyne, Don 57-58

W -
Wachholtz, Kyle 92-93
Waddell, Don 45
Wagner, Lowell 41-42
Walker, Glen 75-76
Walker, James 64-65
Walker, Tommy 47
Wall, Fred 44
Wallace, Larry 89-90-91-92
Ward, Herb 78-79

Walshe, Joe 85-87-88
Walters, Shawn 93
Warburton, Irvine
32-33-34
Ward, John 27-28-29
Ware, Tim 82-83-84
Washington, Al 85
Washington, Dave 60
Washington, Marlon
87-88-89
Washmera, Ray 71
72-73
Watts, Elbert 85
Weaver, Charles 69-70
Webb, David 89-90-91
92
Webb, James 32-33-34
Weber, Scott 71
Weber, Tom 52-53
Webster, Steven 85
86-87-88
Weeks, Charles 51-52
Wehba, Ray 36-37-38
Welch, Harry 51-52
Wellman, Gary 87-88
89-90
Wells, Harry III 64
Welsh, Louis 50-51-52
West, Patrick 44
West, Troy 81-82
Westphal, Richard 54
White, Charles 76-77
78-79
White, Lonnie 85-86
White, Tim 80-81-82
Whitehead, Duane
43-44-45-46
Whittier, Julian 29
Wilbur, Robert 34
Wilcox, Ralph 28-29
30
Wilcox, Thomas 27
28-29
Wilensky, Joe 34
35-36
Wilkins, John 59-60
Willer, Don 40-41-42
Willholte, Elmer 51
52
Williams, Brian 91
92-93
Williams, Britt 59
60-61
Williams, Charles
35-36-37
Williams, Eric 75-76
Williams, Hal 41

Williams, Homer 64
Williams, John 49
50-51
Williams, Kevin 77
78-79-80
Williams, Marv 81-83
Williams, Michael 86
87-88-89
Williams, Rod 82-83
Williamson, Don 45
Williamson, Frank 31
32-33
Williamson, Jack 32
33-34
Williamson, Stanley
29-30-31
Willig, Matt 88-89-90
91
Willingham, Charles
29
Willis, Jack 57
Willison, Gary 85-86
Willott, D.Laird 54
55-56
Wilson, Allan 90-91
Wilson, Ben 61-62
Winfield, John 28-29
30
Winans, Jeff 72
Wing, Paul 34-35
Winslow, Robert 37
38-39
Winslow, Troy 65-66
Wolf, Joe 42-43
Wood, Richard 72-73
74
Wood, Willie 57-58-59
Woods, Ray 40-41-42
Wotkyns, Haskell 32
33-34

Y -
Yary, Anthony 65-66
67
Yary, Wayne 69-70
Youel, Curtis 31-32-33
Young, Charles 70-71
72
Young, John 68-69
Young, Adrian 65-66
67

Z -
Zachik, Don 59-60
Zampese, Ernie 55-56
Zimmerman, Daniel
49-51

UCLA Football Lettermen, 1929-1993

A -
Abdellatif, Hazem 89
Adams, Bryan 90-91-93
Adams, Chuck 86
Adams, Tom 55
Adkins, Bryce 76-77
Agajanian, Larry 66-67-68
Agnew, James 43
Aikman, Troy 87-88
Akers, Arthur 77-78-79-80
Albany, Tony 60
Alder, Eugene 39-40-41
Aldrich, Troy 93
Ale, Arnold 90-91-92
Alexander, Chris 91-92
Alexander, Jim 84-85-86
Alexander, Kelton 84-86-87-88
Alexander, Kermit 60-61-62
Alexander, Kirk 83-84-85-86
Allen, Brian 90-91-92-93
Allen, Dick 60-61-62
Allen, Jimmy 72-73
Allington, Robert 34
Almquist, Glen 57-58-59
Altenberg, Kurt 63-64-65
Alumbaugh, Dennis 68-69
Andersen, Chris 93
Andersen, Foster 59-60-61
Andersen, Norm 73-74-75
Anderson, Aaron 91-92-93
Anderson, Art 40-41
Anderson, Avery 92-93
Anderson, Dave 48
Anderson, Theo 93
Anderson, Wilbert 56
Anderson, Willie 84-85-86-87
Andrews, Bob 43
Andrews, Fred 52

Andrews, Danny 81-82-83-84
Andrusyshyn, Zenon 67-68-69
Anthony, Corwin 87-88-89-90
Arbuckle, Charles 86-87-88-89
Arceneaux, Whitney 50-52
Argo, Stacy 88-89-90-91
Armstrong, Bill 40-41-42
Armstrong, Levi 75-76-77
Armstrong, Ray 64-65-66
Armstrong, Sean 83
Arnold, Jason 93
Arnold, Mike 67
Asher, Tom 44-45-46
Audelo, Dave 89
Austin, Edward 31-32-34
Austin, Randy 87-88-89-90
Avery, Tom 56-57
Ayers, Derek 93
Ayers, Eddie 73-74-75

B -
Baaden, Steve 83
Baggott, Bill 74-75
Baggott, Bryan 76-77-78-79
Baida, John 36-37-38
Bailey, Jeff 88-89-90-91
Bailie, Ed 30
Bajema, Ken 67
Baldwin, Burr 41-42-46
Baldwin, Clarence 32-33-35
Baldwin, Harry 58-59-60
Ball, Eric 85-86-87-88
Ball, Russell 74
Ballard, Bob 54-55
Ballou, Mike 67-68-69
Banducci, Eric 91
Banducci, Russ 63-64-65
Barber, Pete 36

Baran, Dave 81-82-83-84
Barbee, Mike 79-80-81-82
Barkate, Harold 86-87-88
Barnes, John 92
Barnhill, Gordon 36
Barnes, Bruce 70-71-72
Barr, Robert 34-35-36
Bartlett, Bob 68-69-70
Bartlett, Ray 39-40
Bashore, Rick 76-77-78-79
Bashore, Ted 64
Baska, Rick 71-72-73
Bates, Patrick 89
Batchkoff, Frank 83
Bauwens, Joe 60-61-62
Bauwens, Steve 59-60-61
Beamon, Willie 74-75
Beardsley, Harold 46-47
Beban, Gary 65-66-67
Beling, Willard 43
Bell, Ray 75-76-77
Benjamin, Warner 52-53-54
Bennett, Tom 63
Bennett, Tommy 92-93
Benstead, Roy 58
Benton, Carl 46-47
Berg, Jim 70-71
Bergdahl, Bob 54-55-56
Bergdahl, Lenny 30-31-32
Bergdahl, Mike 66
Bergey, Bruce 68-69-70
Bergman, Jim 60-61-62
Bergmann, Paul 82-83
Berliner, Myron 51-52-53
Bernstein, Gary 67
Berry, Joe 32
Betts, Dean 58-59
Beverly, Randy 86-87-88-89
Bickers, Gary 64
Biddle, Brooks 44-45
Billington, Barry 56-57

Birren, Don 55-56
Bischof, Vince 67-68-69
Bishop, Harold 27-28-29
Bleymaier, Gene 72-74
Blinn, Steve 91-92-93
Block, Chris 83-84
Blower, Albert 44
Boermeester, Peter 77-78-79
Boghosian, Sam 52-53-54
Bolden, Bill 67-68-69
Bolin, Greg 83-84-85-86
Bonds, Jim 88-89-90-91
Bono, Steve 80-81-83-84
Boom, Herbert 44-45-46
Borden, Don 43-46
Bosserman, Gordon 67-68-69
Boyd, Brent 75-77-79
Boyd, Jack 43-44-45
Boyer, Verdi 32-33-34
Boze, Dave 73-74
Bradley, Doug 54-55-56
Braly, Harold 48-49
Brant, Michael 77-78-79-80
Braunbeck, Dick 54
Bray, James 85
Breeding, Ed 42-46
Breeland, Oran 51
Breiniman, Ansel 29
Brennan, Brent 93
Bright, Jim 71-72-73
Brigida, Andrew 89
Briley, Dave 73
Brisbin, Kent 76-77-78
Britten, Larry 51-52-53
Broadwell, Brewster 36-37-38
Brockington, Fred 77
Brown, Brian 87-88-89-90
Brown, Carl 27-28-29
Brown, Dave 43
Brown, Don 36
Brown, George 47

Brown, Jack 46-47-48
Brown, Jim 54-55
Brown, Jim 74-75-76
Brown, Joe 38
Brown, John 56-57-58
Brown, Sam 53-54-55
Brown, Theotis 76-77 78
Browne, Henry 86
Bruno, Frank 80-81-82
Bryan, Jack 29
Bryson, Brad 86-87-89
Buchanan, Jim 49-50
Buenafe, Kevin 81-82 83-84
Bukich, Steve 74-76 77-78
Burkley, Laurence 87 88-89
Burks, Raymond 73 74-75-76
Burnett, Anthony 87-88
Busby, Harold 66-67 68
Butler, Dick 57-58
Butler, Homer 76-77
Butler, Ron 80-81-82 84
Butler, Steve 63-64-65

C -
Caldwell, Jack 33
Callies, Gary 62-63-64
Cameron, Paul 51-52 53
Campbell, Craig 70-71
Campbell, Gary 70-71 72
Campbell, Merle 43
Campbell, William 45
Cannon, Glenn 77-78 79-80
Cantor, Izzy 36-37-38
Cantor, Leo 39-40-41
Capp, Don 46-47
Caragher, Ron 86-87 88-89
Cargo, Dave 73-74
Carney, Carmac 80-81 82
Carroll, Frank 38-39
Carter, Kaleaph 89-90 91-92
Carver, Ron 69-70-71
Case, Ernie 41-45-46
Cephous, Frank 80-81 82-83

Chaffin, Jeff 81-83
Chalenski, Mike 90-91 92
Chambers, Bill 46-47
Champion, Cornell 64 66
Champion, John 66
Charles, Russ 72-73-74
Cascales, C. 38-39
Chavoor, Sherman 34 35-36
Cheshire, Chuck 33-34 35
Childers, Marion 45
Christensen, James 91-92
Christensen, Bob 69 70-71
Christensen, Gregg 78-79-80
Chudy, Craig 57-59-60
Claman, Allan 65-66-67
Clark, Gene 71-73-74
Clark, Jamal 93
Clark, Jeff 90-91-92-93
Clark, Walter 32-33
Clayton, Mike 70-71
Clements, Bill 45-46 47-48
Clinton, David 83-84 85-86
Coates, Lee 31-32-33
Cobbs, Anthony 93
Cochran, Mike 71
Cochran, Rod 57-58-59
Coffman, Ricky 78-79 80-81
Cogswell, Don 49-50
Cohen, Jack 39-40
Colbert, Andy 93
Cole, Randy 90-91
Coleman, Dick 43
Colletto, Jim 63-64-65
Collier, Travis 90-91 92-93
Collins, Willie 53
Compton, Lynn 41-42
Cook, Wayne 91-92-93
Cooper, Gwen 67-68 69
Cope, Bill 51
Copeland, Ron 67-68
Coppens, Gus 75-76-77
Comish, Frank 86-87 88-89
Corral, Frank 76-77
Cory, Frank 36

Coulter, Michael 75 76-77
Cox, Chris 84
Cox, Larry 64-65-66
Cox, Robert 84-85
Craig, Bradley 90-91 92-93
Craig, Paco 84-85 86-87
Crawford, Bob 74-75 76
Crawford, Lyndon 80 81-82-83
Crestman, John 68
Cress, Robert 38
Cronin, Kevin 84
Cross, Randy 73-74-75
Cureton, Hardiman 53 54-55
Cureton, Mickey 68-69
Curran, Willie 78-79 80-81
Curry, Dale 73-74-75
Curti, Noah 40-41

D -
Dabov, Dave 59-60
Dailey, Pete 51-52-53
Dalby, Dave 69-70-71
Daluiso, Brad 89-90
Daly, Rick 89-90-91-92
Damron, Jeff 85-86-87
Daniels, Tom 70-72
Dankworth, Jeff 74-75 76
Darby, Matt 88-89-90 91
Dathe, Walt 61-62-63
Davenport, Bob 53-54 55
Davidson, Dick 68
Davis, Bruce 75-76 77-78
Davis, Chuck 62-63-64
Davis, Craig 86-87-88 89
Davis, John 57-58
Davis, Milt 52-53
Davis, Ricky 90-91 92-93
Davis, Ron 77-78-79
Davis, Steve 84
Dawson, Jim 56-57-58
Deakers, Rich 64-65-66
Debay, Terry 51-52-53 54
Debose, Ron 78-79-80

Decker, Jim 54-55
Decker, Robert 30-31 32
DeFrancisco, Nate 39 40-41
Dellocono, Neal 81-82 83-84
DeMartinis, Jack 74-75
Denis, Joe 34
Dennis, Ted 28-29
Denton, Wes 86-87-88
Derflinger, Paul 67
DeWitt, Brad 80
Dial, Allan 84-85-86-87
Dias, Bob 83
Dickerson, George 34 35-36
Dickey, Kevin 91-92-93
Diebolt, Doug 69
Dills, Preston 54-56
Dimas, Mike 31
Dimitro, Mike 46-47 48
Dimkich, Mitch 60-61 62
Dinaberg, Bob 57
DiPoalo, Carmen 61-62
Debrow, David 46-47 48
Donahue, Terry 65-66
Donald, Dick 65-66
Donatelli, Doug 82-83
Dorrell, Karl 82-83-85 86
Doud, Chuck 52-53
Dougherty, James 41 42
Dow, Norm 65-66
Dowling, Mike 83
Dressel, Dennis 56-57
Duddleston, Tom 43
Duffy, Ted 28-29
Duffy, Bill 48
Dufour, Dan 79-80 81-82
Dummit, Dennis 69-70
Duncan, Don 56-57
Duncan, John 29-30-31
Duncan, Norm 29-30 31
Durbin, Steve 64-65-66
Durden, Mike 79-80 81-82
Dutcher, Bob 53-56
Dutcher, Erwin 64-65 66
Dye, Cecil 39-40

E -
Easley, Kenny 77-78 79-80
Eatman, Irv 79-80 81-82
Eaton, Ed 47-48-49
Echols, Reggie 70-71 72
Eck, Keith 74-75-76
Edgar, Anthony 78-79
Edwards, Donnie 92-93
Edwards, Oscar 75-76
Ehrlich, Lyman 51
Elias, Chris 77-78 79-80
Elias, Lou 56
Ellena, Jack 52-53-54
Elliott, Stacey 87-88
Ellis, Allan 70-71-72
Enger, Bob 55
Ennen, Henry 47
Erlich, Mickey 65
Erquiaga, John 65-66 67
Escher, Erik 78
Escher, Werner 50-51
Estwick, Mark 87-88 89
Evans, Mike 70
Evans, Ron 86-87

F -
Fade, Bill 44-45
Fagerholm, Rod 58
Fahl, Matt 73-74-75
Farber, Stu 56
Farmer, George 67-68 69
Farr, Andre 88-89 90-91
Farr, Mel 64-65-66
Farr, Mel Jr. 84-85 86-87
Farr, Mike 86-87-88-89
Fears, Charles 40-41-42
Fears, Tom 46-47
Feldman, Rudy 51-52 53
Fenenbock, Charles 38 39
Ferguson, Donvel 35 36-37
Ferguson, Mark 79-81 82
Ferrell, Bobby 72
Fields, Jerry 49

Fien, Ryan 92
Finlay, Jack 40-41-42
Finstad, Jim 62
Fiorentino, Tony 60 61-62
Fitterer, Scott 93
Flanagan, Mike 93
Fletcher, John 30-31
Flores, Mike 71
Flynn, Ed 50-51-52
Forbes, Ted 40-41
Ford, Jim 68-69
Forge, James 77-78 79-81
Forster, George 28 29-30
Foster, Don 51-53
Fowler, John 75-76-77
Francis, Don 62-63-64
Francisco, Kent 62-63 64
Francois, Greg 83-84 85
Franey, David 86
Frankel, Lorry 71
Franklin, Scott 83-84 85
Frankovich, Lee 36-37
Frankovich, Mike 32 33-34
Frawley, John 36-38-39
Fraychineaud, Chuck 50-51
Frazier, Cliff 74-75
Freedman, Morris 65
Freitas, Steve 68-70
French, Marion 28-29
Florence, John 50-51
Fry, Art 72
Frye, Stuart 36
Fryer, Mike 72-73
Fuller, Rick 89-90 91-92
Funk, Fred 34-35-36
Funke, Sigfried 33-34
Fyson, Ed 45

G -
Gaines, Gene 58-59-60
Galigher, Ed 70-71
Gallagher, Clay 72
Gallatin, Donovan 92 93
Gamble, Robert 90-91 92-93
Garibaldi, Bob 83-84 85-86

Garratt, Mike 67-68-69
Gary, Joe 78-79-80-81
Gary, Richard 34
Gaschler, Randy 70-71 72
Gasser, Joe 82-83-84 85
Gaston, Dave 40-41
Geddes, Bob 68-69
Gelfand, Chuck 55
Gemza, Steve 80-81 82-83
Gertsman, Steve 56-57 58
Ghormley, Dan 62
Gibbs, Dave 61-62-63
Gibbs, John 77-78-79
Gibson, Alfred 28-29
Gideon, Aron 89-90 91-92
Gilbert, Dan 72
Gilbert, Fred 89
Gilmore, Dale 37-38-39
Givens, Quentin 92
Glasser, Jeff 84-85 86-87
Goebel, Joe 83-84-85 86
Gomer, Dave 78
Goodman, Brian 70-71
Goodrich, Paul 67
Goodstein, Maurice 28 29-30
Goodwin, Marvin 91 92-93
Gordon, Ike 78-79-80 81
Gordon, Scott 82-83
Goynes, Chester 80
Graham, Danny 68-69
Graham, Doug 44
Grant, Wes 68-69
Gray, Carlton 89-90 91-92
Gray, Rex 81-82
Greedy, Garrett 90-91 92-93
Green, Gaston 84-85 86-87
Green, Jason 91-92-93
Green, Sandy 65-66-67
Greenwood, Carl 91-92 93
Greenwood, Marcus 84-85-86
Grider, Dallas 65-66

Griffin, Edison 56
Griffin, Harold 66-67 68
Griffith, Kim 67-68
Griswold, Hoxie 42-46
Grosman, Aubrey 29 31
Grounds, Randy 77
Grubb, Gerald 40-41
Gueringer, Ron 77
Gueringer, Tony 78
Guidry, Paul 93
Gunther, Rich 72
Gustafson, Mark 66-67 68
Gutman, Tom 60-61
Guyton, Brent 93

H -
Hackett, Kyle 83
Haffner, Mike 61-63-64
Haight, Leslie 30
Hale, Lynn 49
Hall, Larry 79-80
Hampton, Kerns 30-32
Hampton, Russ 54-55
Hansen, Howard 48-49 50
Hanson, Bob 44-45
Haradon, Howard 34
Harden, Wilbur 75-76
Hardin, Harold 74-75 76
Harmon, Mark 72-73
Harper, Joe 56-57-58
Harris, Earl 35-36-37
Harris, Esker 55-56
Harris, Merle 36-38
Harrison, Morrie 42
Hartmeier, Mike 82-83 84-85
Harvey, Clarence 43
Haslam, Fred 31-32-33
Haslam, Warren 38
Hassler, Edgar 31-32 33
Hastings, John 34-35 36
Hatcher, Orville 46
Hauck, Bill 61-62-63
Helm, John 78-79
Henderson, Othello 90 91-92
Henderson, Scott 71
Henderson, Ted 85
Hendricks, Phil 70
Henry, Wally 74-75-76

Hendry, Robert 31-32 33
Henley, Darryl 85-86 87-88
Hermann, Johnny 53 54-55
Herrera, Andy 65-66 67
Herrera, Efren 71-72 73
Herrera, Mike 75
Hershman, Leo 49-50
Hesse, Don 39
Heydenfeldt, Bob 52 53-54
Hickman, Gale 62-63
Hicks, Chuck 59-60-61
Hicks, Skip 93
Hill, Ernest 37-38-39
Hinshaw, Lynn 67
Hirshon, Hal 36-37-38
Hohl, Mason 43
Hoisch, Allan 46-47
Holcomb, Eric 93
Hollaway, Chuck 55-56
Holman, H.R. 43
Hookano, Steve 71-72
Hopwood, Don 77-78
Horgan, Paul 63-64-65
Horta, Joe 50
Horton, Myke 73-74
Horton, Troy 43
Hosea, Bobby 77-78
Howard, Bob 52
Howard, Jack 43
Howard, Sean 88-89
Howell, Harper 80-81 82-83
Hoyt, Bill 46-47
Hubbard, Phil 76-77 78-79
Hudspeth, Marcus 84 85-86
Huff, Doug 68-69-70
Hull, Ron 59-60-61
Hummel, Ben 87
Hunt, Howard 41-46
Hunt, Don 47-48-49
Huse, Russell 28-29
Hutchins, Adam 83-86
Hutt, Eddie 64-65-66

I -
Inglis, Bill 52
Irvine, Gifford 84-85 86
Irwin, Ed 40-41

Isaia, Sale 91-92-93
Izmirian, Albert 42

J -
Jacobs, Brian 89-90
Jacobson, Don 28-29 31
Jacobson, Keith 88-89
Jacoby, Mike 74
Jackson, Billy Don 77 78-79
Jackson, Melvin 84-85 86-87
Jackson, Warren 62-63
James, Gary 73
Jarecki, Steve 82-83 84-85
Jaso, Jerry 69-70
Jasper, Shane 91-92-93
Jensen, Keith 61
Jensen, Roy 48-49-50
Johns, Gerald 63-64
Johnson, Bret 89
Johnson, Chance 85 86-87-88
Johnson, Ernie 46-47 48-49
Johnson, Jim 58-59-60
Johnson, John 41-46
Johnson, Kermit 71-72 73
Johnson, Mitch 62-63 64
Johnson, Mitch 85
Johnson, Norm 78-79 80-81
Johnston, Dan 67
Jones, Brian 86
Jones, Carl 62-63
Jones, Dick 45
Jones, Eugene 72-73
Jones, Frank 69-70
Jones, Gerald 78
Jones, Gordon 30-31 32
Jones, Greg 67-68-69
Jones, Ike 50-51-52
Jones, Ivory 59-60
Jones, Jimmie 72-73
Jones, Ted 39-40
Jordan, Al 89-91-92
Jordan, Fritz 86-87-88
Jordan, Kevin 92-93
Jordan, Wes 83
Jorgensen, Bruce 68-69

K -

Kahn, Mitch 74-75-76
Kase, George 92-93
Kealey, Pat 72
Keating, David 86-87 88
Keeble, Joseph 31-32 33
Keefer, Robert 44-46 47
Keeton, Rocen 87-88 89-90
Kelly, Brian 88-89 90-91
Kelly, John 89-90
Kendall, Chuck 57-58
Kendricks, Marv 70-71
Kennedy, Paul 91-92 93
Key, R.F. (Ted) 34
Keyes, Luther 50-51
Keyler, Courtney 90 91-92-93
Kezirian, Ed 72-73
Kezirian, Rob 75-76
Kidder, John 84-85 86-87
Kiefer, Ken 44-45-46
Kilmer, Bill 58-59-60
Kimble, Phil 74
King, Bob 57-58
King, Nelson 44-45
Kinney, Jack 40
Kipnis, Howard 77-78
Kirby, Dean 49-51
Kirschke, Travis 93
Kitchen, Bill 41
Kjeldgaard, Kipp 87 88-89
Klein, Jerry 64-65
Kline, Doug 85-86 87-88
Klosterman, Steve 72 73
Knowles, Lee 82-83-84
Knox, Ronnie 55
Knupper, Max 70-71
Kordakis, James 84
Krehbiel, Don 43
Kroeber, George 51
Kroener, Frank 36-37
Kuehn, Art 72-73-74
Kukulica, Rick 73-74
Kurrasch, Roy 42-45 46
Kuykendall, Fulton 72 73-74
Kvitky, Ben 39-40

Kyzivat, Louis 37-38 39

L -
LaChapelle, Sean 89 90-91-92
Laidman, Dan 51-52
Lake, Carnell 85-86 87-88
Lambert, Dion 88-89 90-91
Lane, Herb 50-51
Lang, Walter 80-81-82
Langston, Guy 77
LaRose, Chad 91-92
Lassalette, Tom 88-91
Lassner, Jack 70-71-72
Lauter, Dan 80-81-82
Lawhorn, Kim 90-91 92-93
Lawrence, Teddy 92-93
Leal, Russ 70-71-72
Leckman, Arnold 49
Lee, Eugene 43-44-45
Lee, Kenny 74-75-76
Lee, John 82-83-84-85
Lee, Larry 78-79-80
Leeka, Bill 56-57-58
Leggins, Bobby 79
Lemmerman, Allan 70 71-72
Leonard, Robert 46
Leoni, Eugene 81-82
Lepisto, Vic 64-66-67
Lescoulie, Jack 40-41 42
Lesley, Jason 93
Leventhal, Barry 63 64-65
Levy, Dave 52-53
Lewand, Ray 48-50-51
Lewin, Kurt 57
Lightner, Clifford 33
Linn, Mike 89-90-91
Littleton, Nkosi 90-91 92-93
Livesay, Ransom 32 33-34
Livingston, Cliff 50-51
Lloyd, Glenwood 29
Lockwood, Brian 87 88-89-90
Lo'Curto, John 61-62 63
Lodish, Mike 86-87 88-89
Long, Bob 52-53-54

Long, Don 56-57-58
Longo, Tony 58-59-60
Lott, Sinclair 32-33-34
Loudd, Rommie 53-54
55
Love, Duval 81-82-83
84
Luster, Marv 58-59-60
Lyman, Brad 69-70-72
Lyman, Dell 38-39-40
Lynn, Johnny 75-76
77-78
Lyons, Damion 90

M -
Macari, Frank 59-60-61
Mackey, Clarence 41
MacLachian, Bruce 48
49-50
MacPherson, Don 38
39-40
Maddox, Tommy 90-91
Maggio, Kirk 86-87
88-89
Mahan, Mike 83
Mahlstedt, Don 80-81
82
Main, Jim 76-77-78-79
Maizlish, Bryan 82
Malmberg, Don 42-43
45-46
Malone, James 88-89
90-91
Mancini, Dom 71
Mandula, Francis 49-50
Manning, Bob 68-69-70
Manning, Don 65-66-67
Mannon, Mark 82-83-84
Manumaleuna, Frank
74
Marienthal, Mike 42-43
Markel, Art 43
Markham, Dean 44-45
Markowitz, Barry 74
Marlett, Walter 41
Martinez, Mike 73-74
Marty, Pat 78
Marvin, Joe 49-50-51
Mascola, Lou 76
Mason, Bill 57
Mason, Mike 79-80-81
Massey, Thaddeus 93
Masters, Jim 84-85-86
Matheny, Jim 55-56
Matheson, Martin 38
39-40
Matheson, Tory 67-68

Mathews, Ned 38-39
40
Matthews, West 46-47
48-49
Maurer, Mark 47
Mayer, Vic 78-79
Mayfield, Paul 66
Maxwell, William 31
McAlister, James 72-73
McAteer, Tim 64-65-66
McCabe, Mike 44
McClave, Andrew 91
92-93
McClure, Darren 93
McCullough, Abdul 93
McGaffrey, Mike 66
McChesney, Bob 32
34-35
McConnaughy, James
47
McConnell, Lawrence
34-35-37
McCracken, Brendan
85-86-87-88
McCullough, Jim 82
83-84-85
McDougall, Gerry 54
55
McElroy, Lee 67-68-69
McFarland, Matt 77
78-79-80
McGaugh, Eugene 84
McGill, Mark 86-87
88-89
McGue, Delbert 32-33
McIntire, Ken 63
McKay, Jack 54
McKenzie, Leonard 42
McKenzie, Stuart 40-41
McKinnely, Phil 73-74
75
McLandrich, Greg 68
69
McLaughlin, Leon 46
47-48-49
McMillan, Lloyd 29
30-31
McNairy, Louis 36
McNeil, Freeman 77
78-79-80
McNeill, Fred 71-72-73
McPherson, Pat 88-89
90
McSween, Alton 72-73
Mefford, Frank 43
Mehr, Steve 85-86

87-88
Mena, Xavier 46-50
Menifield, Bobby 85
86-87-88
Merrill, Mike 92
Merrill, William 32
Merten, Bjorn 93
Metcalf, Jack 58-59-60
Mewborn, Gene 81-82
83
Meyer, Rick 86-87-88
89
Mike, Robert 46-47
Milum, Edward 29-30
Miller, Andy 87-88-89
Miller, Chuckie 83-84
85-86
Miller, Ed 50-51
Miller, Jamir 91-92-93
Miller, Jim 63-64-65
Miller, Mitch 93
Miller, Scott 89-90
Miller, Willie 73
Milliner, James 92-93
Michel, Howard 33
Mitchell, Hal 49-50-51
Mitchell, Jim 37-38-39
Mohl, Curt 77-78-79
80
Mok, Vince 70-71-72
Molina, Mike 76-77-78
Monahan, Steve 73-74
Montgomery, Blanchard
79-80-81-82
Montgomery, Jack 36
37-38
Montoya, Max 77-78
Moomaw, Donn 50-51
52
Moore, Bob 50-51
Moore, Michael 90-91
Moore, Reggie 87-88
89-90
Moore, Reynaud 69-70
Moore, Terry 83-84
Moreau, Ismael 92
Morehead, Terry 81-82
Moreno, Gil 53-54-55
Morgan, George 50
Morgan, Karl 79-80
81-82
Morris, Marvin 77-78
Morris, Nate 87
Morton, Dave 76-77
Morze, Mark 72
Moss, Martin 78-79
80-81

Moyneur, Paul 70-71
72
Muir, Larry 90
Mulhaupt, Richard 29
30-31
Muller, Walter 32-33
Munro, Jack 43
Murdock, Lawrence
35-36-37
Muro, Jeff 75-77-78
Murphy, Dennis 65
66-67
Murphy, Rex 48
Murphy, Tom 76
Murphy, William 33
34-35
Myers, Jack 44-46-47

N -
Narr, Joe 46
Nader, Jim 68-69-70
Nagel, Ray 46-47-48
49
Nanoski, John 73-74

UCLA

Vs.

USC

Crosstown

Crossfire

Narleski, Ted 50-51-52
Nash, Robert 36-37
Neighbor, Richard 44
Nelson, Byron 63-64 65
Nelson, Dan 45-46-47
Nelson, Don 45
Nelson, Glenn 29
Nelson, Harvey 28-29
Nelson, Kevin 80-81 82-83
Neuheisel, Rick 81-82 83
Nguyen, Mike 91-92-93
Nichols, Perry 76
Nielsen, Ron 91-92
Nikcevich, John 46-47 48-49
Noble, Eugene 27-28 29
Nordli, Phil 32-33
Norfleet, Greg 72-73 74
Norfleet, Haughton 30 31-32
Norrie, David 82-83 84-85
Norris, Clarence 53-54
Norris, Trusse 57-58-59
Norton, Ken 84-85-86 87
Novitsky, Craig 90-91 92-93
Nowinski, Jeff 84-85
Noyes, Dave 63
Nuttall, Dave 66-67
Nwoke, Ted 92-93

O -
Obbema, Rick 76-77
Obidine, John 41-42
Oesterling, Tim 69-70
O'Garro, Pete 51-55-56
Ogden, Beverly 29
Ogden, Jonathan 92-93
Oglesby, Paul 57-58-59
Okuneff, Gerry 53-54
O'Leary, Prentice 62 63-64
Oliver, Al 72-73
Oliver, Homer 30-31 32
Oliver, Jim 67
Olmstead, Remington 33-34-35
Olson, Carl 34-35-41
Onwutuebe, Emmanuel

88-89-90-91
O'Quinn, Carrick 90
91-92-93
Oram, Phil 60-61-62
Otey, Dave 77-78 80-81
Overlin, Bill 38-39-40
Owen, Dave 51-52
Owens, James 75-76 77-78
Oxford, Rex 41

P -
Pace, Gayle 49-50-51
Page, Charles 47
Page, Kenny 80-82-83
Pagni, Mike 92
Pahulu, Otieni 86
Paige, Bill 86-87-88-89
Painter, Earl 30
Palmer, Steve 53-54-55
Pankopf, Tory 83-84 85-86
Paopao, Tony 76
Pardi, Don 43
Parker, Vaughn 90-91 92-93
Parslow, Phil 56-57-58
Pastre, George 46-47 48-49
Paton, George 88-89 90-91
Paton, Tom 59-60-61
Patterson, Ernest 32-33
Patton, Marvcus 86-87 88-89
Paul, Don 43-44-46-47
Paul, Rick 65-66
Pauly, Ira 51-52-53
Pavich, Mike 69-70-71
Pearce, Kent 73-74
Pearman, Greg 69-70 71
Pearson, Wade 65-66 67
Pederson, Don 73-75 76-77
Pedrini, Tom 43
Peeke, Gerald 72-73
Peers, Ray 35-36
Pele, Pete 75-76
Penaranda, Jairo 79-80
Penner, Gerald 55-56
Pentecost, John 62-63 64
Perez, Louis 91-92
Pernecky, Paul 90-91

92-93
Person, Barney 74-75
Pertulla, Rick 68
Peters, Doug 54-55
Peterson, Cal 71-72-73
Peterson, Dan 55-57
Peterson, Dan 82
Peterson, Dave 56-57 58
Peterson, Dick 62-63 64
Peterson, Earl 70-71
Peterson, John 51-52 53-54
Peterson, Marion 45
Petrie, Roger 86
Pfeiffer, George 36-37 38
Phifer, Roman 87-88 90
Phillips, Art 57-58-59
Phillips, George 41-42 44
Phillips, Tony 82-83 84-85
Phinny, Sherm 37-38
Pickert, Joe 85-86-87
Pierovich, John 57-58 59
Pierson, Ray 41-42
Pifferini, Bob 69-70-71
Pike, Charles 34-35-36
Pinkston, Pat 56
Pitts, Ron 81-82-83-84
Piver, Arthur 32
Plemmons, Brad 77-78 80-81
Polizzi, Ignatius 46-48
Porter, Jack 45
Potter, Ken 82-83-84
Preston, Steve 68-69
Price, Dennis 84-85 86-87
Primus, James 84-85 86-87
Profit, Mel 61-62-63
Pryor, John 86-87-88-89
Purdy, Rick 66-67-68
Putnam, Bill 44

Q -
Quarles, Bernard 79

R -
Rae, James 88
Raffee, Alan 51
Rafferty, Thomas 31

32-33
Ramsey, Herschel 72 73-74
Ramsey, Tom 79-80 81-82
Randle, David 82-83 84
Rainey, Jack 33
Rasmus, Bob 27-28-29
Ray, Billy 85-86-87-88
Ray, Joe 52-53-54
Record, Clayton 70
Reece, Severn 75-76 77-78
Reed, Jack 62
Reel, Stanley 32-33
Reemsten, Brian 90
Reese, Floyd 67-68-69
Reeves, Doug 80
Reichle, Art 35-36
Reid, Scott 77-78
Reidt, Eric 93
Reiges, Ben 46-47
Reinhard, Robert 29
Reilly, Paul 86
Remsberg, John 29
Reyes, Bob 73-74-75
Rice, Dan 71
Richards, Brian 92-93
Richards, David 87
Richardson, Bob 63-64 65
Richardson, John 64 65-66
Richardson, Paul 88 89-90-91
Riddle, Everett 41-42
Riggs, Darrell 48-49-50
Rile, Glen 35-36
Riley, Avon 79-80
Riskas, Mike 57-58
Roberts, Dick 45
Roberts, Gerry 72-73
Roberts, Howard 29 30-31
Robinson, George 35 36
Robinson, G.H. 43
Robinson, Jackie 39-40
Robinson, Jerry 75-76 77-78
Robinson, Raymond 78-79
Robotham, George 42 45
Roesch, Johnny 43-44 46-47

Rogers, Don 80-81 82-83
Rogers, Eric 83-85-86
Rohlinger, George 88
Rohme, Mike 92-93
Rohrer, Robert 43
Roof, Mike 64-65-66
Rosenkrans, Joe 59-60-61
Ross, Ben 34
Rossi, Cal 44-45-46-47
Rowell, Russell 80-81
Rowland, Gene 45-46-47-48
Ruckman, Jeff 93
Ruettgers, Joe 38-39
Rumbaoa, Phil 79
Russell, Bob 44-45-46-47
Russo, Mario 41
Russom, Jerry 27-28-29
Rutledge, Craig 83-84-85-86
Ryland, John 36-37-38

S -
Sabol, Joe 50-51-52
Saenz, Ernie 77
Saipale, Toa 78-79-81-82
Salsbury, Jim 51-52-53-54
Sanchez, Chris 92
Sanchez, Lupe 79-80-82-83
Sandifer, Bill 72-73
Sandifer, Dominic 88-91
San Jose, Bobby 87-88
Sargent, Earl 35-36
Sarpy, James 75-76-77
Sarver, Joe 33
Schager, Darren 91-92-93
Schell, Walt 35-36-37
Schexnayder, Anthony 87-88-89-90
Schmidt, Mark 86-87

Schmidt, Pat 75-76
Schneider, Bert 46
Schoner, Bob 63
Schroeder, Cliff 48-49
Schroeder, Jay 80
Schroeder, Robert 34-35-36
Schroller, Karl 92-93
Schuhmann, Charlie 72-73-74
Schwartz, Randy 62
Schwenk, Vic 46
Sciarra, John 72-73-74-75
Scribner, Rob 70-71-72
Scott, Burness 81-82
Selecky, Mark 87
Senteno, Rick 78-79
Settles, Gene 72-73-74
Shah, Sharmon 92
Sharpe, Luis 78-79-80-81
Shaw, Meech 89-90
Sheley, Dale 74
Sheller, Henry 44-46
Shelton, Ken 91-92
Sherrard, Mike 82-83-84-85
Shinnick, Don 54-55-56
Shinnick, Josh 82-83-84-85
Shipkey, Jerry 44-46-47
Shipman, Travis 92-93
Shirk, Marshall 59-60-61
Shoemaker, Steve 75
Short, Dick 48-49-50
Shubin, John 37
Shubin, William 39
Simmons, John 44
Simpson, Clifton 27-28-29
Simpson, David 85
Simpson, Robert 39-40-41
Simpson, Sherwood 49
Simms, Arthur 70
Sindell, Steve 63-64
Singleton, Ezell 60-61-62
Slagle, Larry 65-66-67
Smalley, Rod 91-92-93
Smalley, Steve 67-68
Smith, Arthur 26-29
Smith, Bobby 59-60-61

Smith, Brian 79
Smith, Charles 30-31
Smith, Chester 29
Smith, Dave 57
Smith, Earl 59-60
Smith, Earl 84-85
Smith, Eric 84-85-86-88
Smith, Frank 43
Smith, Hal 55-56
Smith, Jeff 74-75
Smith. John 45
Smith, John (Cappy) 50-51-52
Smith, John 53-55
Smith, Julian 33-34
Smith, Kevin 88-89-90-91
Smith, Lee 77
Smith, Mark 76
Smith, Milt 40-41-42
Smith, Nathan (Skip) 58-59-60
Smith, Ray 57-58-59
Smith, Rob 61-62
Smith, Vic 41-42-44
Smith, Willie 65-67
Snelling, Ken 41-42
Snyder, Greg 69-70-71
Soenksen, Matt 92-93
Solari, Al 41-42
Solid, Ken 44-45
Solomon, Edward 27-29-30
Soltis, John 90
Sommers, Jack 38-39-40
Sosnowski, Steve 76-77
Spalding, Scott 88-89-90-91
Sparlis, Al 41-42-45
Spaulding, Bill 34-36
Spielman, Art 42
Spindler, Rich 65-66-67
Spurling, Dennis 68-69
Stalwick, Don 51-52-53
Stamper, Bill 45-48
Stanley, Jim 60-62-63
Stanley, Steve 65-66-67
Stauch, Scott 77-78-79-80
Stawisky, Sam 33-34-35
Steele, Greg 73
Steele, Scott 68
Steffen, Art 45-46

47-48
Steffen, Jim 57-58
Steiner, Les 46-47-48
Stephens, Frank 75-76-77
Steponovich, Tony 67
Stevens, Bob 59-60-61
Stevens, Derek 90-91-92-93
Stevens, Matt 83-84-85-86
Stevenson, Scott 86-87
Stickel, Walter 31-32
Stiers, William 43
Stiles, Bob 65
Stits, Bill 51-52-53
Stockert, Ernie 50-51-52
Stoeffen, Howard 29
Stokes, J.J. 91-92-93
Story, Al 59
Storey, Sam 33-34
Stout, Dave 60-61-62
Strawn, Dean 44
Stretz, Grady 92-93
Strode, Woody 37-38-39
Stroschein, Breck 48-49-50
Sullivan, John 73-74-75
Sullivan, Tom 79-80-81-82
Sutherland, Lester 36-37-38
Svensgaard, Ira 45
Sweetland, Pat 73-74
Swick, Jim 73-74
Sykes, Jim 64

T -
Taber, Norman 35-36
Tamborski, Steve 70
Tawscheck, Russell 44-45
Tautolo, John 77-78-79-80
Tautolo, Ray 79
Tautolo, Terry 74-75
Taylor, Eric 64
Taylor, Greg 74-75-76
Taylor, Tommy 82-83-84-85
Tennell, Derek 83-84-85-86
Tenningkeit, Tim 74-75-76
Tetrick, Steve 75-76-77
Theodore, Terry 82-83-84-85

Thoe, Rueben 28-29-30
Thomas, Cliff 78-79
Thomas, Jewerl 75-76
Thomas, Jim 51-52
Thomas, Larry 80-81-82
Thompson, Almose 60 61
Thompson, Danny 85 86-87-88
Thompson, Harry 48-49
Tibbs, Burt 51
Tiedemann, Bill 63
Tiesing, Scott 79-81
Tighe, Brian 91-92-93
Tinsley, Phil 46-47-48
Titensor, Glen 76-77
Toland, Don 40
Townsell, Jojo 79-80 81-82
Toy, Maury 88-89-90-91
Treadaway, Jim 82
Treat, Ben 58
Trembley, Vic 72
Tretter, Ron 66-68-69
Tritt, Bill 45
Trotter, Harry 33-34
Troxel, William 37
Truesdell, Steve 61 62-63
Tuala, Siitupe 89-90
Tuiasosopo, Manu 75 76-77-78
Tuinei, Mark 78-79
Tumey, Terry 84-85 86-87
Turner, Eric 87-88-89-90

Turner, Jimmy 78-80 81-82
Turner, Marcus 85-86 87-88
Tyler, Ed 42
Tyler, Randy 70-71-72
Tyler, Wendell 73-74 75-76

V -
Vannatta, Chuck 43-44
Vassar, Brad 75
Veal, Zeno 71
Velasco, Alfredo 86-87 88-89
Vena, Dan 59-60-61
Vernoy, Terry 70-71-72
Versen, Walter 46
Viger, Joe 38-39
Villalobos, Ray 86-87
Villaneuva, Primo 53-54
Vlack, Russ 46
Von Sonn, Andy 60-61 62
Vujovich, Roy 48-49

W -
Waddell, Tom 72-73-74
Wagner, Jim 88-89-90
Wahler, Jim 85-86-87-88
Wai, Francis 37-38-40
Walen, Mark 82-83-84 85
Walker, Bruce 90-91-92
Walker, John 61-62-63
Walker, Ken 76-77-78
Walker, Kevin 93
Walker, Rick 74-75-76
Walker, Rob 92-93
Wallace, Jim 57-58-59
Wallen, Dick 56-57-58
Walton, Bruce 70-71-72
Walton, Gary 92-93
Ward, Phillip 93
Ware, Tom 65-66
Wargo, John 71
Warnick, Russ 84-85 86-87
Washington, Daron 91 92-93
Washington, Kenny 37 38-39
Washington, James 84 85-86-87
Wassell, Doug 84-85 86-87
Waterfield, Bob 41-42

44
Watson, Bob 48-49-50
Watts, Jack 44-46
Way, Guy 50
Wayland, Cory 89-90-91
Weeden, Bob 57-61
Weisstein, Julie 49-50 51
Welch, Herb 83-84
Wellendorf, Leonard 29-30-31
Werner, Matt 90-91 92-93
West, Bert 44-45-46
West, Doug 81-82-83
Westland, Duke 36
Wetzel, Warren 63
Wheeler, Bob 44-45
White, Brett 74-75
White, John 62-63
White, Roger 53-54-55
Whitebook, Milt 39-40
Whitenight, Tom 85 86-87
Whitfield, Clint 56-57 58
Whitney, Jerry 47
Widmer, Don 67-68-69
Wiener, Herb 40-41 42-43
Wilcox, Bryan 87-88
Wilder, Marc 88-89 90-91
Wiley, Bryan 81-82 83-84
Wilkes, Rick 69-70
Wilkinson, Bob 48-49 50
Wilks, Deon 90
Williams, Billy Bob 35 36-37
Williams, Dave 50
Williams, Dokie 78-79 80-82
Williams, Greg 73-74
Williams, Jim 74-76
Williams, Kevin 89-90 91-92
Williams. Lewis 52
Williams, Michael 89 90-91-92
Williams, Robin 39-40
Williams, Steve 73
Williams, Steve 81-82 83
Willoughby, Howard 30
Wills, Duane 59-60

Wills, Shawn 88-89 90-91
Wilson, Al 84-85
Wilson, Kirk 56-57-58
Wilton, Wilt 33-34
Windom, Glenn 78-80 81
Wingle, Blake 80-81-82
Winnek, John 88-89 90-91
Witcher, Dick 64-65
Witt, Dean 43-44-46
Woefle, Rod 42-45
Wollard, Ron 76-77
Womble, Wendell 34
Wood, John 32
Woodfin, London 91 92-93
Woods, Bill 44-47
Woolley, Don 76
Wrightman, Tim 78-79 80-81
Wyrick, Clestine 36-37 38

Y -
Yearick, Clayton 32-33
Yelich, Chris 80-81-82-83
Young, Chuck 44
Young, H.M. 43
Young, Mike 81-82-83-84
Yurosek, Gary 56

Z -
Zaby, Carl 74-75
Zaby, John 36-39
Zarubica, Mladin 37-38-39
Zelinka, Bob 50-51
Zeno, Eric 87
Zeno, Joe 60-61-62
Zeno, Lance 87-88-89-90
Zeno, Larry 62-63-64
Zilinskas, John 88-90
Zimmerman, Kurt 65-66
Zimmerman, Meyer 29
Zwaneveld, Onno 83 84-85-86